Catholic Social Thought
and the New World Order

Catholic Social Thought and the New World Order

Building on One Hundred Years

Oliver F. Williams, C.S.C.,
and John W. Houck
Editors

University of Notre Dame Press
Notre Dame   London

Library of Congress Cataloging-in-Publication Data

Catholic social thought and the new world order : building on one
    hundred years / Oliver F. Williams and John W. Houck, editors.
        p.   cm.
    Papers presented at a symposium hosted by the Notre Dame Center
for Ethics and Religious Values, University of Notre Dame, April
14–17, 1991.
    Includes bibliographical references.
    ISBN 0-268-00797-7 (alk. paper)
    1. Catholic Church and world politics—Congresses. 2. Sociology,
Christian (Catholic)—Congresses. 3. Church and social problems—
Catholic Church—Congresses. 4. World politics—1989—
Congresses. I. Williams, Oliver F. II. Houck, John W.
III. Notre Dame Center for Ethics and Religious Values in Business.
BX1793.C37   1993   92-56866
261.8'08'822—dc20   CIP

To the extent that earthly progress can contribute to the better ordering of society, it is of vital concern to the Kingdom of God.

(*Gaudium et Spes,* par. 39)

Contents

Part III

The New World Order and the Challenge for the Church 125

Part IV

The New World Order and the Plight of Developing Countries 199

Part V

The New World Order: Shaping a Just Community 265

Preface

From its earliest origins the Catholic church has tried to influence society, and society has, to varying degrees, shaped the church. Recently, with the demise of the Marxist alternative to capitalism, Catholic social teaching has assumed the role of the major international force challenging free enterprise to be more humane. What does the church have to say about the world's current situation and the possibility of a new world order, and how has this message evolved over the past one hundred years? To answer these and related questions, The Notre Dame Center for Ethics and Religious Values in Business hosted a symposium on April 14–17, 1991. The twenty essays in this volume are updated versions of the 1991 papers and reflect on the development and evolution of Catholic social teaching and analyze its practical application for a new world order.

The idea of a new world order was given prominence by former President Bush during the Gulf War and the last years of his administration. President Clinton clearly demonstrated his resolve to carry forward that theme in his Inaugural Address on January 20, 1993:

> To renew America, we must meet challenges abroad as well as at home. There is no longer a clear division between what is foreign and what is domestic. The world economy, the world environment, the world AIDS crisis, the world arms race—they affect us all.
>
> Today, as an old order passes, the new world is more free but less stable. Communism's collapse has called forth old animosities and new dangers. Clearly, America must continue to lead the world we did so much to make.
>
> While America rebuilds at home, we will not shrink from the challenges nor fail to seize the opportunities of this new world. Together with our friends and allies we will work to shape change lest it engulf us.

Before taking office, Clinton had set some of the contours of his vision of the new world order, speaking of a "pro-democracy foreign policy" and a "new covenant for american security" where "our definition of security must include common threats to all people." The premise of this volume is that the Catholic social thought developed over the past hundred years has much to offer our times in providing the concepts and shaping the vision of a new world order.

We are most grateful for the financial assistance provided by John Caron, William Lehr, Jr., and the Hershey Foods Corporation. The support of our colleagues at the University of Notre Dame Press, James R. Langford and E. Ann Rice, made our task much lighter. We extend our thanks to Sue Barnett and Madeline Day, symposium and manuscript coordinator, for their typing and editorial work. Finally, this volume is dedicated to all those men and women who labor for a new world order that promises more peace and justice for all.

The Center for Ethics and Religious Values in Business

The Notre Dame Center for Ethics and Religious Values in Business seeks to build bridges among business, business studies and the humanities. Its programs are designed to strengthen the Judeo-Christian ethical foundations in business and public policy decisions by fostering dialogue between academic and corporate leaders, and by research and publications. The Center is under the co-directorship of Oliver F. Williams, C.S.C. (theology), associate provost, and John W. Houck (business), professor of management, College of Business Administration.

In 1978 the Center published *Full Value: Cases in Christian Business Ethics*, which was the inaugural volume of Harper & Row's Experience and Reflection series. Michael Novak commented that the book "quite successfully juxtaposes the power of the Christian story, in its biblical immediacy, to concrete problems Christians in the world of business are likely to meet." James M. Gustafson wrote about *Full Value:* "Religious traditions provide, as these writers observe, a story, for example the Christian story, which informs our moral outlook, creates our moral vision, sustains our moral loyalties, and nurtures our moral character."

In 1980 the Center hosted a national symposium, *The Judeo-Christian Vision and the Modern Business Corporation.* The *Los Angeles Times* contrasted "the competitive success-oriented style necessary for corporate promotion with the traditional Christian view of the virtuous person." The *New York Times* reported that "there would be no facile resolution to the conflict between the values of a just society and the sharply opposing values of successful corporations."

A second symposium, *Co-creation: A Religious Vision of Corporate Power,* followed in 1982, focusing on Pope John Paul II's encyclical letter, *Laborem Exercens. Newsweek* characterized the conference as a "free marketplace of ideas" exploring a religious vision of corporate power.

In December 1983 the Center assisted the U.S. Bishops' Committee charged to write a pastoral letter on the economy by convening a three-day symposium, *Catholic Social Teaching and the American Economy.*

The *Los Angeles Times* observed: "About one-third of the major speakers represented conservative viewpoints, the remainder voiced moderate-to-liberal positions." The *New York Times* reported that "contentiousness is commonplace here at Notre Dame.... And when dozens of business leaders, theologians, and academics lined up against each other at the university this week, the debate over the economy was fought as hard as any gridiron encounter." More than 250 people attended the meeting, including the five bishops who were to draft the letter.

Catholic Social Teaching and the Common Good was the theme of a 1986 symposium to explore the possible retrieval of the notion of "the common good" in philosophical-economic discourse. Ralph McInerny saw the concept of the common good as needed "to draw attention to flaws in our economic thinking and policies as well as to make positive suggestions that will be manifestly in line with our tradition." *New Catholic World* wrote: "A collection of eighteen essays...by social scientists, theologians, philosophers, business faculty, and television producers. The essays represent different points of view from both theoretical and practical perspectives.... It would be a valuable contribution to Catholic social teaching if all it did was to make people aware that a concept of the common good once was alive and well. It does much more than that."

The 1987 symposium focused on *Ethics and the Investment Industry*. Much has been written in the eighties about the misdeeds of actors in the investment community; suggestions for legislative reform abound. Very little has been said about the ethical vision and institutional bonding that form the context for a humane capitalism. It is these themes, as well as the appropriate market and legal aspects, that were explored at Notre Dame. *America* said of *Ethics and the Investment Industry* that it "will be an important reference for future participants in the international business community."

In 1992 the Center published *A Virtuous Life in Business* from a 1990 conference. Important scholars from a variety of disciplines discussed the recent trends in narrative theology and the theory of virtue, which may have much to contribute to the literature on the ethical dimension of business life. *Commonweal* wrote: "I highly recommend *A Virtuous Life in Business: Stories of Courage and Integrity in the Corporate World*.... The book is not only valuable, it is readable and gets progressively better."

Publications by the Center include:

Full Value: Cases in Christian Business Ethics
Matter of Dignity: Inquiries into the Humanization of Work
The Judeo-Christian Vision and the Modern Corporation

Co-Creation and Capitalism: John Paul II's "Laborem Exercens"
Catholic Social Teaching and the U.S. Economy
The Common Good and U.S. Capitalism
The Apartheid Crisis
Ethics and the Investment Industry
The Making of an Economic Vision
A Virtuous Life in Business: Stories of Courage and Integrity in the
*   Corporate World*

Articles have appeared in *California Management Review, Business Horizons, Theology Today, Business and Society Review, Horizons, Journal of Business Ethics* and *The Harvard Business Review.*

Oliver F. Williams, C.S.C.
John W. Houck
University of Notre Dame
Notre Dame, Indiana 46556
1993

Part I

The New World Order and the Resources of Catholic Social Teaching

Robert S. McNamara, former Secretary of Defense in the Kennedy and Johnson administrations, in a recent address captured a sentiment that is shared by many today:

> We need a vision of a world no longer dominated by the East-West rivalry which for more than 40 years shaped the foreign policies and defense programs of Western nations.... If East and West and North and South dare break out of the mind-sets of the past four decades, we can reshape international institutions, as well as relations among nations, in ways that will lead to a far more peaceful world and a far more prosperous world for all the peoples of our interdependent globe.[1]

The times require a new world order and there is no question that such a new vision is slowly emerging as leaders formulate new ideas and policies to meet contemporary needs.

The premise of this volume is that the resources of Catholic social teaching developed over the last hundred years can play a part in providing some of the concepts and the vision for this new world order. New political and economic realities are emerging around the globe and the time is ripe for shaping a new consensus on how to fit nations into a global network.

The first essay is by a theologian who has written extensively on the challenge of bringing ethical values into the business world. Oliver Williams focuses on how the resources of Catholic social teaching might influence a global economy in the direction of a communitarian democratic capitalism. Although, as Paul Sigmund notes, the congruence of the idea of a communitarian democracy and the Catholic tradition was advanced by Jacques Maritain in 1950, the full-blown intellectual movement known as communitarianism has developed only in recent years.

1

The common theme of communitarianism is to retrieve the focus on community needs and civic obligations, a focus which many believe was lost because of an overemphasis on individual rights. President Bill Clinton echoes this theme throughout his speeches:

> When I think of how I want to change America during the next four years, I want most of all to restore the link between rights and responsibilities, opportunities and obligations; the social contract that defines what we owe to one another, to our communities, and to our country.[2]

Citing primarily from the 1991 encyclical, *Centesimus Annus*, Williams argues that Catholic social teaching offers a vision of moderate communitarianism that has much in common with that of leading secular thinkers searching for a new economic and social paradigm. As the countries of Africa and the peoples of the former Soviet Union and Eastern Europe begin to search for new answers, the hope is that this vision might take hold. Developing countries as well as the developed countries might find much that is helpful in Catholic social teaching, with its focus on a more person-centered economy with a communitarian vision.

The second essay is by J. Bryan Hehir, a distinguished priest-scholar who served as an ethicist and theologian on the staff of the U.S. Catholic Bishops Conference for a number of years. Hehir provides an analysis of the three major contributors of that body of knowledge known as Catholic social teaching: Pope Leo XIII, the Second Vatican Council, and Pope John Paul II. He offers an insightful discussion of four dimensions of the church's social role: political, economic, international and ecclesiological. The study then examines how the social question has been shaped in the United States by examining four key characteristics: the secular state, a pluralistic society, a capitalist economy, and a post-cold war world.

Hehir concludes by considering three proposals for the new world order that are being discussed widely in the United States: a unipolar world, the reemergence of a multipolar world, and a revival of a fully developed United Nations system. While Hehir favors the third option, he sees an important role for Catholic social teaching in exploring these options and engaging the geopolitical debate.

Chapter Three is by an eminent political scientist, Paul E. Sigmund. Sigmund helps the reader understand the resources of Catholic social thought at a more profound level by his careful study of the relationship between Catholicism and democracy. Starting with the early Christian communities, he shows how the ideas developed through the medieval times to the present where we have a church which has a formal commitment to democracy and human rights. Jacques Maritain is singled out as a significant pathfinder:

He was responsible for a new development in Catholic thought...the argument that democracy was not simply one of several forms of government, all of which were acceptable to the degree that they promoted "the common good," but was the one political structure most in keeping with the nature of man[kind] and Christian values.

Today, while the church does not support uncritically all the democratic outcomes, especially in the area of sexual morality, it does give strong support to democratic political structures for the new world order. In Latin America and Eastern Europe the church has been an important force for human rights and democratic institutions. Sigmund suggests that contemporary liberal culture may find the emphasis on community and participation in Catholic social teaching a valuable corrective.

The fourth chapter is by the noted French Catholic scholar, Jean-Yves Calvez, S.J. While admitting that the central concerns of Catholic social teaching are all stated in *Rerum Novarum* and revolve around "the concern about a deep division of society on the basis of the economy," Calvez outlines how the church's approach to meeting these concerns has evolved over time. Both the church and society have changed. The church, now all the people of God and not just the hierarchy, is more internal to society; advances in human and social values are seen as furthering the Kingdom of God. Society now assumes that human rights should be a reality for all and there is a growing awareness of the possibility of an international community. Calvez is hopeful that Christians can change the world in the direction of Catholic social teaching if they have a church that instills the confidence and knowledge that is the very soul of the Christian message, particularly as it was renewed by the Second Vatican Council.

The final chapter in the section is by a retired chief executive officer of a business and a man who has long had an active interest in the social teaching of the church. John Caron makes a persuasive case that the people who write church documents, and more specifically the U.S. bishops' pastoral letter on the economy, *Economic Justice for All*, do not take the time to understand the world of the business manager. Consequently, the teaching is not very influential in the business world. While it is true that some of the specific proposals of the economics teaching have fallen on deaf ears, a case might be made that the fundamental vision of Catholic social thought is finding an echo in more and more of the statements of the top managers of our public and private institutions. For example, President Clinton is quite explicit in his support of the basic vision:

> I also share the values expressed in the Bishops' pastoral letter on
> the economy: that every institution and every economic decision in
> our society must be judged by whether it protects or undermines the

dignity of the human person. And, for everyone who can work, human dignity is first and foremost the opportunity and the obligation to support oneself and contribute to society.[3]

However, as Jean-Yves Calvez notes: "The U.S. bishops are aware, as they have said in their pastoral letter *Economic Justice for All* (1986), that when they enter the more specific fields of economic reality their recommendations are more controversial." Caron points to the negative consequences of controversial proposals and clearly he is speaking for many. To be sure, his suggestion that there be more opportunities for dialogue between theologians and business leaders is well taken. If there is to be a new world economic order, it will be realized only with the active leadership of the business community.

Notes

1. Robert S. McNamara, "A Vision of a 'New World Security Order," *Report of the Joan B. Kroc Institute for Peace Studies*, Notre Dame, Ind., Fall 1992, p. 1.
2. Governor Bill Clinton, "Remarks Prepared for Delivery: University of Notre Dame," September 11, 1992, p. 5.
3. *Ibid.*, p. 6.

One

Catholic Social Teaching: A Communitarian Democratic Capitalism for the New World Order*

Oliver F. Williams, C.S.C.

Harvard Business School professor George C. Lodge (1976; 1983) has long championed what he calls communitarianism, and he believes this position is implicit in Catholic social teaching, especially in the writings of John Paul II. In presenting communitarianism to the business community, Lodge proceeds as follows:

> The community—New York City, for example—is more than the sum of individuals in it; the community is organic, not atomistic. It has special and urgent needs as a community. The survival and the self-respect of the individuals in it depend on the recognition of those needs. . . . In the complex and highly organized America of today, few can live as Locke had in mind. (1983, p. 245)

This chapter will argue that contemporary Catholic social teaching, in particular, the most recent document, *Centesimus Annus*, offers a vision of a new communitarian democratic capitalism that is a humane and ethical alternative to the present state of affairs. It will outline the central communitarian features of Catholic social teaching and some of their implications for the reform of democratic capitalism.

Communitarianism

Centesimus Annus (CA) was issued on May 1, 1991, the hundredth anniversary of *Rerum Novarum*, a treatise generally considered the church's first formal reflection on the social and political implications of the biblical teaching. Catholic social teaching has developed consciously its positions in opposition to those of the influential philosopher John

---

*Also published in a 1993 issue of the *Journal of Business Ethics*.

Locke (1632–1704) and the school of thought known as liberalism. In "liberal" thought, society is understood as a collection of individuals who have come together to promote and protect their private rights and interests. For Locke (1963) the law of nature is the basis for commutative justice which provides the norms for contractual and exchange relationships between atomistic individuals.

> The *state of nature* has a law of nature to govern it which obliges everyone: and reason, which is that law, teaches all [hu]mankind, who will but consult it, that being all equal and independent, no one ought to harm another in his [or her] health, liberty, or possessions. (P. 311)

In Locke's state of nature, however, the rights to liberty and to property are in perpetual jeopardy, and thus there is need for a political body and a government; in this regime, however, government can curtail freedom or property rights only when defending the liberty or property of another citizen. These rights override all others.

Communitarianism, on the contrary, holds that the person is social by nature, not by choice. The need for others, for community, is a constitutive dimension of the person. Thus, the "law of nature" grounds not only a commutative justice but also a distributive and a social justice as well. *Centesimus Annus* is based on this premise.

> Even prior to the logic of a fair exchange of goods and the forms of justice appropriate to it, there exists something which is due to man because he is man, by reason of his lofty dignity. Inseparable from that required "something" is the possibility to survive and at the same time to make an active contribution to the common good of humanity.[1]

This passage goes on to note that many developing countries still have not realized the basic communitarian vision of *Rerum Novarum* and lack such important safety net policies as unemployment insurance and social security (par. 34). While much of the developed world enjoys these benefits, there are many who still slip through the cracks and go without adequate food, shelter and health care. It is this group that is the focus of much of the religious social teaching.

To be sure, communitarianism is not without its critics. Luttwak (1990) identifies communitarianism as one of the "new antagonisms that could shape world politics through the end of the millennium and beyond" (p. 17). Luttwak characterizes communitarians as those

ready to subordinate democratic majority rule to their own imperatives. As with Lenin's vanguard that must be willing to ignore the
expressed will of the people to serve its real interests (which the
people are too ignorant to recognize), the communitarian vanguard
is prepared to impose its preferences on majorities too backward to
appreciate their superior merits. (P. 25)

He cites environmentalists who use the courts to thwart the pro-
growth decisions of elected government officials as an example of communitarian arrogance. For Luttwak, communitarianism is "a serious
challenge to capitalism and democracy." His point follows that of Joseph
Schumpeter (1940), that is, that the social disruption ("creative destruction") caused by a market economy will be less palatable as people grow
more and more affluent from that very economy. Luttwak fears that, in the
name of community and humane values, communitarians might well
destroy a market economy by inappropriate government intervention.

However, *Centesimus Annus* displays a profound appreciation of the
tension. On the one hand, there is a recognition of the wealth-creating
capacity of a market economy and the need for that economy to be as free
as possible to be efficient. On the other hand, there is the reminder that
Schumpeter's creative destruction has serious human costs when people
lose jobs, businesses fail and whole cities are depressed because of movements of capital, new technology or new markets. The goal is to try to
maintain the benefits of economic growth while trying to address the
human concerns that come with creative destruction. A modest role is
suggested for government and the private sector in cushioning this suffering while building community. Of course, the problem is that it is often
impossible to predict in advance what really is a "modest" intervention by
government. Intervention may do more harm than good if higher prices
and taxes slow growth and cause more social disruption. In one sense,
Centesimus Annus wants to have it both ways: economic efficiency with
all the advances it enables in the moral, social and political worlds, as well
as a humane community insulated by government and private-sector
intervention from the suffering entailed with a free economy's creative
destruction. While this is a noble vision—and one I share—a fresh reading
of Schumpeter's *Capitalism, Socialism and Democracy* highlights the
magnitude of the challenge.

It is not clear that capitalism and democracy cannot appropriate the
communitarian perspective. In fact, to the contrary, Phillips (1991) argues
that communitarianism is a much more appropriate philosophy than individualism to undergird our way of life as it is actually lived. His point is
that the Declaration of Independence embodies the values of the nation,

and this founding document guarantees not only crucial rights such as life and liberty but also the pursuit of happiness. This pursuit of happiness entails "all those things necessary to achieve a life of genuine human flourishing" and this surely includes a humane community. Contemporary liberal philosophers, however, have many reservations about communitarianism as an ethical theory.

The debate today between contemporary liberal philosophers (for example, Rawls, 1971; Dworkin, 1977; Nozick, 1974) and communitarians (for example, Sandel, 1982; MacIntyre, 1984) most often focuses on what each position perceives the other to be lacking. The liberal philosophers argue that communitarians neglect adequate grounding for individual rights, while the communitarians stress the omission of sufficient attention to community obligations and civic and personal virtues in the liberal agenda.[2] A number of scholars have adopted a "moderate communitarianism," a position which appropriates a stress on individual rights as well as a focus on the context for those rights, a community of character and virtue. For example, Bellah (1991) in *The Good Society* argues in this fashion. To be sure, communitarians still have significant differences among themselves. Lasch (1992) finds the communitarianism in *The Good Society* "difficult to distinguish from social democracy.... They have a great deal to say about responsibility, but it is social responsibility, not the responsibility of individuals, that mainly concerns them" (p. 10).

Centesimus Annus offers an account of "moderate communitarianism" which does justice both to the individual and the community and which holds much promise for a more humane democratic capitalism, especially as a New World Order is taking shape. To make this case, four features of Catholic social teaching that clearly embody a moderate communitarianism are outlined below. The features identified, while not an exhaustive description, are the core of what many communitarians espouse (see, for example, Bellah, 1991; Glendon, 1991).

1. *Rights, while important, are not always viewed as absolute but are seen in the context of their role of promoting and protecting human dignity in community.*

Catholic social teaching always has understood that, although the right to private property is important, the worker's right to a "just wage" takes precedence over an employer's right to bargain for the cheapest wages possible. Settling wages below a just or living wage simply because the market will tolerate it is censured as "thoroughgoing individualism . . . contrary to the twofold nature of work as a personal and necessary reality" (par. 8). This teaching was stated first in 1891 when Pope Leo XIII, in *Rerum Novarum* (Byers, 1985), put the church squarely on the side of the workers in the struggle for recognition of trade unions. Since workers have a right to a living wage, they have the additional right to join labor unions to secure this right. This right is considered essential even today (Oswald, 1984; Fitzgerald, 1983; Cunningham, 1987; and Ghilarducci, 1991). *Rerum Novarum* also indicated that the state has the right and duty to ensure that this right and others are promoted and protected by legislation.

Monsignor John A. Ryan was perhaps the most influential scholar in U.S. Catholic circles, writing *A Living Wage* (1906) and *Distributive Justice* (1916). Ryan drafted a crucial document of the National Catholic Welfare Conference (the predecessor of the United States Catholic Conference) issued in 1919 by the U.S. bishops and often cited as the forerunner of some of Franklin Roosevelt's New Deal policies. Titled *Social Reconstruction: A General Review of the Problems and Survey of Remedies*, Ryan's document offered a moral perspective on the economy and made suggestions for a humane community, including such reforms as minimum-wage laws, child-labor laws, the right of labor to organize, and unemployment and health insurance. For the most part, Ryan's suggestions have become public policy in the United States and his vision is still a powerful one.

It is important to note that the notion of a living or just wage has taken on different meanings as the "background institutions" have evolved (De George, 1986). The background institutions, or the make-up of the social order, determine the criterion of fairness or justice of a wage. In the context of the 1930s, for example, fairness was largely determined by need and the cry was for market restraints against exploitation. In the light of a whole array of state interventions such as minimum-wage laws, unemployment insurance, welfare programs and trade union empowerment, there is a consensus that the system is generally a just one and labor transactions are free and not coerced. Today, most developed countries are thought to have a relatively just system and, hence, wages produced by market forces are usually accepted as just. Where there is injustice it concerns issues of equality and discrimination. In less developed countries, however, where there are few, if any, background institutions, there is still a pressing need for legislation to prevent starvation wages that preclude any life but bare subsistence. In these extreme situations, because of the unfair or underdeveloped system, the burden of determining a just wage cannot be left to the market but falls upon those who manage private and public institutions (Tavis, 1991). To be sure, this is no easy problem to resolve.

Catholic social thought is ever vigilant against the collectivist tendencies which tend to stifle individual freedom and obliterate legitimate mediating structures. This defense of personal rights clearly is evident in the *Centesimus Annus* where Pope John Paul II vigorously defends the solidarity of workers and their right to come together in organizations to defend common interests as well as numerous other rights. Eschewing the model of interest-group pluralism in democratic politics, which tends to view the world exclusively through the prism of one set of interests, Catholic social thought repeatedly returns to the notion of the common good as the appropriate context in which to consider one's own interests. While the concept of the common good is found helpful by many Protestant (West, 1987; Wogaman, 1987) and Catholic scholars (Curran, 1987; McInerny, 1987), McCann (1987) argues that the term is "so nebulous that nothing very well focused by way of a moral agenda can be inferred from it" (p. 159). He suggests a more procedural and historical perspective with the phrase "the good to be pursued in common." John Paul II uses the term in a way sympathetic to McCann's analysis.

A good example of what McCann has in mind is the process used by the U.S. Catholic bishops in writing their 1986 document on economic ethics, *Economic Justice For All*. Public hearings were held throughout the country and several draft documents published to solicit comments. Similar to *Centesimus Annus,* the final document is decidedly empirical and clearly shows evolution from previous statements. All this is done in an attempt

> to situate particular interests within the framework of a coherent vision of the common good. The latter is not simply the sum total of particular interests; rather it involves an assessment and integration of those interests on the basis of a balanced hierarchy of values; ultimately, it demands a correct understanding of the dignity and the rights of the person. (Par. 47)

Catholic social teaching's position that individual rights are not absolute is illustrated also in the teaching on the right to private property; Chapter 4 of *Centesimus Annus,* titled "Private Property and the Universal Destination of Material Goods," concludes with a succinct summary: "Ownership morally justifies itself in the creation, at the proper time and in the proper way, of opportunities for work and human growth for all" (par. 43). The point here is that income and wealth differences are justified under the rubric of private property; however, possessing wealth entails obligations to the community. Although those obligations are not spelled out in any detail, the teaching does put the burden on the consciences of those with resources to use their ingenuity and entrepreneurship to create jobs and communities where all have the opportunity to flourish.

The society envisioned by Catholic social teaching is one where private property is respected. Following the medieval scholar Thomas Aquinas, the church assumes that private property enables the human development intended by the Creator. Yet the teaching has always insisted that private property has a social dimension which requires that owners consider the common good in the use of property.[3] This vision of society assumes that some persons will have more material goods than others but that the affluent will provide for the less fortunate, either through the channels of public policy or other appropriate groups of society. The emphasis is always on respect for the human dignity of the poor, even in their unfortunate situation. The ideal is to structure society so that all those who are able might provide for themselves and their families by freely employing their talents.

2. *The market has an important though limited function in society.*

Catholic social teaching has a teleological understanding of human institutions and so the constant refrain is to ask the *purpose* of the market economy in society. The key premise is that development entails much more than producing goods and services; development is a matter of enabling people to follow their unique personal vocation, to be creative, to participate and to work and thus "to respond to God's call" (par. 29). The market, in this vision, plays an important role in that it provides the material conditions for all these moral, spiritual and political ideals to be realized. It is not, however, the be all and end all.

While the writings of Catholic social teaching have not always seemed to understand the market system (Pichler, 1983, 1984), *Centesimus Annus* marks a dramatic change and explicitly endorses the value of a market economy, although with one important *caveat*, that is, that the market should not become an idol (par. 40). The significant point, however, is that although heretofore economic self-interest was equated largely with greed in church teaching, *Centesimus Annus* explicitly recognizes the virtues of a market economy in harnessing self-interest for the material betterment of society.

The moral philosopher Adam Smith (1723–1790) is perhaps most responsible for helping people understand the fundamental dynamic of what today is called a market system. Smith asked a very simple but ingenious question: Why are some nations noticeably wealthier than their neighbors? In his famous work, *An Inquiry into the Nature and Causes of the Wealth of Nations* (1776), Smith related his observations. Some nations were wealthier because they used an effective division of labor in making products and because they used the free competitive market. His notion of the market mechanism continues to underpin what have become known as capitalist economies (Smith, 1976).

When each person pursues his or her own self-interest, the common good is enhanced. The baker bakes the very best bread possible and sells it at the lowest price feasible so the proceeds of his sale can be used to buy what he wants. Although motivated by self-interest, the net result is that the community has quality products at a reasonable cost. What Smith did was to show how economic action based on self-interest could be beneficial for the community. This was indeed a remarkable turn of events, for economic self-interest had not been thought to be responsible.

Reflecting on the commerce of his time, Smith concluded that goods will be produced more efficiently and cheaply for all if each person strives to maximize his or her self-interest in the marketplace. Producing attractive goods at competitive prices will be in the self-interest of the producer and in the best interest of the public. Smith speaks of "an invisible hand" which guides self-interested behavior to be of benefit to the whole society. His hope was that if governments would understand the real source of the wealth of nations, they would forgo all tariffs and other measures which provide protection to the producers and advocate a free market.

The prevailing mercantile view looked to the quantity of precious metals to measure wealth. Smith rejected this understanding, for he saw that real wealth was a nation's productivity, "the value of the annual produce of its land and labour." Increased productivity (wealth) was not an *end* in itself but a *means* to increase the quality of life of people. Smith accepted the Judeo-Christian vision which portrayed a land where all might enjoy the good things of creation. His insight was that this vision, although far from realized in any nation, was gradually becoming a reality in those places that used incentives, economic action based on self-interest (profit motive), and a market economy. In my view, Smith assumed that the *self* that was self-interested would be shaped by moral forces in the community so that economic self-interest would not always degenerate into a crass selfishness.[4] The virtues Smith celebrates are those of the Judeo-Christian vision and are articulated clearly in his earlier treatise on ethics; I contend that this earlier work forms the context for the later remarks on self-interest in *The Wealth of Nations*. Consider Smith's position:

> And hence it is that to feel much for others and little for ourselves, that to restrain our selfish and to indulge our benevolent affections constitutes the perfection of human nature and can alone produce among [hu]mankind that harmony of sentiments and passions in which consists their whole grace and propriety. (1969, pp. 71–72)

Thus, in my view, Smith's vision was one of a market economy enabling a humane community (Williams, 1986). Catholic social teaching is one attempt to speak to problems of the day and provide an ethical and religious dimension to economic life and, hence, foster the humane community envisioned by Smith. *Centesimus Annus* makes this point as a recurring theme. In particular, the document argues that what is lacking in our time is a moral culture capable of informing economic life so that it has a context in a humane community. What is needed is a revitalized ethical and religious dimension (par. 39).

One way to view church statements which reflect on and offer guidance to capitalist economies is as an attempt to provide a religious vision. The church strives to influence the institutions of society so that they might be the moral force assumed by Adam Smith, ensuring that a market economy does not so blind a people that it becomes an acquisitive society. This blindness happens when the *means* of developing the good society, wealth creation, becomes an *end* in itself. Moral institutions can influence minds and hearts and, thus, individual choices. The point is not to eliminate consumer sovereignty but, rather, to strengthen it. The goal is growth, with all having some share, and the perennial target of condemnation by Catholic social teaching is materialism, acquisitiveness for its own sake. Church teaching has never seen fit to condemn capitalism as intrinsically evil, although some theologians have (Baum, 1982), but rather has aimed its guidance at the reform of institutions, structures and personal life involved with the free market economy. The key criticism of capitalism focuses on what it does to people.

> It is not wrong to want to live better; what is wrong is a style of life which is presumed to be better when it is directed toward "having" rather than "being" and which wants to have more not in order to be more, but in order to spend life in enjoyment as an end in itself. It is therefore necessary to create lifestyles in which the quest for truth, beauty, goodness and communion with others for the sake of common growth are the factors which determine consumer choices, savings and investments. (Par. 36)

3. *The state has an important though limited function in society.*

Paragraph 42 of *Centesimus Annus* is the strongest affirmation of a market economy that Catholic social teaching has ever made. Yet within this affirmation there are qualifications which go to the core of the church's tradition on economic matters. The paragraph notes that now that communism is a failure, the question arises as to what economic system should be recommended as the model for all those developing countries struggling for economic and political progress. Clearly, the answer is a market economy, but a mixed economy with government regulation that strives to cushion the inevitable destructive side of the market. While the concern for people is not new in Catholic social teaching, what is new is an *explicit* recognition that this concern is best exercised by taking into account the basic dynamic of the market system.

Paragraph 42 reflects the central concerns found throughout the history of Catholic social teaching since the publishing of *Rerum Novarum* in 1891. Catholic social teaching offers a vision of this world that is religious and ethical. It is a world where a huge gap between the rich and the poor is seen as a problem and where all, especially the poor in developing countries, ought to have the opportunity of earning a living wage (Hehir, 1991; Bartell, 1991; Vogel, 1987). The implicit assumption here is that some version of capitalism can narrow this gap (Wilber and Jameson, 1982, 1983). It is a vision of society where the state has a role in influencing the economy toward the common good, but one where the state is not all powerful in the economic realm; in fact, the goal is for the state to encourage and enable "mediating institutions," those groupings between the individual and the state that foster freedom and initiative, such groups as professional associations, churches, corporations, trade unions, universities, families and so on (Berger, 1976). While some communitarians would advocate a more comprehensive role for the state (for example, Bellah [1991] calls for a "global New Deal"), most are concerned that state power should be limited. The fear is that inordinate power concentrated in either the market or the state would stifle initiative and freedom and generally not serve the human community.

In 1931 Pope Pius XI issued *Quadragesimo Anno* (Byers, 1985). Although its proposed alternative model of society is of dubious value today, the role of the church as an agent of change in the sociopolitical order clearly was established. Three principles enunciated in the document have been dominant in all subsequent Catholic social theory: the need to protect the dignity of the person; the concern that organizations be no larger than necessary—subsidiarity (Schall, 1982, pp. 121–125); and the focus on the necessity for mediating structures (family, professional associations, church, etc.) between the person and the state.

Quadragesimo Anno outlined a vision of society and its relationship to the state that has continued to develop in Catholic social thought. Society is a community of communities comprised of all the various groupings that people find necessary or helpful—families, churches, unions, professional associations, business corporations, social clubs, neighborhood associations, and so on. The role of the state is to be *in the service of* society, that is, its role is primarily to facilitate the cooperation and well-being of all these groupings or "mediating structures" as they are often called today. The encyclical uses the verbs *direct, watch, urge* and *restrain* "as occasion requires and necessity demands" when describing the role of the state (par. 80). The 1961 encyclical of Pope John XXIII, *Mater et Magistra* (Byers, 1985), employs similar terms: the role of the state is to "encourage, stimulate, regulate, supplement and complement" (par. 53).

Centesimus Annus reiterates the teaching for our time:

> It is the task of the state to provide for the defense and preservation of common goods such as the natural and human environments, which cannot be safeguarded simply by market forces. Just as in the time of primitive capitalism the state had the duty of defending the basic rights of workers, so now, with the new capitalism, the state and all of society have the duty of defending those collective goods which, among others, constitute the essential framework for the legitimate pursuit of personal goals on the part of each individual. (Par. 40)

Catholic social teaching is very cautious about advocating big government as the answer to social problems, even to the point of harshly criticizing the "welfare state." On the question of the right of everyone to work, *Centesimus Annus* illustrates the typical understanding of the role of the state in the context of the principle of subsidiarity.

> Another task of the state is that of overseeing and directing the exercise of human rights in the economic sector. However, primary responsibility in this area belongs not to the state, but to individuals and to the various groups and associations which make up society. The state could not directly ensure the right to work for all its citizens unless it controlled every aspect of economic life and restricted the free initiative of individuals. This does not mean, however, that the state has no competence in this domain, as was claimed by those who argued against any rules in the economic sphere. Rather, the state has a duty to sustain business activities by creating conditions which will ensure job opportunities, by stimulating those activities where they are lacking or by supporting them in moments of crisis. (Par. 48)

What becomes clear is that the document gives little in the way of concrete policy guidance. For example, what is the best way to create jobs? Is the best policy that advanced by the liberal Democratic or the conservative Republican wing? Both groups can find statements that seem to support their ideology and this is both the strength and the weakness of

Catholic social teaching. The truth of the matter is that the document is not intended to *close* the discussion on job creation or any other matter of public policy, but rather to *open* discussion, to motivate people of good-will to keep seeking solutions to what often appear to be intractable problems.

This vision underpins all the economic teaching of the church. While accepting the value of a market economy, religious social thought argues that one must have a conscious concern for the common good of all, and not depend on unconscious workings of the market, the "hidden hand" to solve all problems. Some disciples of Adam Smith believed in God's providence working to ensure the common good, a self-regulating economy. Religious social thought says, in effect, that we must make God's work our own, that we must have a conscious care for the common good. This sometimes requires government regulation of the market. To be sure, regulation is tricky business and the good consequences sought are often elusive. For religious social thought, failure in a particular regulation is no argument against regulation, however, but rather one for better regulation. The continual refrain of Catholic social teaching is that we must learn how to do it right. Deciding on appropriate social regulation entails much debate and often trial and error (see De George, 1989; Walton, 1989; and Shriver, 1989, for a discussion of appropriate regulation in the investment industry).

4. Individuality is shaped by social institutions, and institutions that corrupt people's character need to be reformed while those engendering desirable character traits ought to be strengthened.

To understand Catholic social teaching on economic life it is necessary to see it in the context of a religious view of earthly existence. The overarching Catholic vision was stated in systematic form by Thomas Aquinas (1225–1274) and this perspective continues to guide the church today. Aquinas, drawing on the biblical teaching and the writings of the Church Fathers, wove an enduring tapestry with an Aristotelian and neo-Platonic philosophic framework. All of creation flows from God and finally will return to God. The goal of life on this earth is to become the kind of person who will finally enjoy the vision of God in the next world. "Man's ultimate happiness consists solely in the contemplation of God" (*Summa Contra Gentiles*, III, 37).

Becoming a person who might enjoy this vision, becoming virtuous, is only thought to be possible because of a gift of God (a supernatural gift of grace). Appropriating the virtues over a lifetime is the *means* to the *end* of human life, then one is oriented properly to God and may see God in the next life. For Aquinas, however, all creation is fundamentally good, and being properly oriented to God entails as well the appropriate orientation toward the natural good. *Centesimus Annus* says: "People lose sight of the fact that life in society has neither the market nor the state as its final purpose, since life itself has a unique value which the state and the market must serve" (par. 49). Aquinas highlights the key biblical virtues—faith, hope and charity—but he stresses also the need to form character in Aristotle's four cardinal virtues: wisdom, justice, temperance, and fortitude.

For Aquinas, then, moral and spiritual nourishment were crucial, for this was the way one prepared for life in the next world. The focus was on personal morality and in this context the medieval theologians wrote much about just prices, trade and usury (Noonan, 1957). The efforts of the moralist were directed largely to individual Christians and were designed to insure that each kept faithful to a path of personal virtue.

While the churches have never forsaken their role of shaping the character of individual Christians through preaching, teaching and liturgy, there has been a new realization that the Christian mission also entails shaping the character of social structures and transforming the world. Aquinas lived in an era when it was generally assumed that society was static. People most often remained in the socioeconomic group where they were born as lord, peasant, craftsman or merchant. "Justice" was understood to mean that each person was entitled to whatever their particular role in society required. Thus, in "justice," a lord had considerably more material goods than a peasant. Viewing the world in terms of the analogy of the human body, each class of society was seen to have a different role to perform in society, but all were united in an organic unity.

In our time, transforming institutions and hence involvement in social and political issues have come to be understood, in the words of the official 1971 church document *Justice in the World* (Byers, 1985), as a "constitutive dimension of the preaching of the Gospel" (p. 250).

In the area of economic ethics, the church has had much to say in the last hundred years. While it is true that the skill of producing wealth is a relatively new one in the history of the human race, and that this skill has the potential to create a more humane life and hence advance the plan of God, the church insists that wealth creation always be carried out in the context of the end of life on this earth, *the formation of virtuous persons.* Economic activity is only a means, and it must be guided by reference to the moral ends. This is the heart of the teaching of Thomas Aquinas, and it continues to form the basis of church documents. Some seven hundred years later, the Second Vatican Council decree, "The Church in the Modern World," (Byers, 1985) restates the point clearly: "Economic activity is to be carried out according to its own methods and laws but within the limits of morality so that God's plan for humankind can be realized (par. 64).

The insight of Catholic social teaching, applied in various circumstances throughout the last century, is that capitalism without a context in a humane community seems inevitably to shape people into greedy and insensitive human beings. Thus, the church teaching accepts the market economy but with a key qualification, that the state intervene where essential to promote and protect the human dignity.

A major theme of the criticism of capitalism by the church is summed up well by Pope John Paul II in speaking of alienation. He notes that the Marxist analysis of alienation is false, but there is a type of alienation in our life today. The point is that it is quite possible for people in a market economy to lose touch with any real meaning or value in life (par. 4). This can happen in two ways, the first is called "consumerism," an easily misunderstood term. Consumerism, as a pejorative term, is certainly not referring to the consumption of material goods, which is, after all, required for a market economy to function and for people to have employment. Consumerism refers to that aberration where people are led to believe that happiness and self-fulfillment are found solely in acquiring material goods. The values of friendship, music and beauty, for example, come to pale in importance and because basic, non-materialistic needs are not met, there is alienation. Consumer advocates in the United States have long been critical of certain kinds of advertising because of its adverse cultural and social effects similar to those described above. *Centesimus Annus*, rather uncritically, judges the market to be the cause of consumerism. This may be the case, but the issue needs much more research. Meaning and value typically would be the domain of the other major institutions of society, especially the family, the school and the church. How can these institutions exercise more influence? Is this problem to be solved by more ethical marketing and advertising (Williams and Murphy, 1992)? I believe it is at least a partial solution.

Alienation can also be traced to the workplace when the workers perceive their work as meaningless and have no sense of participation (par. 41). There is considerable research in this area of job satisfaction and the quality of work life, and most find that worker productivity hinges on experienced meaningfulness. It is significant that it is only in the most advanced market economies that this research is being conducted and that the workplace is beginning to be humanized, a point that religious social teaching often overlooks.

To be sure, Catholic social teaching recognizes that participation in market economy can be a great aid toward developing character. While the market seldom teaches one how to love, the habits and virtues required to participate in the market—honesty, industriousness, patience, deferred gratification, for example—are ones extolled by the church. *Centesimus Annus* reiterates this point (par. 32). Thus, participation in the market need not, in principle, have a deleterious effect on character but, on the contrary, can transform the person thus creating the greatest resource and the ultimate source of wealth (Williams, 1992).

One of the roles of the state, according to this religious perspective, is to facilitate the growth of desirable character traits and mute those that are less noble. Yet there is a confidence in the goodness, the cooperative dimension of the person, so that the social constraints of the state and the shape of institutions, including a market economy, are designed to enhance human freedom and curtail selfishness for the common good. *Centesimus Annus* makes these points well.

> Moreover, man, who was created for freedom, bears within himself the wound of original sin, which constantly draws him toward evil and puts him in need of redemption. Not only is this doctrine an integral part of Christian revelation, it also has great hermeneutical value insofar as it helps one to understand human reality. Man tends toward good, but he is also capable of evil. He can transcend his immediate interest and still remain bound to it. The social order will be all the more stable the more it takes this fact into account and does not place in opposition personal interest and the interests of society as a whole, but rather seeks ways to bring them into fruitful harmony. In fact, where self-interest is violently suppressed it is replaced by a burdensome system of bureaucratic control which dries up the wellsprings of initiative and creativity. (Par. 25)

As indicated above, Catholic social teaching, and specifically *Centesimus Annus*, evidence an understanding of Adam Smith and his use of "self-interest" in analyzing the dynamics of a market economy.

The society envisioned by Catholic social teaching is one where the human dignity of all is given attention, especially the poor. Aiding the poor means assisting them so that they might make good use of their capacity for work (par. 28). Serving the poor will enhance one's personal traits and may even lead to a change of horizon so that one advocates major changes in lifestyle and institutional life for a new world order.

In discussing the role of profit, Catholic social teaching, in principle, views it with approval. Yet, if the quest for profit destroys the personal character traits that are essential for the human community called business, then the cost is too high (par. 35). *Centesimus Annus*, in stating that there are limits to what one should do for profit, finds an echo in much of the management ethics literature.

A key concern of communitarians is to strengthen the character-forming institutions which provide the discipline that develops that trait so essential for civic life and public trust. Institutions such as the family, the church, the neighborhood and school are eroded when the market dominates life in society. Catholic social teaching is clear in distinguishing its social doctrine from socialism, where the social nature of the person is "completely fulfilled in the state." For Catholic social teaching, the social nature of the person is "realized in various intermediary groups, beginning with the family and including economic, social, political and cultural groups (par. 13). The family is where the person "first receives formative ideas about truth and goodness and learns what it means to love and to be loved, and thus what it means to actually be a person (par. 39).

Catholic social teaching is particularly concerned that the family be supported and strengthened by social policies of the state. The role modeling in the family is taken to be the primary vehicle for developing the character essential for the good society.

> In order to overcome today's widespread individualistic mentality, what is required is a concrete commitment to solidarity and charity, beginning in the family with the mutual support of husband and wife and the care which the different generations give to one another. (Par. 49)

Contemporary liberal philosophers understandably are concerned that communitarians, especially the religious variety, will strive in dogmatic fashion to reorient society and ignore individual rights in the process. Catholic social teaching holds that both individual rights and the requirements of the community have equal moral status but that rights must be viewed in the light of community and the community in the light of individual rights. For example, in the case of the "living wage" discussed above, there is agreement that the employer has the right of private property but also that the community should have the power to protect and promote the human dignity of the worker and his or her family by shaping a just social system with its background institutions or, in developing countries, by regulating a living wage. Thus, the community is charged to protect this substantive good, human dignity.

Crucial to the moderate communitarian position of Catholic social teaching is the conviction that although individuals ought to shape their institutions in ways that form fulfilling communities, this shaping ought to be a product of rational public discussion. This is true whether the issue is curtailing individual rights to ensure competition in the marketplace or controlling pornography or illicit drug traffic or changing unjust governments. For example, in discussing unjust governments, Catholic social teaching tries to steer a course between simply supporting the *status quo*, where it may be unjust or corrupting, and unabashedly encouraging violent revolution. To the rich and powerful, the teaching counsels concern for the poor and the environment that nurtures them; to the poor, it preaches "solidarity" by taking a stand and collectively reacting to exploitative situations and systems. In speaking of the momentous changes in Eastern Europe and the U.S.S.R., *Centesimus Annus* exemplifies this approach.

> Also worthy of emphasis is the fact that the fall of this kind of "bloc" or empire was accomplished almost everywhere by means of peaceful protest, using only the weapons of truth and justice. While Marxism held that only by exacerbating social conflicts was it possible to resolve them through violent confrontation, the protests which led to the collapse of Marxism tenaciously insisted on trying every avenue of negotiation, dialogue and witness to the truth, appealing to the conscience of the adversary and seeking to reawaken in him a sense of shared human dignity. (Par. 23)

In our time, strong disagreements among people of goodwill over issues such as abortion continue to challenge our confidence in rational discussion as a feature essential for a humane community. In my view, however, fidelity to the vision of Catholic social teaching demands allegiance to public, rational discussion as *the means* to form a more humane community.

Moderate Communitarianism: Realizing the Vision

In the area of economic ethics, Catholic social teaching today is trying to develop a moral consensus and to establish and strengthen those institutions which foster morally constrained behavior. The teaching calls the church to be a community that calls people to higher values and obligations. It offers an integrative vision, but it is not naive about the power of economic rationality in the workplace. The recent spate of hostile akeovers and plant closings serve as a reminder of the power of economic rationality. Catholic social teaching realizes that to have compelling power, its teaching must be matched by concrete proposals for institutional arrangements which might overcome the distrust inherent in the dynamic of self-interest in the market. Thus, for example, *Centesimus Annus* "recognizes the legitimacy of workers' efforts to obtain full respect for their dignity and to gain broader areas of participation in the life of industrial enterprises" (par. 43). Institutional changes that may overcome distrust and harness greed and selfishness are suggested.

To be sure, there are some scholars who argue that voluntarism in ethical areas and social responsibility of business is stymied by economic rationality, for the "same competitive process which prevents laziness or incompetence also precludes voluntarism on any significant scale" (Baumol, 1991, pp. 50–53). Charles Schultze has pioneered these ideas, for the most part advocated by *Centesimus Annus*, in his *The Public Use of Private Interest* (1977). Baumol, for example, argues for the state to use the price mechanism to achieve social goals "so that the behavior we desire becomes *more profitable* than the activity patterns we want to modify." Catholic social teaching is more hopeful about the prospect of voluntarism in the business community; it does, however, see merit in Baumol's argument and suggests that new institutional arrangements be explored to enable more respect for the person and the health of the community.

The U.S. bishops' 1986 pastoral letter on the economy, *Economic Justice for All*, is more specific than *Centesimus Annus* in making suggestions for new institutional arrangements that might enhance a communitarian democratic capitalism. The rationale is stated as follows:

> The virtues of good citizenship require a lively sense of participation in the commonwealth and of having obligations as well as rights within it. The nation's economic health depends on strengthening these virtues among all its people, and on the development of institutional arrangements supportive of these virtues. (Par. 296)

While recognizing that there are strengths and weaknesses to each of these proposals, the documents suggest some trial and error experimentation. The proposals include, among others, the following: new structures of accountability so that not only stockholders but all the stakeholders ("workers, managers, owners or shareholders, suppliers, customers, creditors, the local community, and the wider society") are considered in important decisions; cooperative ownership of a firm by all workers; and participation of workers in plant closing decisions or decisions on movement of capital. The U.S. bishops' document, as well as *Centesimus Annus*, also champion the United Nations as an indispensable international agency which can serve to overcome distrust among nations and move the world toward a global community. While some of the above suggestions may prove wanting, the point is still valid. That is, a new vision is not feasible without new structures that will help overcome distrust and facilitate the birth of a communitarian democratic capitalism. A communitarian democratic capitalism could blossom from a vision that respects both individual rights and a virtuous community, values an essential but not all-powerful role for the state and the market, and supports a conscious effort to sustain and enhance those institutions that develop and support character. While this vision is far from being realized, it is the vision of contemporary Catholic social teaching.

What clearly is revealed from the texts cited in this article is that Catholic social teaching now supports a market economy and understands the values and virtues entailed with participation in such an economy. Before the publication of *Centesimus Annus*, such support and understanding was not entirely clear to many, particularly those in the business community.

The texts cited above also reveal that Catholic social teaching strongly supports a socially regulated capitalism. Of course, the mixed economy of the United States and many other nations has much social regulation. The great debate today concerns how much and what kind of new social regulations is appropriate. Here, *Centesimus Annus* is not particularly helpful. It offers general principles on the role of government but few specifics on what constitutes "good" or "bad" government. Although partisans on both sides of the aisle quote the document to bolster their case, most scholars would argue that the role and function of the teaching is to offer a vision for believers and people of goodwill, not to offer concrete particulars.

On the one hand, the encyclical makes a shocking proposal: "sacrificing the positions of income and power enjoyed by the more developed economies" to aid the economies of the less developed countries (par. 52). On the other hand, the teaching is very cautious about advocating big government as the answer to social problems, even to the point of harshly criticizing the "welfare state" (par. 48). The encyclical displays an understanding of the trade-off between efficiency and equity and constantly reminds decision makers to focus on the dignity of the person. It does not, however, enter into specifics, leaving the prudential decisions about social regulation to those qualified to make them. The thrust of the encyclical, however, is to be unyielding on basic moral objectives such as concern for the poor and less fortunate. Those sympathetic with Arthur Okun's thesis in *Equality and Efficiency: The Big Tradeoff* (1975) will find much that is congenial with Catholic social teaching.

In my view, Catholic social teaching and all religious and moral teaching play an important role in society. Perhaps Max Weber (1864–1920) said it best. In the final pages of his classic *The Protestant Ethic and the Spirit of Capitalism* (1958), he candidly expressed doubts that capitalism could survive once it lost religious roots.

> Where the fulfillment of the calling cannot be directly related to the highest spiritual and cultural values, or when, on the other hand, it need not be felt simply as economic compulsion, the individual generally abandons the attempt to justify it at all. In the field of its highest development, in the United States, the pursuit of wealth, stripped

of its religious and ethical meaning, tends to become associated with purely mundane passions. . . . For of the last stage of this cultural development, it might well be truly said: "Specialists without spirit, sensualists without heart." (P. 182)

From this perspective, religious social thought that reminds us of the plight of the poor and the powerless in society is capitalism's best friend. Its appeal to the consciences of people of goodwill keeps alive the vision of a just and wholesome community and, consequently, puts the roles of business and government in proper perspective.

If people without food, housing, jobs, participation, etc., are ever to have the quality of life envisioned by the encyclical, it will be because the highly skilled managers of today's complex institutions directed their time and talent to this challenge. Post (1991) offers an insightful "theory of institutional responsibility" to assist managers in this task (see also Tavis, 1991; Sethi and Steidlmeier, 1991). The pressing need is for cooperation so that, together, visionaries and managers might begin to lay the groundwork for a more just world. If the encyclical can bring people together for discussion and action on this matter, it will go down in history as a great success.

Notes

This article includes an updated version of some material previously published. For more elaboration on the history of Catholic social teaching, see articles by O. F. Williams in J. W. Houck and O. F. Williams, eds., *Catholic Social Teaching and the U.S. Economy: Working Papers for a Bishops' Pastoral* (Washington, D.C.: University Press of America, 1984); and in O. F. Williams and J. Houck, eds., *The Judeo-Christian Vision and the Modern Corporation* (Notre Dame, Ind: University of Notre Dame Press, 1982).

1. Unfortunately, exclusive language prevails throughout papal encyclicals. Since it is a reminder of justice issues yet to be tackled, I have let it stand. All citations of *Centesimus Annus* are to the text published by the United States Catholic Conference, Washington, D.C.

2. For a summary and bibliography of this debate as it focuses on the relationship between the individual and the community, see Etzioni (1991).

3. For the view of Thomas Aquinas on private property, see *Summa Theologica* II–II, 66, 2. For a summary of the tradition, see E. Duff, "Private Property," *New Catholic Encyclopedia*, 2:849–55.

4. Note that I interpret Adam Smith by relying on his earlier work in ethics and thus suggest that Smith assumed that the good citizen would promote the common good. Cf. Adam Smith, *The Theory of Moral Sentiments*

(Indianapolis, Ind.: Liberty Classics, 1969; originally published in 1753, twenty years earlier than *The Wealth of Nations*). For more discussion of Adam Smith see my earlier essay, "The Professional Disciplines: Business and Management," *Justice and Peace Education: Models for College and University Faculty*, David M. Johnson, ed. (Maryknoll, N.Y.: Orbis Books, 1986), pp. 141–156.

Bibliography

Bartell, E. J., "John Paul II and International Development," *The Making of an Economic Vision*, Oliver F. Williams and John W. Houck, eds. (Washington, D.C.: University Press of America, 1991), pp. 217–239.

Baum, G., *The Priority of Labor* (New York: Paulist Press, 1982).

Baumol, W. J., *Perfect Markets and Easy Virtue: Business Ethics and the Invisable Hand* (Cambridge, Mass.: Blackwell, 1991).

Bellah, R., *The Good Society* (New York: Knopf, 1991).

Berger, P., "In Praise of Particularity: The Concept of Mediating Structures," *Review of Politics*, pp. 130–144, July 1976.

Byers, D. M., *Justice in the Market Place: Collected Statements of the Vatican and the U.S. Catholic Bishops on Economic Policy, 1891–1984* (Washington, D.C.: United States Catholic Conference, Inc., 1985).

Cunningham, W. J., "The AFL-CIO Looks at the Common Good," *The Common Good and U. S. Capitalism*, Oliver F. Williams and John W. Houck, eds. (Washington, D.C.: University Press of America, 1987), pp. 344–363.

Curran, C. E., "The Common Good and Official Catholic Social Teaching," *The Common Good and U.S. Capitalism*, Oliver F. Williams and John W. Houck, eds. (Washington, D.C.: University Press of America, 1987), pp. 111–129.

De George, R. T., *Business Ethics*, second edition (New York: Macmillan Publishing Company, 1986).

———, "Ethics and the Financial Community: An Overview," in *Ethics and the Investment Industry*, Oliver F. Williams, Frank K. Reilly and John W. Houck, eds. (Savage, Md.: Rowman & Littlefield, 1989), pp. 197–216.

Dworkin, R., *Taking Rights Seriously* (Cambridge: Harvard University Press, 1977).

Eagleson, J., and Scharper, P., eds., *Puebla and Beyond* (Maryknoll, N.Y.: Orbis Press, 1979).

Ellis, J. T., *American Catholicism*, second edition (Chicago: University of Chicago Press, 1969).

Etzioni, A., "Liberals and Communitarians," *A Responsive Society* (San Francisco: Jossey-Bass Publishers, 1991), pp. 127–152.

Fitzgerald, M. J., "Focus on Labor," *Co-Creation and Capitalism: John Paul II's Laborem Exercens*, John W. Houck and Oliver F. Williams, eds. (Washington, D.C.: University Press of America, 1983), pp. 254–280.

Ghilarducci, T., "John Paul II and American Workers in the Emerging Fourth World," *The Making of an Economic Vision*, Oliver F. Williams and John W. Houck, eds. (Washington, D.C.: University Press of America, 1991), pp. 361–376.

Glendon, M. A., *Rights Talk: The Impoverishment of Political Discourse* (New York: Free Press, 1991).

Hehir, J. B., "John Paul II and the International System," *The Making of an Economic Vision*, Oliver F. Williams and John W. Houck, eds. (Washington, D.C.: University Press of America, 1991), pp. 67–73.

Kasper, W., *Jesus the Christ* (New York: Paulist Press, 1977).

Lasch. C., "Communitarianism or Populism?" *New Oxford Review*, LIX, No. 4, 5–12.

Locke, J., *Two Treatises of Government*, Peter Laslett, ed. (New York: Cambridge University Press, 1963).

Lodge, G. C., *The New American Ideology* (New York: Alfred A. Knopf, 1976).

_____, "Managers and Managed: Problems of Ambivalence," *Co-Creation and Capitalism: John Paul II's Laborem Exercens*, John W. Houck and Oliver F. Williams, eds. (Washington, D.C.: University Press of America, 1983), pp. 229–253.

Luttwak, E., "The Shape of Things to Come," *Commentary*, 89(6), 17–25, 1990.

MacIntyre, A., *After Virtue*, second edition (Notre Dame, Ind.: University of Notre Dame Press, 1984).

McCann, D. P., *Christian Realism and Liberation Theology* (Maryknoll, N.Y.: Orbis Press, 1981).

_____, "The Good to be Pursued in Common," *The Common Good and U.S. Capitalism*, Oliver F. Williams and John W. Houck, eds. (Washington, D.C.: University Press of America, 1987), pp. 158–178.

McInerny, R., "The Primacy of the Common Good," *The Common Good and U.S. Capitalism*, Oliver F. Williams and John W. Houck, eds. (Washington, D.C.: University Press of America, 1987), pp. 70–83.

Miranda, J., *Marx and the Bible*, John Eagleson, trans. (Maryknoll, N.Y.: Orbis Press, 1974).

Neuhaus, Richard John, "The Pope Affirms the 'New Capitalism,'" *Wall Street Journal*, A14, May 2, 1991.

Niebuhr, H. R., *Christ and Culture* (New York: Harper, 1951).

Noonan, J. T., *The Scholastic Analysis of Usury* (Chicago: University of Chicago Press, 1957).

Novak, M., *Freedom With Justice* (San Francisco: Harper & Row, 1984).

Nozick, R., *Anarchy, State, and Utopia* (New York: Basic Books, 1974).

Oswald, R., "The Economy and Workers' Jobs, The Living Wage and a Voice," *Catholic Social Teaching and the U.S. Economy: Working Papers for a Bishops' Pastoral*, John W. Houck and Oliver F. Williams, eds. (Washington, D.C.: University Press of America, 1984), pp. 77–89.

Phillips, R. L., "Communitarianism, the Vatican, and the New Global Order," *Ethics and International Affairs*, 5, 135–147, 1991.

Pichler, J. A., "Business Competence and Religious Values—A Trade-Off?" *Co-Creation and Capitalism: John Paul II's Laborem Exercens*, John W. Houck and Oliver F. Williams, eds. (Washington, D.C.: University Press of America, 1983), pp. 101–123.

————, "Capitalism and Employment: A Policy Perspective," *Catholic Social Teaching and the U.S. Economy: Working Papers for a Bishops' Pastoral*, John W. Houck and Oliver F. Williams, eds. (Washington, D.C.: University Press of America, 1984), pp. 37–76.

Post, J. E., "Managerial Responsibility and Socioeconomic Systems: Assessing the Papal Encyclicals," *The Making of an Economic Vision,* Oliver F. Williams and John W. Houck, eds. (Washington, D.C.: University Press of America, 1991), pp. 312–331.

Rawls, J., *A Theory of Justice* (Cambridge: Harvard University Press, 1971).

Ryan, J. A., *Distributive Justice*, third edition (New York: The Macmillan Company, 1942).

Sandel, M. J., *Liberalism and the Limits of Justice* (Cambridge: Cambridge University Press, 1982).

Schall, J. V., "Catholicism, Business, and Human Priorities," *The Judeo-Christian Vision and the Modern Corporation*, Oliver F. Williams and John W. Houck, eds. (Notre Dame, Ind.: University of Notre Dame Press, 1982), pp. 107–140.

Schriver, D. W., "Ethical Discipline and Religious Hope in the Investment Industry," *Ethics and the Investment Industry*, Oliver F. Williams, Frank K. Reilly, and John W. Houck, eds. (Savage, Md.: Rowman & Littlefield, 1989), pp. 233–250.

Schultze, C. L., *The Public Use of Private Interest* (Washington, D.C.: The Brookings Institution, 1977).

Schumpeter, J., *Capitalism, Socialism and Democracy* (New York: Harper & Row, 1940).

Sethi, S. P., and Steidlmeier, P., "Radicalization of the Socioeconomic Environment of the Third World—Conflicting and Cooperative Roles for the Catholic Church and Multinational Corporations," *The Making of an Economic Vision*, Oliver F. Williams and John W. Houck, eds. (Washington, D.C.: University Press of America, 1991), pp. 332–360.

Smith, Adam, *The Wealth of Nations*, Edwin Cannan, ed. (Chicago: University of Chicago Press, 1976).

_____, *The Theory of Moral Sentiments* (Indianapolis, Ind.: Liberty Classics, 1969).

Tavis, Lee A., "Papal Encyclicals and the Multinational Manager," *The Making of an Economic Vision*, Oliver F. Williams and John W. Houck, eds. (Washington, D.C.: University Press of America, 1991), pp. 289–311.

Vogel, D., "The International Economy and the Common Good," *The Common Good and U.S. Capitalism*, Oliver F. Williams and John W. Houck, eds. (Washington, D.C.: University Press of America, 1987), pp. 388–409.

Walton, C. C., "Investment Bankers from Ethical Perspectives," *Ethics and the Investment Industry*, Oliver F. Williams, Frank K. Reilly and John W. Houck, eds. (Savage, Md.: Rowman & Littlefield, 1989), pp. 217–232.

Weber, Max, *The Protestant Ethic and the Spirit of Capitalism*, Talcott Parsons, trans. (New York: Charles Scribner's, 1958).

West, C. W., "The Common Good and the Participation of the Poor," *The Common Good and U. S. Capitalism*, Oliver F. Williams and John W. Houck, eds. (Washington, D.C.: University Press of America, 1987), pp. 20–49.

Wilber, C. K., and Jameson, K. P., "Goals of a Christian Economy and the Future of the Corporation," *The Judeo-Christian Vision and the Modern Corporation*, Oliver F. Williams and John W. Houck, eds. (Notre Dame, Ind.: University of Notre Dame Press, 1982), pp. 203–217.

_____, *An Inquiry into the Poverty of Economics* (Notre Dame, Ind.: University of Notre Dame Press, 1983).

Williams, O. F., "Can Business Ethics Be Theological? What Athens Can Learn from Jerusalem," *Journal of Business Ethics*, 5, 473–484, 1986.

_____, "Who Cast the First Stone?" *Harvard Business Review* 62(5), 151–160, 1984.

_____, "Religion: The Spirit or the Enemy of Capitalism," *Business Horizons*, 6–13, November/December 1983.

_____, "The Professional Disciplines: Business and Management," *Justice and Peace Education: Models for College and University Faculty*, David M. Johnson, ed. (Maryknoll, N.Y.: Orbis Press, 1986), pp. 141–156.

Williams, O. F., and Murphy, P. E., "The Ethics of Virtue: A Moral Theory for Business," *A Virtuous Life in Business*, Oliver F. Williams and John W. Houck, eds. (Lanham, Md.: Rowman & Littlefield Publishers, Inc., 1992), pp. 9–27.

Wogaman, J. P., "The Common Good and Economic Life: A Protestant Perspective," *The Common Good and U.S. Capitalism*, Oliver F. Williams and John W. Houck, eds. (Washington, D.C.: University Press of America, 1987), pp. 84–110.

Two

The Social Role of the Church: Leo XIII, Vatican II and John Paul II

J. Bryan Hehir

This chapter examines three contributions to the understanding of the social role of Catholicism, and to test the content of that social role in light of the experience of the church in the United States. The three contributions are those of Pope Leo XIII (1878–1903), the Second Vatican Council (1962–1965), and Pope John Paul II (1978–). The argument of the paper will move in three steps: (1) first a discussion of the categories needed to define the church's social role, (2) an assessment of the three contributions to that role, and (3) an examination of the social teaching in light of questions facing one local church.

Defining the Social Role of the Church: Themes in the Catholic Tradition

This conference, like scores of others throughout the church, is focused on the centenary of *Rerum Novarum* (1891); the significance of this text is understood to be both its own content and the catalytic role it played in shaping the "social encyclical" tradition of the past century. *Rerum Novarum*, therefore, is rightly never examined in isolation. It is seen in the wider context of its successor documents stretching through the several social texts of John Paul II. This broader historical and analytical approach is the proper hermeneutic for the social teaching.

When one approaches the topic of this paper, however, even the broader encyclical tradition is an insufficient lens for analysis. A more adequate framework for assessing the church's social role involves four distinct categories: (1) a political dimension, (2) a socioeconomic dimension, (3) an international dimension, and (4) an ecclesiological definition. In this section of the paper my objective is to locate the resources within the Catholic social tradition for addressing these four questions. The next section will assess more specifically the three contributions of Leo XIII, Vatican II and John Paul II to the wider tradition.

The Political Dimension

The church's relationship to the political order is addressed primarily in its teaching on church and state. Because this relationship is so central to understanding the social role of Catholicism, and because it is only marginally included in the social encyclical tradition, it is necessary to add the church-state teaching to the church-society issues found in the social encyclicals.

The church-state themes have a different historical framework from that of the 1891–1991 period encompassing the social encyclicals. The full scope of the church-state history reaches back to the patristic writings of Ambrose and Augustine; the relevant modern history reaches from Gregory XVI (1830–1846) through Vatican II.[1] In this modern narrative Leo XIII played a pivotal role, but different from the one he played in the social encyclical tradition.

Leo XIII inherited the church-state argument from Gregory XVI and Pius IX (1846–1878); in contrast he initiated the social encyclical themes, opening a new engagement of the church and society. Moreover, his contribution to the church-state question—crucial as it was—primarily consisted in redefining the issues without moving toward resolution of them. Essentially, Leo XIII put to rest the nineteenth-century papal style of addressing the church-state issues. The combined effect of his two predecessors had been (1) to deny any legitimacy to the democratic revolutions of the eighteenth century, (2) to set the church against the right of religious freedom, and (3) to affirm "the Catholic state" as normative for defining the church's relationship to the political order.[2]

Leo XIII did not change any of these conclusions. As John Courtney Murray demonstrated, Leo XIII's contribution lay in recasting the church-state question so that both institutions and their relationship were to be seen and judged in light of the welfare of the citizen. But Leo XIII did not move from a new definition to new conclusions. He opened the door to such a redefinition of the church's social role, but he was too much a part of the historical argument of the nineteenth century to step through the door himself. In retrospect, however, one can draw a line from Leo XIII to Pius XII and then on to John XXIII and *Dignitatis Humanae* of Vatican II. On church and state Leo XIII prepared for change; he did not effect change on specific issues. But Pius XII did. He reversed the first of the nineteenth-century conclusions, affirming the value and validity of democratic governance in his Christmas addresses during World War II.[3] On the other two questions Pius XII resembled Leo XIII; his teaching of the Christmas addresses on human dignity, human rights and democracy produced the resources to move beyond earlier Catholic teaching on religious liberty and the Catholic state. He moved to the threshold of change with his 1953 address to Italian Catholic jurists, but stopped short of recasting the conclusions.

John XXIII used the foundation of Pius XII in *Pacem in Terris* to reaffirm the new relationship of Catholic teaching and the democratic state, and then to affirm cryptically "the right to honor God according to the dictates of an upright conscience, and therefore the right to worship God privately and publicly."[4]

The full development of this papal affirmation found expression in *Dignitatis Humanae*. This document, taken with the chapter on "The Life of Political Community" in *Gaudium et Spes*, brought the definition of the church's relationship to the political order to a new term. The political dimension of the church's social role now could be summarized as: (1) affirming the right of religious liberty for each person as a result of his/her human dignity, (2) accepting a positive but limited definition of the role of the state in society (what Murray termed "the constitutional state"),[5] and (3) reducing the previously normative status of "the Catholic state" to a contingent application of more general principles, i.e., it might be useful in certain historical and cultural settings. John Paul II has added his own teaching to this conciliar consensus but that will be considered below.

The Economic Dimension

The social role of the church in the economic order is the church-society teaching of the social encyclicals. The centennary we are celebrating is the appropriate history and two distinct phases of development are evident. Leo XIII, Pius XI and the early Pius XII addressed "The Social Question" created by the Industrial Revolution. Beginning with Pius XII, the scope of the analysis widens because of the growing interdependence of the international community. Paul VI summarized the focus of the second stage of social teaching when he said the social question had become "worldwide."[6] In the first phase, the Industrial Revolution yielded questions about the proper role of the state in the economy, the content, scope and exercise of workers' rights, and, with Pius XI, the analysis of the social system of a nation. In the second phase, the relevant system is the content of the international economic order; the issues are broader and deeper— how individuals and nations are affected by patterns of trade, monetary policy and foreign investment.

In both stages of development the social teaching on economic issues has been articulated over against the two dominant economic options of the century: capitalist and socialist modes of economic organization. The dominant note of the teaching was a critique of the premises and consequences of both systems. At times there was the hint that the social teaching sought to articulate a "Third Way," but this has been rejected decisively by John Paul II.[7]

Summarizing the church's teaching on the economic order is more complex than the political questions, but several themes are clear: (1) the unit of moral analysis must be the international economy, with national and local questions retaining their intrinsically important role, but situated in the larger pattern of economic relations; (2) the classical principle of the universal destination of the goods of creation sets the norm for assessing the international order; the principle of distributive justice is articulated in light of this universal destination; (3) within nations the state has a positive role to play in achieving economic justice; (4) the justice of the economy at every level is judged by its ability to meet basic standards of welfare for each person; the standards are specified by the teaching on human rights and the theory of social and distributive justice; (5) the principle of subsidiarity seeks to preserve a sphere of freedom and initiative in society; in turn subsidiarity is balanced by the demands of socialization which require a positive conception of the state's socioeconomic responsibilities toward the poor; (6) the poor, in turn, have a central role in assessing the justice of any social system; recent Catholic teaching has identified that role in terms of an obligatory "option for the poor."

The International Dimension

The economic teaching moved by necessity into the international arena, but that does not exhaust the full range of Catholic teaching on international affairs. Since Pius XII the older Catholic teaching about sovereignty, war and peace and the unity of the human family have been significantly expanded and developed in terms of four issues: international order, human rights in world politics, the morality of war, and economic justice. From John XXIII to John Paul II these international themes have established the horizon for the rest of the social teaching.

The social role of the church implied by this teaching is an expression of its theological conviction about the common origin, nature and destiny of the human family, and an expression of a transnational community which ministers across the international system. Both its doctrine and structure call the church into an active international role. For centuries that role has been expressed through the church's diplomatic engagement. Today, this presence of the church is greatly expanded, but is also complemented by interaction between local churches and the Holy See. The involvement of local churches in issues of human rights, war and peace and national policies affecting international justice has developed since Vatican II. Together, the formal diplomatic engagement and the more activist social ministry provide distinct channels for making use of the international social teaching.

The international teaching reflects on a broader scale the way questions have been addressed within nations. The economic issues of rights and duties, distribution and ownership have counterparts among nations; the teaching on church and state domestically is played out in terms of issues of sovereignty at the international level. In defining the church's social role, its character as a transnational actor, with local, national and international capacities, will grow in importance in an increasingly interdependent world.

The Ecclesiological Dimension

The social role of the church is, at its foundation, an ecclesiological question. But for much of the century being commemorated in 1991 the social teaching did not possess a strong ecclesiological basis. If pressed, the response would have been that the ecclesiology was presumed and the social teaching should be interpreted as an extension of the church's life. But the failure to spell out the relationship between the nature of the church and its social ministry resulted in the latter being treated as an optional or secondary dimension of the church's life and work.

The emergence of an explicit theological basis for all the social teaching was the achievement of Vatican II, particularly the relationship of *Lumen Gentium* and *Gaudium et Spes.*[8] Moreover, since the Council, a substantial concern of the theology of social ministry has been focused on the ecclesiological question. The issues at stake have been how to identify the place social ministry should have in relationship to the other foundational ministries of the church, how to conceive of the church-world and church-state relationships, and how to describe the proper role for bishops, laity, priests and sisters in the fulfillment of social ministry.

The responses to these questions, which have been far from unanimous, have been shaped in terms of the conciliar teaching, but also in the perspective of political theology and the theology of liberation. The answers given to the ecclesiological questions, some of which are discussed below, have shaped both social teaching and social ministry.

The Social Role of the Church: Three Contributions

The overview of the Catholic social vision in the first section of the paper concentrated on categories and themes. In this section I will comment synoptically on three contributions to the tradition, which have influenced significantly Catholicism's view of its social role. The three contributions share certain characteristics: each has been decisive in providing overall direction for the social tradition, and each was shaped in light of a larger "grand design" concerning the church's relationship with the world. In all three cases, Leo XIII, Vatican II and John Paul II, the specific social teaching they have produced has been a response to a larger conception each has had about the public social challenge facing Catholicism. The challenges differed significantly, but the scope of the social project in these three moments of the tradition is what ties them together.

My purpose is to sketch on a broad canvas, not to delineate details. In each of the three cases, I will identify the substance of the "grand design," and then seek to illustrate how these three contributions influenced the conception of the church's social role.

Leo XIII

All the commentators on Leo XIII take note of the scope of the pastoral vision he brought to the papacy. One source depicts "The World Plan of Leo XIII"; another describes his pontificate in terms of "a watershed in the history of the modern papacy."[9] It is no exaggeration to say that this aristocratic intellectual conceived of his ministry as responding in the name of Catholicism to three revolutions: the intellectual one of the Enlightenment, the political one of the eighteenth-century democracies, and the social one of the Industrial Age. Leo had inherited from his two predecessors (Gregory XVI and Pius IX) a situation in which the church was on the defensive in Europe (the setting of all three revolutions as Rome saw them) on all three fronts. Leo XIII was not about to repudiate the popes of the nineteenth century, but neither was he prepared to imitate them. He understood the fragility of the Catholic position, not only because it was isolated increasingly (e.g., only four nations sent diplomatic representatives to Leo XIII's installation), but because the resources for a Catholic response were not well developed. His task involved both formulating a strategy *and* preparing the raw material for the strategy.

Leo XIII defined his challenge broadly and he set afoot a comprehensive response: intellectual, social and political. The intellectual task was fundamental; the response of the papacy to the tumultuous pattern of nineteenth-century Europe had been timorous and uninspiring. Joseph Moody's comment on Pius IX's pontificate as a "Time of Resistance" is revealing: "He condemned many contemporary movements of thought and action, but he did not provide well-constructed alternatives. . . . There was no examination of the new social conditions and no positive proposals. The most profound of modern movements was scarcely reflected in papal declarations up until 1878."[10]

Leo XIII was determined to respond himself to "modern movements" in a different tone from his predecessors, and he understood that his personal leadership had to be part of a wider pattern of Catholic life. His chosen instrumentality for the latter was a return to his mentor, Thomas Aquinas. The neo-scholastic movement is rooted in the pontificate of Leo XIII, inaugurated by *Aeterni Patris* (1879); the movement was the major inspiration for Catholic philosophical and theological thinking until Vatican II.

The social response of Leo XIII was embodied in *Rerum Novarum*. The encyclical reflected Leo XIII's understanding that a profound, systematic moral challenge faced Catholicism in the socio-economic order, and it illustrated his conviction that Scholastic philosophy was the church's best resource in the face of this authentically new reality of industrialization. *Rerum Novarum*, with its natural law structure and organic theory of society, set the direction of the Catholic social response for the next sixty years. Concepts such as the common good, the intrinsic dignity of work, the positive role of the state and the principles of distributive justice remained the basic elements of the social tradition's defense of workers.

Leo XIII's political response had two dimensions: his teaching on church and state, and his diplomatic initiatives. The church-state teaching has been noted above; suffice here to note that the intellectual foundation of the teaching again was Thomistic in categories and traditional in affirming the "dyarchy" of power (spiritual and temporal) which should begin all discussions of church and state.[11] Here Leo XIII faced a fundamental threat from the post-revolutionary direction of political thought in Europe. The drive of the secular state to encompass all aspects of society met firm resistance from Leo XIII. It was the specter of this threat which made it impossible for Leo XIII to distinguish the value of the eighteenth-century democratic revolution from its nineteenth-century manifestations. Leo XIII's double achievement on church and state was to move away from the style of his predecessors on the question and to provide a philosophical critique of the pretensions of Jacobin political thought in the nineteenth century.[12] His limited sense of democracy meant that Catholic teaching had to wait for a less conflicted time to address democratic polity at the level of principle.

Diplomatically, Leo XIII inaugurated his papacy by writing to heads of state, most of whom had ignored his election. He did not contribute substantially to Catholic teaching on international relations, but his skillful diplomacy reestablished the church's presence in the diplomatic arena.

He reached out to heal the post-revolution rift in French Catholicism and he faced down Bismarck's challenge in the *Kulturkampf*. Leo XIII was the pope of labor not the international teacher his successors would be.

In summary, Leo XIII's contribution to the social tradition was his catalytic role in inaugurating the church-society teaching of the encyclicals; he shaped this teaching further in a decisively philosophical direction, providing Catholicism with the mediating concepts and language which could relate religious vision to the empirical complexity of the socioeconomic order. In time the purely philosophical teaching would be seen as lacking biblical richness, but this would be the insight of Vatican II.

Leo XIII's perspective, ecclesial and socially, was thoroughly hierarchical. This limited his own teaching; he recast the church-state question in the name of the citizen, taking the emphasis off the institutional conflict to focus on the person both should serve. But he could not find in the citizen a source of initiative or a possibility for creative contribution. Society was shaped from the top down by princes and popes. In his economic teaching, the strong emphasis on distributive justice did not diminish Leo XIII's attachment to maintaining an aristocratic conception of class relations. Later papal teaching, as David Hollenbach has shown,[13] had a stronger egalitarian emphasis. Finally, Leo XIII's neo-scholasticism helped to form and guide thinkers such as Jacques Maritain, John Courtney Murray and John A. Ryan. But the limits of neo-scholasticism became clear as each of these thinkers and others used and transcended its conclusions.

Leo XIII shaped the church's social role philosophically and socially; he made the church a voice in the struggle for the rights of labor. He restored a Catholic voice in the public life of Europe, and he opened the way for the church to address democracy and to develop a broader social teaching than he produced himself.

Vatican II

The Second Vatican Council technically does not stand in "the social tradition"; it is broader in scope and less focused on specific issues than the encyclical teaching. The argument for its inclusion is that it provided the social teaching with an ecclesiological foundation which had been absent, and constituted a fundamental weakness for the church's social ministry. The Council, shaped by John XXIII and Paul VI, had its own "grand design." The challenge it faced, as John XXIII made clear in his opening address, was fundamentally different from the one that confronted Leo XIII. He had inherited a church under siege, threatened and isolated by intellectual and political forces which sought to drive the church from a public presence in culture and society. John XXIII, criticizing "the prophets of doom," defined the challenge of Vatican II as an opportunity, a chance to present the Gospel in clearer, more compelling terms.

To respond to this opportunity the Pope and the Council adopted a strategy of dialogue. Paul VI articulated the tone and themes of this strategy in his encyclical *Ecclesiam Suam.* The dialogue was multidimensional and produced a social role for Catholicism which was not only different from Leo XIII's conception but significantly changed from that of Pius XII's strategy of the 1940s and 1950s.

The "grand design" involved moving the church from a posture of being "over against" major movements in society to engaging them in conversations which would be learning and teaching opportunities for the church. From the sixteenth to the twentieth centuries Catholicism had defined itself over against three movements: the Protestant Reformation, the Democratic Revolutions, and the Enlightenment. Leo XIII, as noted, had two of these in his "world plan," but even Leo's shift from his predecessors did not involve the style of dialogue found in the conciliar texts. The response to Protestantism falls outside the scope of this paper; the dialogue with the political and intellectual movements of democracy and the Enlightenment (particularly the world of culture and science) is found in the conciliar texts *Dignitatis Humanae* and *Gaudium et Spes.* The first addressed the political order, moving beyond both Leo XIII and Pius XII, and the second involved a broader intellectual address to "the world," understood as the secular order of politics, knowledge, economics and international affairs.

The tone of *Gaudium et Spes* was set early: It desired to provide "eloquent proof of its solidarity" with the world by engaging it in conversation about "the signs of the times." The conversation ranged across many of the topics already found in the church-state and church-society teaching. The distinctive contribution of Vatican II was not to address a specific social question. Rather, it was the way in which it joined the entire social ministry to the center of the church's life.

The key texts were paragraphs 76 and then 40–42 of *Gaudium et Spes.* I have spelled out the meaning in other writings;[14] here, it is sufficient to note the structural contribution they make to the Catholic social vision. Paragraph 76 identifies the church's social role as standing as "a sign and safeguard of the transcendence of the human person." This sentence takes the major theme of the social teaching—protecting human dignity—and gives it *ecclesial* standing. The fulfillment of this role is tied to the church's nature and mission. Paragraphs 40–42 clarify *how* the church is to fulfill this social role. She is always to remain a *religious* institution, directed toward the Kingdom and in service of the life of the Kingdom. But the Kingdom is partially realized in history, and the Council calls the church to fulfill its religious ministry in a way that protects human dignity, fosters human rights and contributes to the unity of the human family. This mandate then must be articulated on the specific levels of social ministry—local, national and international—which are found in the social encyclical tradition.

The ecclesiological contributions of the Council were matched by one other fundamental influence. The teaching of *Gaudium et Spes* takes on a definite biblical and theological tone, quite different from the social tradition of Leo XIII to Pius XII. Although the natural law categories are much in evidence in *Dignitatis Humanae*, they are not very visible in *Gaudium et Spes*. This more theological tone becomes a staple of Catholic social teaching under John Paul II.

The substance and style of the conciliar teaching have had a direct, long-term impact on the social role of the church in the last twenty-five years. The title of *Gaudium et Spes*, "The Church *in* the World," as well as its method of learning from empirical data ("the signs of the times"), and its description of the church's role of putting at the disposal of the world "the saving resources" the church has received from Christ, have produced a distinct form of Catholic engagement. While it differs by social situation, the servant church model of active involvement in the life of society has increased markedly since the Council. While Leo XIII shaped the church's social role with moral categories, Vatican II gave the moral tradition new depth and meaning by joining it to ecclesial themes. Together, the moral and ecclesial have shaped a post-conciliar Catholic activism which has been a dramatic shift for the church, with far-reaching social implications for the world.

John Paul II

From the moment of his election, John Paul II raised sociopolitical expectations. Tad Szulc, writing two months after the election said, "The elevation of the 58-year-old Polish prelate to the Holy See as Pope John Paul II constitutes a global political event of vast proportions."[15] The pope has denied vigorously any political intentions or strategy on the part of the church, but he has projected a "grand design" since early in his pontificate. The design is cast first in chronological terms. In his first encyclical, *Redemptor Hominis* (1979) he identified the year 2000 as a focus of his concern, describing the time approaching it as an image of a "New Advent." His words and deeds must be taken together to grasp the design. His continuous travel to local churches—often caught in political conflict—is joined to an expansive conception of the church's social teaching. Together, the words and deeds constitute the most activist papacy since the High Middle Ages.

The media, fascinated by the pope's Polish origins, his intimate knowledge of Marxism and his crucial role in the dissolution of Soviet rule in Central and Eastern Europe, focus on his role in that area of the world. But the papal design is global in scope and ecclesial in nature. John Paul is convinced, with the conviction of biblical faith, that religion has a public role to play, and he understands that role in light of his conception of an increasingly interdependent world. He came to the papacy with the post-conciliar consequences of an activist church in full tide. While determined to distinguish the church's role from that of political institutions, he has intensified its social mandate and activity. Three major characteristics of his social teaching build upon previous themes, but go beyond them in scope and specificity.

First, in distinguishing the ecclesial and the political, the pope continually denies a political role for the church, but he presses a social agenda with immense political consequences. His rationale is rooted in *Gaudium et Spes*, paragraphs 40–42. The conciliar distinction fits John Paul II perfectly: a religiously grounded ministry exercised in the name of human dignity and human rights. From his U.N. address on human rights, to his Latin American and Polish visits, this ecclesial-rights theme has been his message. He understands it as fulfilling paragraph 76, safeguarding human dignity, an ecclesial task. But the political results are not confined to the ecclesial arena. While resisting political identification between the church and any secular institution, he presses the human dignity-human rights agenda with more specificity than any of his modern predecessors.

Second, the theological shift in the social teaching initiated by *Gaudium et Spes* is carried forward by John Paul II. His social theology is cast in four interconnected themes: anthropology, Christology, ecclesiology and social ethics. The person is the foundation of the church's social concern, but the full meaning of human dignity is only understood in Christ. Christ's ministry, in turn, is the model for the church in the service of humanity and social ethics is the guide for the conduct of this ministry. Throughout his social teaching John Paul II combines the philosophical stream of the earlier encyclical tradition and the theological ideas of the post-conciliar period.

Third, the pope's conception of international order builds upon the work of Pius XII, John XXIII and Paul VI; like them he seeks to provide a moral structure for the still decentralized international system. From the U.N. address in 1979 to *Sollicitudo Rei Socialis* in 1987, his social teaching is focused on the international system. He is more willing than his predecessors to join a geopolitical critique of existing patterns to his moral teaching on world politics. The basic thrust of the teaching has these key themes:

1. He demands a concept of order which takes seriously the needs of states and people unable to demand attention (e.g. sub-Saharan Africa);
2. He has called for a devolution of superpower control of world affairs (now increasingly likely);
3. The devolution of the big powers is designed to create space for others to surface, particularly the developing countries and a united Europe;
4. While concerned about the nuclear threat and the political life of nations, his most urgent demand is a revision of the rules and practices of international economic relations as they affect developing countries;
5. The test for international relations, as for domestic affairs, is a person's human rights.

While still in the midst of this papacy, it is clear that John Paul II already has stamped the social teaching of Catholicism for decades. His global perspective, his theological grounding of the teaching, his willingness to reduce principles to specific conclusions and his conception of the church as an actor within nations and among nations have proven Tad Szulc correct: "By electing Poland's Karol Cardinal Wojtyla to the papacy the Roman Catholic church has thrust world politics into a wholly new dimension with extraordinary and far-reaching consequences that can be fully measured only with the passage of time."[16]

The Social Role of the Church: A Local Test

In 1991 the social role of Catholicism was shaped by several forces (many of them not addressed in this chapter), but the joint impact of the social teaching of the popes and the conciliar teaching of Vatican II has been decisive. One characteristic of both conciliar and recent social teaching has been an awareness of the need to understand and apply the teaching within the specific demands of each local church. The theme was best stated by Paul VI: "It is up to the Christian communities to analyze with objectivity the situation which is proper to their own country, to shed on it the light of the Gospel's unalterable words and to draw principles of reflection, norms of judgment and directives for action from the social teaching of the church."[17]

This passage invites social teaching from "the bottom up"; it calls the local church to be a creative source of insight, experience and ideas as it mediates the values and principles of the social tradition in the specific conditions of a given society. This sensitivity to the contingent conditions in which Christians live is reflected also in the appeal of *Gaudium et Spes* to the "signs of the times" as a way to understand how the social teaching is to be lived and applied.

It is at the level of application that I wish to test the social role of the church in the United States. The goal is both to examine the setting within which the church functions and to assess the strengths and limits of the social teaching in responding to this setting. The four characteristics which significantly shape the social question of the 1990s for the church in the United States are: (1) a secular state, (2) a pluralistic society, (3) a capitalist economy, and (4) a post-cold war world.

Secular State

The church in the United States has lived with a secular state since its inception; secularity was the native condition and it did not connote opposition to religion. The European churches, however, had known a state that was not secular, and when secularity came, it arrived often with an anticlerical or antireligious edge.

The essence of the secularity of the state, reflected in the First Amendment to the Constitution, is that religious communities would experience neither favoritism nor discrimination at the hands of the state. Secularity, in this sense, means equal treatment through law and policy. Many have argued (and I tend to agree but do not wish to discuss the matter here) that equal treatment toward specific religious communities does not mean that the state has to be neutral or indifferent to religion as a social good.

From Leo XIII through Pius XII the teaching on church and state treated the fact of a secular state as tolerable but not desirable. The "thesis/hypothesis" norm developed in the nineteenth century prevailed in Catholic teaching, so anything less than "a Catholic state" was, at best, tolerable. The change in church-state teaching discussed earlier provided a foundation in principle for relating to a secular state. The principles of the Council were not designed only for this situation; indeed they applied to a range of church-state relationships from Eastern Europe to Latin America to Asia. But the principles of the Council changed the judgment on a secular state from toleration to acceptance, provided that the full meaning of the right to religious liberty would be guaranteed to all citizens and each religious community.

In the 1990s the test that a secular state poses for the church is not at the level of principle. The teaching is developed to a point where no further modification seems indicated. At the level of practice, however, the secular state and the social consensus which supports it pose a continuing challenge for the social role of the church. The effect of secularity is to establish the church in a zone of protected freedom; the right to religious liberty, understood in its personal and corporate dimensions, means that the church is free to fulfill all aspects of its ministry. The essential challenge this freedom creates is that the social significance of the church, its role, relevance and influence, is only as good as its witness.

There is neither special status nor significance accorded in principle to the religious perspective in American public life. The social role of the church in this setting depends on its capacity to contribute to a public sense of meaning and purpose using religious resources which are not *a priori* the basis for shaping public institutions or public policy.

The test of the religious vision in such a secular context is its capacity and to translate the religious vision into a usable wisdom for the wider civil community. This double test—within the congregation and in the broader public debate—was the standard the bishops had in mind in preparing the two pastoral letters of the 1980s.

The social role of the church is not totally exhausted by its teaching. Throughout the world today, religious communities and institutions play a crucial role in social development, and individual religious leaders have made decisive interventions in public life. Clearly, the possibility for such an institutional or personal role is open in U.S. society. But there are some differences, not rooted in the secular state as such but in the style of the culture which sustains it. It is difficult for me to conceive of any situation in which a Catholic prelate in the United States would hold the social position of a Cardinal Silva in Chile, a Cardinal Sin in the Philippines or a Cardinal Wysznski in Poland. While each of these bishops is/was a formidable personality, the point of the comparison is not with the personal attributes of bishops in the United States. There is, rather, a role these men played in their society which would be very difficult (probably not desirable) to replicate in the United States. The social role of the church, in this secular setting, cannot be grounded in this kind of powerful leadership.

Part of the reason is structural. In each of the cases cited, authoritarian regimes had dismantled effectively the societal structures which protect democratic governance, and the effect was to leave the church in

Santiago, Manila and Warsaw in a classical church-state confrontation. In that setting, the charismatic leadership of these three bishops emerged.

In the United States the multiplicity of social, political and religious institutions in the society makes the church one actor among others. Leadership in social issues is possible, but is dependent upon fulfilling a role on a level playing field with several competing players. Even in times of significant social conflict (e.g., civil rights in the 1960s, Vietnam in the 1970s) or in major policy debates (e.g., the Persian Gulf), the religious voice is part of a larger chorus. It would take a social and constitutional crisis of extreme proportions to produce the kind of church-state confrontation that has occurred repeatedly in other parts of the world over the last thirty years. The combined effect of a secular state and the existence of several strong, mediating institutions between the citizenry and the state has the effect of relativizing a distinctive, singular ecclesial witness. There is clearly a social role for the church, but in the setting of a complex social structure where no single voice dominates the field for very long.

A Pluralistic Society

The combination of a secular state, which is also constitutionally a limited state guaranteeing religious freedom for all, produces a pluralist culture. Two different kinds of pluralism are present in U.S. society and bear upon the church's social role: religious pluralism and a pluralistic structure of power.

Religious pluralism is the direct result of the secular state and the right of religious freedom. The consequence for the church's social role is the challenge such pluralism poses for the moral teaching of Catholicism. Catholic teaching traditionally has been wary of pluralism. John Courtney Murray argued convincingly that the combined effect of *Dignitatis Humanae* and *Gaudium et Spes* was to accept religious pluralism as the "normal" setting for the church's ministry.[18] The state of contemporary Catholic teaching, therefore, is strikingly different from that of the previous century. Through Pius XI, pluralism was acknowledged but it was to be resisted. After Vatican II the acceptance of religious pluralism as a fact calls for the church in pluralistic cultures to develop a style of teaching and pastoral practice that can witness effectively in the midst of pluralism.

The major challenge religious pluralism poses for the church in the United States is in the area of its moral teaching. Catholic moral theology is systemic in scope, comprehensive in content and public in style. All three characteristics bring it directly into confrontation with a religiously pluralistic environment. Because it is systemic, Catholic teaching addresses personal and social issues, private and public morality. Because of its comprehensive concern, Catholic teaching cannot be single-issue; it articulates a sexual, social and international ethic which includes most of the major policy issues in the U.S. public debate. Because of its public style, Catholic teaching engages not only the community of faith but the civil society as a whole.

These three characteristics of Catholic moral vision and teaching style were exemplified in the 1980s as the Catholic bishops simultaneously pressed an ecclesial and public debate about abortion, nuclear weapons, economic justice and human rights in Central America. The responses—within and outside the church—were multiple: some criticized the bishops for imposing their religious views on the private choices of U.S. citizens (i.e., abortion); others opposed the bishops interfering in the public policies of the government (nuclear strategy); others argued that they squandered their religious authority by addressing issues beyond their competence (economic justice).

This is not the place to enter the substance of these arguments; the point here is functional. Religious pluralism guarantees difference of positions on the ultimate questions of meaning and morality. Catholic teaching that has "accepted" the challenge of pluralism must be supplemented by a pastoral presence which can function effectively in a pluralistic context. The double challenges which must be met are: (1) how to address the wider civil society by using a religiously grounded tradition to produce moral wisdom persuasive to those outside the community of faith, and (2) how to maintain a coherent community of faith when its members are influenced significantly by the wider cultural pattern of pluralism. Abortion has been the most dramatic test for this double challenge; twenty years into the debate Catholicism has maintained a coherent position but has not persuaded the wider culture. But abortion is simply an example of a range of issues where religious pluralism tests the church's social role.

A different kind of pluralism in U.S. society, the pluralism of power, presents an opportunity for the social role of the church. The opportunity is identified by a basic principle of Catholic social teaching—the principle of subsidiarity. Subsidiarity views a pluralistic structure of power in society as a positive characteristic since it contains the power of the state, provides space for "intermediary associations" (voluntary associations) and opens the possibility for creative public-private initiatives on social issues. The point to be stressed here is, again, a functional one: the variegated institutional structure of Catholicism in the United States (including schools, universities, health care systems and social welfare organizations) fits well with the idea of a pluralism of power. A pluralistic social structure invites collaboration from nongovernmental agencies. In addition, a multiplicity of social issues in the United States today, from housing to health care to drugs and day-care, requires both public funding and private engagement to address these issues effectively.

Over the last twenty-five years U.S. social policy has swung precariously from a view that government was the answer to social crises to the current view that government is the major social problem. Neither view is in accord with Catholic teaching and neither view can respond to the present range of social policy needs. Catholic teaching combines a positive conception of the state's social role with an equally positive view of the need for other agencies in the social arena.

But the principles of the teaching do not provide creative strategies for using the church's institutional presence creatively. This is a task which is properly that of a local church—to shape the principles into a workable policy. Catholic social potential in the United States outstrips the strategies we have designed so far to match public and private resources. Facing the domestic social issues of the 1990s, a fitting celebration of the Catholic social tradition would be a concerted, collaborative effort of major Catholic agencies at the national and diocesan levels to think through a strategy for the social presence of Catholicism in a pluralist social structure. The prime topics would be housing and health care. Both would require an aggressive public policy seeking the investment of public funds, but these efforts should be matched by a clear strategy of how Catholic institutions are prepared to play a larger social role in concert with public institutions.

Capitalist Economy

At the heart of the social encyclical tradition, from Leo XIII through John Paul II, runs a critique of the two models of socioeconomic organization which have dominated the twentieth century: liberal capitalism and Marxist socialism. (Between the two "ideal types" there have been a variety of options, but the ecclesial teaching has focused primarily on the theoretical examples.) Regarding both, Catholic teaching has criticized the premises, sought to limit the negative consequences, and found a way to live in the midst of systems it would not have designed or recommended.

This mode of teaching is not used in the 1991 encyclical, *Centesimus Annus* because the Marxist model of socioeconomic planning has collapsed substantially; it is being dismantled by its primary representatives in the Soviet Union and by the people who have lived under it in Eastern

Europe. Having acknowledged this primary fact, two other comments are needed. First, the collapse of Marxist-socialism in the East does not necessarily mean that, in the different circumstances of some developing countries, all socialist options will be forsaken. Second, John Paul II has gone out of his way to make clear that the collapse of Marxism—to which he substantially contributed by word and deed—does not, in his view, mean the moral triumph of capitalism. His critique of the capitalist premises and some of its consequences are well documented and, I suspect, will continue.

Nonetheless, the context for the ethical evaluation of socioeconomic systems has shifted. The encyclical commentary on the capitalist model has always been the more pertinent topic for the church in the United States. Moreover, there have been two levels of the evaluation: (1) the consequences of capitalism within the United States, and (2) the role of capitalist theory and policy as reflected in international institutions and structures that affect the developing world. (It is interesting that church teaching has had little to say about the relationships among the advanced industrialized countries, i.e., the United States, the European Community and Japan.)

In the 1990s, how should the encyclical tradition be read and used in the United States? In both the economic and political orders, change has been so profound and rapid that much of the analysis of *Sollicitudo* has been by-passed. Domestically, in the United States, I believe there will be much continuity in terms of the relevance of the encyclical tradition. The basic problem faced, if not resolved, has been to address the consequences of capitalism for those left behind or left outside the circle of economic security. In one sense the issues are old ones: housing, health care, the vulnerability of women and children, and the intersection of poverty and minorities. In another sense, these old issues have new dimensions: the way in which family breakdown, drugs and the danger of permanent economic disenfranchisement threaten sectors of society. These characteristics do not dissolve the economic justice dimension of the problems, but make an adequate address to poverty more complicated. In addition to addressing the consequences of poverty, John Paul II continues to stress the problem of consumerism as a moral test of capitalism.

The international dimension of Catholic economic teaching is the area where more attention is needed in the United States. The collapse of Marxism virtually guarantees that the basic structure of economic policy— trade, monetary, investment and aid—will be framed in capitalist terms. Individual developing countries may have socialist systems, but they will fit into a larger pattern of a capitalist order.

The need, therefore, is to design and implement a moral strategy which takes seriously the structure, policies and consequences of those institutions that undoubtedly will control much of the immediate future of the international economy. This is not a new issue, but it deserves more intense attention, because other countries virtually have no choice but to relate to these international institutions and regimes such as the International Monetary Fund, the General Agreement on Tariffs and Trade, the World Bank and various bilateral aid programs. How these are designed, how they function, and how the negative consequences can be mitigated (e.g., structural adjustment) demands a new effort of assessment and advocacy. Because the church lives in countries affected by these institutions, and because the church lives in United States and the other industrialized countries that have a dominant voice in these institutions, information can be shared, a division of labor can be established and local churches can address distinct dimensions of the international economic justice issues.

Post-Cold War World

In the field of international relationships, the year 1990 stands as an historical fault-line, similar to 1648, 1815 and 1945. At each point, fundamental changes in world politics occurred. The year 1990 qualifies due to changes in the U.S.-Soviet relationship between 1985–1990, because of the revolutions in Eastern Europe of 1989, and because of the reunification of Germany in 1990. Catholic teaching on the international order had developed from Pius XII to John Paul II as an effort to provide moral direction for the post-World War II international system. As noted earlier in this paper, the basic moral category was the concept of order, within which the popes then addressed three issues: war and peace, the protection of human rights, and international economic justice.

The post-cold war world presents the universal and local churches with a new challenge and with new choices. The "logic of the blocs," which dominated world politics in the cold war and which was severely criticized by John Paul II in *Sollicitudo*, has gone. But most of the problems addressed in Catholic social teaching over the past fifty years remain. While the cold war is over, nuclear arsenals remain. The condition of developing countries is not easily summarized, but for large numbers of them the observation of John Paul II in *Sollicitudo*, that their problems have moved from deciding on how to develop to agreeing on how to pay their growing debt, is still valid; regional conflicts—often rooted deeply in local realities—still ravage Central America, Southern Africa and, of course, the Middle East. Finally, the removal of the strait-jacket imposed by the cold war has brought to the surface the unfinished business of nineteenth-century ethnic and national rivalries throughout Europe.

In the face of this changing empirical picture, one would expect Catholic teaching to maintain its basic concerns. The constant theme, particularly clear since *Pacem in Terris*, is the gap between the needs of the universal common good and the structure of authority—both political and legal—in the international system. The ending of the cold war does not promise a fundamental change in this theme, although the growing interdependence of the world has generated the growth of "regimes," in which states pool their sovereignty claims on specific issues of trade, finance, and arms control. The growth of regimes is an incremental approach to enhancing the possibility of a more adequate structure of authority and governance in world politics.

The fundamental Catholic concern about the *moral order* of the international system must engage the multiple proposals now being offered about the direction for a new empirical order in world affairs. This debate is very intense in the United States, and should be of particular concern to this local church. Three proposals are already being discussed at the policy level. One is that the emerging structure of power is a unipolar world—the immediate result of the collapse of the Soviet Union. In my view, this unipolar proposal is undesirable, empirically and morally. Empirically, the world is too complex for it to succeed; morally, it moves in exactly the opposite direction from John Paul II's concept that breaking the logic of the blocs should provide space for others in the system.

A second proposal, the reemergence of a multipolar world, is more likely empirically, but it will take time and will be a more complicated multipolarity than the nineteenth-century model. The new multipolarity will have not only several actors but distinct kinds of power at different poles. Multipolarity reflects some of the vision of *Sollicitudo*, a pluralist structure of powers, but it does not guarantee the fundamental concern of John Paul II and his predecessors: that the concept of order be designed so that the needs of *all* the nations and peoples of the international system are included from the outset. A multipolar world still could be a world designed only for those with some form of power to claim.

The third proposal, a renewal and revival of the U.N. system in all its possible forms—political, security, economic and human rights—is clearly the idea which most closely approximates the papal teaching of the last five decades. But it will be necessary to look beyond slogans and formulas to see how the system would actually work. A renewal of the notion of collective security, in a world where aggression is still very possible and where internal conflicts are very likely, would be a clear benefit. But it is not useful to have a collective security concept where the United States becomes the sheriff for the Security Council. Such an outcome could be the unipolar world under another name.

Giving specific content to a revitalized U.N. system is a useful idea to pursue for the church universal and at the local level. But it may not be the only possibility; clearly my sketch has not exhausted the discussion. What is needed is an effort at several levels of the church to do, in a 1990s version, what John Paul II did in *Sollicitudo*: engage the geopolitical debate about the future of world politics with the resources of Catholic moral vision.

Notes

1. For a survey of the history cf: J. C. Murray, "The Problem of Religious Freedom," *Theological Studies* (T.S.) 25 (1964) p. 503–575; J. N. Moody, ed., *Church and Society: Catholic Social and Political Movements 1789–1950* (New York: Arts Inc., 1953) p. 21–92.

2. Murray, pp. 507–508; 512.

3. V. Yzermans, ed., *The Major Addresses of Pope Pius XII,* vol. II: *The Christmas Messages* (St. Paul, Minn.: The North Central Publishing Co., 1961) esp. pp. 51–66; 78–90.

4. John XXIII, *Pacem in Terris,* (1963), no. 14.

5. Murray, pp. 545–546.

6. Paul VI, *Populorum Progressio* (1967), no. 3.

7. John Paul II, *Sollicitudo Rei Socialis* (1987), no. 41.

8. Vatican II: *Lumen Gentium* (1963); *Gaudium et Spes* (1965).

9. O. Koehler, "The World Plan of Leo XIII: Goals and Methods," in H. Jedin, ed., *History of the Church: The Church in the Industrial Age* (N.Y.: Crossroad Publishing Co., 1981) p. 3–25; J. N. Moody, cited, p. 41.

10. Moody, *Church and Society.*

11. J. C. Murray, "The Church and Totalitarian Democracy," *Theological Studies,* 13 (1952), pp. 555–560; and "Leo XIII on Church and State: The General Structure of the Controversy," *T. S.,* 14 (1953), pp. 1–30.

12. *Ibid.*

13. D. Hollenbach, *Claims In Conflict: Retrieving and Renewing the Catholic Human Rights Tradition* (N.Y.: Paulist Press, 1979), pp. 45–46. On Leo XIII's sense of hierarchy in church and society, cf. Murray, "Freedom, Authority, Community," *America* (December 3, 1966), pp. 734–741.

14. J. B. Hehir, "Church-State and Church-World," *Proceedings of the Catholic Theological Society of America* 41 (1986), pp. 54–74; "Vatican II and

the Signs of the Times: Catholic Teaching on Church, l State and Society," in L. Griffin, ed., *Religion and Politics in the American Milieu* (Notre Dame: *Review of Politics*), pp. 57–78.

15. T. Szulc, "Politics and the Polish Pope," *The New Republic* (October, 28, 1978), p. 19.

16. *Ibid.*, p. 19.

17. Paul VI, *Octogesima Adveniens* (1971), no. 4.

18. J. C. Murray, "The Issue of Church and State at Vatican II," *Theological Studies*, 27 (1966), pp. 585–586; 602.

Three

Catholicism and Liberal Democracy

Paul E. Sigmund

It has been only a little over four decades since Sidney Hook stated, "Catholicism is the oldest and greatest totalitarian movement in history."[1] Ten years after this statement Paul Blanshard declared, "You cannot find in the entire literature of Catholicism a single unequivocal endorsement by any Pope of democracy as a superior form of government."[2] Much has happened—both in theory and in practice—to mitigate the suspicion of the inherent authoritarianism of Roman Catholicism on the part of Americans of Protestant, Jewish, and secular backgrounds. Yet there is still a lingering suspicion that there remains what Max Weber called an "elective affinity" between a hierarchical church organized around a single non-elected leader and authoritarianism in politics, a basic opposition between Catholicism and liberal democracy. While the stereotyped thinking of a Hook or a Blanshard receives little credence today, still it may be useful to examine the historical and contemporary record on the relationship between Catholicism and democracy to arrive at a more nuanced view.

Historical Relationship between Catholicism and Democracy

When we examine the record of the early church, it appears to be neither a democracy nor a centralized hierarchical structure, but something in between. Peter and his successors were understood to have received a special commission from Christ, "Thou art Peter and upon this rock I will build my church" (Mt. 16:18), but the apostles and their successors, the bishops, were also given a universal mission by Christ ("Going therefore teach ye all nations," Mt. 28:19) and the early Christian communities were seen as direct recipients of divine grace and inspiration ("Where two or three are gathered in my name, there am I in the midst of them," Mt. 18:20). The Christian communities often acted as quasi-independent, self-governing entities to make decisions, especially in times of persecution. The apostles elected a replacement for Judas and, in the Council of

Jerusalem that was to decide on whether circumcision was required for Gentiles, Peter was corrected by Paul and decisions were made by consensus. The government of the early church partook of elements of all three of the classic forms—monarchy, aristocracy, and democracy—and when later Christians looked back to it as a model they could find evidence of all three forms of government.[3]

Also relevant to later ideas of limited government that were important in the development of liberal democracy was the dualism of loyalties and of institutional structure implied by Christian belief in an independent source of legitimation of government that gave both a special religious character to political authority and limited its area of authority ("There is no power but of God. The powers that be are ordained of God," Rom. 13:1–2. "We must obey God rather than men," Acts 5:29).

When the church emerged from the catacombs in the fourth century and was tolerated and then formally established as the religion of the Roman empire, there was a danger that it would be swallowed up in the imperial bureaucracy, and indeed something close to that process took place in the Eastern church. Yet even there collegial decision-making structures existed, notably the ecumenical councils, seen principally as assemblies of bishops and patriarchs, although usually called by the emperor and with a special place for the representative of the pope. In Western Europe and North Africa, councils of bishops enacted legislation with or without participation of temporal authorities, and Rome demanded—but did not always receive—a special role in resolving disputes. Bishops were selected in various ways, most commonly by a vote or consensus of the diocese, and while the episcopal dioceses were in communion with Rome, the pope was not seen as exerting a strong governing role in the diocese. Often the strongest influence was the local ruler but, in theory, as argued explicitly by Pope Gelasius (c.590 A.D.) "there are two" structures of rule: a dualism of spiritual and temporal authority.

The centralization associated with the modern Roman Catholic church dates from the twelfth century. A revitalized papacy developed a system of law, courts, records, and bureaucracy that made Rome increasingly important in the government of the church. Neo-Platonic hierarchical models ("The Great Chain of Being"), particularly as mediated through the writings of Pseudo-Dionysius who was mistakenly believed to be the convert of St. Paul mentioned in Acts 17:34, were seen as an earthly reflection of the order of angels, a view reinforced by feudal theory and practice that conceived of medieval political and social life in terms of ranks and orders. John of Salisbury (1120–1180) and others employed classical organic analogies to describe the organization of society along lines analogous to the structure of the human body, and medieval canon and civil lawyers used analogies between head and members to describe the organization and legal status of emerging "corporate" groups such as guilds, cathedral chapters, religious orders, etc.

Yet there were also more democratic elements in the practice and theory of medieval Catholicism. Gratian's *Decretum*, a twelfth century compilation of earlier church documents that was used by all medieval canon lawyers, insisted that "Bishops are to be elected by the clergy and requested by the people" (D. 62, c.1) and "No bishop should be assigned to the people against their will" (D. 62, c.1), and cited as a condition for the validity of a law that it must be "approved by the practice of those under them" (D. 4, c.2). A Roman law phrase that originally applied to water rights "What touches all, should be approved by all" was incorporated in the official canon law collection, the *Liber Sextus*, in 1298, and new religious orders such as the Dominicans developed elaborate systems of election and representation for their internal governance. In the church-state conflicts between the spiritual and temporal powers, each side appealed to the legitimizing role of the consent of the people to weaken the claims of the other side, and in the fourteenth and fifteenth centuries, the writers of the conciliar movement appealed to the democratic elements in the church tradition (elections, consent to law, and even original equality in natural law) to argue that the council as representative of all the members of the church was superior to the pope.[4]

Yet in standard university courses on "Western Civilization" or "The History of Political Thought," the classic expression of medieval Catholic political thought is taken to be *Unam Sanctam* (1302), the papal bull of Boniface VIII, which, appealing to "Blessed Dionysius," concludes that "every human creature must be subject to the Roman pontiff." A more accurate version of the medieval Catholic political tradition is contained in the writings of St. Thomas Aquinas who combines both hierarchical and democratic elements. On the one hand, law is made by "the whole community or the person who represents it" (*Summa Theologiae*, I–II, qu. 90, art. 3) and the best form of government is one in which "all participate in the selection (*electio*) of those who rule" (*ST* I–II, qu. 105); on the other hand, government by a monarch is best because it promotes unity and follows the pattern of God's monarchical government of the universe (*De Regimine Principum*, ch. 3). The pope leads the church to a higher spiritual goal of man, but (at least in one interpretation—there are conflicting texts) he can intervene only in temporal affairs "with respect to those things in which the temporal power is subject to him" (*ST* II–II, qu. 60. art. 6). Law is morally obligatory and reflects the divine purposes in the world, but an unjust law that violates natural or divine law is no law at all but an act of violence (*ST* I–II, qu. 96, art. 2). All people are equal in the sight of God and even slaves have rights, but "there is an order to be found among men" according to which even before the Fall the more intelligent were to lead the less intelligent (*Summa contra Gentiles*, 4, 81 and *ST* I, qu. 92, arts. 3–4). Authoritarian, constitutionalist (Aquinas as "the first Whig"), and democratic conclusions can be drawn from Aquinas's writings—and from the tradition of medieval Catholicism.[5]

The process of papal centralization that had been initiated in the twelfth century was carried much further in the period of the Counter-Reformation with the imposition of a common liturgy ("the Roman rite"), discipline, and control over appointments of bishops (in the Middle Ages, exerted principally through the requirement of papal confirmation of episcopal elections). That control was shared with Catholic monarchs through the *jus patronatus*, the right to name candidates for episcopal sees to the Vatican, and through concordats (i.e., treaties) that guaranteed the rights of the church, especially state support for Catholicism and enforcement of religious uniformity as well as special rights in the areas of education and marriage. Yet this apparent endorsement of absolute monarchy was qualified by the Jesuit and Dominican opponents of the theory of "the divine right of kings," including Robert Bellarmine and Francisco Suarez who argued that political authority came from God through the people. Some of their arguments for a conditional transfer of authority contributed to the constitutional tradition that led ultimately to Locke's *Second Treatise of Civil Government*, but none of the Catholic writers argued as Locke did for religious toleration. The Catholic writers still endorsed religious uniformity and the rule of the monarch while arguing for moral and constitutional limits on his exercise of rule. In a comfortable but corrupting arrangement, the Catholic church in Western Europe was the state church in the principalities and kingdoms of southern and central Europe, while Protestantism held a similar position in northern Europe ("the union of throne and altar"). In Italy the pope was also temporal ruler of the Papal States which cut diagonally across the peninsula from just south of Venice and Padua to the area north of Naples.

In the eighteenth century, what was seen as another threat to Catholicism emerged—the Enlightenment. Voltaire exclaimed, "*Ecrasez l'infame*," and Rousseau proposed an obligatory civil religion viewing, as Locke had (by implication) in his *Letter on Toleration*, the Vatican's religious authority as a threat to civic loyalty.

The republican movement associated with the French Revolution was opposed to the privileges of the church, and Italian republican-nationalists saw the papal states as the major obstacle to Italian unification. Reacting to an uprising in the papal states that he had suppressed with the aid of Austrian troops, Pope Gregory XVI (1831–1846) in his encyclical

Mirari Vos (1832) recommended "trust and submission to princes" and denounced those who "consumed with the unbridled lust for freedom are entirely devoted to impairing and destroying all rights of dominion while bringing servitude to the people under the slogan of liberty" and attempting "to separate the Church from the state and to break the mutual concord between temporal authority and the priesthood."

In the next pontificate, Pius IX (1846–1878) reacted to the seizure of the Papal States in 1860 by denouncing liberal ideas (quoting Gregory XVI) as "insanity" and "injurious babbling" in his encyclical *Quanta Cura* (1864) which was accompanied by a compilation of past papal statements on related topics, the *Syllabus of Errors*. Among the errors condemned were the proposition that "it is no longer necessary that the Catholic religion be held as the only religion of the state" and (the most famous error) "that the Roman pontiff can and ought to, reconcile himself to, and agree with, progress, liberalism, and modern civilization."[6]

When Rome was seized by the Italian nationalists, Pius IX imposed a ban on Catholic participation in Italian politics. His successor, Leo XIII, did not lift that ban but he encouraged French Catholics who had opposed the Third Republic because of its anti-clericalism to involve themselves in French political life through the so-called *ralliement* policy. In Bismarckian Germany too, Catholics organized the Catholic Center Party in resistance to the Iron Chancellor's anti-Catholic *Kulturkampf.* The Vatican's opposition to democracy was modified somewhat with the publication of Leo's encyclical *Immortale Dei* (On the Christian Constitution of States) in 1885. Leo wrote that "no one of several forms of government is to be condemned. . . . Neither is it blameworthy in itself in any manner, for the people to have a share, greater or less, in the government; for at certain times and under certain laws, such participation may not only be of benefit to the citizens, but may even be of obligation" (no. 36). Yet this does not mean that Leo had suddenly become a liberal democrat. In both this encyclical and in *Libertas Humana* (Human Liberty) issued in 1888, he reaffirmed his predecessors' denunciations of freedom of worship, of expression, and of teaching, accusing the liberals of making "the state absolute and omnipotent" and of proclaiming "that man should live altogether independently of God." Indeed, the pope denounced liberalism as "the sullied product of a revolutionary age of man's unbounded urge for innovation." Yet having opposed religious freedom in principle, he then added that the church "does not forbid public authority to tolerate what is at variance with truth and justice, for the sake of avoiding some greater evil or preserving some greater good."[7] (This is the passage that gave rise to the distinction later made by Catholic theologians between the "thesis" or ideal situation of Catholicism as the established true religion, and the "hypothesis" or pragmatic compromise of religious toleration in a situation of religious pluralism.)

Liberal democracy was identified by the nineteenth century papacy with the separation of church and state, the removal of public support for Catholicism, the secularization of education and marriage, and efforts to replace the Catholic religion with an all-encompassing rationalism and anti-clericalism. The Vatican was only vaguely aware that in the Anglo-American world liberalism did not take on the anti-Catholic stance of the liberals on the continent, if only because Catholics were a small—although increasing—percentage of the population with no pretensions to public recognition or financial support. Nevertheless, the Vatican was suspicious of ecumenical developments in the United States and, in 1895, the Apostolic Delegate saw to it that the rector of the Catholic University of America was removed and that the "naturalism" of the American church and its tendency to minimize its differences with Protestantism were condemned.

The establishment of the Center Party in Germany was followed by the creation of Catholic parties in Holland, Belgium, and Austria, which also were concerned primarily with the protection of the rights of the church. Those parties, however, began to take a more active social role with the publication in 1891 of Leo's encyclical *Rerum Novarum*, which, while it rejected Marxist notions of the class struggle and argued for the natural law status of private property, focused mainly on the plight of the working classes in a rapidly industrializing Europe. The encyclical's call for a living wage to enable the worker to support himself and his family, its assertion of the right of the laboring man to form (preferably Catholic) trade unions to defend his rights, and its argument for the promotion of intermediate groups between the individual and the state formed the basis of the development of the social teaching of the church with important effects in Europe and Latin America.

Yet this social Catholicism should be distinguished from Christian Democracy, the political movement to form parties that endorsed pluralistic democracy as the form of government most in keeping with Christian teaching. In France, racked by the Dreyfus affair that had divided the country along religious lines and by the controversies that accompanied the separation of church and state, a French Catholic leader, Marc Sangnier, established *Le Sillon*, a movement to encourage Catholic participation in French political life. Pius X, Leo XIII's successor, suppressed *Le Sillon* because "to justify their social dreams, they appeal to the gospel, interpolated in their own manner, and what is still more grave, to a disfigured and diminished Christ." *Le Sillon* had fallen afoul of the general suspicion of the heresy condemned by Pius as "Modernism" which the pope accused of "proposing a reform of church government to bring it into harmony with men's conscience which is turning toward democracy."[8]

Thus, while in other European countries with parliamentary governments, such as Belgium, Holland, Germany, and Austria, Catholic parties participated in political life—in the German case, the Center became one of the bulwarks of the Weimar Republic after World War I—in France and Italy parties of Catholic inspiration were not active because of Vatican opposition. After the *Non Expedit* ban on Catholic participation in Italian politics was lifted in 1919, a socially oriented priest, Don Luigi Sturzo, organized the Popular Party which had spectacular success but was, in effect, dissolved in 1924 by the Vatican after Mussolini came to power and Sturzo went into exile. In France many Catholics (including the young army officer Charles de Gaulle) were monarchists and opposed to the parliamentarism of the Third Republic, but a small party of Christian Democratic inspiration, the Popular Democratic Party, was organized in the 1930s and involved young leaders who were later to be active in the Resistance to Nazism and in the creation of a Christian Democratic party, *le Mouvement Republicain Populaire* (MRP) after World War II.[9]

Under Pius XI (1922–1939) the church entered into ill-fated agreements with Mussolini and Hitler—the Lateran Treaty in 1929, establishing Vatican City and guaranteeing religious instruction in the Italian schools, and a Concordat with Hitler's Germany in 1933, both soon violated by the dictators. Pius XI's social encyclical *Quadragesimo Anno* (1931) further developed Leo's arguments in *Rerum Novarum*, endorsing the encouragement of intermediate groups between the individual and the state, which the pope called the principle of subsidiarity. His support for vertical vocational groups ("orders") in industry and the professions, involving cooperation of labor and management, seemed to resemble the corporatism adopted by authoritarian regimes in Portugal, Italy, and Austria in the twenties and thirties. However, as the totalitarian character of the German and Italian regimes became evident, the pope issued two denunciatory encyclicals, *Non Abbiamo Bisogno* (1931) and *Mit Brennender Sorge* (1937).

It was an indication of the state of Catholic political thought in Latin Europe and of the continuing tensions between Catholicism and European liberalism that, in Spain in the early 1930s, the Falange, organized by José Antonio Primo de Rivera, the son of the former dictator, could appeal to Catholicism for support for a third position between Marxist collectivism and liberal parliamentarism in politics, and between socialism and capitalism in economics. There seemed to be an affinity, not between Catholicism and totalitarianism, but between the Vatican and authoritarian regimes willing to grant the church certain rights in the areas of education and marriage. The ease with which Francisco Franco could take over the Falange as his official party, and the support he received from Spanish ecclesiastical authorities, seemed to prove this.

The single person who did the most to relate democracy and human rights to the Catholic tradition and to argue against a link between Catholicism and authoritarianism was the French philosopher, Jacques Maritain. Converted to Catholicism in 1906 and to Thomism in 1912, Maritain only began to write about politics in the late 1920s, following the condemnation by Pius XI of *Action Francaise*, a right-wing movement with which Maritain had been sympathetic.[10] In his writings, Maritain argues that "integral" or "personalist" and "communitarian" democracy is the best application of Christian and Thomist political principles, and that the modern democratic state is the result of the "leavening influence of the Gospel principles in human history."[11]

Maritain distinguished his religiously based personalism from what he considered to be the egoistic individualism of "bourgeois liberalism" and the collectivism of Marxism—thus maintaining a continuity with early papal "third positionism." However, he drew from the Thomist tradition to argue for a religiously pluralistic and socially concerned democratic state that was almost indistinguishable from the contemporary democratic welfare states of Europe. Along with other Catholic political thinkers of European background, such as Yves Simon[12] and Heinrich Rommen,[13] he was responsible for a new development in Catholic thought that had been anticipated but not articulated by earlier European writers—the argument that democracy was not simply one of several forms of government, all of which were acceptable to the degree that they promoted "the common good," but was the one political structure most in keeping with the nature of man and with Christian values.

Maritain's writings on democracy were read, quoted, and used by the leaders of the incipient or revived Christian Democratic parties in Europe after World War II and in Latin America in the 1950s and 1960s. For the MRP in France, the CDU-CSU in the German Federal Republic, and the *Democrazia Cristiana* (DCI) in Italy, Christianity implies democracy, and Maritain's personalism and communitarianism provided the theoretical justification that drew on Catholic and Thomistic conceptions of human nature to argue for free institutions, the welfare state, religious pluralism, and political democracy.

During World War II the Catholic integralists and authoritarians were discredited because of their support for fascism, and the Vatican began to take a more positive attitude toward democracy. Pope Pius XII, in his Christmas messages, drew direct links between political freedom, democracy, and the Christian tradition. His well-known 1944 *Christmas Message* stated that "a democratic form of government appears to many people as a natural postulate imposed by reason itself." However, he maintained some continuity with earlier papal criticisms by distinguishing between "the people," and "the mass," describing the latter as "the main enemy of true democracy and of its ideal of liberty and equality," since "a democratic state left to the arbitrary will of the mass" acts as if "the authority of the state is unlimited . . . and there is not left any appeal whatsoever to a superior and morally binding law." "A sound democracy," the pope insisted, must be "founded upon the unchanging principles of natural law and revealed truths."[14]

It was ironic that just as the Vatican and Catholic Europe were finally opting for democracy, a bitter debate broke out in the United States over the relation of Catholicism and democracy. The immediate policy issue was whether Catholic schools could receive financial support from the government. The Supreme Court had argued in the New Jersey Bus Case (*Twining versus Ewing Township Board of Education*, 1947) and in the *Everson* case (1948) that the First Amendment forbade even non-discriminatory aid to church-related schools, although it allowed "aid to the child" in the form of bus transportation. The appearance of Blanshard's *American Freedom and Catholic Power* in 1949, just at the time the U.S. bishops were making a drive for aid to their schools, attempted to provide evidence to American liberals that the growing influence of American Catholicism constituted a fundamental threat to American democracy. For a time the editorial and letters pages of the *Washington Post* were full of references to nineteenth century papal encyclicals and quotes from such otherwise unknown works as John Ryan and Francis Boland[15] to demonstrate that Catholics believed only in religious toleration when they were in a minority and that once they reached power they would establish Roman Catholicism as a state religion. It did not help that Ryan and Boland printed extracts from *Immortale Dei* in their text, following them with an argument that although "error has not the same rights as truth . . . the foregoing propositions have application only in a completely Catholic state" nor that there were still restrictions on the rights of Protestants to proselytize in Colombia and Spain.

Beginning in 1948 John Courtney Murray wrote several articles criticizing the theory that the establishment of a state church was the Catholic ideal, and arguing that indeed the American arrangement was closer to that ideal than Franco's Spain. Cardinal Alfredo Ottaviani, head of the Holy Office in Rome, publicly attacked Murray's view[16] and it was extensively debated in the *American Ecclesiastical Review*. In 1955 Murray was advised by his superiors in Rome to discontinue his writing on the subject and he cleared his study of all books related to the topic. Yet ten years later he was one of the principal influences upon the preparation of the Second Vatican Council's Declaration on Religious Freedom (*Dignitatis Humanae Personae*).

As the Latin title indicates, the Vatican statement bases its argument for religious freedom on the dignity of people as free moral beings. During the intervening ten years, European historians and theologians such as Joseph Lecler had prepared the way for the Declaration, but the most important breakthrough in the official Vatican position was the publication of Pope John XXIII's encyclical *Pacem in Terris* in 1963. After what appears to be a classically conservative beginning, a discussion of "order between men," the pope states that every human being is a "person" by virtue of which "he has rights and duties of his own, flowing directly and simultaneously from his very nature." Among those rights is "the right to worship God according to one's conscience," which the pope describes as "the right to honor God according to the dictates of an upright conscience, and therefore to worship God privately and publicly."[17] The reference to public worship seems to indicate a change in the official position that had endorsed (see the Ottaviani letter) the policy of Franco's Spain that tolerated non-Catholic worship only in private.

The encyclical makes a similar argument on democracy, stating that "the dignity of the human person involves the right to take an active part in public affairs and to contribute one's part to the common good of the citizens" and that "the human person is entitled to the juridical protection of his rights." In the next section the pope says, "It is impossible to determine, once and for all, the most suitable form of government," but he refers again to the advantages of participation and of ministers holding office only for a limited time, in effect arguing for periodic elections.

The encyclical swept away the single most important obstacle to the acceptance of democracy by the Vatican—its belief in the theoretical superiority of the union of church and state. The liberal democratic state necessarily entails religious freedom, and it took until the 1960s for the Vatican to accept its desirability on philosophical and theological grounds. (Indeed, Father Murray had been "disinvited" as an expert [*peritus*] at the first session of the Council and only came in that status to the second session at the insistence of Cardinal Spellman.)

A similar link between religious freedom and endorsement of democracy is evident at the Second Vatican Council (1962–1965). The same session that adopted the Declaration on Religious Freedom also voted the Pastoral Constitution on the Church in the Modern World (*Gaudium et Spes*) that included the following formal commitment of Catholicism to democracy:

It is in full accord with human nature that juridical-political structures should, with ever better success and without discrimination, afford all their citizens the chance to participate freely and actively in establishing the constitutional bases of a political community, governing the state, determining the scope and purpose of various institutions, and choosing leaders. (No. 75)[18]

The Declaration on Religious Freedom restated in more forceful terms what Pope John had said in *Pacem in Terris*. Arguing that "the human person has a right to religious freedom," the Council declared that "the right to religious freedom has its foundation in the very dignity of the human person." The Council defined that right as freedom

from coercion on the part of individuals or of social groups and of any human power in such wise that in matters religious no one is to be forced to act in a manner contrary to his own beliefs. Nor is anyone to be restrained from acting in accordance with his beliefs, whether publicly or privately, whether alone or in association with others, within due limits. (No. 2)[19]

Religious freedoms were not the only liberties endorsed by the Council. Again drawing its arguments from the development of "a keener awareness of human dignity"—and repeating what had been argued in *Pacem in Terris—Gaudium et Spes* endorsed the contemporary aspirations for

a political-juridical in which personal rights can gain better protection. These include rights of free assembly, of common action, or expressing personal opinions, and of professing a religion privately and publicly. For the protection of personal rights is a necessary condition for the active participation of citizens, whether as individuals or collectively, in the life and government of the state. (No. 73)

Applications

The formal commitment of the official church to democracy and human rights as well as to religious freedom meant, in effect, the abandonment of the long-standing opposition between the Vatican and liberal democracy. The Council's statement on democracy contained footnotes to

Pius XII's wartime Christmas messages but it marked a much clearer and unambiguous commitment to democracy and political participation than ever before. While there remained a suspicion, indeed a moral critique of economic liberalism, the opposition to liberalism's political program—much of it fueled by now obsolete struggles over education and financial support—had disappeared. While in many ways this was simply a recognition of political changes that had taken place at the grass roots and in the national communities in Europe and Latin America, the fact that now it was endorsed formally at the highest level had an important impact on the conduct of church leaders and clergy in subsequent decades. The bishops themselves had received a kind of political and moral education as a result of their attendance at the Council from September until December for four years (1962–65) and it affected their attitudes toward their own role as moral leaders. Catholic seminaries and educational institutions used the Council's decrees as an educational reference point, and old-line conservatives and integralists no longer could cite the Vatican to legitimate their political views.

In countries such as France, Germany, Italy, and the Low Countries the battle already had been won. The election of Charles de Gaulle in 1958 marked the beginning of the end of the division between Catholic monarchists and anti-clerical republicans that had begun with the French Revolution. Before that, the collaboration of conservative Catholics with the Vichy regime during World War II had discredited the anti-republican cause, and the MRP had become the largest party in France until its ranks were split open by the creation of the Gaullist party. The Gaullist regime and later the Socialists finally were able to work out compromises on the vexing question of state financial aid to church schools. In Germany the Christian Democratic Union included Catholics and Protestants among its leaders and no longer saw its primary function as the defense of the rights of the Catholic church. Similarly, the Christian trade unions and their international confederation signified by changing their names that no more was there a direct link to the church.

While, for geographic and historical reasons, Italian Christian Democrats were more concerned with the role of the church, they too began to lose their confessional character and to make compromises and alliances with republicans, liberals and socialists who earlier had been sworn enemies.

All this had begun to take place well before the Council. A more measurable impact of the Council's commitment to democracy can be discerned in Spain, Portugal, and Latin America. In Spain the tight link between the hierarchy and the Franco regime began to loosen—especially among Catholic student and labor groups and the younger clergy and bishops. By the time of the transition that followed Franco's death, Catholics, socialists and communists could work out constitutional solutions to problems that had caused a civil war forty years earlier. In Portugal the church was less prepared for the downfall of the authoritarian regime, but once the mid-seventies radicalism of the military and the peasantry wore off, it too developed a system that involved compromise and cooperation among liberals, Catholics, and socialists.

The most striking impact of the change was in Latin America. In the Alliance for Progress period of the early 1960s, the Christian Democratic parties were seen as "the last best hope" (the title of a book by Leonard Gross, published in 1967) for Latin America. In Chile and Venezuela large and well-organized Christian Democratic parties emerged to challenge the old link between conservatism and Catholicism with programs of agrarian reform, and improved housing, education, and welfare that appealed to Maritain and the social encyclicals. Christian Democratic parties also were founded in Central America and were to play a significant role in the coming decades.

By the time of the Conference of Latin American Bishops (CELAM) in Medellín in 1968, however, many of the elected civilian governments of Latin America had been overthrown—often in the name of Western and Christian values. The church's public endorsement of democracy prevented the military regimes from using Catholicism as a source of legitimacy as earlier authoritarian rulers had been able to do. More importantly, the church became an umbrella under which human rights groups and opponents of the regime could find protection and support. In post-1973-coup Chile, for example, the church set up the ecumenical Committee for Peace and later the Vicariate of Solidarity to aid victims of the repression, and a Human Rights Commission was established headed by Jaime Castillo, a Thomist theorist and former minister of justice of the Christian Democratic government of Eduardo Frei (1964–1970). In Brazil the National Conference of Brazilian Bishops became an outspoken critic of government repression in the 1970s, and in El Salvador and Nicaragua the hierarchy repeatedly denounced instances of torture and murder by authoritarian regimes. The single exception was Argentina where, except for the activities of a Catholic layman, Adolfo Perez Esquivel, the Catholic church was strangely silent in the face of the disappearances of 9,000 Argentines between 1976 and 1979.[19]

The pattern continued in the 1980s. The Guatemalan church which had previously been supportive of the military encouraged and assisted the transition to an elected government in 1983. The Haitian church was one of the few institutional structures that could operate to assist that troubled country's search for a stable democratic government after the departure of the Duvaliers. In Chile a church-inspired group promoted a massive registration campaign that was a major factor in the defeat of Augusto Pinochet's 1988 bid for an extension of his mandate until 1997. In the Philippines Cardinal Jaime Sin played a central role in the defeat of the Marcos government at the polls and Marcos' subsequent departure from power. In Panama the Catholic hierarchy wrote a pastoral letter in June 1987, calling for democracy and so began the process of popular mobilization against General Manuel Noriega. In Brazil the church promoted the transition from military rule, and a leftist candidate from the trade unions with strong connections to the Ecclesial Base Communities (CEBS) came close to winning the presidency in December 1989.

Catholic conservatives now found it more difficult to justify their position by appealing to order, hierarchy, and property as intended by God. Latin American conservatism in general began more and more to resemble its North American counterpart, arguing for efficiency, law and order, economic freedom, and the importance of the private sector and private property. In Chile there was a curious amalgam of two previously antithetical traditions in the argument of Chilean Catholic conservatives (e.g., Jaime Guzman) that the encouragement of the market economy was an example of Pius XI's principle of subsidiarity. The Latin American neo-conservatives' ideological shift is important because, besides endorsing market capitalism, now they accept the necessity and even the desirability of a democratic political system. Since many of them have been educated in Catholic schools, the shift in Catholic theory and practice has been an important influence in their change of attitude.

Returning to Europe in the eighties, one is struck again by the salience of the church in the political openings in Eastern Europe. The link between the Catholic church and the Solidarity movement in Poland is an evident one, and it should not be surprising that a democratized Poland is in the process of reintroducing (optional) religious instruction in the government schools. A somewhat less obvious but nevertheless important role was played by the Catholic church in Czechoslovakia while, in East Germany, the Evangelical (Lutheran) Church ministers emerged as important leaders in 1989.

In the United States, while there was never any doubt about the commitment of American Catholics to democracy, there were important changes in the relationship of Catholics to the American political process. Since the election of John Kennedy in 1960, Catholics no longer felt discriminated against in the American life. The close historical link to the Democratic Party has been broken, and the ideological spectrum in American Catholicism runs from the *National Catholic Reporter* on the left through the *National Catholic Register* in the center, to *The Wanderer* on the right. The two Catholic senators from New York, Daniel Patrick

Moynihan and Alfonse D'Amato symbolize in their differences the range of contemporary Catholic political views. While there are lingering problems, mostly centered around the abortion issue—especially some bishops' efforts to impose ecclesiastical sanctions on those who favor legalized abortion—the public attention given to the Catholic bishops' pastoral letters on nuclear weapons and on the U.S. economy are an indication that, although this may not be Richard Neuhaus's *Catholic Moment*,[20] the church and its spokesmen are regarded as respected contributors to national political debate—especially when its leadership takes account of differing opinions and makes appeals to rational norms—as it did in the two letters. Both those letters evoked strongly critical responses by Catholic conservatives, notably Michael Novak, confirming for the case of American Catholicism Robert Wuthnow's thesis in *The Restructuring of American Religion*[21] that the divisions in American religion are now more along ideological than sectarian lines.

Catholicism and Liberal Democracy Today

The endorsement of liberal democracy by the institutional church has not been a wholly uncritical one, and there has been an attempt to maintain continuity with earlier statements. This is particularly true in the case of economic liberalism or free market capitalism. In 1967, for example, Pope Paul VI wrote an influential encyclical, *Populorum Progressio* (On the Development of Peoples), that attacked capitalism as a system "which considers profit as the key motive for economic progress, competition as the supreme law of economics, and private ownership of the means of production as an absolute right that has no limits and carries no corresponding obligation." The Pope quoted Pius XI on "the international imperialism of money" and argued that "unchecked liberalism" is itself a form of dictatorship (para. 26). The encyclical focused on the economic relations of rich and poor countries and called for action to favor the Third World, since "development is another name for peace" (para. 30). In the following year, the Medellín Conference of Latin American Bishops denounced both liberal capitalism and Marxism as "against the dignity of the human person" with Latin America "caught between the two options" (para. 10, Document *On Justice*). It is not surprising, therefore, that the liberation theology movement was able to use the conference's description of the "institutionalized violence" in Latin America to extend the traditional just war criteria to include revolutionary counter-violence against capitalism.[23]

Pope John Paul II often is described as a conservative in theology and ecclesiology, but he has maintained a critical attitude toward liberal individualism and free enterprise economics, which was expressed in the encyclical *Laborem Exercens*, written in 1981 on the anniversary of *Quadragesimo Anno*, that endorsed the priority of labor in economics. *Libertas Conscientiae*, the Second Vatican Instruction on Liberation Theology (1985) sums up the state of contemporary Catholic social thought in its commitment to solidarity—man's obligation to contribute to the common good—against individualism, and to *subsidiarity*—the promotion of the initiative of individuals and intermediate communities—against collectivism (para. 73). The Instruction reiterates the church's commitment to democracy, arguing that there can only be "authentic development in a social and political system which respects freedoms and fosters them through the participation of everyone," while guaranteeing a "proper pluralism in institutions and social initiatives" (para. 95).

Papal criticism of capitalism is modified in John Paul II's encyclical *Sollicitudo Rei Socialis* (On Social Concern), issued in 1988 in observance of the twentieth anniversary of *Populorum Progressio*. Perhaps for the first time in papal documents, it lists among the human rights that everyone should be guaranteed, "the right of economic initiative . . . which is important not only for the individual but for the common good" but it balances this with a denunciation of the international economic, financial, and social mechanisms "that accentuate the situation of wealth for some and poverty for the rest" (para. 15), adding that there is a "social mortgage" on property and "the goods of this world are originally meant for all" (paras. 22 and 42). The pope emphasizes once again the importance of democratic and participatory institutions, since the "free and responsible participation of all citizens in public affairs" and "respect for the promotion of human rights" are necessary conditions of authentic development (para. 44).[24]

Are we to conclude from this review that, after a long history of opposition, Catholic social thought has now not only reconciled itself to liberal democracy but has embraced it? Not exactly. A number of tensions and conflicts remain between the views of most liberal democrats and contemporary Catholic thinking on politics.

Some would hold that a central difference is that contemporary liberalism is relativistic and skeptical, while Catholicism is committed to a transcendent source of absolute religious and moral values. This understanding of liberalism seems to me to be an excessively reductionist one, since it lumps all liberals into the camp of what I would call "procedural" or "value-neutral" liberals such as (the early) John Rawls, Robert Nozick, or Ronald Dworkin (and, much earlier, Thomas Hobbes), as distinct from what I might call "substantive" liberals like John Locke, Immanuel Kant, or among contemporary writers Joseph Raz,[25] for whom liberal democracy is grounded in absolute values intrinsic to the human person, whether derived from a conception of the free individual in "the state of nature which has a law of nature to govern it" (Locke, *Second Treatise*, no. 6), from the nature of a free self-legislating moral person (Kant), or from the freely-choosing, morally committed, and socially-oriented individual (Raz). In the case of natural law liberal democrats such as John Hallowell,[26] democracy is based on a view of the nature of the person that closely resembles the views of Catholic theorists. For them, to use Rawlsian terminology, liberal democracy is not just about the right, but also "a thick theory of the good."[27]

Thus, there is a convergence of contemporary Christian Democrats and those liberals who argue that something more than a commitment to individual freedom—i.e., a moral and social view of the human person is necessary to undergird social cooperation in a democracy. In the case of the Christian, that something more is the nature of the person as endowed with an immortal soul and a special right and duty to make moral and social choices for which he or she is responsible to the Creator. In the case of "substantive liberals" it is a conception of a human person as moral, free, and aware of his or her responsibility to respect the equal moral rights of other human beings. The differences are not that great between the two. Both believe that the state should respect human rights and resolve differences democratically—and both do so for moral reasons—as distinct from the "procedural liberal" who supports democracy because he is skeptical about the possibility of knowing the good.

There still remain areas of tension, however, between liberalism and Catholicism. Several come to mind. In the area of sexuality and the family, liberalism tends to tolerate—and even in some cases, endorse—greater diversity of "life-styles" than does Catholicism. The church continues to oppose abortion, contraception, divorce, homosexuality and pornography, while for most liberals these are matters of individual "choice." Historically and even today, the church has extended its opposition to such practices to support for the enactment of coercive legislation against them—whatever liberals may think of those practices (and some liberals, certainly most Catholic liberals, believe that they are wrong) they are opposed to the legislation of morality. It is true there is a long tradition in Catholic social thought that permits the toleration of evil to avoid a greater evil (e.g., St. Augustine on houses of prostitution), and that leading contemporary Catholic politicians often distinguish between their personal moral views on abortion or homosexuality and the advisability of enacting coercive legislation.

However, the Catholic church has been reluctant to leave to the area of individual choice what it considers to be serious moral ills. It has long since ceased to press for legislation outlawing contraception, and only in a few countries is it still fighting a losing battle to prevent the enactment of legislation permitting divorce. In the areas of pornography, homosexuality, and abortion, however, it is still hostile to liberal permissiveness—viewing these practices as fundamental violations of natural law—the murder of the fetus and the corruption of family values that are important to a stable democracy. In a democracy any group is entitled to make an argument on philosophic grounds on the areas of morality that are essential to a stable society and, provided the results are arrived at after open debate and by majority rule, it seems to many Catholics that there is nothing wrong with legislation in these areas.

Liberals however—including Catholic liberals—would argue that the area of sexual conduct is a matter of private choice and not for public legislation. Their opposition as liberals is reinforced by their opposition as democrats to the pressure tactics used by some members of the hierarchy—and more generally to what they see as an undemocratic structure of authority and decision making in the church itself.

It is true that Vatican II's Dogmatic Constitution on the Church (*Lumen Gentium*) defined the church as "the people of God" and stated that "the order of the bishops is successor to the college of the apostles in teaching authority . . . together with its head, the Roman pontiff and never without this head" (chs. II and III) and that there has been a partial decentralization of the internal structure of the church. Since Vatican II national councils and international synods of bishops have taken a more active role, and the laity has been more deeply involved. However, the church has not become a democracy and those who have argued, like the Brazilian liberation theologian, Leonardo Boff, for an increase in internal democratization have had difficulties with the Vatican. There is still a tension, and there always will be, between a hierarchical church that sees itself as a guardian and interpreter of divine revelation and a sociopolitical structure that decides public questions on the basis of free discussion, majority rule, and individual rights.

A second area of tension between Catholicism and liberal democracy is that of education. Arguing that common schooling is essential to promote the cultural preconditions of democratic coexistence, most liberal democrats in the United States have opposed direct support to church schools, although compulsory education laws recognize that they are performing a valuable social service. The tortured state of contemporary constitutional law in the area of church and state, as it applies to aid to religious schools, demonstrates that a rigid application of the "wall of separation" doctrine is neither historically, philosophically, nor practically valid. More generally, the recent church-state cases seem to demonstrate, as William Galston and others have argued, a doctrinaire commitment by many judges to the privatization of religion as well as a refusal to recognize that in a pluralistic society, religious beliefs are an important source of moral and social insights.[28]

A third area of tension in the past, which has been mentioned earlier, is the historic hostility of Catholicism to capitalism, the economic system of all Western democracies. It is true that now there is much less resistance in Catholic circles to free markets than in the past. Christian Democratic parties worldwide, from the CDU in Germany to the PDC in Chile, have moved from an initially anti-capitalist position to one that accepts and even endorses market freedom, provided it is supplemented by a substantial program of social legislation ("the social market economy"). Michael Novak and others have tried to make a stronger religious argument for the virtues of capitalism, but there remains in the Catholic tradition a belief that capitalism is based on greed and exploitation, and suspect from a moral point of view so that it requires state action to limit its excesses.

The social orientation of Catholic political thought derived from a belief in humanity's common creation by God and in an objective common good has meant that, historically, it has been more favorable than has liberalism to welfare programs, unionization, and government action. Here again, however, there has been a convergence in this century as contemporary liberals, at least in the English-speaking world, have accepted and endorsed welfare legislation. In theory, however, as the communitarian theorists like to remind us, liberalism's model of a person, while not quite as starkly individualist as Michael Sandel's "unencumbered self,"[29] seems to arrive at social obligations from premises that are initially more individualist than Catholic in concept.[30]

Since Vatican II, as I have argued earlier, official Catholic commitment to political democracy and human rights has been added to the church's earlier support for social legislation. Recent statements by the Vatican and by national episcopates in Latin America and the Philippines have stressed the moral duty of political participation that goes beyond the more permissive attitude of liberalism. Public service is lauded as a morally praiseworthy and religiously legitimate calling. From being a critic, and even opponent of democracy, the church has become its strong supporter and, while there may be differences concerning the morality of some democratic outcomes, there is no dissent on the moral superiority of democratic political structures and the religious grounding of human rights. As recent events in Latin America and Eastern Europe have demonstrated, the church now provides an important reinforcement for democracy and is an institutional refuge for human rights activists in times of oppression. In addition, at least some critics of contemporary liberal culture would endorse the efforts of the church to warn of the corrosive social and moral effects for democracy of materialism, rampant sexuality, and declining family values.

The relationship now between Catholicism and liberal democracy, then, has become a positive and, one would hope, a mutually reinforcing one, even if there are a number of continuing tensions between them. The "Naked Public Square" is not yet bereft of religious people committed both to democracy and to fundamental moral values. If, as Robert Bellah and others have argued, an inherent problem for democracy is the lack of moral commitment to community and to participation that seems to result from the individualism and pluralism of the liberal society, the changes we have traced in this chapter will provide significant support for the future of democracy in the contemporary world.

Notes

1. Sidney Hook, *Reason, Social Myths and Democracy* (1984), p. 76.

2. Paul Blanshard, *American Freedom and Catholic Power* (1958), p. 64

3. On the documentary evidence for and against papal claims, see James T. Shotwell, ed., *The See of Peter* (New York: Columbia University Press, 1940). On the emergence of the monarchical episcopate, see Elaine Pagels, *The Gnostic Gospels* (New York: Harper and Row, 1979), ch. 2. For more general accounts, see Maurice Goguel, *The Primitive Church* (London: Allan & Unwin, 1984) and Wayne Meeks, *The Moral World of the First Christians* (Philadelphia: Fortress Press, 1986).

4. See the documents in Brian Tierney, ed., *The Crisis of Church and State* (1050–1300) (Englewood Cliffs, N.J.: Prentice-Hall, 1964) and Tierney, *Religion, Law, and the Growth of Constitutional Thought, 1150–1650* (New York: Cambridge University Press, 1982), as well as Paul E. Sigmund, *Nicholas of Cusa and Medieval Political Thought* (Cambridge, Mass.: Harvard University Press, 1963), ch. 4, and Antony Black, *Council and Commune: The Conciliar Movement and the Fifteenth Century Heritage* (London: Burns and Oates, 1979), chs. 16–17.

5. See the selections in Paul E. Sigmund, ed. and trans., *St. Thomas Aquinas on Politics and Ethics* (New York: W. W. Norton, 1988).

6. For the English texts, see Claudia Carlen, ed., *The Papal Encyclicals (1740–1878)* (Raleigh: McGrath Publishers, 1981), pp. 235–240 and 381–385. For the *Syllabus of Errors*, see Henry Bettenson, ed., *Documents of the Christian Church* (New York: Oxford University Press, 1960), p. 382.

7. All quotations are taken from the translations of Leo XIII's encyclicals in Joseph Husslein, *Social Wellsprings*, vol. 1 (Milwaukee: Bruce Publishers, 1940).

8. Quotations are from Alex Vidler, *A Century of Social Catholicism* (London: Society for the Promotion of Christian Knowledge, 1964), p. 138.

9. See Michael Fogarty, *Christian Democracy in Europe, 1820–1953* (London: Routledge, 1957).

10. The best known of his books applying Thomist principles to democracy are *Integral Humanism*, French edition (Paris: Aubier, 1936); *Scholasticism and Politics* (New York: Macmillan, 1940); *The Rights of Man and the Natural Law* (New York: Scribner's, 1943); and *Man and the State* (lectures delivered at the University of Chicago in 1950 and published by its press the following year).

11. On the development of Maritain's political theory, see my article "Maritain on Politics" in Deal Hudson and Matthew Mancini, eds., *Understanding Maritain* (Atlanta: Mercer University Press, 1987). Maritain's early writings were critical of liberalism and capitalism, but after a lengthy stay in the United States, he wrote a book that praised the most bourgeois liberal of all modern states as the best application of Christian principles; see his *Reflections on America* (New York: Scribner's, 1958).

12. Yves Simon, *The Philosophy of Democratic Government* (Chicago: University of Chicago Press, 1951).

13. Heinrich Rommen, *The State in Catholic Thought* (St. Louis: Herder, 1945).

14. See the 1944 Christmas Message in Michael Chinigo, ed., *The Pope Speaks: The Teachings of Pope Pius XII* (New York: Pantheon, 1957), pp. 292–299.

15. John Ryan and Francis Boland, *Catholic Principles of Politics* (New York: Macmillan, 1940), pp. 318–319.

16. *New York Times*, July 23, 1953.

17. Pope John XXIII, *Pacem in Terris* (Peace on Earth) (Huntington, Ind.: Our Sunday Visitor Press, 1963), *passim*.

18. Walter Abbott, ed., *Documents of the Second Vatican Council* (New York: Herder and Herder, 1966), p. 285.

19. *Ibid.*, pp. 678–679.

20. See Eric O. Hanson, *The Catholic Church in World Politics* (Princeton: Princeton University Press, 1981), ch. 7; Brian Smith, *The Church and Politics in Chile* (Princeton: Princeton University Press, 1982); Thomas C. Bruneau, *The Church in Brazil: The Politics of Religion* (Austin: University of Texas Press, 1982); Philip Berryman, *The Religious Roots of Rebellion: Christians in the Central American Revolutions* (Maryknoll, N.Y.: Orbis Books, 1984); Emilio Mignone, *Witness to Truth: The Complicity of Church and Dictatorship in Argentina* (Maryknoll, N.Y.: Orbis Books, 1988); and Paul E. Sigmund, *Liberation Theology at the Crossroads: Democracy or Revolution?* (New York: Oxford University Press, 1990).

21. Richard Neuhaus, *Catholic Moment* (New York: Harper & Row, 1987).

22. Robert Wuthnow, *The Restructuring of American Religion* (Princeton: Princeton University Press, 1988).

23. See my *Liberation Theology at the Crossroads* for a discussion of the relationship between revolution and democracy in liberationist thinking. In the 1980s the liberation theologians moved away from the socialist revolutionism of the 1960s to an endorsement of grass-roots democracy, because, in the words of Hugo Assmann, long regarded as one of the most radical of the liberation theologians, "Democratic values are revolutionary values" (quoted on p. 175).

24. The text of *Sollicitudo Rei Socialis* appears on Gregory Baum and Robert Ellsberg, eds., *The Logic of Solidarity* (Maryknoll, N.Y.: Orbis Books, 1989), pp. 1–62.

25. Joseph Raz, *The Morality of Freedom* (Oxford: Clarendon Press, 1986).

26. John Hallowell, *The Moral Foundations of Democracy* (New York: Cambridge University Press, 1954).

27. See the discussions in R. Bruce Douglass, Gerald M. Mara, and Henry S. Richardson, eds., *Liberalism and the Good* (New York: Routledge, 1990), esp. ch. 11.

28. William Galston, "Public Morality and Religion in the Liberal State," *P.S.*, vol. 19, 1986, pp. 807–824.

29. Michael Sandel, *Liberalism and the Limits of Justice* (New York: Cambridge University Press, 1982).

30. For an example of the difference in reasoning patterns compare John Rawls' use of a quasi-contractual theory in *A Theory of Justice* (Cambridge: Mass.: Harvard University Press, 1970) to argue for a constitutional system that only tolerates inequalities that benefit the least advantaged, with the more communitarian, scriptural and philosophical arguments given by the bishops of Latin America for the "preferential option for the poor."

Four

Is the Social Role of the Church Changing?

Jean-Yves Calvez, S.J.

As we celebrate the hundredth anniversary of *Rerum Novarum*[1] and read the old encyclical again, we discover that the main concerns of the social teaching of the church all begin with that encyclical and are already present in it: the concern about a deep division of society on the basis of the economy. There is the search for corrective social justice, the quest for a just salary (which is not necessarily the salary agreed upon in contracts), concern about a reasonable intervention of the state in the economy, and the hope that associations (even corporations or professional organizations) can be revived so the social texture can be reconstructed.

The church at successive stages will, of course, adapt to new sets of circumstances, to the wider social issues of a Third World in the throes of development, to new cities and the immense metropolitan areas in all parts of the world, to new financial techniques, and to the ecological problems. But the church will be faithful all through the century to the same chapters of its social doctrine and to the same principles of subsidiarity and solidarity, personal initiative and action in the name of the common good, association, and participation.

At the same time, the social role of the church, or its role with regard to social, economic and political life, has changed or has begun to change. This has much to do with the style in which the church and Christians deal with the social side of their lives. *Role* is the right word here insofar as it reflects a way of acting within a more general framework than the church—it is society. However, the word role is inadequate for a reality, the church, that cannot be conceived only in terms of social service or social organization. The church does not have "a mission in the political, economic or social order"; it has a broader goal, "a religious one," said the Council.[2]

In Leo XIII's perception, the church must be allowed the freedom to bring Christian values, views and a Christian formation to bear upon the critical social situation in which humankind finds itself. Without the church and the contribution it can make, there is no prospect of healing the terrible social illnesses of the day. The contribution of the church consists of a teaching, a system of formation of the personality by cult, sacraments and discipline (Christian morals or way of life), by social institutions and agencies set up by the church itself. "These agencies alone can reach the innermost heart and conscience, and bring men and women to act from a motive of duty, to control their passions and appetites, to love God and their neighbours with a love that is outstanding and of the highest degree" (RN no. 22).

Such a view, at times, has been called integralist because the church has tried to influence from outside economic and social reality, including political reality. For example, after having been stripped by the liberal states of the power to govern or indirectly control the political world, it tried to gain control of civil society or of the socioeconomic world. However, this was not the real tone of Leo XIII, whatever the situation of the church may have been at the time; rather, the church wants to *help* and *serve* humankind. But Leo XIII certainly believed that, short of the church's help, no remedy could be found for the deep, social division of the time. He admitted, of course, that others could help and contribute—governments, workers and employers could pool their efforts to practice justice.

At the time of Pius XI's *Quadragesimo Anno* (1931), the atmosphere had not yet changed profoundly but there was a better acceptance of the church. The church offered to the world a global model, of a corporativist nature, as the solution to the new crisis—capitalism and socialism (communism), both in grave disrepute as they had treated people inhumanely. True, according to Pius XI, there was no longer the explicit claim that a solution could be entertained without the contribution of the church. Nor perhaps was there in the surrounding world the view that the church was not needed or wanted, as was the case at the end of the fifteenth century, that is, during the time of Leo XIII. After the First World War, the socialist director of the newly founded International Labor Office (ILO), Albert Thomas, decided that he needed at his side someone in the capacity of an international civil servant to advise him on the social views of the church and who would be in touch with church authorities, a practice even today.

But more changes were to come with the Second World War and with the reconstruction period that followed. The church in the Western world contributed immensely to the varied aspects of social reconstruction given through many Christian politicians and trade union leaders, as well as by Popes Pius XII and John XXIII.[3]

"The Catholic social doctrine," said John XXIII, "is an integral part of the Christian conception of life."[4] This implies that the church is not only offering help in a crisis but that Christian daily life itself has a social dimension and the gospel message is not distant from social existence. The pope's statement may seem an obvious one today but at that time it was not so common.

From then on, the church has not just been playing a role in society—it has shared in the very life of society. A Christian cannot think of being separate from that social life as he or she may have an essential contribution to make to the solution of a given crisis. The important sentence is at the beginning of *Gaudium et Spes*, which definitely strikes a new note: "The joy and hope, the grief and anguish of the men of our time . . . are the joy and hope, the grief and anguish of the followers of Christ as well" (no. 1). "The Council can find no more eloquent expression of its solidarity and respectful affection for the whole human family, to which it belongs, than to enter into dialogue with it about the problems touching man's individual and collective endeavour" (no. 3). The church can "furnish mankind with the saving resources which the church has received from its founder" (*ibid.*) but it can do so only in a dialogue as it shares the same experiences as all humankind. The church, the Council continues, "offers to cooperate . . . with mankind, in fostering a sense of brotherhood to correspond to this destiny of theirs. . . . The church is not motivated by an earthly ambition but is interested in one thing only—to carry on the work of Christ." What is that work? It is "to bear witness to the truth, to save not to judge, to serve not to be served" (*ibid.*). A reference is made here to many passages of the Gospel: Jn 3:17, 18:37; Mt 20:28, Mk 10:45.

"To save not to judge, to serve not to be served," these words indicate that the church's social pronouncements can no longer have the nature or even the semblance of inflexible, imposed conclusions. Rather, it is acknowledged that many men and women have thought about the problems already and that all this input has to be used. Then the church can bring the light of Christ's message to bear upon the various social situations. The Vatican II Council says that its religious mission is a "source of commitment, direction and vigor to establish and consolidate the community of men according to the law of God" (GS no. 42). But the church as a body, the church represented by its bishops in their official capacity, does not pretend to have all the solutions. Similarly, the Council tells lay people they should turn to the clergy for guidance and spiritual strength but, at the same time, realize "that their pastors will not always be so expert as to have a ready answer to every problem (even every grave problem) that arises" (no. 43).

In addition, "the church is able, indeed it is obliged, if times and circumstances require it, to initiate action for the benefit of all men, especially of those in need, like works of mercy and similar undertakings" (GS no. 42). Examples of such action are cooperatives set up by the church, a trade union started by a priest, and a political party (an exceptional case) also started by a priest.

Concerning the social teaching, one should pay attention to the expressions recently used by John Paul II: "The Church's social doctrine is not a 'third way' between liberal capitalism and Marxist collectivism, . . . Nor is it an ideology, but rather the . . . results of a careful reflection on the complex realities of human existence . . . in the light of faith."[5] A few paragraphs earlier, John Paul II said that the church has no program or system of a more technical nature, that it has no preference among systems, provided they serve the basic needs and heed the fundamental rights of people.

Finally, John Paul II has these very important, more general statements on what constitutes the social teaching of the church: "An application of the word of God to people's lives, and the life of society . . . offering 'principles for reflection,' 'criteria for judgment,' and 'directives for action'" (SR no. 8). But all this, he says, is to guide in a discernment which is to be made by each person or each group "to respond, with the support also of rational reflection and of the human sciences, to their vocation as responsible builders of earthly society" (no. 1).

The image is that of a church which is part of the social world and accompanies people with its light in a discernment and action that can only be theirs, and that feeds itself also on rational light and scientific findings (scientific even if they are of a precarious, provisional nature).

The church, meaning this time all the faithful, is not in this new view more distant from the social scene than when Leo XIII claimed that no social solution could be found without the church's contribution. It is rather more present, through its members as they act in a Christian way in their ordinary social lives. The U.S. bishops are aware, as they have said in their pastoral letter *Economic Justice for All* (1986), that when they enter the more specific fields of economic reality their recommendations are more controversial. The prudent judgments they make do not enjoy the same authority as their declarations on principles. But they said too, "We feel obliged to teach by example how Christians can undertake concrete analysis and make specific judgments on economic issues" (pastoral message presenting the pastoral letter). That means, the church, including those with responsibility in the church, have to be there: "The Church's teaching cannot be left at the level of appealing generalities."

This has been the practice of John Paul II of late, even though he has insisted that the church cannot offer programs as such or take a stand among systems. Indeed, there are many concrete recommendations in his *Laborem Exercens* and *Sollicitudo Rei Socialis* on solidarity, trade unions, initiatives in the economy, and democracy in the Third World states to give the clear impression of a church that accompanies people in their endeavors but which leaves particular decisions to their consciences.

Not everything the church does in human society is successful, nor is every step taken by the church well conceived. One should note, however, how Christians have contributed in recent years to the protection of human rights, for example, in Chile and Brazil, or to the peaceful reestablishment of democracy in the Philippines, Haiti (particularly in 1987), Poland, Czechoslovakia and East Germany. The church and Christians exercise a constant pressure, felt at the international level, in the direction of solutions favorable to Third World countries and to their positive development. Consequently, Christians are often accused of being ingenuous or naive; previously, some were labeled "Marxists." One can bear such accusations without much inner turmoil when one does not give reason for them, which most frequently is the case. As is well known, John Paul II has played a formidable role in the process of detotalitarianizing Eastern Europe.

All such elements make up a picture of the present social role of the church and the present relationship of the church to society. The church is more internal to society than it used to be, or pretended to be. Even where it was persecuted recently in Eastern Europe, clearly it was part of the picture. And part of the problem. If the church enjoys this new presence, it is because both the church and society have changed.

The church has changed. An important traditional view has been revived in today's church: The basic trust, in spite of pessimism (see *The Closing of the American Mind*) or the faith that human activity in the universe, "individual and collective activity, that monumental effort of man through the centuries to improve the conditions of the world . . . corresponds in itself to the plan of God" (GS no. 34). Social values cultivated by men and women—"human dignity, brotherly communion, freedom"—can be "transfigured" and thus become eternal wealth, elements of God's very kingdom, elements of that great work, his life and death, that Christ gives and offers to his Father at the end of time, as the Vatican II Council has explained. This is the most crucial tenet of faith for a world of human achievements (or a world where achievement and endeavor count).

But society has altered too and, in part, the transformation made change of the church possible. The church has taken notice of those changes in many ways. John XXIII was remarkable at that; he always took note of what was in progress in humankind. For instance, he saw all the positive effects of social and economic promotion of the working classes (PT no. 40)—they were more aware of their rights and could claim to be treated humanely and to have access to the cultural goods, and so forth. He saw also the progress resulting from the entrance of women into social and public life; he stressed the fact of a new consciousness of their dignity which makes them insist on being treated everywhere as persons, at home as well as in the public sphere. Again, John XXIII said that people no longer tolerate the distinction of dominated and dominating nations;

he saw the end of colonialism (at least of the formal type of colonialism). "The idea of the natural equality of all men" is gaining ground (no. 44).

A little later, the Vatican II Council speaks in the same tone, not only when it says, "A deeper aspiration: man as an individual and a member of society craves a life that is full, autonomous, and worthy of his nature as a human being. . . . Among nations there is a growing movement to set up a worldwide community" (GS no. 9), but also in the Declaration on Religious Freedom.[6] On what does the church build its new statement here? The first consideration it explicitly refers to is the progress of human conscience at large. The Council writes: "Contemporary man is becoming increasingly conscious of the dignity of the human person; more and more people are demanding that man should exercise fully [his] own judgment and a responsible freedom in [his] actions and should not be subject to the presence of coercion but be inspired by a sense of duty" (DH no. 1). People also demand constitutional limitation of the powers of governments so that governments cannot restrict the rightful freedom of individuals and associations. "The demand for freedom in human society," the Council continued, "is concerned chiefly with man's spiritual values, and especially with what concerns free practice of religion in society" (ibid.). All these are important "spiritual aspirations" and the Council recognizes that they are in accord with the Christian message.

John Paul II agrees with this concept when, for instance, he notes that "peoples and individuals both aspire to their liberation" (SRS no. 46) and that there is a greater consciousness today of the contradiction inherent in a development which limits itself to its economic aspect (no. 33). He sees that the respect for human rights is growing in importance in almost every country (ibid.). He has been accused of taking a very dim view of development—he sees no real progress during the last twenty years, rather, a regression. However, after long, negative descriptions, John Paul comes to the positive aspects of his panorama. He stresses again the fact that "many men and women are coming to a full conscious[ness] of their dignity and of that of every human being" and are concerned with the respect of human rights (no. 26). There are, he notes, many associations working for that purpose—obviously, he had Amnesty International in mind.

John Paul II also stresses the fact of a growing consciousness of interdependence and, consequently, the necessity for solidarity. Respect for life is growing too, in spite of the temptations against it concerning abortion and euthanasia in particular, and there is growing concern about ecological problems (SRS no. 26).

What I want to emphasize is that, according to those in authority in the church, people and societies change (many times for the better) as they discover human rights and dignity, the impossibility of discrimination, the basic fact of pluralism, and the necessity to widen the place of freedom in social life. In such societies the church is at home, it feels freer to participate and freer to acknowledge that it belongs there—ready to help and accompany people. The whole picture has changed a great deal since the tense times in which Leo XIII lived.

This is not to say, however, that the social situation has become easier for the church. The situation may become at times even more difficult for the individual Christian because it is often through the exercise of a person's responsibility that the church will be present and capable of playing the role it must play, especially in areas where the basic Christian view is not at one with common opinion. The Vatican II Council reflected on this problem: In a pluralistic society more than anywhere else, one has "to distinguish between the activities of Christians acting individually or collectively in their name as citizens guided by the dictates of Christian conscience and their acting along with their pastors in the name of the Church (officially . . . or as a body)" (GS). This text means that there is more scope in a pluralistic society for the first kind of action, that is, Christians discerning and acting on the basis of their individual consciences but guided by the Christian message. The text also means that people have to be trained to discern and act in such a way.

The role of the church in this freer environment is not a lesser one, nor are Christians as the church less present. They can be even more effective if they have a thorough assimilation of the Christian message in their personal and common discernment, provided they remain fully faithful to the incarnational view that was revived by Vatican II and they do not fall back into the dualistic representations which were common earlier. Such differing views are sometimes offered again today, unconsciously, or out of fear because of the aggressiveness of certain trends of the world in which we live and try to escape. If there is a practical conclusion to be drawn, it should be to make oneself capable of avoiding criticizing the forms of escapism that appear, preventing the church from taking advantage of the possibilities of a real deep unity of Christian life and social existence that present themselves nowadays.

Notes

1. Leo XIII, encyclical *Rerum Novarum*, May 15, 1891.
2. Second Vatican Council, *Gaudium et Spes*, December 7, 1965, no. 42.
3. I am thinking in particular of the social teachings of Pius XII, which were expressed in many addresses to all kinds of social and professional

groups, and of the two social encyclicals of John XXIII, *Mater et Magistra* (1961) and *Pacem in Terris* (1963).

4. *Mater et Magistra*, no. 222.

5. John Paul II, encyclical *Sollicitudo Rei Socialis*, no. 41.

6. Second Vatican Council, Declaration on Religious Freedom, *Dignitatis Humanae*, December 7, 1965.

Five

A New Ministry to the Business Community: The Challenge

John B. Caron

U.S. business executives are not listening to the social teachings of the Catholic church. Even American *Catholic* business executives are not listening. Why do barriers exist between the church and its social teachings and the Catholic business executive?

Catholics live in a pluralistic society so they are influenced by many value systems, not just the Catholic church. Bishops and priests often come from different socioeconomic backgrounds from those of the typical Catholic executives, so their dissimilar life experiences can influence how they think and act. Anti-business rhetoric and stereotypes also are stumbling blocks to productive dialogue. I want to discuss these problems and make suggestions to overcome them.

In the 1950s and 1960s the church's authority was unquestioned. Pluralism brought an end to unquestioned authority. Now most people want to know the reasons behind a decision, and if they do not know, understand or agree with the reasons, they will not cooperate. I was brought up in one of those Catholic ghettos. I went to Catholic schools. Most of my friends were Catholic. When Sister or Father spoke, but especially when the pope spoke, we listened and accepted the directives without questioning.

Several movements in the 1950s and 1960s were based on the concept of the Mystical Body of Christ. The Christian Family Movement (CFM), which had a big influence in my life, was based on this understanding of lay people becoming the arms and legs of Christ. We studied Scripture and discussed how the scriptural messages could be applied to our everyday lives.

The National Conference of Christian Employers and Managers (NCCEM) began about this time; some of the members had participated also in CFM. We used a case study approach on how Catholic social teaching could be applied in our own businesses. In addition, we had an informal affiliation with UNIAPAC, the European organization of Catholic business people, and groups were established in Chicago, Rockford,

Minneapolis–St. Paul and Detroit, but the movement never really became popular.

In both CFM and NCCEM we sought and received church approval. We had chaplains, some of whom were strong influences because they represented the ultimate authority. I remember a talk that Monsignor Hillenbrand, a priest of considerable prominence in social action in those days, gave to our NCCEM group. It was profound and we listened intently as it was coming from an "authority," but I do not think we understood what he was saying—we were on different wavelengths.

When change exploded on our society in the late 1960s—the civil rights movement, the Vietnam war, the sexual revolution—it affected all of us. The Catholic ghetto disappeared.

Business people do not want to be separated from the mainstream because they are Catholic. They are better educated and not exclusively in Catholic colleges. Country club quotas on Catholics have broken down. We are part of the entrepreneurial class. We are Americans.

Pluralism diminished the role of ecclesiastical authority. Priests and bishops no longer are considered the authorities and many Catholic business people feel the church does not have a good understanding of how the economy works.

The business community's reaction to the U.S. bishops' pastoral letter on the economy was largely negative. Why? One explanation is that bishops and business look at issues from different perspectives. There is an old saying, "You stand where you sit." Where do I stand? What influences my decision and thoughts? I am a businessman and a textile manufacturer. I view situations from a businessman's perspective. Regarding unions, I see them as a threat to productivity because of their restrictive work rules. I see unions resisting change and that resistance inhibits a company's ability to respond to challenges. Such opposition and restrictive work rules can adversely affect costs and the ability of a firm to compete.

A major issue in the recent *New York Daily News* strike was "feather bedding." Look at the problem the U.S. automobile industry has had with restrictive work rules and job classifications that make the auto manufacturers less competitive than their Japanese counterparts. How many years did it take to remove the fireman, who stoked the coal for the steam engine, from the diesel engine crew where he had nothing to do? Often a financial analysis of a company for investment purposes will say the company is a good buy because it is nonunion, not because they pay lower wages but because they are more flexible and can produce more competitively. I am a business executive so I view the role of the unions from that perspective.

What is the bishops' perspective? What background influences their thinking?

Several years ago, I participated in an afternoon-long meeting with a small group of Catholic businessmen and three prominent U.S. bishops. One of the bishops said that this was the first time he had ever sat down to talk informally with a group of businessmen. Another bishop talked about being on welfare when he was young. All three bishops came from blue collar working-class families and their growing-up experiences were unlike those of most business executives. The bishops are aware of the problems of working-class people because they observed them first-hand in their own families.

When the first draft of the bishops' pastoral letter on the economy was published, each diocese was encouraged to study and comment on the letter. I live in Fairfield County, Connecticut, which is the headquarters of more Fortune 500 companies than any other area except New York and Chicago. I wrote to my bishop and offered to have a dinner meeting for him and some prominent Fairfield County Catholic business people to discuss the issues raised in the pastoral letter. His reply was that he had assigned that topic to an assistant professor at Fairfield University. Reading between the lines, I inferred that he was uncomfortable talking about economics with a group of well-informed people. In this case, not even an attempt was made to bridge the gap between a bishop and his business leaders.

But why such an adverse reaction from business people to the bishops' pastoral letter on the economy? Whether intended or not, business people heard criticism. Our economic system has created a higher standard of living for more people, with less class conflict than any other country. Certainly there are problems. Anyone involved in business knows you cannot stand still. If you do not keep improving and solving problems, someone else will and you could be out of business. U.S. business learned the hard way. The Japanese came up with better quality and cheaper prices. The consumer preferred their products. U.S. business learned that you have to keep improving or else someone will overtake you.

Business leaders were not saying our economic system could not be improved; however, the pastoral letter was seen as criticism and the proposed solutions as counterproductive. The role of government was emphasized in the letter, whereas most business people feel the strength of the U.S. economy has been the initiative and the responsiveness of individuals.

The lessons of Eastern Europe have shown dramatically that reliance upon government destroys the initiative of individuals, and that attempts to control and plan the economy and allocate resources are counterproductive. The government may be well meaning, but the plans do not work.

What was my reaction to the bishops' letter on the economy? They spent a lot of time getting input and I felt they were really trying to listen.

I participated in the three-day meeting at Notre Dame with the five bishops who were chairing the group that prepared the letter. I made a point of having a meal with each of the five bishops to get a better understanding of them as individuals and to get some insight into their thought processes on our economy.

My reaction was similar to many other business people, in that I thought there was too much reliance upon government intervention, but I took it more as a challenge rather than a criticism of our economic system. The bishops said we had produced unprecedented prosperity, but there were some obvious inequities. We could and should do better.

I heard the bishops say that if we do not agree with their specific suggestions on how our economic system could benefit more people, then we should come up with better ideas. I do not think there was disagreement over the end to be achieved—an economic system that benefits people. What means are taken to achieve that end remains the question.

A brief comment on papal teachings. Even papal messages on social teachings are getting little attention in this country. We have a charismatic pope, but he sends out confusing signals. He speaks of justice, but his actions emphasize the importance of orthodoxy—and the press in this country focuses on the issues of orthodoxy.

Another obstacle to acceptance of the social teaching by business is the rhetoric directed against business. The words "exploitation" and "capitalism" can hardly be separated in many circles. This makes me angry. These are examples of that rhetoric:

- Capitalism depends upon exploitation of workers.
- Economics is a zero-sum game. If someone gains, someone must lose.
- Socialism is the preferred economic system as it is more egalitarian.
- The problems of the Third World are due primarily to exploitation by capitalist countries. (This rationalization takes attention away from the real problem of incredible corruption, mismanagement and civil wars in Third World countries. It is always easier to blame someone else, but it does not solve the problem.)

Underlying this rhetoric is the feeling that profit is bad; profit is taking advantage of someone else.

Most executives believe that the rhetoric about exploitation does not reflect reality and that many critics of capitalism are like the person who says, "Don't bother me with the facts, my mind is already made up." Many business people, therefore, feel it is useless to try to engage in dialogue.

I have been involved for many years with the *National Catholic Reporter*, for a number of them as chairman of the board; I continue to serve as a director. Here are some quotes from the NCR, representing only the particular writer's viewpoint but which is held, I think, fairly widely:

Not only is capitalism founded on exploitation, but that exploitation inexorably divides society into antagonistic classes.

There is seldom a discussion of Third World countries without a comment on exploitation by the developed countries. What is the definition of "exploitation"? My litmus test for an economic system or policy is: Are people better off with what they have now than before, and are there reasonable prospects for continued improvement?

Many of the writers in the NCR consider economics to be a zero-sum game—if there is economic growth somewhere, it must come at the expense of someone else. There is more concern with egalitarianism than with economic growth.

Obviously the gain of any particular capitalist would be offset by the loss of another.

From a letter to the editor:

A large percentage are suffering because of the prosperity of others.

I thought Henry Ford put that idea to rest a long time ago when he said a well-paid worker was a better customer. That is why it is in the interest of the United States to have economic growth in the Third World. Everyone benefits. It is not a zero-sum game.

Despite the collapse of socialism in Eastern Europe there is still wishful thinking for a perfection of socialism. The West urges Eastern European countries to impose merciless economic policies that have never worked in their own countries, nor have they worked in the United States or in Germany.

Under socialism people would liberate themselves from a demonic pursuit of money.

Evil motives are implied:

What banking interest fueled the rush into the Gulf War?

Bankers are always good targets.

The rhetoric of socialism is good—people count. The rhetoric of capitalism is bad—the bottom line. But the reality is often just the opposite. Capitalism is certainly not perfection but the capitalist economies have higher standards of living; people participate more and individual talents are used more fully in companies in capitalist countries.

The shrill rhetoric turns off the business community which feels it is creating jobs, not exploiting people. It feels it is making the economic pie bigger, not dividing up a no-growth pie in a zero-sum game. So when the bishops' letter came out, the atmosphere was not receptive because of the concern that the letter was a continuation of the rhetorical bashing.

This concern was evident in the first few meetings of the Notre Dame Program on Multinational Companies and World Poverty which was initiated about twelve years ago by Father Hesburgh and Professor Lee Tavis of the University of Notre Dame. The invitees included executives from multinational corporations, academics and clerics. Some executives were reluctant to attend because they did not want to be subjected to "the usual bashing," but a good number did come. Although everyone was trying to be polite, people talked right past each other because each had a mental stereotype of the other; nobody heard what the other was saying. The stereotype of the business executive is a hard-hearted person who cares about nothing but the bottom line, no matter how those results are achieved. The stereotype of the academics and clerics is an impractical, unrealistic theoretician with simplistic solutions to complex problems.

Over the years since this program was started, mutual suspicions have been overcome. At least there is a better understanding of where the other person is coming from, although there might not be acceptance of that person's point of view. As the rhetoric was modified, understanding improved.

I have talked about some of the difficulties that lessen the impact of Catholic social teaching—the different perspectives of the bishops and the executives due to differing backgrounds and life experiences, and the rhetoric that discourages dialogue. What can be done to increase understanding?

We must recognize that shrill rhetoric and assumptions of stereotypes, from both sides, antagonize people and create higher barriers. We have to develop a forum where the theoretician and the practitioner can learn from each other. It is tragic that more U.S. Catholic business people did not participate in the various conferences celebrating the hundredth anniversary of the Catholic social teaching. If the teacher is not reaching those people who need to be taught, what good is the teaching?

Someone asked me the other day, "Does business have a conscience?" Business is made up of people. People have consciences, but the problem is in maintaining a balance and a focus.

One of the problems I have had is in maintaining a balance among my responsibilities to my business, my family, and as a member of a community. Running a business can be all-consuming. The achievement, the creativity involved can be exciting and exhilarating. It can also be depressing when things do not go right. The business world is very competitive.

Your performance is being measured constantly by the profit and loss statement. A business person must be constantly on the ball.

An executive can lose balance in life because of concentration on the day-to-day involvement in business. Family relationships can suffer. Extra-curricular activities can become superficial.

So there is a need for periodic reevaluation of the purpose in life, to sit back and reflect on the big picture. This is where the church can be helpful. Most people want to feel their religion influences the way they lead their lives. There is need for a forum to discuss what it means to be both a Catholic and a business person. That forum does not exist because I feel that neither the bishops nor the business community really want it— they are too far apart philosophically. The church and the business person are not far apart regarding the ultimate end of a better life for more people, but the term "better" needs to be defined.

It is interesting to note that I am the only business person in this volume. We must have more interaction between the theorists and the practitioner if we are to put principles into practice. There is a big gap now but I am aware of two groups trying to bridge that gap: the Woodstock Center at Georgetown and the Center for the Laity in Chicago. However, if the tradition of Catholic social thought is to have an influence upon our society, the dialogue between the church and business people must be expanded. The follow-up on the bishops' letter on the economy has been disappointing.

The Woodstock conference is raising these issues. The following are quotes from the minutes of a meeting at the Woodstock Center in which I participated recently, regarding what business would like to say to church leaders:

> Do you know me and my work experience? How can you preach to me if you do not know me, and what I experience, do, and feel? How otherwise can you know the relevance of religion to my life?
>
> On the other hand, perhaps church leaders are sometimes confused and intimidated by business leaders. Some feel they are treated condescendingly, whereas they too, especially Cardinals and Archbishops, run "major corporations." In that sense they are business leaders in their own right.
>
> Business can be all-consuming. It is exciting; you are driven by achievement, the thrill of the game. Competence is the key to success in business, in doing good. How can we formalize the instinct to do good into the virtue of doing well?
>
> The business executive is confronted with competing values: how do you manage them when they confront one another in a particular decision?

The business executive is constantly experiencing change. How do corporations relate to change? Conversion and change also are the business of religion. What can religion tell us about how we can be in a process of continuous change? How do we get people to change? How do we change an environment, a culture?

These are good questions and the church can have helpful input.

I said at the beginning that U.S. business executives are not listening to Catholic social teaching. The need for dialogue and change and teaching is there. The business executive lives in a complex and competitive environment. The church has something helpful to say. Perhaps this meeting will lead to actions that will further the dialogue.

Part II

The New World Order and a Focus on International Authority

Part two focuses on what the term "New World Order" means, how the vision of such an order relates to Catholic social thought and the various proposals for international structures to form and sustain such an order.

Opening this section is chapter six, an essay by a distinguished elder statesman of the church of our time, Theodore M. Hesburgh, C.S.C. Hesburgh notes that Pope John XIII in his 1963 encyclical *Peace on Earth* outlines the need for new global structures for social justice and world security, a new world order. In Hesburgh's view, the New World Order refers to "the reorganization of the United Nations and especially its Security Council." He offers five major changes to the organization of the Security Council which will enable a new world order to come about. While hopeful for such a future, Hesburgh notes that without this paradigm shift we may face global disaster.

Chapter seven is by Cardinal Agostino Casaroli, the former Vatican Secretary of State and the renowned architect of the church's strategy in Eastern Europe. Casaroli follows Hesburgh in his strong support of a "perfected" United Nations as *the* new international authority. He notes that there is a remarkable congruence between the responsibilities assigned to the international community by Catholic social thought and the actual agencies of the United Nations. The chapter discusses the work of some of the key UN agencies: the United Nations Conference on Trade and Development (UNCTAD), the General Agreement on Tariffs and Trade (GATT), the United Nations Children's Fund (UNICEF), the United Nations High Commission for Refugees (UNHCR), the International Labor Organization (ILO), the United Nations Food and Agriculture Organization (FAO), the United Nations Industrial Development Organization (UNIDO), the International Agency for Atomic Energy (AIEA), the World Health Organization (WHO), and the United Nations Educational, Scientific and Cultural Organization (UNESCO).

While not uncritical of the present operations of the United Nations, Casaroli stresses that this organization has the potential to be the international authority that our interdependent world sorely needs. He is hopeful that all will rise to the challenge.

Chapter eight concludes this section with a most provocative thesis: this talk of a new world order "rests on the uncritical transposition of American national experience to the international scene." The learned international journalist William Pfaff is skeptical that the United Nations can function as a new world authority. "In fact, the vast majority of members of the United Nations are unrepresentative governments, class- or interest-bound oligarchies or dictatorships, or outright despotisms." Pfaff is critical of progressive political thought that assumes an inevitable development towards more virtuous forms of political organization and behavior. He counsels a sober analysis of the current state of affairs and suggests rejecting the hopelessly flawed United Nations and opting for the organizations of the "community of democracies." What he has in mind is forging new forms of "international cooperation based on shared democratic values."

Just as Eastern Europe and the Soviet Union were attracted to the democratic values of Western Europe and the United States, so might other non–democratic nations be attracted to a new "commonwealth of democracies." Pfaff echoes some of the themes of Paul Sigmund's essay in chapter three when he notes that although "the church made its peace with democracy . . . after more than two centuries of hostility," its leaders "are still often attracted to utopian and absolutist political formulations." Thus, Pfaff would have Catholic social teaching avoid faulty solutions such as the United Nations and advocate a "creative internationalism, . . . making use of the building materials of nation and nationalism." Pfaff's argument is controversial, but it is certain to be repeated again and again as the public policy discussion continues.

Six

A New World Order: What It Will Need for Survival

Theodore M. Hesburgh, C.S.C.

During the Gulf War, on almost every occasion that our former president, George Bush, spoke of the purposes of the war, he mentioned "a New World Order." He did not say what this New World Order is, or was going to be, but just mentioning it so often put it in a special category of good results that should emerge from the successful prosecution of the war.

Now that the Gulf War is over and we have a new president, Bill Clinton, what are we to expect from this often-mentioned goal: a New World Order?

Lance Morrow, an astute observer of the national scene, had this to say:

> Bush has never been comfortable with what he calls the "Vision Thing," but in the context of the Gulf War and its aftermath his mind has grown fairly visionary. Three times in his speech [to a joint session of Congress] Bush conjured up a phrase he has used much in recent months—"New World Order."
>
> What does New World Order mean in George Bush's mind?... some deeper American ambition—a pattern of the Persian Gulf intervention to be extended elsewhere in the world as occasions arise? Nearly everyone is puzzled by the idea of a New World Order. In his State of the Union speech Bush honored the collaborative aspects of his vision: "What is at stake is more than one small country. It is a big idea, a new world order, where diverse nations are drawn together in common cause to achieve the universal aspirations of mankind: peace and security, freedom and the rules of law."[1]

On the basis mainly of that final presidential statement, I want to say what I hope this New World Order means, how it relates to Catholic social doctrine, and what we must do for a New World Order to be born and to grow successfully. Before doing that I will explain why a New World

Order is unique to our times and was impossible earlier during the post-World War II decades.

Recent events surrounding the condemnation of Saddam Hussein's actions in invading Kuwait were absolutely unique, even for the United Nations. The original idea for the United Nations, that saw birth in San Francisco, never really worked because of the active and ongoing competition of the superpowers who used every issue to gain a point or win a victory. The result was a score of brush wars all over the world and millions of violent deaths.

The most widespread of these surrogate wars were in Korea, Vietnam, Afghanistan, Cambodia, Angola, Nicaragua and San Salvador. Korea would never have been a United Nations war had not the Soviets absented themselves from the Security Council during an important vote to take the "police action" which the Soviets would have vetoed if present.

The mutual antagonism of the U.S.–U.S.S.R. during almost fifty years since the end of World War II resulted in a disastrous arms race in which even the Third World nations, with U.S. and U.S.S.R. support and financing, spent over $330 billion dollars in 1990. The U.S. and U.S.S.R. and our allies brought the total expenditure for armaments worldwide to over a trillion dollars.

All this was happening while hunger and malnutrition were devastating about a billion people, mainly in the Third World, while 40,000 children died needlessly each day, a Hiroshima or Nagasaki every five days, while a billion people were illiterate and without schooling and while housing was becoming ever more miserable in the great urban slums throughout the world. Worldwide development schemes and initiatives were thwarted by dwindling financial support. Pope Paul VI offered an inspiring vision in *Populorum Progressio*, saying that "Development is the new name for peace" and peace, of course, is at the heart of any true world order, but that vision was not to be realized in his lifetime.

While all of this constitutes a fairly dismal picture in terms of justice, peace and world order during the postwar years, the one salient new political fact that makes a New World Order possible today is the great change in the relationship between the superpowers, due mainly to [former] President Gorbachev's *glasnost* and *perestroika*—he launched this new era of openness and restructuring and ended the cold war.

Nowhere was this new political situation more significant than in the voting of the UN Security Council following Iraq's invasion of Kuwait. For once, the five key members with the power of veto voted together to declare Iraq's action unjust, imposing an embargo also universally applied, demanding quick and complete withdrawal from Kuwait and finally (China abstaining) approving military action after January 15 if Iraq had not withdrawn. An extraordinary alliance of over twenty nations, several former enemies, supplied the requisite armed forces, and others agreed to share the costs in billions of dollars, until justice was reestablished.

All of this was unique and unprecedented in the history of the past five decades and gave rise, I believe, to new hopes on the part of former President Bush and others for a New World Order, still as yet formally undefined. Even as late as January 15, 1991, I visited [former] President Gorbachev with some Soviet and American colleagues. He had just concluded a long telephone conversation with Bush, and remarked during an hour-and-a-half rambling talk that we all had to see reason rise over emotion, that we needed more stability and order, that we are now living in a newly recognized interdependent world, that we can cut nuclear weapons to almost zero and cease all nuclear testing to preclude new third generation nuclear weapons, that the superpowers and their allies and everyone else can now work together to help create a New World Order seeking peace and justice.

With all of this unusual encouragement, and despite some discouragement from eminent scholars who question the idea "that the Gulf War could determine a New World Order,"[2] I want to consider the idea of a New World Order as it is proposed in Catholic social teaching, particularly in Pope John XXIII's *Pacem in Terris*.

As Joseph Gremillion notes in his magisterial book, *The Gospel of Peace and Justice* (p.47), most of the papal social encyclicals before World War II had concentrated on workers' rights and social justice in the industrialized Western world. In post-World War II, concern for social justice has become worldwide, and at the heart of the social question is the consideration of how to achieve worldwide justice and peace. Pope Paul VI makes this point in the opening paragraphs of *Populorum Progressio* (no. 3). While many conservative Americans of all faiths would blanche at the thought of new planetary structures for social justice and collective security, that is precisely the direction in which a New World Order is heading and must head. Vatican II's *Gaudium et Spes* has a whole chapter on "the Fostering of Peace and the Promotion of a Community of Nations" and that was declared more than a quarter of a century ago.

Pope John XXIII, the convener of Vatican II, produced a marvelous encyclical which he addressed to "the faithful of the whole world" on April 11, 1963, shortly before his death. This encyclical, *Pacem in Terris*, has five parts. The first part is entitled, appropriately enough for our subject, "Order among Men." The second statement in Part I is really the foundation for all Catholic social teaching:

Any human society if it is to be well ordered and productive, must lay down as a foundation this principle, namely that every human being is a person, that is, his nature is endowed with intelligence and

free will. By virtue of this, he has rights and duties of his own, flowing directly and simultaneously from his very nature. These rights are
therefore universal, invaluable and inalienable. (No. 9)

Shades of our Declaration of Independence!

Part II of the encyclical *Peace on Earth*, to use its English title, deals
with relations between individuals and public authority within a single
state, Part III is on relations between states and, in the final theoretical Part
IV, John XXIII finally turns to the world community or, if you will, a New
World Order.

John XXIII's argument for a New World Order is precise and so clear
that I give it in his own words; this is really the heart of his thesis:

> As a result of far-reaching changes which have taken place in the
> relations of the human family, on the one hand the universal com-
> mon good gives rise to problems which are complex, very grave and
> extremely urgent, *especially as regards security and world peace*. On
> the other hand, the public authorities of the individual political com-
> munities—placed as they are on a footing of equality one with the
> other—no matter how much they multiply their meetings or sharpen
> their wits in efforts to draw up new juridical instruments, are no
> longer able to face the task of finding an adequate solution to the
> problems (of security and world peace) mentioned above. And this
> is not due to a lack of good will or of a spirit of enterprise, but
> because of a structural defect which hinders them. (No. 134)
>
> It can be said therefore, that at this historical moment, the pre-
> sent system of organization and the way its principle of authority
> operates on a world basis no longer correspond to the objective
> requirements of the universal common good. (No. 135)

What John XXIII is reflecting here is the fact that we have had scores
of wars, large and small, with millions of deaths, despite the fact that we
have had a United Nations and a Security Council.

Since Bush served as the U.S. Ambassador to the United Nations, I
would guess that it is precisely the reorganization of the United Nations
and especially its Security Council that he has in mind when he speaks of
a New World Order. It would operate much as the current Security
Council operated during the Persian Gulf crisis, but it would need reorganization to do so regularly and not just luckily as it recently did.

Several major readjustments would be required:

1. The current veto power by five states would have to be eliminated
and changed to a two-thirds vote of the membership. For all the years of

the United Nations until the recent Gulf crisis, veto action by one of the superpowers, engaged in a cold war, has paralyzed the Security Council and prevented common action for security and peace, not to mention justice which is the first condition for peace. Serious world decisions must always require a serious majority vote by those who are willing to implement their decisions.

2. I believe that the membership of the Security Council should be changed so that all who vote for a peacemaking action would be required to back up that decision, by military action if necessary, as a last resort. This would require member nations of sufficient size and means to keep in readiness a brigade of 25,000 paratroopers, professional soldiers on call when needed, even as a threat, ready to be sent anywhere in the world by stand-by means of rapid deployment. The members must also be of sufficient economic stature to make an unusual boycott meaningful and reasonably universal.

Armed forces should be used by turns, *seriatim*, and selected by the Security Council with political sensitivity (i.e., no Muslim troops into India or vice versa). This would keep the United States from becoming the global peacekeeper, while recognizing that the world will not avoid dozens of brush wars or even bigger wars like the Gulf War, without a police force, or at least one might hope, the police threat eliminating largely the need for its use.

This requirement of about twenty stand-by forces of 25,000 each would give muscle to the decisions of two-thirds of the Security Council. If there should be need for the half million troops who reinforced the Gulf War resolutions, all of the stand-by troops would add up to the required force. Naval and air forces are less numerous and could be factored into this equation, as required of Security Council members.

Incidentally, there was provision for such a military council in the original UN organization. It could be reactivated now to provide for unified command of multiple forces and possible annual maneuvers to make these forces visible and respected. One might even nominate General Schwartzkoff as the first UN commanding general since he successfully commanded over twenty such units in the Gulf War.

3. I suggest the following twenty larger powers as prime candidates for membership on the new Security Council, with two-thirds vote required for decisions and action:

U.S.S.R.	Germany
China	France
Japan	U.K.
Indonesia	South Africa

India	Nigeria
Pakistan	Egypt
Argentina	Turkey
Brazil	Iran
Mexico	U.S.
Canada	Australia

I would hope that for most of these countries the stand-by force of 25,000 professional soldiers would constitute the maximum armed forces they would need for domestic problems and any occasional external call to peacemaking by the United Nations.

4. Part of the reorganization should involve deep cuts in nuclear warheads and delivery systems, possibly down to 100 if not all. In the case of chemical and biological weapons, we had enough worry in the Gulf War to insist upon zero chemical and biological weapons for everyone. Again, there should be a strict non-proliferation agreement for nuclear arms, with periodic mandatory inspection for all banned arms. No more Saddam Hussein surprises.

5. This will be most difficult because of the greed of the major arms suppliers and dealers (the sleaziest group in the world)—there should be a worldwide embargo on arms trading; no more, never again.

Given the problems of world development, especially in the Third World, it is insane for major and minor countries to spend a trillion dollars a year on deadly instruments of high technology and at enormous cost. We have seen the folly of arming Iraq, and are concerned about possible use of nuclear, chemical and biological weapons. The time has come to admit worldwide that high technology has rendered obsolete the classical saying of Clausewitz, that war is simply political action by another means. The time has come to declare war obsolete as a solver of problems.

Is this utopian? Consider the alternative—widespread death and destruction on a continual basis, possibly the obliteration of the human race and all our dreams for the future. We now have the means of doing just this, many times over. One Triton submarine with D-5 missiles has eight times the destructive power of all the explosions of World War II, which caused fifty million deaths. Do we need twenty Tritons plus the other two legs of our defensive triad, air and ground power plus the surface navy, all in enormous numbers? There comes a time when the billions of suffering and underdeveloped humans simply scream, Stop! Now is the time.

Can it happen? Can world development really be the new name for peace? The odds are bad at the moment. The Gulf War was hardly over when we (the United States) started talking of an $18 billion arms package for Middle Eastern countries. This is not just foolish, it is insane. Have we learned nothing? Is there no limit to this ugly greed of the arms dealers?

We may have at this moment of enlightenment, in a still volatile region, a scintilla of hope, particularly since our leaders are still using that pregnant phrase, a New World Order, or its equivalent. I hope I have not read too much into this New Vision. Maybe we can still realize what needs to be done to create this New World Order realistically, a new security system involving justice and peace, an end to war, violence and destruction. Maybe, just maybe. If not, we will continue to march to the destruction of humankind and the good earth that God has given us.

If we really believe, as both our former and present presidents apparently do, that a New World Order is both necessary and possible, then we must do what needs doing to make a New World Order possible, feasible and operative. I claim no special wisdom as to what is needed to create a New World Order, but at least I have specified the steps I believe to be necessary and useful. The idea of a New World Order has been addressed increasingly and everywhere since the conclusion of the Gulf War. I believe that whatever one thinks of the Gulf War, it is quite likely that its greatest result could be to push at an accelerated rate towards a New World Order, however one structures it, so long as it represents a constructive and realistic system for achieving world justice and peace. If someone has a demonstrably better scheme than mine, I would be happy to hear it. At least let us make the possibility of a New World Order the center of our creative conversation and the object of our best efforts. I think also that John XXIII would be applauding from heaven.

Notes

1. *Time*, March 18, 1991, pp. 19–23.
2. *Chronicle of Higher Education*, February 20, 1991, pp. 1, 6.

Seven

The Functions and Future of International Institutions

Agostino Cardinal Casaroli

In 1991 the Catholic church—but we might also say the entire world—commemorated the centenary of a papal document of the greatest importance not only for those who believe in Christian revelation but also for the moral conscience of all humankind.

The encyclical, *Rerum Novarum*, which Pope Leo XIII published on May 15, 1891, was the result of lengthy preparation and consultation on the part of the pope with the pioneers of Catholic thought and social action in Europe and North America. While the encyclical's purpose was to shed the light of the gospel on problems of social and economic life, it hearkened back constantly to "human nature" and the "natural law," in other words, to a basis which should have allowed then and should allow even today for the broadest possible consensus on the part of all people who strive to be guided on this point by "right reason."

In 1931 Pius XI, commemorating the fortieth anniversary of Leo's encyclical with the publication of *Quadragesimo Anno*, felt secure in affirming that this "apostolic voice" had been received with great favor even by a good many people of other faiths—indeed, he added, by "nearly all who since then either in private study or in enacting legislation have concerned themselves with the social and economic question." Favor, yes, but also "hold suspect by some, even among Catholics, and to certain ones it even gave offense." On the one hand, *Rerum Novarum* rejects the socialist theory because "besides failing to resolve the social question, it only harms the workers themselves, while furthermore being unjust on many counts" (RN no. 3). Still, as Pius XI observed (QA no. 15), "it boldly attacked and overturned the idols of liberalism, gave no weight to long-standing prejudices, and was in advance of its time beyond all expectation."

Thus, for Catholics especially, *Rerum Novarum* appeared as a true manifesto which continues to remain a foundation for Catholic social doctrine and teaching. It is an object of study, of debate and of further investigation, so that indications can be drawn from it for trade union and legislative proposals in social questions.

Various successors to Leo XIII—from Pius XI to Pius XII, John XXIII, Paul VI and up to the present John Paul II—have taken advantage of each ten-year anniversary of the encyclical's publication to devote important documents to it, seeking to clarify certain issues under debate while expanding and updating its teaching.

On March 26, 1967, quite apart from these ten-year intervals, Paul VI published another encyclical, *Populorum Progressio*, which was destined to leave a mark no less profound than that left by the encyclicals *Mater et Magistra* (1961) and *Pacem in Terris* (1963) of John XXIII. John Paul II commemorated the twentieth anniversary of *Populorum Progressio* with the encyclical *Sollicitudo Rei Socialis* (1987), after he had celebrated the ninetieth anniversary of *Rerum Novarum* with the encyclical *Laborem Exercens* (1981). In May 1991 a new social encyclical, *Centesimus Annus*, was published to commemorate the centenary of *Rerum Novarum*.[1]

Like the popes, various episcopates have made presentations of Christian social doctrine, generally with reference to the different situations and problems faced by their respective countries. Here I cannot fail to mention the masterly pastoral letter of the U.S. bishops: "Economic Justice for All: Catholic Social Teaching and the United States Economy" (1986).

* * * * *

At the heart of Christian social teaching there is *the human person*—man and woman with that natural and irreplaceable complement of theirs which is the family—with his or her dignity and rights, including those in the economic and social fields; each more important than the state or the collectivity; each with obligations and responsibilities to others and to the community.

Let me very briefly summarize the "cardinal points" of this doctrine: the right to private property and the social mortgage which weighs upon it; the just (family) wage; the right of personal initiative and freedom of association; solidarity among classes, peoples and countries; the right and duty of the state to provide for the attainment of the "common good" through the prohibition of abuses, and the promotion in opportune ways of economic development and just economic and social relations, with particular concern for the weaker members of society.

Against a system of uncontrolled profit seeking and unbridled competition, where the weak always risk being crushed, and the temptations of a centralization which deadens both the economy and the freedom of the citizenry in particular, Christian social doctrine points out the principles and criteria to be followed for ensuring in the best way possible that all people will enjoy freedom without license, protection without oppression, advancement without the initiative of individuals or social groups being stifled, and cooperation and solidarity rather than conflict.

* * * * *

The social question had been addressed by Leo XIII in view of the internal situation of individual political communities, particularly those in Europe.

In *Quadragesimo Anno*, Pius XI turned his gaze even farther, passing beyond "the more civilized and wealthy countries" to those "countless regions, not only in the countries called new, but also in the realms of the Far East," where "manufacturing and industry have so rapidly penetrated" that "the number of the non-owning working poor has increased enormously" (no. 66). The pope also referred to the struggles taking place on the international level, "not only because countries employ their power and shape their policies to promote every economic advantage of their citizens, but also because they seek to decide political controversies that arise among nations through the use of their economic supremacy and strength" (no. 116).

Instead, the pope emphasized how appropriate it would be that "since the various nations largely depend on one another in economic matters and need one another's help, they should strive with a united purpose and effort to promote by wisely conceived pacts and institutions a prosperous and happy international cooperation in economic life" (no. 96).

* * * * *

As a consequence of the Second World War, new sources of misery and problems came to be joined to those already existing. To counteract these, more generous cooperation and a more courageous effort was needed to achieve a vision and to make political decisions on the world level. This was demanded because of solidarity, both human and Christian, a solidarity which cannot be limited by the frontiers of states or continents. It was demanded also by common interest. Increasingly, new bonds of interdependence were linking the fortunes of various countries and parts of the world because the great ideological divide between East and West created, along with extremely serious problems of the political order, growing economic and development difficulties, due especially to the immense military expenses involved.

Even then, the truth lay in what the Second Vatican Council later would observe in its pastoral constitution *Gaudium et Spes* (1963): "In order to work effectively and more successfully for the universal common good at a time when the close ties of mutual dependence are on the increase between all citizens and peoples on earth, the community of nations now needs to provide itself with an order which will correspond to modern challenges, particularly those concerning the many regions which are still suffering from intolerable want" (no. 84).

* * * * *

Mutual dependence—common good. These two terms recur constantly in the language of the popes and of the church. Interdependence is the need that an individual, a social group or state has of others to achieve its proper purpose, a need that is all the greater the more lofty and arduous the purpose which must be achieved. Common good, a concept which, according to John XXIII (MM no. 65) consists of "all those social conditions which favor the full development of human personality" (hence we speak also in a general way of an integral common good, one corresponding, that is, to persons in the fullness of their being, both physical and spiritual). Promoting the common good within the context of a state is the duty of the public powers which exercise their authority in that state.

If we lift our gaze beyond the borders of individual states, what authority would be capable of and have responsibility for ensuring their advancement? In *Pacem in Terris* John XXIII observed that in times past the governments of various countries could seek solutions through conventions or treaties. He continued:

> In our own day, however, mutual relationships between States have undergone far-reaching change. On the one hand the universal common good gives rise to problems of the utmost gravity, complexity and urgency—especially as regards the preservation of the security and peace of the whole world. On the other hand, the rulers of individual nations, . . . largely fail in their efforts to achieve this, however much they multiply their meetings and their endeavors to discover more fitting instruments of justice. And this is no reflection on their sincerity and enterprise. It is merely that their authority is not sufficiently influential. (No. 134)

The universal common good, the pope concluded, presents us with problems which are worldwide in their dimensions and which cannot adequately be confronted and resolved except by public authorities with the extension, organization and means proportionate to meeting them— by public authorities, in other words, that are capable of acting effectively on a worldwide level. "The moral order itself demands the establishment of some such general form of public authority" (no. 137).

* * * * *

The international community was not deaf to this need. The establishment of the United Nations organization and the gradual development of its complex system give eloquent proof of this. A central purpose of the United Nations is to safeguard peace and security in the world. But as part of its will to safeguard peace, the organization proposed "working to achieve international cooperation in the solution of international problems of an economic, social, cultural and humanitarian character as well" (United Nations Charter, July 26, 1945, art. 1).

If, according to the well-known expression of Paul VI (PP no. 87), "development is the new name for peace," it is easy to see how essential it is for a positive promotion of peace to resolve the economic and social problems which hold so much of the world in their grip. Previously, the pope had emphasized the danger for world security, represented by lengthy delays and excessive disparities in the development of peoples: "Extreme disparity between nations in economic, social and educational levels provokes jealousy and discord, often putting peace in jeopardy" (PP no. 76).

John XXIII earlier had highlighted a similar fact: "Given the ever increasing interdependence between peoples, a lasting and fruitful peace cannot reign among them when the imbalance in their economic and social conditions is too severe" (MM no. 1667).

If we glance at the complete array of goals the United Nations set for itself in the San Francisco Charter and to which it has slowly but surely given concrete form throughout the forty-seven years of its existence, we cannot but remain struck by the complexity and commitments involved.

A similar impression is had when we look at the whole framework of the UN system (the United Nations itself and the international governmental organizations that constitute its specialized agencies of a universal character), to say nothing of the international organizations of a regional or group character with which the United Nations is associated. This impression becomes all the stronger if we compare the UN organization with that of the League of Nations which, in 1919, at the end of the First Great War, was the forerunner of the modern organization of the world community; it too had the purpose of "promoting international cooperation and achieving the peace and security of states."

From the League of Nations, however, the United Nations in some way has inherited an organization of remarkable importance in the field which most concerns us. I am referring to the International Labor Organization (ILO) that emerged as a distinct institution the same time as the League itself, in 1915.

* * * * *

I certainly cannot claim to be an expert in the functioning of the United Nations and its associated agencies, so my reaction, in facing a reality with such demanding and varied purposes and such complex structures, is that of someone deeply interested in issues of peace and development and who shares in a lively way the widespread desire that good solutions be found to these questions, with the cooperation of all. It is a reaction of satisfaction and hope. Indeed, for the first time in its long history, humankind has set up a system of agencies for research and action which is capable of confronting, at least in theory, practically all the problems associated with peace and development.

If we look in particular at the problem of economic and social development, we really get the impression that between the General Assembly, the highest organ of the United Nations, its appropriately named Economic and Social Council, and its existing specialized institutes or agencies, the fields of possible interest in this sector receive adequate coverage. It is interesting to note also the correspondence between the institutionalized competencies and functions attributed to these different agencies and the responsibilities which Christian social doctrine attributes to the international community. (This is not to say that every one of the directions in economic and social policy adopted by those agencies is always in harmony with the Christian vision; here I would refer pointedly to certain criteria followed in the field of economic development and family policy.)

In regard to decisions directly taken by the General Assembly, I recall the Special Sessions of April-May 1974 and September 1975, dedicated to the realization of the so-called "New International Economic Order"; the XI Special Session of August 1980 on the critical situation in many developing countries; and the XIII Special Session of April 1990 on "International Economic Cooperation."

Beginning in 1960 the United Nations announced a series of "decades" devoted to development, which John Paul II acknowledged in *Sollicitudo Rei Socialis* (no. 12).

If we pass to the activities of the Economic and Social Council that serves to program and coordinate the United Nations' activity on behalf of international development and cooperation in the economic, social and humanitarian field, the panorama becomes much more varied and complex. Within this panorama, given their well-known importance, are the activities related to the United Nations Conference on Trade and Development (UNCTAD) and the General Agreement on Tariffs and Trade (GATT).

But it is even more necessary to recall two agencies which, as far as social advancement and humanitarian activities are concerned, represent a particularly outstanding source of honor for the organization of the international community:

• United Nations Children's Fund (UNICEF) and
• United Nations High Commission for Refugees (UNHCR).

The first of these was responsible for the recent Summit for Children that took place in the UN headquarters in September 1990 with the participation of seventy-one heads of state or government, and concluded with the solemn signing of a declaration, with an apposite plan of action, on behalf of the world's children.

The High Commission for Refugees, the descendent of an office established in 1921 by the League of Nations and reestablished by the UN General Assembly in 1950, has the task of confronting one of the very trying problems that come in the wake of wars, political upheavals, and great natural calamities like drought and famines. Vast regions of Africa and Asia have been and continue to be struck grievously by this problem: the tragedy of the refugees from Mozambique, Ethiopia, the Sudan—among others—and those of the Vietnamese boat people or the refugees from Cambodia or China. Europe, too, has known this calamity. Yesterday, it was the East Germans; in these recent times, it has been the thousands of Albanians who have sought refuge from their country along the Adriatic coast of Italy, in heart-rending conditions and generating problems which bring to mind scenes from a post-war period that once seemed long distant. The activity of the High Commission and that of the analogous UN agency for Palestinian refugees are worthy of distinction as being among the most noble efforts the international community has made on behalf of the most defenseless and needy members of the human family.

* * * * *

In the vast constellation of the international governmental organizations that are part of the UN system as specialized agencies, a place of honor, as I have mentioned already, goes to the International Labor Organization, which also has a particular character in that it is made up, in equal measure, by representatives from workers, employers and governments.

John XXIII, in *Mater et Magistra* (no. 103), wished to express his "heartfelt appreciation" to this organization which "for many years now ... has been making an effective and valued contribution to the establishment in the world of an economic and social order marked by justice and humanity, an order which recognizes and safeguards the lawful rights of the working man." Even more ample recognition went to the ILO from Pope John's successor, Paul VI, and from the present pope. Both visited the headquarters of the organization in Geneva, speaking words of praise and encouragement.

In the encyclical mentioned above, John XXIII has shown equal appreciation to another organization of the United Nations, its Food and Agriculture Organization (FAO), stressing the extremely beneficial work it has undertaken "to establish effective collaboration among nations, to promote the modernization of agriculture especially in the less developed countries, and to alleviate the suffering of hunger-stricken peoples" (MM no. 156).

Along with agriculture, the United Nations devotes great attention to the problems of industrial development, particularly through the activity of the United Nations Industrial Development Organization (UNIDO).

* * * * *

To give an overview of the other specialized agencies of the United Nations would take too long and perhaps be unnecessary, even though more than a few of them carry out functions of the highest interest in international cooperation on behalf of the development of humanity. Who is unaware of the importance of the International Agency for Atomic Energy for peaceful purposes (AIEA), with its responsibility for ensuring that so powerful and potentially dangerous an energy source not be used without indispensable safeguards for other than peaceful purposes? Likewise, who is not aware of the vital function carried out by the World Health Organization (WHO) which is involved at the same time in the areas of science, technology, welfare and even morality?

But a special expression of high regard must go to an organization that plays an outstanding role within the context of humanity's "integral development." It is concerned with that hunger of the spirit and that thirst for knowledge which are distinctive of the human being and which still remain unsatisfied in so much of the human family. The United Nations Educational, Scientific and Cultural Organization (UNESCO) represents the joint determination of the peoples of the world finally to vanquish illiteracy and ensure that all people receive that minimum of education and culture which corresponds to every individual's fundamental dignity, at the same time promoting the development of a higher culture and the progress of the sciences. The church, and the Holy See in particular, have always sensed that the aims of UNESCO are congenial to her own. Eloquent witness to this is borne by the words of the most recent popes, Paul VI and John Paul II, who visited, almost as "a pilgrim of the spirit," that organization's headquarters in Paris.

A general recognition, yet one of particular significance because it came from representatives of the Catholic church from all over the world, was expressed by the 1971 Synod of Bishops in the document, "Justice in the World":

> We stress also the importance of the Specialized Agencies of the United Nations, in particular those directly concerned with the immediate and more acute questions of world poverty in the field of agrarian reform and agricultural development, health, education, employment, housing and rapidly increasing urbanization. (No. 22.5)

The United Nations and its system are not the only international institutions in the world, but they are certainly the most "organized" and have the greatest influence in the affairs of the world community. The functions are fundamental for the political, economic and social life of all humankind and are practically all-embracing. But how have they lived up to, and do they continue to live up to, their lofty purposes and the hopes of humanity?

The 1991 "Gulf crisis" raised a number of questions in the minds of many people. We all know what they are, and this would not seem the place to deal with them at length. The hundredth anniversary of the encyclical *Rerum Novarum* has directed our attention to the role of the United Nations and of its specialized agencies in the field of economic and social problems, rather than on the—certainly no less central—problem of peace and international security. Nevertheless, the grave problems raised by the Gulf crisis in regard to the one also touch the other, albeit indirectly.

But to pause, again, at economic and social problems, what are we to say of the efficiency of the activity undertaken by the United Nations and its specialized agencies throughout its history? Paul VI, during his visit to the UN headquarters in October 1965, presented his message primarily as "a solemn moral ratification" of that institution, stating, "We know how intense and ever more efficacious are the efforts of the United Nations and its dependent world agencies to assist those governments which need help to hasten their economic and social progress."

Yet, at the close of 1987, little more than twenty years after that visit, John Paul II, commemorating *Populorum Progressio*, observed that "the hopes for development, at that time so lively, today appear very far from being realized," despite certain results obtained throughout two decades by UN-promoted development. The pope pointed in particular to "the persistence and often the widening of the gap between the areas of the so-called developed North and the developing South" (SRS nos. 12–14). Since then, those problems have probably increased.

What should be said?

There come to mind the words addressed by Paul VI in October 1965 to the UN General Assembly: "The edifice which you have built must never fail; it must be perfected and made equal to the needs which world history will present. You mark a stage in the development of mankind, from which there must be only advance, no going back."

* * * * *

Perfected. Made equal to new needs. As history, in its often disorderly rhythm, faces both new problems and some old ones which grow more acute, it can present new demands as well as bring to light other demands that had not been taken into account sufficiently (I am thinking particularly of eventual structural defects which experience can reveal).

A just assessment obliges us objectively to recognize inadequacies or possible failures, but it must not make us overlook the virtualities lodged deep within an institution that remains fundamentally responsive to the challenges of an ever more interdependent world, one in rapid evolution.

* * * * *

The current international organization represents the greatest and most systematic effort made thus far by the entire world community to guarantee peace and security in justice for itself and for each of its members in the face of every attempt at oppression by means of force, and to favor an ordered development for all, against the self-centeredness of some.

All this involves a constant convergence of will and judgment on the part of all, or at least of such a majority as to be almost unanimous. Because this type of convergence is not easy to attain, it is not rare in the church's social teaching that we find the desire expressed that there be established a universal authority capable of ensuring unity—a world government, set up by analogy with those governments which rule individual political communities, and provided with similar executive means.

John XXIII, as I mentioned above, affirmed the need for this. And Paul VI, addressing the UN General Assembly, exclaimed, "Is there anyone who does not see the necessity of coming thus progressively to the establishment of a world authority, able to act efficaciously on the juridical and political levels?"

* * * * *

We are speaking of a goal which, although it can be envisioned, still seems far away.

In the meantime, we must make use of the existing institutions. We need to perfect them, making them adequate in their structures and in their functioning to meet new needs that arise; disappointment or lack of confidence must not be allowed to weaken seriously an instrument which is so useful, not to say indispensable. It is essential, in any case, that every effort be made to ensure, in the best way possible, the credibility of international institutions. It should always appear clearly, to those who look at them without bias or hostility, that those organizations really are involved in the service of the "universal common good" in the face of attempts to impose, by trick or force, the particular interests of one nation or of a group of nations.

This tack is not always easy. Let us look, for example at the whole gamut of problems relative to development.

The popes and the church insist that "economic progress ought to remain within the control of people and not be committed to the sole decision of a few or to groups possessing too much economic power, or to a single political community or to some more powerful nations" (GS no. 65). Opposed to this clear and courageous statement, there are powerful forces and pockets of resistance, often hidden, or veiled by an appeal to "economic laws." The competent international institutions must be able to single out these forces and combat them when they result from self-interest, or correct them when it is a question of economic or financial "mechanisms" (the expression is that of John Paul II in SRS no. 16) which "although they are manipulated by people," that is, by certain people, "often function almost automatically, thus accentuating the situation of wealth for some and poverty for the rest."

Another heading of extreme difficulty and complexity is the so-called "international debt" which weighs upon the economy of so many countries and menaces their hopes of development, or at least of survival, and the prospect of an ordered economic and social progress, as well as peace, throughout vast areas of the world. The United Nations has been committed to the search for solutions that are in everyone's interest, and it should be sustained and supported by all.

Nor must we forget the whole ecological problem, for which all the members of the world community must feel responsible so that all will not later be victims of the disaster predicted by scientists. Here is a social problem of a deeply moral and technical nature, one which *Rerum Novarum* could not foresee, yet one which enters fully into that perspective of the centrality of humananity that grounds all of Christian social doctrine as well as the UN Charter itself.

* * * * *

The future of international institutions which the community of peoples has provided for itself on the regional, continental or world level will depend upon effective cooperation, not only in making complaints or criticism (although these are always useful when they are truly constructive) but in the realm of thought and action. This is especially so for member countries, but it is true also of institutions that, like the Holy See and the Catholic church, constantly monitor their painstaking progress.

I wish my final word to be one of trust and hope. Beyond the level of technical concerns and the problems of a complex bureaucracy (which can sometimes appear to be too weighty), it is essential that institutions that claim to serve humanity should not forget the real people involved.

Let me conclude by making my own the desire which John XXIII expressed with regard to the United Nations, but which could be extended to the whole array of international institutions operating in the world.

It is our earnest wish that the United Nations Organization may be able progressively to adapt its structure and methods of operation to the magnitude and nobility of its tasks. May the day not be long delayed when all human beings can find in this organization an effective safeguard of the rights which derive directly from their dignity as persons; rights which are therefore universal, inviolable and inalienable. This is all the more desirable since people today, while taking an ever more active part in the public life of their own nations, are showing an increased interest in the affairs of other peoples and are more deeply aware of being living members of a world community. (PT no. 145)

Notes

1. John Paul II, encyclical *Centesimus Annus*, May 1, 1991.

Eight

A Reconsideration of
Internationalism and Nationalism

William Pfaff

Progressive political thought in the twentieth century, as in the nineteenth, has rested on the unChristian assumption that people experience a natural development toward higher and, implicitly, more virtuous forms of political and social organization and conduct. The troubled past is interpreted as the product of ignorance, unscientific thought, or superstition, and its manifestations of willful cruelty, greed, and vengeance are assumed to be the product of backwardness.

One might think such figures as Adolph Hitler, Joseph Stalin—or Saddam Hussein, if one seeks a contemporary example—as obstacles to the progressive interpretation of history. Theoretically, they are dealt with by demonizing them—in a secularized manner, to be sure—so as to place them outside the mainstream of progressive history. As outsiders, their defeat enables that history to resume; they are not part of it. The proposition that such people are contemporary history's insiders, so to speak, not its outsiders, and that they are not unrepresentative figures of contemporary history, not isolated and defeatable exceptions, is widely rejected. We saw this in the recent U.S. refusal to consider the Iraqi president in a context of secular Arab nationalism and the upheavals of the Middle East since the Ottoman collapse. We see it in the frequent insistence upon separating Stalin, the demonic figure, from Lenin, the supposed progressive one, when considering Soviet history, and in the claim that Hitler's genocidal attack upon the Jews was a unique event, uniquely evil, concerning only the Jews and different from the other racial and social proscriptions and murders of the Nazi regime: those of Gypsies, Poles, homosexuals, etc. One has to remark that if the Shoah was indeed unique, there is nothing to learn from it because it is by definition unrepeatable. I do not think this is so.

There is another view of history which is unprogressive, in the sense in which the term is commonly used, although it does not and could not deny the obvious development of human institutions toward more and more complex and sophisticated forms: the substitution of contract for blood and kinship obligations, the progress of institutions of justice and the protection of human rights, the extension of democratic political institutions, etc. This view certainly would recognize that the political and material conditions of life have grown better for those fortunate enough to live in North America, Western and Central Europe, and a part of Asia. It would suggest also that the conditions have grown markedly worse in much of Africa, another part of Asia, and parts of Latin America, and for specific groups even in the advanced states. It sees that societies progress but also decline: Europe today is not what it was in the Middle Ages or the Renaissance, nor are China or the Islamic world, for whom our Middle Ages were periods of prosperity, intellectual and scientific advancement, and stable government—all of which they lack today.

This view of history says that some things get better and some get worse, that moral as well as institutional progress takes place but also institutional and moral regression; hence, that the balance of good and evil in the world—of high-mindedness and low-mindedness—is today about what it always was, all the way back to neolithic times. A friend of mine, an ethnologist and explorer (Michel Peissel), has written of a community of hunters and simple agriculturists he came across in an isolated Himalayan valley. He believes them to be neolithic—essentially unaffected by the outside world since neolithic times. They even make rock drawings of ritual significance, resembling those found in the caves of southwestern France, our earliest examples of human art. His Himalayan people are indistinguishable from "modern" people in basic conduct and outlook. I find this very consoling: the moral constancy and continuity of humanity through the millennia.

Modern European and U.S. thought has sought fairly consistently to identify moral progress with institutional development and material improvement in society, their model being the progress of science and technology, in defiance of the fact that twentieth-century progress in those fields, stunning in pace, was accompanied by the rise of totalitarian political systems of unprecedented savagery and institutionalized, industrialized, genocide. We have left totalitarianism behind for the moment, or mostly so, but who can say what still lies ahead?

However, history is a complicated matter and these remarks are simply an introduction to the subject I want to address, which is how the progressive view of history has affected our understanding or misunderstanding of the fundamental unit in modern political society, the nation-state, and hence our understanding, or misunderstanding, of the force of nationalism. These matters, in turn, bear upon our expectations of the future and how we see our possibilities for influencing the future of international relations toward an institutional structure more humane in its consequences than today, and less conducive to the settlement of disputes by war.

Nowadays, many are concerned with the loss of that relative international stability, founded on stalemate, which was provided by the bipolar power relationship of the cold war. In the aftermath, one has witnessed a dramatic revival of the expression of ethnic and national hostilities in the Balkans—in Serbia, Croatia, Slovenia, Slovakia, Bulgaria. The ancient quarrel between Romanians and Hungarians over Transylvania has reopened. The former Soviet Union has experienced disintegrative forces produced by the mutual hostilities of its component nations (worsened by Stalin's Russification policies and punishment of politically suspect peoples by forcibly transporting them to implantation among other national groups, hence the difficulty today of finding settlements based on "national" or ethnic frontiers—there are few such that cannot be contested).

In the Middle East, Saddam Hussein in the fall of 1990 explosively reopened the hundred-year-old question of the "Arab Nation," making evident the fragility of existing boundaries in the Middle East. The fictions of African national frontiers have been apparent since the Berlin Conference of 1884–85, which drafted most of them. They are virtually all arbitrary, while the frontiers of the continent's real "nations," which is to say its tribal, clan, or ethnic communities, contradict these political frontiers, provoking persistent conflict.

* * * * *

The hypothesis that a progressive historical trend exists, tending to render nations and nationalisms obsolete and produce closer and more peaceful forms of international community, is sustainable only with heavily qualified arguments. In Europe, where the modern nation originated, the past was considerably more "international" than the present. Nations are a late invention. Even the people of the earliest historical nations— England, France, Poland, for example—considered themselves part of a larger Christendom, successor to the Roman empire. The mass of people obviously were rooted in small communities, and stayed there, but clergy, scholars, the nobility, moved freely through Europe and communicated with those abroad by means of the universal Latin, considering themselves part of a "universal" community whose essential frontiers were those where Christianity ran against the Muslims in the south and east, and pagan societies in the east and north. As late as the sixteenth century, after the Reformation had begun to harden national definitions in Europe by producing an identification of religious with political identity, Polish Lutherans took for granted sending their sons to study at Wittenberg, and

Calvinists to Basel, while Catholics went to Italy—Jagiellon University being in temporary decline. Between 1501 and 1605, Adam Zamoyski writes, "Polish students consistently made up at least a quarter of the whole student body at the University of Padua." Italian architects produced the Renaissance buildings of Poland and Bohemia as well as those of Germany and France. Even Charlemagne had Italian and Spanish advisers, as well as German and French. The twelfth century saw major Romanesque monuments in existence from central Norway and Kirkwall in the Orkneys to Palermo in Sicily, and from Santiago on the Spanish Atlantic coast to Crakow. The Gothic influence was even wider.

* * * * *

At the origin of civilization were cities where exchange and specialization developed as well as professionalization and written language (as in Mesopotamia)—cooperative and collective structures. Cities, dominating a region, evolved into empires under god-kings as in Mesopotamia, Egypt, China—Rome in its decadence (after the republican experiment, learned from the Greece of city-states). Frontiers were inclusive, not exclusive like national frontiers.

Christianity and Islam, the great Mediterranean monotheisms which emerged in succession to the monotheism of the Jews—who were, to be sure, a nation, an identified and exclusive people possessing a covenant with God—claimed universal moral authority and universal missions. The dynastic monarchy or empire which was the characteristic political institution of Europe from the Roman decline until the French Revolution, was typically multicommunal or multinational and polyglot. It divided territorially and communally according to dynastic successions or crises, recombined by marriages, alliance, or war. The English and French nations, the first West European nations, were defined by their dynastic wars with one another and by the struggle between Norman French and Anglo-Saxon languages (English replaced Norman French in the law courts of England in 1362).

One need scarcely continue. The Hapsburgs, inheritors of the Holy Roman Imperial title, ruled a major part of Europe from the thirteenth to twentieth centuries, not only German Austria, Hungary, Bohemia, Poland, Lombardy and Tuscany, and a part of the Balkans, but Spain, Belgium, and the Netherlands. The Bourbons ruled France, Sicily, Naples, Parma, and Spain—where they intermarried with Hapsburgs. Juan Carlos of Spain is a Bourbon, as is the consort of the unlucky claimant to the throne of Romania today—Michael.

The Eastern Roman Empire, in Constantinople, dominated the Balkan peninsula (modern Greece, Macedonia, and a part of Turkey) and most of the south Mediterranean coast. The Muslim Arab and Ottoman empires which took its place were even more inclusive and un-national than their predecessor, easily accommodating Christians and Jews as well as Moslems—Arabs, Spaniards, French, Egyptians, Greeks, Bulgars, eventually Hungarians, Bosnians, Albanians, etc.

The European nations of the twentieth century that have a more or less coherent history of independent existence within roughly their present borders are fairly few: Ireland, Scotland and England, France, Sweden (for a time also a European empire), Denmark, Spain and Portugal (empires as well), Russia (Muscovy—Czarist and Soviet expansion into Asia is modern), Poland (which disappeared from the map between 1795 and 1918), Bohemia. For most, independent existence has been intermittent over the centuries. The Roman empire was Italian, but Italy did not exist until the nineteenth century. Lombardy, the Kingdom of Sicily, the Kingdom of Naples, the Venetian Empire, the Papal States, Savoy and Piedmont existed. Greece vanished into the Roman Empire before the birth of Christ and reemerged from the Ottoman Empire only in the nineteenth century.

* * * * *

Nationalism is connected with the existence of modern nations but more with their non-existence. A violent "nationalism" is the product of unachieved nationalism, the absence of nation, the search to achieve nationhood or to separate a would-be nation from another political body encompassing it. The nation struggling to be born is, in the nature of its situation, compelled to combat the party which refuses to recognize its claim, occupies what it regards as its national territory, or blocks the expression of its national culture or the use of its language. Nationalism rests on the moral and emotional attachments of a group.

There surely is nothing reprehensible about that. Without a loyalty we are anonymous. The flight from anonymity produces nationalism. Yet nationalism, tribal loyalty, exists before consciousness exists of the possibility of exclusion and anonymity. It appears to be the primordial factor in political existence, inextinguishable as well, yet transferable. The expatriate does not live without loyalties. The act of expatriation is produced by loyalties—disabused loyalties, or disappointed ones perhaps, betrayed. One never is indifferent to what one has left. The new attachments which come are as unreasonable as the attachments abandoned, and as likely to be disappointed.

When in the *anno mirabilis* of 1989 the countries of Central and Eastern Europe and the Balkans were freed of Soviet military and political domination, the "old demons" of nationalism were spoken of with much reference to the origins of first and second world wars, the first touched off by the Hapsburg Archduke Franz Ferdinand's assassination by a Serbian nationalist, the second beginning with Hitler's exploitation of pan-German sentiments in Austria and the Sudetenland so he could annex Austria and dismember Czechoslovakia. It was clear in 1989 that many national groups in the east of Europe remained unwilling to accept their condition as minorities in countries dominated by other nationalities. It is equally clear that many of these majorities are unwilling to accept secession by those minorities. Thus, Yugoslavia today is engaged in civil war. The Transylvania issue threatens again to become as important as it was between the two world wars. The position of the Turks in Bulgaria remains in contention. The Soviet Union has disintegrated, in considerable part because of national feelings.

* * * * *

On the other hand, the forms of internationalism dominating the twentieth century have proven more dangerous than nationalism. Nazism exploited national feeling and resentment in interwar Germany but was essentially an internationalist ideology based on racialist theory. It conceived of itself as the vehicle of Aryan "Nordic" (not specifically German) supremacy over inferior races, of which the Jews were only one. The Slavs also were inferior, thought fit only to be laborers under Nordic domination. Gypsies, like sexual deviants, were "degenerate" and deserved extinction, as did the Jews. The Nazi program envisaged the unification of Europe under the Nordics: Germans, Scandinavians, the Dutch—the English. This, of course, is why Germany's occupation of the Netherlands, Denmark, and Norway was "correct," mostly respecting recognized norms of military occupation, while in the East it was genocidal. It is why Hitler so bitterly resented the refusal of the British, under Churchill, to agree to a settlement after Dunkirk that would have left Britain with the seas and its empire—its own sovereignty over "inferior" peoples—and left Europe to Germany. Hannah Arendt has observed that the fact that "so small (and, in world politics, so unimportant) a phenomenon as the Jewish question and anti-semitism could become the catalytic agent for first, the Nazi movement, then a world war, and finally the establishment of death factories," is an "outrageous fact." However, it is no more outrageous than that an avowedly humane undertaking to rescue the industrial working class from powerlessness and exploitation should have resulted in the Gulag, vast purges of the innocent, and the political institutionalization of lies and betrayal.

The second internationalist source of Nazism, Arendt argued, was imperialism, where the limits of the nation were slipped and power sought internationally—transnationally. "Expansion is everything," Cecil Rhodes said, despairing at the stars, "these vast worlds which we can never reach. I would annex the planets if I could." The realists of nineteenth-century government opposed imperialism. They were not inconsiderable figures. Bismarck, Clemenceau, and Gladstone all opposed the imperialist parties in their countries because, as Arendt says, they grasped that imperial expansion "could only destroy the political body of the nation-state," since the nation-state, "based upon a homogeneous population's active consent to its government," could not integrate a colonial population as the earlier forms of inclusive and non-national empires could. (The observation obviously is an important one with respect to the tensions many European countries experience today as a result of immigration from their former colonies. It also emphasizes the overall success of the United States in creating a kind of internal, inclusive "empire" in which immigrants have until now nearly all been successfully integrated. Whether this will continue to be the case is a question of the greatest importance for the United States. There is some contemporary evidence that it will not be so.)

As the colonialism of modern empires did not invite its African or Indonesian or Indian subjects to say *"civus Romanus sum,"* but instead merely to submit to foreign domination, its essential tendency was toward inequity and tyranny, however powerful the paternalistic and missionary impulses of the colonizers also may have been.

Nazism had its idealists, even though it all ended appallingly. In his wartime novel, *Arrival and Departure*, Arthur Koestler (himself Jewish and a Zionist) has one of his characters, a young Nazi diplomat, describe Nazism as

> a real revolution and more internationalist in its effects than the storming of the Bastille or of the Winter Palace in Petrograd. . . . Every new, cosmopolitan idea in History has first to be adopted by one particular nation, become a national monopoly as it were, and become formulated in nationalist terms before it can begin its universal expansion.

The young Nazi speaks of the future integration of Europe's resources, industries, energy, and transport, the stripping away of restrictions and abolishing of frontiers, in a way that would delight a European commissioner planning the European Single Market today. "We are experimenting," he concludes, "but experimenting on a scale never dreamt of before. We have embarked on something—something grandiose and gigantic beyond imagination. There are no more impossibilities for man now."

Communist internationalism was the product of Enlightenment and progressive thought (as well as bearing the powerful and fateful influence of religious messianism). It held that a dialectical process governed history by which higher forms of social organization replaced lesser ones, with the determined eventual outcome of a millennial rule of justice, embodied in the rule of the proletariat—a secular paradise. This doctrine proved capable of enlisting generations of the idealistic, exploiting and squandering their idealism in what one might think the self-evidently absurd proposition that a decisive break with the human past could be produced, an abolition of the human condition—even, in a significant respect, of human mortality itself, since the triumphant proletariat would prove immortal. From the later nineteenth century to the 1980s, death or appalling suffering was inflicted on millions as a consequence of this doctrine. At the same time, tens of thousands willingly and selflessly gave themselves to its propagation—Jesuits of revolution, believers in the possibility of temporal salvation, missionaries for the proposition Auden stated (and later retracted):

> The conscious acceptance of guilt in the necessary murder; . . .
> We are left alone with our day, and the time is short, and
> History to the defeated
> May say Alas but cannot help nor pardon.

In Auden's defense one must add that the vocation of the poet is to be a witness to his time, not its political analyst. This was the sentiment of a very large portion of the European and even U.S. intelligentsias of the period. (It is not, I think, without significance in explaining the power Marxism exercised over its adherents that both Marx and Engels had "set out in their youth to be poets." They chose politics as their medium—as Hitler, the painter and architect *manque* was to do later. In Hitler's case, he had first to level his building site.)

*   *   *   *   *

What destroyed both these specifically modern forms of injustice, Nazi and communist totalitarianisms, was the nationalism of those upon whom they were imposed, for a time with success. Resistance to Hitler was fundamentally nationalist: Churchill's indomitable Englishness and ability to mobilize the British people, the patriotism of the Dutch, Norwegians, Czechs, Poles, Free French, and others who were prepared to fight in 1940 and 1941 when victory was impossible to foresee without—as then seemed remote or implausible—Russian or U.S. entrance into the war on the allied side. In the event, both those countries entered the war only for nationalist reasons: for national survival (in Russia's case) when Hitler (Russia's then ally) invaded, and only after Japan's attack upon the United States at Pearl Harbor. (Would the United States have entered the European war had Hitler not first declared war on the United States in solidarity with Japan?)

The Soviet system equally has been ended by outraged nationalism in Eastern Europe. It was outraged nationalism, hatred for foreign occupation and domination, that powered the waves of protest in Eastern Europe in 1989, and finally broke down the Berlin Wall and freed all the East. (It must be observed also that communism's postwar successes in Asia, its only real successes after the Bolshevik Revolution itself, were derived from its success in identifying itself with the nationalist causes in China and Vietnam.)

What happened in Soviet-controlled Europe was essentially a series of profoundly nationalist upheavals against foreign oppression, by peoples who indeed wished to be prosperous, democratic, even capitalist, and to rejoin a European cultural as well as political community from which they felt themselves excluded. These people wanted first of all and most of all to rid themselves of Soviet occupation and the agents of Soviet occupation, to become free again to be themselves. This logically implied, of course, the possibility of their becoming again, as many of them had been in the past, not at all democratic, but authoritarian in government, intolerant of difference, and belligerent toward their neighbors. Some of them did indeed demonstrate the latter qualities—which is not surprising, people being what they have proven to be. However, the remarkable factor in the great liberation of 1989 was the moral victory achieved: Moral energy had inspired forms of political and material resistance that sapped and finally destroyed communist authority. This moral quality remained a significant element in the legitimacy of the new leaders who emerged.

The nineteenth and twentieth century left has been destroyed by nationalism. We are witnessing communism's collapse. The socialist Second International, founded in Paris in 1889 on the centenary of the French Revolution, was destroyed effectively in 1914 when the German Social Democratic Party rallied to Germany's war. German and French Socialists, and the majority of the British Labour movement, went to war against one another in 1914 with enthusiasm. The Third International, created in 1919 by the Soviet Communist Party, was merely an instrument of Soviet foreign policy, which is to say of Russian national policy. Theory and the internationalist idealism of the left were consistently overtaken and destroyed by primordial forces of communal solidarity and identification—and no doubt by the force of Thanatos as well—that dark willingness, even eagerness, to die as well as to kill, which erupts in human communities and remains a permanent force at work in history. This is witnessed to by Christianity, which is willing to name the evil that modern secular thought would deny.

The United States is surely as ferociously nationalist a society as Serbia or Transylvania; its national integrity luckily has never been challenged seriously, whereas theirs has been, for centuries. The separatism, (or nationalism), of the American South, capable of provoking a civil war a century and a half ago and still powerful as recently as the 1950s, today has virtually vanished into the larger U.S. nationalism. The nationalism of Quebec, primarily but not entirely cultural and linguistic, jeopardizes the survival of the Canadian federation. On the other hand, there has been significant success in containing the pernicious consequences of nationalism in the European Community and the larger associations grouping the parliamentary democracies, the functional international organizations dealing with security, trade, economic development, international finance. The future development of "Europe" seems extremely promising, although it is difficult to believe it will end in the creation of a real political authority capable of taking the place of the European national governments.

* * * * *

Nationalism is a problem, but also an answer. Such, at least, is my argument which I do not state as a paradox but as a complexity, inadequately appreciated. One of the large assumptions made in U.S. political discussion, certainly since the First World War—though the idea in its modern form comes from the eighteenth century—has been that internationalism not only should but would, eventually, replace nationalism: "the war-drum throb . . . no longer, and the battle-flags . . . furled/in the Parliament of man, the Federation of the world." It is a curious case of dual consciousness, given that the American people are surely as assertively nationalistic and exclusivist as any in the contemporary world, flying flags and yellow ribbons, chanting "We're number one," mobilizing against one demonized enemy after another—Russian, Cuban, Libyan, Panamanian, Iraqi—and maintaining military forces vastly more sophisticated and powerful than those of any other nation on earth. Yet the avowed end of U.S. policy is a new and cooperative world order.

Recently, this policy aim has been stated forcefully again by former President George Bush, in connection with his policy in Iraq and his ambitions for the future. It remains an extremely sketchy conception and not, perhaps, a very serious one, although it is a promise easily made because new orders are familiar terrain for an American people whose experience began in the Enlightenment ambition to establish a *"novus ordo seclorum."* Mr. Bush's ambition is in the direct line of U.S. reformist internationalism which began with Woodrow Wilson's invention, in 1917, of the principle of national self-determination and his proposal of a League of Nations. It is a policy tradition which rests on the uncritical transposition of American national experience to the international scene, assuming that an association or congress of the world's states, like that of the American states, can represent legitimately the will of the world's people (or indeed that there is such a coherent will of the people): hence, that an assembly of governments provides a form of world democracy. In fact, the vast majority of members of the United Nations are unrepresentative governments, class- or interest-bound oligarchies or dictatorships, or outright despotisms. Of the UN's Security Council, two of the five permanent members are single-party dictatorships with abominable records of human rights abuse. It seems scarcely a suitable agency for establishing world democracy and international respect for human rights. But one may doubt that world democracy or international respect for human rights will be established.

The Bush proposals faithfully express the liberal reform tradition which has put forward two forms of solution to the problems of national and nationalist conflict: universal national self-determination on the one hand and, on the other, internationalism, the construction of higher political authorities able to mediate or adjudicate national claims or evoke a loyalty superior to national loyalties. One must note that the internationalist "solution" actually existed in the fairly recent past, in the Austro-Hungarian and Ottoman-Arab cases (the causes of the two empires' nineteenth-century deterioration and early twentieth-century collapse merit reconsideration and reflection). The League of Nations, the United Nations, the Union of Soviet Socialist Republics, and the European Community are twentieth-century attempts to substitute international for national communities. The League abjectly failed. The Soviet system proved a menace to humane political values. The UN has substantial accomplishments to its credit and enjoys a provisional revival of fortunes, but has no chance of becoming the true world authority many expected during the enthusiastic months of its creation. The construction of Europe has been successful in the economic and commercial domains but is not, so far, a serious affair with respect to political union. The European

Economic Community is, however, the most complex, interesting, realistic, and successful effort we have yet seen to establish modern international community, and it is notable that it has been constructed on the basis of existing nations, with abiding respect for national differences and national feeling. It was from the start a moral enterprise, inspired by the conviction of Jean Monnet and his associates that the cycle of European war had to be broken and the integrity of European civilization affirmed. It has been constructed pragmatically, from the bottom up, organically, according to needs and problems that had to be met, extended when previous steps had been consolidated. Most important in the success of this enterprise has been the fact that the European nations do possess a common civilization and common political values. And, of course, the effort to create "Europe" is incomplete; it goes on today.

There is another successful international community whose existence tends to be overlooked. There is a practical community of the democracies which possesses an immense and complex web of practical associations that also rest on the foundation of shared political values. Largely since the Second World War, the democracies have created an extensive network of cooperative institutions and associations dealing with the economy (the EEC itself, the European Free Trade Association, the Organization of Economic Cooperation and Development—which originated as the agency directing the use of Marshall Plan aid—the World Bank, the International Monetary Fund, the Group of Seven finance ministers' meetings, the annual economic "summits," etc.), trade (the General Agreement on Trade and Tariffs, GATT), security (NATO, West European Union, etc.), and political cooperation (the North Atlantic Council, the Council of Europe, the European Community itself, the regular gatherings of heads of states). In addition, there are thousands, possibly hundreds of thousands, of semi-public or private institutions of cooperation acting across the frontiers of the democracies, from multinational corporations to academic seminars and journals, some self-interested, some devoted to the public interest, but together providing a dialogue among the democracies of unprecedented intensity, complexity, and breadth.

This amounts to an unacknowledged Commonwealth of the Democracies and is, perhaps, the crucial achievement of the postwar years. Yet it is taken for granted, or even ignored, by those in quest of other and more glamorous forms of institutionalized world order. I believe we neglect this achievement to our risk, because it is possible for us to falter in this intense cooperation and lose our best chance for a steadily widening yet utterly realistic form of international cooperation based on shared democratic values. This achievement already has demonstrated its ability to draw the nondemocratic states toward the values of the democracies. The magnetism of our cooperative successes proved the force which irresistibly drew Eastern Europe and the Soviet Union toward Western European and U.S. political values in the last few years. Here, surely, lies our best opportunity for creative internationalism in the years to come, making use of the building materials of nation and nationalism. It is a not unrealistic vision, although whether we will continue in this way, extending our Commonwealth, remains to be seen. In my view it is clearly the course the church should encourage. The church made its peace with democracy in the Second Vatican Council's deliberations, after more than two centuries of hostility, but churchmen are still often attracted to utopian and absolutist political formulations, more often of the left in recent years, than of the right, as in the past. The church continues to have difficulty reconciling the authority, or authoritarianism, inherent in its doctrinal and teaching missions, with the modalities of discourse and debate of the democratic societies. But this is a matter others can address, and have addressed, better than I.

I have been asked merely to offer a reflection on the character of the international society in which we live, and on the direction in which that society may develop. I have spoken about the future with an uncharacteristic optimism, by suggesting that a Commonwealth of the Democracies might extend its influence and radiate its values to that larger world which remains caught in oppression and violence. The truth may prove to be the reverse. The democracies—as we have every reason to know, from 1914 to 1992—also know the power of Thanatos. And this is a matter, surely, where the church may speak, warn, and prophesy. This is the domain of the church, the spiritual order, a domain to which secular modern individuals are characteristically strangers, and where their greatest dangers still lie.

Part III

The New World Order and the Challenge for the Church

The common theme of the three chapters of part three is that the church has some unique responsibilities in light of the dawning of a new world order. These responsibilities have to do with the life of the church, applying the social teachings of the church to the church itself.

Chapter nine is by the respected philosopher, Richard T. De George. A scholar of Marxism as well as Catholic social thought, De George, through a careful textual analysis, argues that most of the major social encyclicals (*Rerum Novarum, Quadragesimo Anno, Mater et Magistra*, and *Laborem Exercens*) were written in reaction to Marxist socialism. Now that the threat of Marxist social theory has passed, De George is concerned that the church will retreat from its moral critique of international capitalism. He argues that the church must become much more proactive and less reactive for "now it has a greater rather than a lesser role to play."

As a new world order emerges, De George suggests five principles from the social encyclicals to provide guidance: the dignity of the human person, subsidiarity, the common good, justice and charity. He concludes with a mandate for the church: "Freed from the necessity of attacking communism, it cannot serve only as a gadfly and as an outspoken moral critic of the excesses of capitalism. It must articulate Christian principles in concrete and pertinent ways to help remake the global economic and social order."

Richard P. McBrien offers a brilliant and succinct ecclesiological analysis of Catholic social thought in chapter ten. He notes that in light of the documents of the Second Vatican Council, Catholic social teaching is seen to be part of the very mission of the church and not simply a matter of Christian moral behavior. McBrien's recurring theme is that the social teaching of the church must now be applied to the life of the church itself. "It is time these one hundred years of Catholic social teachings should begin to make some real, practical difference inside the church as well as outside." Questions of freedom and authority and related concerns are especially highlighted.

McBrien concludes the essay with five items that remain part of the "unfinished agenda" for Catholic social teaching as it moves into the twenty-first century.

Chapter eleven is by a prominent social psychologist, communications theorist and leader of female religious, Joan Chittister, O.S.B. The power of her oratory skills clearly comes through the pages of the written text. The focus of Chittister's remarks is summarized: "The question is, who are we choosing to be as church now, in our time, and what does the choosing imply for the masses waiting to see what Christians say being Christian today is all about?" Is the role of the church primarily political, pastoral or prophetic?

For Chittister there is little doubt that our call today is to be a prophetic church, criticizing social structures that impede the cause of the poor, building global solidarity, planning a global economy and educating for world citizenship. She offers a ringing endorsement for a prophetic church in the New World Order.

Nine

Neither the Hammer and Sickle Nor the Eye of the Needle: One Hundred Years of Catholic Social Thought on Economic Systems

Richard T. De George

The Catholic church has a two-thousand-year history of coexisting with a great variety of different economic systems. In not identifying itself with any particular economic system, it has followed successfully the norm of rendering to Caesar the things that are Caesar's and to God the things that are God's.

Although the church has always been solicitous of and has ministered to the poor, the downtrodden, and the oppressed, it has emphasized salvation hereafter rather than happiness in this vale of tears, where suffering is to be endured and legitimate authority obeyed. In its early days it helped slaves, but did not condemn slavery. In the middle ages it condemned usury, but it did not seek to free the peasants from the tyranny of the lords. With the development of the industrial revolution and the rise of capitalism, it was solicitous of the poor and preached charity but it did not condemn the system, seek structural improvements, or lead the workers in an effort to change their conditions. These things were not its job, nor was it competent to do any of them.

Yet, with the appearance in 1891 of *Rerum Novarum*, the church's position changed dramatically. Since then, papal encyclicals dealing with economic systems have developed progressively the Catholic church's teaching in this area.

In considering the evolution of this doctrine, I shall defend two claims. First, the development of Catholic social teaching on economic systems as found in four key encyclicals has been reactive rather than proactive. That teaching cannot be understood adequately without the backdrop of Marxist socialism. Marxism forced the church to engage in the moral evaluation of economic systems. Written in reaction to Marxist initiatives and doctrines, these encyclicals accepted and modified many of the Marxist criticisms of capitalism. Throughout this period Marxism has been the chief target as well as the driving force behind these encyclicals. Second, if this is true, then with the demise of Marxist socialism, the church now stands at a crucial juncture. No longer does it need to battle Marxist social theory, and it is not threatened by capitalism. It can, but should not, revert to its earlier indifference to economic systems. Now it has a greater rather than a lesser role to play in the moral critique of economic systems, especially that of international capitalism. It has the moral resources for that task. Yet it is an open question as to whether, without the threat of communism, it has the mission, the motivation and the will to pursue it.

Catholic Social Teaching: The Influence of Marxism

The claim that the church's social doctrine on economic systems developed in response to the threats of Marxism, and the claim that the doctrine that developed was influenced significantly by that threat, is not widely acknowledged. Yet that influence provides a vital key to understanding the evolving teaching and the present challenge.

To look for the church's social policy prior to 1891 is to look for something very amorphous. Prior to *Rerum Novarum* the church had no articulated social policy or stand on economic systems, except for its concern for the needy and its preaching of charity. Certainly it held and championed moral values that could be applied to social issues but, strictly speaking, it did not see as one of its tasks the formulating of what we call now a social policy. It is for this reason that *Rerum Novarum* is hailed, cited and quoted when one asks about the church's social policy. That document Pope Pius XI referred to as the Magna Carta "upon which all Christian activity in the social field ought to be based"[1] is the acknowledged foundation of Catholic social policy. It was the church's answer to what euphemistically is called the "social problem." That watershed document ironically owes its appearance as much to the socialism it sought to counter as to its concern for the workingman's plight, which the socialists had done so much to expose.

At the time *Rerum Novarum* appeared, the Marxists definitely were in the forefront of social and economic criticism, had done the most to underline the dreadful conditions of the working masses, and were the most successful force in raising the consciousness of the working class to the possibility of organizing and changing its situation. The church had not done this. Clearly, there was a social problem before Leo XIII's celebrated encyclical, and certainly the church had carried on its work and its ministry to the poor, as it conceived it, prior to that encyclical. Why did the church's position change when it did, and why did it enunciate its social doctrine as it did?

The answer is incomprehensible without considering the condition of Europe and especially the growing threat of socialism when *Rerum Novarum* was written. The evils of *laissez-faire* capitalism had been present and growing for over a century by the time the pope came forward to condemn, as part of the church's social policy, those evils and abuses. In doing so he was a Johnny-come-lately. During the previous forty years Marx and his followers had excoriated the evils of capitalism: they had described the alienation, exploitation and oppression of the worker, and they had established the International Workingman's Association to improve his lot. They called also for the violent overthrow of existing institutions, the seizure of power by the masses, the elimination of private property to be replaced by social property, and the establishment of socialism, the first stage of communism.

Marxist socialism contained a powerful social doctrine, and by 1891 it was a growing movement and a political force. Marxism promised happiness here, not hereafter. It was basically atheistic and saw established Christianity as an enemy that preached acceptance of one's lot in life, happiness in an afterlife, and justification of established authority. In 1888 Frederich Engels in his work *Ludwig Feuerbach and the End of Classical German Philosophy* divided the great ideologies of the world into two camps and pitted Marxism against religion, especially organized religion, of which Catholicism was the obvious and most powerful rival. That book made explicit the choice that workers of the world had to make. Thereafter there could be no doubt about the threat of Marxism to Catholicism. Both sides knew who the enemy was, and acted accordingly.

Socialist doctrine carried with it moral force and moral power that made it attractive to many. It was active and not passive. In preaching its doctrine it sought the souls and hearts of the workers. Marxist socialism thus posed a threat to the church that slave-holding societies, feudalism, mercantilism, and other economic systems did not pose. The church could and did coexist with all of those. It could not coexist with the emerging socialism which saw the church as an opponent whose worldview socialism sought to replace.

By way of contrast, capitalism posed no threat to the teachings of the church and sought neither to supplant it nor to attack overtly its doctrines. The church, which had lived with a variety of economic systems in the past, found no threat in capitalism. The church's concern for the plight of the poor did not seek to substitute one economic system for another. To that extent, the Marxist charge that the church sought to alleviate the ills of the poor and oppressed without changing the economic structures that produce poor and oppressed peoples was not entirely off the mark.

Leo XIII saw that he had to answer the socialist challenge. Not only had he to condemn socialism, but he had also to formulate an explicit, positive Catholic social doctrine to counter it. Without understanding this background it is easy to miss the importance of socialism to the development of the church's social doctrine, it is easy to fail to see how successive popes formulate their critiques of capitalism in reaction to developing socialist doctrine, and it is easy to overlook the crucial juncture at which the church stands today with respect to its social doctrine on economic systems. What started as a reaction to socialism has produced positive developments in the church's teaching.

Marxism provided a trenchant critique of capitalism. In the name of the workers of the world, it sought to change social conditions. Although Marxist socialism was atheistic, it was and still is perceived by many as proposing a social and economic system morally superior to capitalism. Papal documents never have acknowledged that moral superiority. Catholic social teaching for the past hundred years, as embedded in the papal encyclicals of *Rerum Novarum, Quadragesimo Anno, Mater et Magistra, Laborem Exercens* and *Centesimus Annus*, consistently have hewn the same line. They have continued to reject Marxism but, at the same time, they have not and could not embrace or defend *laissez-faire* capitalism. Those who question the driving force of Marxist social doctrine on Catholic social teaching need look only at those papal encyclicals.

Five Encyclicals as Responses to Marxism

Rerum Novarum

In the Preface to the German Edition of the *Communist Manifesto* of 1890, Engels boasted that the *Manifesto* was "the common programme of many millions of workers of all countries, from Siberia to California."[2] The boast was neither frivolous nor idle. In 1891, a year later, and three years after Engels's challenge in *Ludwig Feuerbach*, Pope Leo XIII's encyclical *Rerum Novarum* appeared.

Ironically, much of the moral appeal of Marx's socialism—its concern for the poor, the downtrodden, the working class—came in no small part from Christianity. To this the socialists added a revolutionary doctrine and an ideal of communism—a type of heaven on earth. Having seized that moral ground, they placed Leo XIII in a difficult position. While he refused to cede concern for the poor to the socialists, he was compelled to defend that concern in what both then and now appear as conservative terms, because they are traditional and not radical. It has taken close to a hundred years of dialectical interaction between these two opposing giants for Catholic social doctrine to regain the active and progressive championship of the working class that Marxist socialism usurped.

Rerum Novarum was not only clearly a reply to socialism but also it invited comparison with the *Communist Manifesto*. The invitation was not accidental, and it is easy to read *Rerum Novarum* as an almost point-by-point response to the Manifesto, as I shall show.

The first three paragraphs of *Rerum Novarum* implicitly accept the economic analysis of the conditions, the plight and the misery of the working class detailed in Marx's *Capital*. The encyclical adopts the vocabulary of "capital" and "labor" and the sociological analysis in terms of class that comes from Marx. From the point of view of one interested in defending free enterprise against Marxist attacks, this ceded too much. But that was not the pope's aim. He was not interested primarily in defending free enterprise but in countering atheistic Marxist socialism, which he begins to do in paragraph number four. It is clear that he presupposes the reader's knowledge of the context in which he is writing, since he moves so quickly to the heart of the socialist program. He directly counters the socialist attack on private property and the socialist goal of making "individual possessions the common property of all, to be administered by the State or by municipal bodies."

Although the real issue is atheism versus Christianity, the pope joins battle on the issue of property. He bases his defense of private property both on the Bible[3] and on natural law.[4] His defense is not unlike that of Locke in his *Second Treatise on Civil Government*. The only possible explanation for the pope's emphasis on private property is the fact that Marx sees it as the source of alienation, exploitation, oppression and class conflict, and its abolition as the means to achieving a good society. Private property as such has no intrinsic relation to Catholic doctrine. The vow of poverty taken by those in monastic orders, in fact, precludes their owning private property. Property held in common is not antithetical to Catholic doctrine, and it was popular in the early days of the church. Hence, the reason for the pope's defense of private property, as well as the basis for calling socialism unjust, must be sought elsewhere other than in the inherent moral value of private property.

Marx claimed that the worker was being forced to a lower and lower level of life, that he had no hope of increasing his resources, and that he could only better his condition in life by abolishing private property and changing the existing economic system. With great prescience, the pope warned that if private property were abolished and all property owned by the state, "the working man himself would be among the first to suffer." With hindsight, we see that the pope was right and Marx was wrong. However, the alternative presented by the pope was at best a conservative one, urging the workingman to live "sparingly,"[5] save his money, and invest it in land.

The pope's language and the points he makes track those of the *Manifesto* almost item for item. The *Manifesto* attacked bourgeois family and marriage. The pope replies with a defense of marriage,[6] and goes on to defend the right of inheritance, also attacked by Marx. In opposition to Marx's ideal of a society of equality, and to his claim that the wells of social wealth will flow abundantly, the pope warns that socialism will lead to envy, discord, and a leveling down "of all to a like condition of misery and degradation."[7] Although now we can see that his predictions of what would happen have come true in Eastern Europe and the USSR, one might argue that they have come true because the revolution that Marx anticipated never took place in the advanced industrial countries where he thought it would.

Marx put great emphasis on equality, which is also an ideal of many who are democratically inclined. Yet, although the equality of all before God is a powerful basis in Christianity for championing equality, the pope argues against an ideal of equality. He holds correctly that people differ in their capacities, conditions and fortunes, and claims that this is not disadvantageous for either the community or—implausibly—for individuals.[8] The attack on equality makes sense only as a reaction to the Marxist doctrine he is countering.

In reply to Marx's claim to end oppression, the pope takes a realistic, but negative line:

> To suffer and to endure . . . is the lot of humanity; . . . no strength and no artifice will ever succeed in banishing from human life the ills and troubles which beset it. If any there are who pretend differently . . . they delude the people and impose upon them, and their lying promises will only one day bring forth evils worse than the present.[9]

The most plausible rationale for preaching passivity in suffering hardships rather than activity in reducing them is that the pope makes this statement in the context of responding to the *Manifesto*.

Nor does the pope shrink from reiterating precisely the religious message that Marx attacked:

> When we have given up this present life, then shall we really begin to live. God . . . has given us this world as a place of exile, and not as

our abiding place. As for riches . . . whether we have them in abundance, or are lacking in them—so far as eternal happiness is concerned—it makes no difference; the only important thing is to use them aright.[10]

By denying the importance of wealth, the pope undermines the motives of envy and greed on which Marx plays.

The *Manifesto* presented all of history as the history of class conflict. To this the pope answers that the two classes, the wealthy and the workers, are "ordained by nature" to "dwell in harmony and agreement so as to maintain the balance of the body politic. Each needs the other."[11] What then of the conflict that, in fact, seems to be present? The Christian solution to that conflict is to be found in Christian institutions and in each class' assuming its proper duty. Interestingly, the pope condemns in different language the same ills that Marx had condemned: exploitation, failure to consider human beings as ends in themselves, child labor, inhumane working conditions, fraud, and pressing people down to lower and lower levels in their standard of living. Whereas Marx's alternative was to change the system, abolish private property and expropriate the expropriators, the pope's solution is to preach economic justice. He asks rhetorically, "Were these precepts carefully obeyed and followed out, would they not be sufficient of themselves to keep under [sic] all strife and all its causes?"[12] His implicit answer is yes. The difficulty is to motivate everyone to follow the precepts. The pope does not look to changing structures but to individual action, character, and morality. In opposition to the state's assuming the role of guardian and leader of society, holder of public wealth, and employer of all, the pope presents a limited role for the state, much like that of the European governments of his day.

He warns the rich that God will hold them to strict account for all they have.[13] One thinks of Christ's warning that it is harder for the rich man to enter heaven than it is for a camel to pass through the eye of a needle. The pope's remedy for class division and the plight of the worker is essentially Christian charity, which will unite the respective classes in brotherly love.[14]

Marx argued forcefully that wages necessarily involve exploitation, and that the solution to exploitation was not higher wages but the abolition of wages and wage slavery. In response, the pope defends the wage system but presents the idea of a just wage, namely, one sufficient "to support a frugal and well-behaved wage-earner," his wife and his children.[15] For Marx a just wage is a contradiction in terms. Ahead of his time, the pope rejects the doctrine that we know as employment-at-will, and he argues that this is only half of what needs to be considered. For (although the pope does not say so) Marx rightly states that, since the laborer has nothing to sell but his labor so he can live, he may be forced to work for less than he ought.

Marx started the workingman's movement and established the First International Workingman's Association. The *Manifesto* calls for the workers of the world to unite. The pope defends unions but opposes those run on Marxist and socialist principles, the joining of which exposes the workers' religion to peril.[16] The alternative is to establish Christian unions.[17]

The encyclical's answers to the false promises of Marxist socialism, and the solution to the exploitation and oppression depicted by Marx, are Christian morals and Christian charity. Marx saw the church and religion as offering solace to the oppressed but as doing nothing to change their condition. Insofar as *Rerum Novarum* is so clearly and directly a reply to Marx, and especially to the *Communist Manifesto*, it takes nothing away from the doctrine or the message to note that it was prompted by Marxism. We have seen that it was prescient in outlining the consequences of adopting Marxist teachings. Undoubtedly, it played a role in lessening the influence of the socialist parties in Europe. But it was more successful in countering communism than in controlling the excesses of capitalism. Although it attacked socialism head-on and point-by-point, its analysis and critique of capitalism was derived mostly from the Marxist attacks, and too amorphous and general to supply much direction.

Quadragesimo Anno

Forty years later, in 1931, Pope Pius XI returns to the "social question." In the interim the world had lived through the First World War, the October Revolution in Russia had ushered Marxist socialism into power, and the industrial countries were in the midst of the Great Depression. Pius XI notes that liberalism has proven itself unable to solve the social problem and that socialism proposes a remedy worse than the illness. Liberalism was the doctrine of *laissez-faire* capitalism which was the only kind of capitalism to have emerged by 1931. The remedy that Pius XI proposed, as had Leo XIII, was "the Christian reform of morals."[18]

Pius XI attacks both liberalism and socialism, but socialism remains the main target because, in its basic outlook, it is opposed to religion. By contrast, Christian charity can reform the liberal state which is not inherently anti-religious. Nonetheless, while defending the institution of private property, the pope reiterates that "the rich are bound by a very grave precept to practice almsgiving, beneficence, and munificence"[19] and he emphasizes the social character of ownership and the common good. He is clearly aware of the growing appeal of social ownership.

Socialism had changed during the intervening forty years, and had split into two sections. One section is communism which preaches class warfare and the abolition of private property and is "openly hostile" "to Holy Church and to God Himself."[20] The other section is socialism whose programs and ends are similar to those held by the church but which seeks human good entirely in material advantage and subordinates the individual to society in the production of goods. The pope concludes that "Religious socialism, Christian socialism, are contradictory terms; no one can be at the same time a good Catholic and a true socialist."[21] Although both socialism and liberalism are to be censured, only socialism is incompatible with Christianity, and hence only socialism is to be condemned rather than reformed. *Quadragesimo Anno* precedes the New Deal. The pope never considers the possibility of keeping the social programs of socialism while reconciling the basic doctrine with Christian virtues and respect for religion. This complete rejection of socialism foreshadows the views of later popes on liberation theology. Because Pope Pius XI admits the similarity of many socialist programs to Christian programs, the heart of the condemnation of socialism is its antagonism to Christianity, which he sees as a central and necessary tenet of socialism.

The pope defends the principle of subsidiarity, which means letting subordinate groups handle what is within their capabilities, yet he admits that free competition needs legal limits, evidently imposed on the national level. Competition, he says, must be guided by social justice and social charity on the international as well as on the national level. Yet Pius XI was still looking primarily to the West, even though he notes the poverty of the Far East. His remedy for both socialism and liberalism is not a change in economic structures but a return to Christian principles and to the law of charity, which is needed to supplement justice if the union of people's minds and hearts are to be achieved.[22] This last point is a crucial one, and one that Pope John XXIII will reiterate.

Mater et Magistra

Another thirty years had passed, the Second World War had taken place, and the Soviet Union had brought socialist and communist governments into Eastern Europe, when Pope John XXIII updated the doctrine begun in *Rerum Novarum.*

The pope starts by emphasizing that "though the Church's first care must be for souls . . . she concerns herself too with the exigencies of man's daily life . . . and his general, temporal welfare and prosperity."[23] Concern for temporal welfare and prosperity is a shift from Leo XIII's advice to frugal workingmen. The countries of Western Europe and the

United States had, in fact, replaced the theme of frugality with one of access to consumer goods, and the picture of what free enterprise could produce had not been lost on the rest of the world nor on the pope.

In reviewing *Rerum Novarum*, John XXIII attacks free and unrestricted competition, the disparity between the enormous riches of a few and the poverty of so many, and the growth of socialism and communism which he condemns as contrary to Christian teaching. Like his predecessors, he defends private property while tying it to "social obligation."[24] Important for him are human solidarity, Christian brotherhood, and the subordination of individual and group interests to those of the common good.[25]

Although the pope reiterates the doctrine of the just wage and the importance of a wage sufficient to support a family, he suggests also sharing ownership with workers.[26] He makes that socialist doctrine part of the church's social teaching.

In this encyclical, Catholic social teaching, which is the teaching of the universal church, finally notices the global interrelation of nations and understands that the economic problem is worldwide as well as national. In 1848 Marx called on the workers of the world to unite. In 1898 Lenin had already formulated his theses on world capitalism in *Imperialism: The Highest Stage of Capitalism* and had attacked colonialism. In 1961 the pope finally addresses these issues. He is still ahead of his time when compared to most other commentators in the West; but he is not the first, nor is he even a leader in the international critique of capitalism. His call is not for a new social order or for new economic structures on the international level but rather, as on the national level, his recommendation is to avoid unfair competition, to foster mutual cooperation and goodwill, and to exercise charity.[27] Justice is important and necessary. But justice is not enough to heal the wounds of those who have been treated unjustly, or to bring together the parts of humankind separated by injustice. Charity is needed as well, not charity understood as alms-giving but as Christian love. Anticipating the charge of vagueness he adds, "It is not possible to give a concise definition of the kind of economic structure which is most consonant with man's dignity and best calculated to develop in him a sense of responsibility."[28]

Laborem Exercens

Twenty years later, in 1981, Pope John Paul II updated the church's social teaching begun in 1891. The enemy was still communism. Just as *Rerum Novarum* invited comparison with the *Communist Manifesto*, *Laborem Exercens* invited comparison with other writings of Marx.[29] Like

Leo XIII in *Rerum Novarum,* John Paul II was still fighting to recapture the moral initiative from the Marxists, dealing with such issues as labor, alienation, and exploitation associated with Marxist doctrine. The dignity of labor and the rights of labor are now the critical norms, with work the fundamental concern.[30]

Whereas previous popes rejected the notion of class conflict, *Laborem Exercens* discusses the "Conflict Between Labor and Capital" in part II as if it were a fact, and traces the conflict to the desire for maximum profit.[31] In opposition to capitalism and its ideology—liberalism—the pope asserts the priority of labor over capital, which he equates with "the principle of the primacy of person over things,"[32] and which he claims differs radically from both Marxist collectivism and liberalism.

The problem of just remuneration for work remains the key social teaching the pope enunciates, and with this go concern for the family, family allowances, concern for mothers and their mission, health care, the right to rest, the right to safety in the workplace, the right to form unions, the right to strike, and care in times of unemployment and old age. These are now familiar claims, widely recognized in both socialist and capitalist societies. But the pope's point is that they are only implemented on any scale in the more developed countries; conditions in the less developed countries remain pitiful. The globalization of the economy is now center stage, and the pope's critique of international capitalism follows closely the charges made earlier by Marxist critics. Yet communism is still the main object of attack, even if capitalism falls far short of the Christian moral ideal.

Centesimus Annus

One hundred years after *Rerum Novarum* appeared, the communist regimes of Eastern Europe had collapsed and Pope John Paul II both marked the encyclical's anniversary and took the opportunity to reflect on the dramatic changes that had taken place.

Centesimus Annus, like the four encyclicals that preceded it, was prompted by Marxism—only this time by its demise. It is noteworthy that only after this demise does the pope comment favorably on authentic democracy in a state ruled by law[33] and on a "market economy" or "free economy" that is "circumscribed within a strong juridical framework which places it at the service of human freedom."[34] The aim is not to praise Western institutions but to offer guidance to Central and East European countries, while warning them of the mistake of thinking that, having rejected Marxist socialism, the only alternative is liberal capitalism which he sees primarily as the system Marx described. Thus he says, "The church offers her social teaching as an indispensable and ideal orientation, a teaching which . . . recognizes the positive value of the market and of enterprise, but which at the same time points out that these need to be oriented toward the common good."[35] He warns against the evils of consumerism, alienation, exploitation and individualism, all of which also form the core of the Marxist critique of capitalism. At the same time, he reiterates John XXIII's position that "the church has no models to present."

Many in the West were heartened that the pope finally endorsed authentic democracy; the notion of a balance of legislative, executive and judicial power, a free market, and human rights. Yet, as encouraging as this is to those who have championed these institutions, such endorsement was long overdue; the church has been characteristically careful, taking all due deliberative time to endorse them. That the pope does so only after the fall of totalitarian socialism is not without significance and should be taken in that context. The pope also calls for "a concerted worldwide effort to promote development,"[36] for "international agencies which will oversee and direct the economy to the common good,"[37] and for the transfer of "know-how, technology and skill"[38] to the less developed countries that are marginalized in the global economy. These, too, are goals worth pursuing, even though they are not new and their endorsement, although appropriate and laudatory, remains vague.

Marxism surely was and is defective. But one of its strengths was uniting theory and practice. It criticized capitalism, offered socialism and communism as an alternative, and proposed a means by which one might move from one system to the other. In answering Marxism over the past hundred years, successive popes have countered by pointing out the evils of communism and have warned simultaneously against the evils of capitalism. They have played the role of critic. They have not, and John Paul does not, suggest a third way, nor consider except in the broadest terms how to achieve a morally acceptable system, even though some interpreters seem to think he has endorsed their view of the good society.[39]

The Challenge of the Future

For many critics 1989 marks the end of communism, the termination of the cold war, and the victory of capitalism. The collapse of socialism in Eastern Europe may bring satisfaction both to defenders of capitalism and to champions of the church's social teaching. But during the past hundred years the primary impetus for articulating the church's social teaching in papal encyclicals had been the desire to counter atheistic communism. With the Marxist threat gone, the pope no longer has to attack that ideology. What is left of the original bifurcated attack on socialism and liberal-

ism is the critique of liberalism in its present-day capitalist or free enterprise garb.

Originally, the position articulated by four different popes was a centrist one between what was generally acknowledged to be the liberal *laissez-faire* capitalist position on the right and the Marxist socialist position
on the left. With the Marxist socialist position discredited, only the centrist
and capitalist positions remain. If the church continues its critique of capitalism, its social teaching will appear necessarily leftist to many adherents
of present-day liberal capitalism. That is a label with which many in the
church may feel uncomfortable. Yet whatever the label, if the church is
consistent in its social teachings, by default it inherits the role of moral
critic of capitalism.

We have noted that the economic system of capitalism poses no
threat to Catholicism. The church can live with it as it has lived with so
many other economic systems of which it could be justly critical. Why
attack capitalism since it poses no threat? Is it the church's role to enter
into the details of economic life as a moral critic when its vital interests are
not challenged? Is it not enough to preach charity and Christian virtues,
and to let people of goodwill apply these precepts to the critique of economic systems? Or, alternatively, has the church's social teaching matured
sufficiently so that even when its religious interests are not threatened it
will pursue vigorously a moral critique of economic systems, as did the
U.S. bishops' pastoral letter on the U.S. economy? Those are the crucial
questions. The answers are by no means a foregone conclusion.

The progressive development of Catholic social doctrine requires a
response to four related challenges: the challenge of a non-hostile economic system, the challenge of productivity versus distribution, the challenge of global morality, and the challenge of moral systemic analysis.

The Challenge of a Non-hostile Economic System

The practical discrediting of communism (even the Italian Communist
Party has changed its name to the Democratic Party of the Left and quotes
the pope instead of Marx)[40] leaves the church without its long-time antag-
onist. The church must now change its approach. In the past the church
often simply accepted and adapted the Marxist description and critique of
capitalism; today, the challenge for the church is to develop its own moral
critique of capitalism, especially on the international level. Since the first
social encyclical in 1891, the church has developed the resources it needs
for taking on the endless and thankless burden of social and economic
critic. Because it is positioned so strongly as a global institution to assume
that role, it is arguably a role that it should assume. The need for it to do

so stems from present-day moves toward capitalism in Eastern Europe, from the dangers to the common good inherent in liberalism, and from the contrast and inequalities between developed and less developed nations. *Centesimus Annus* touches on each of these issues, but it remains too general and abstract to provide much guidance on any of them.

As Central Europe turns into a market economy, it is open to the carpetbagger syndrome, i.e., to the implementation of the *laissez-faire* capitalism characteristic of the early days of capitalism in the United States and Western Europe. This syndrome prevailed before adequate background institutions were developed to control capitalism's tendency to value profit and goods above people. Gross exploitation, fraud, deception, and corruption were all too prevalent. The developments in Central Europe point to the need for a renewed critique of such *laissez-faire* capitalism, and for a moral check on the negative aspects of capitalism until adequate background institutions can be developed. Whether or not the church has the will to take up that task, since capitalism does not challenge its principles or its role as did socialist ideology, the need for it to do so clearly exists.

Yet, since 1989, in Poland where it played such a key role in countering communism, the church has placed its chips not on defending legislation protecting workers and consumers or on promoting the economic common good but on anti-abortion legislation. That issue is a traditional one on which the church leaders feel secure. By contrast, is their silence on the Polish and Eastern European economic chaos an indication of future priorities and a retreat from playing the role of economic critic?

At the same time, Pope John Paul II, who has addressed the problem of the division between developed and underdeveloped countries, is still fighting the remnants of Marxism present in liberation theology, a fight whose importance and centrality many question. The perceived threat in liberation theology is the same as it has been for a hundred years, namely, the threat of socialism and the oft-proclaimed incompatibility of socialism and Catholic doctrine. The pope's battle against liberation theology may seem minor and misplaced, until we consider the logic of the development of the papal encyclicals over the past hundred years. Except possibly for China and Cuba which pose no threat to Catholic interests taken in historical perspective, liberation theology remains the only traditional impetus for the pope to examine critically the moral dimensions of capitalism. To counter that threat, he must pay attention to liberation theology's charges of domination, dependence, and neo-colonialism fostered by international capitalism. Ironically, liberation theology may provide the church with the necessary bridge between following the Marxist critique of capitalism to developing a moral critique of its own.

The church cannot ignore what it has learned during the past hundred years and revert to exclusive concern for religious matters as understood prior to *Rerum Novarum*. It cannot fail to see that religious concerns include concern for the conditions in which people live. Capitalism does not threaten the church nor challenge its teachings. But the church's concern for the poor and oppressed will be credible only if it takes on the task of moral critic of liberal capitalism and helps give a voice to the silent oppressed.

The Challenge of Productivity versus Distribution

The social teachings of the popes since Leo XIII have emphasized charity and the distribution of wealth. Their concern for the just distribution of wealth paralleled Marxism's; however, both ignored the creation of wealth and were concerned almost exclusively with its distribution. In socialist countries the result was a leveling down in the name of equality. Catholic doctrine has not preached a leveling down, but it has given very little thought as to how wealth is produced. Arguably that is not its concern, while charity and just distribution are, which explains the call for charity and the emphasis on the doctrine of a just wage. But that approach is no longer adequate, if it ever was.

Pope John Paul has emphasized the priority of labor over capital. He has not followed through with a comprehensive discussion of freedom both for individuals and markets, nor has he developed the relationship between goods and freedom. Respect for persons certainly includes their living at a decent level of life. But that is not all that is required. The role of freedom in creating wealth is also important. Conditions need to be developed so that both human dignity and the production of wealth can be promoted. Such conditions require more analysis and moral guidance than Catholic social thought has thus far provided.

This challenge of balancing increasing productivity with just distribution requires the church to go beyond Marxism and to consider capitalism and market economics on their own merits. The task is not to justify or identify with capitalism, nor is it to develop economic guidelines. It is to develop and articulate moral guidelines more adequate than those so far enunciated for the task of morally evaluating capitalism, considering its many strengths as well as its weaknesses. Relying primarily on Marx's negative descriptions of capitalism and the church's principles of charity and a just wage will no longer make Catholic social teaching either appear relevant or be relevant to the needs of the times.

The Challenge of Global Morality

Since business is now worldwide, there is a pressing need for global background institutions capable of providing the restraints that laws, social legislation, unions, consumer groups, and articulate public opinion in the advanced industrial countries provide on the national level. The church's self-proclaimed universal mission gives it the adequate global moral perspective to match global capitalist expansion. Even the United Nations, important as it is, is more a grouping of individual nations than an organization with a global view. The need for a worldwide moral perspective is evident.

The church, which has always claimed universality, carries no allegiance to any particular economic system. This lack of commitment to any economic system makes it an ideal institution to exercise the moral leadership required to provide the basis for a new global social and economic order. No individual country can do so without appearing to impose or, in fact, imposing its national stamp on that order. The church's position arguably gives it the responsibility to fill the need.

International capitalism is partly, but not totally, responsible for the present disparity between rich and poor countries and between industrially developed and less developed countries. Adopting free enterprise has helped many countries and people achieve higher standards of living. Only a balanced and impartial moral analysis of international capitalism will carry moral weight now that socialism is no longer a viable alternative. The moral critique of capitalism from a global perspective involves three kinds of evaluation: an evaluation of the structural components of capitalism, an evaluation of their negative tendencies if unrestricted by laws or other effective background institutions, and an evaluation of the end state that results from adopting capitalism on the global level.[41]

Five principles enunciated in the papal encyclicals—the principle of the dignity of the human person, the principle of subsidiarity, the principle of the common good, the principle of justice, and the principle of charity—are the keys to a new global order that can emerge from the social encyclicals. But telling the wealthy nations not "to look with indifference upon the hunger, misery and poverty of other nations" is not enough. Nor is it enough to point, as *Centesimus Annus* does, to the need for "effective international agencies which will oversee and direct the economy to the common good."[42] Although the traditional role of charity in Catholic social teaching often has seemed equivalent to alms-giving, history has shown that on the global level, as on the national level, alms-giving will not solve "the social problem." Critics have emphasized strongly the obligations of justice because the role of charity, in the sense of voluntary giving, has been insufficient. Justice is crucial, but exactly what justice demands is far from clear.

By applying its five principles, the church has the resources to mediate conflicting claims of justice on the part of rich and poor nations. It is not enough to argue obligations exclusively in terms either of justice or of charity, but only of both together. Only justice infused with charity—in the sense of love of neighbor—can heal the gaping division between rich and poor, and between developed and less developed countries. Justice needs tempering by love, a sense of human sharing and solidarity, an appreciation of the oneness of the human family, and an understanding of the fragility of the globe we inhabit. This theme, raised by Pope John XXIII in *Mater et Magistra*, provides the approach to charity that must accompany the increasingly insistent call for international justice. An immediate need is the articulation of actions and structures that join justice and charity in ways acceptable to both the givers and the receivers of transfers of knowledge, goods or wealth, and that enable all people to develop, increase their productivity, and live together as equals.

To provide leadership in the creation of such an order requires more than the enunciation of the principles, even though that is a crucial first step. Although the principles must be fleshed out, their appeal must remain a moral appeal. The articulation of moral principles, the development of guidelines for their implementation, and a non-self-interested global moral perspective are what the church's social teachings can and should provide. Providing them is the step to which the five encyclicals lead. But taking that step will be as great a departure from the traditional role of the church as was the step *Quadragesimo Anno* took in enunciating a Catholic social doctrine.

The Challenge of Moral Systemic Analysis

The church has emphasized the reformation of individuals, in the belief that good individuals make a moral world. That is only half the story. Moral structures are needed also, including moral economic structures. The church as an institution has survived for two thousand years. It has survived poor leaders and even bad leaders, thanks to the strength of its structures. It should remember that lesson as it approaches "the social question." The Marxist critique was effective because it saw that capitalism was not infected by evil people, but by bad structures that inevitably led even well-meaning people into exploitation and oppression. Emphasis on personal reform and virtue is not enough. Although good people are clearly needed, they must form morally sound structures, including economic structures, if serious reforms are to occur.

It is easier to be a critic of what is wrong and unjust than it is to be the creator of just and workable structures. The creation of the structures may not be the work of popes but of people; the principle of subsidiarity suggests that the structures should not be imposed from above. Intermediate international structures that create just background institutions, comparable on the international and global levels to the systems of law present on national levels, is the greatest need in the economic realm. Instead of charity to less developed and poor nations, we need international structures that provide equitably for the sharing of wealth and that enable poorer countries to develop their productive capacities and become self-sufficient rather than dependent on alms. These structures will presuppose that wealth is already shared in the recipient as well as in the donating countries.

One hundred years after *Rerum Novarum* the church is placed ideally for taking the leadership in developing a truly global community, working with international bodies, working through its members, and helping to develop intermediate as well as higher level bodies and structures.

The role of the church is not to propose specific economic or political systems, and the encyclicals repeatedly point out that different countries may adopt different systems so long as they are not contrary to Christian principles. But clearly, it is not enough today to encourage charity, to suggest the subservience of workers to management, and to promote an ideal of frugality. Fortunately, the tradition of the encyclicals provides more.

The church has won at least part of the battle against communism. Various communist regimes have been toppled and much of communist doctrine has been discredited. Yet many of the moral ideals championed by socialism are still strong, viable and attractive. Divorced from atheistic communism, these ideals can be claimed—and in some instances reclaimed—by Catholic social teaching. They are a necessary antidote to international *laissez-faire* capitalism and radical individualism.

The task is to develop a positive Catholic social doctrine adequate to the times, rather than just a negative doctrine that is driven by the specter of communism. The church has learned or should have learned that an appeal to salvation cannot ignore social evils, and the preaching of subservience and acceptance in the name of patience and humility will no longer work. The appeal to salvation and virtue are important but not enough. One must work to ameliorate social conditions for the masses of humankind as well as to save each soul and, not infrequently, attempts to do the latter will depend on attempts to do the former.

Similarly, the key to changing social conditions lies in changing social and economic systems. If Marxism has taught us anything, it is the need to evaluate social and economic structures, not simply individual actions. If the social encyclicals have taught us anything, it is the need for Christian virtues. They must not only be adopted by individuals but built into the new international economic systems and structures.

Conclusion

The present void caused by the collapse of the communist ideal will be filled, and it may be filled by liberalism and radical individualism under the label of *laissez-faire* capitalism. Other than communism, the church has often been the only critic with a global perspective on the excesses of those doctrines. On the hundredth anniversary of *Rerum Novarum* the church has a unique opportunity to fill the role of global moral leader. Freed from the necessity of attacking communism, it cannot serve only as a gadfly and as an outspoken moral critic of the excesses of capitalism. It must articulate Christian principles in concrete and pertinent ways to help remake the global economic and social order. It is a challenge it can ignore. But it is a challenge it must not ignore.

Notes

1. *Quadragesimo Anno*, no. 39.
2. Karl Marx and Frederick Engels, *Selected Works* (Moscow: Foreign Languages Publishing House, 1958), p. 31.
3. *Rerum Novarum*, no. 5.
4. *Ibid.*, no. 8.
5. *Ibid.*, no. 9.
6. *Ibid.*, "No human law can abolish the natural and original right of marriage," no. 12.
7. *Ibid.*, no. 15.
8. *Ibid.*, no. 17.
9. *Ibid.*, no. 18.
10. *Ibid.*, no. 21.
11. *Ibid.*, no. 19.
12. *Ibid*, no. 20.
13. *Ibid.*, no. 22.
14. *Ibid.*, no. 25.
15. *Ibid.*, nos. 45–46.
16. *Ibid.*, no. 54.
17. *Ibid.*, no. 56.
18. *Quadragesimo Anno*, nos. 10, 15.

19. *Ibid.*, no. 50.

20. *Ibid.*, no. 112.

21. *Ibid.*, no. 120.

22. *Ibid.*, no. 137.

23. *Mater et Magistra*, no. 3.

24. *Ibid.*, no. 19.

25. *Ibid.*, nos. 23, 34, 37.

26. *Ibid.*, no. 75.

27. *Ibid.*, no. 80.

28. *Ibid.*, no. 84.

29. For a detailed study of this, see my paper, "Decoding the Pope's Social Encyclicals," *The Making of an Economic Vision*, Oliver F. Williams and John W. Houck, eds. (Lanham: University Press of America, 1991.)

30. *Laborem Exercens*, no. 3.

31. *Ibid.*, no. 11.

32. *Ibid.*, no. 13.

33. *Centesimus Annus*, no. 46.

34. *Ibid.*, no. 42.

35. *Ibid.*, no. 43.

36. *Ibid.*, no. 52.

37. *Ibid.*, no. 58.

38. *Ibid.*, no. 32.

39. See William E. Simon and Michael Novak, "Pope points toward economic third way for common good" who hail the pope for his strong endorsement of democracy and the market economy, for his diagnosis of the collapse of socialism, for his surprising critique of the welfare state and for his emphasis on the limitations and dangers of state power, *National Catholic Reporter*, May 24, 1991, p. 32.

40. *New York Times*, February 4, 1991, p. A3.

41. For a fuller discussion of the evaluation of economic systems, see Richard T. De George, *Business Ethics*, 3rd ed. (New York: Macmillan, 1990), ch. 6, 7, 19.

42. *Centesimus Annus*, no. 58.

Ten

An Ecclesiological Analysis of Catholic Social Teachings

Richard P. McBrien

This chapter is limited in scope and content. It offers only an *ecclesiological* analysis of Catholic social teachings; consequently, it is concerned exclusively with the understanding of the nature and mission of the church that is either explicit or implicit in Catholic social teachings, from Pope Leo XIII's *Rerum Novarum* to the present.

The chapter begins with a question, proper to ecclesiology, whether we should refer to the subject matter as Catholic social *teachings*, as Catholic social *doctrine*, or, following the example of the symposium organizers, simply as Catholic social *thought*.

Secondly, the chapter provides an overview of the ecclesiological development which has taken place in Catholic social teachings over the past hundred years.

Thirdly, the chapter offers a critical synthesis of this ecclesiology, organizing the material according to various theological and pastoral categories.

Finally, the chapter suggests some important areas for further ecclesiological development during the last decade of the twentieth century and into the third Christian millennium.

Catholic Social "Teachings," "Doctrine," or "Thought"?

Some commentators have made an issue of the way one speaks about the body of papal, conciliar, synodal, and episcopal statements on the social question, from the time of Pope Leo XIII to the present.[1] Some of these commentators find the term "social teachings" preferable to "social doctrine" because the latter suggests a "timeless dogmatism" or "a corpus of unchanging teaching . . . particularly inappropriate to Third World situations in that it [tends] to impose Western categories unsuited to local situations,"[2] while the former seems more open to change in teaching as circumstances warrant. Still other commentators object to "doctrine" and "teachings" alike on the grounds that both suggest, unacceptably, that the church has a body of principles and a model of society that amount to a "third way" between capitalism and socialism.[3]

Those for whom the question of terminology is both sensitive and important were disturbed by Pope John II's reference to "the social doctrine of the church" in his opening address at the Third General Conference of Latin American Bishops in Puebla, Mexico, on January 28, 1979, just four months after his election to the papacy.[4] On the other hand, in three of his subsequent social encyclicals, *Laborem Exercens* (1981), *Sollicitudo Rei Socialis* (1988), and *Centesimus Annus* (1991), Pope John Paul II moved easily between both expressions: social "teaching" and social "doctrine."[5] In any case, even Vatican II's *Gaudium et Spes* employed the language of "social doctrine" (no. 76).

The U.S. Catholic bishops, in their pastoral message to mark the centenary of *Rerum Novarum*, refer primarily to "Catholic social teaching," but they also use the term "social doctrine" as well as "Catholic social *tradition*" and "Catholic social *vision*."[6]

I disagree with those who resist the use of the word "doctrine" to describe the corpus of the church's social teachings. The objection may be based, in fact, on a confusion of doctrines with dogmas. A doctrine is an official teaching of the church. But not all doctrines are dogmas. In fact, very few doctrines have dogmatic status. A dogma is a doctrine which has been promulgated with the highest authority. It is a definitive teaching and, as such, is infallible. No one, including John Paul II, has claimed definitive or infallible status for the church's social teachings. Indeed, if he had, his action would have caused considerable consternation for some of his strongest supporters, among whom Catholic social teachings/doctrine have never been especially popular.

In this chapter I use the term "teaching" rather than "doctrine" because "teaching" and "doctrine" are roughly equivalent (a doctrine is an *official* teaching), and because the term "teaching" is generic enough to avoid provoking objections unnecessarily. Furthermore, there are many specific elements in the corpus of Catholic social teachings which are too tentative to be called doctrinal.

Those who prefer even more generic terms like "tradition," "vision," or "thought" are free to employ them, so long as they do not intend to deny the authentically magisterial and formally doctrinal elements of that tradition, vision, or thought.

To the suggestion, finally, that no body of Catholic social teachings even exists, one can only react with some astonishment. Many of the church's official teachings and pastoral activities over the past hundred years have been directed to the "social question." Indeed, the popes themselves consistently refer to papal teachings antecedent to their own to establish continuity in the development of the Catholic social tradition. Pope Pius XI's *Quadragesimo Anno* ("The Fortieth Year") was published forty years after *Rerum Novarum*. Pope John XXIII's *Mater et Magistra* (1961) was published on *Rerum Novarum's* seventieth anniversary. Pope Paul VI's *Octogesima Adveniens* ("The Eightieth Anniversary") was released in 1971, eighty years after *Rerum Novarum*. In 1981 Pope John Paul II presented those teachings and activities as the context for his own *Laborem Exercens* which commemorated the ninetieth anniversary of *Rerum Novarum*,[7] and in 1991 he marked the centenary of *Rerum Novarum* with a new encyclical of his own, *Centesimus Annus* ("The Hundredth Year").

The U.S. Catholic bishops, in their turn, insist that Catholic social teaching is "more than a set of documents. It is a living tradition of thought and action" which encompasses issues such as "developments in human work, new economic questions, war and peace in a nuclear age, and poverty and development in a shrinking world." While the content of this teaching and action may have changed over the last century, there are certain basic principles and themes which have emerged within this tradition: the dignity of the person, the rights and responsibilities of the person, the call to family, community, and participation, the dignity of work and the rights of workers, the option for the poor and the vulnerable, and global solidarity and interdependence.[8]

In the end, this collection of documents is, by turns, exhortative, analytical, didactic and doctrinal. Thus, it can be described by any and all of the terms employed heretofore.

An Ecclesiological Overview

The corpus of Catholic social teachings under consideration in this paper include the following documents:

Papal Encyclicals, Apostolic Letters and Apostolic Exhortations:

Leo XIII's *Rerum Novarum* (1891)
Pius XI's *Quadragesimo Anno* (1931)
John XXIII's *Mater et Magistra* (1961) and *Pacem in Terris* (1963)
Paul VI's *Populorum Progressio* (1967), *Octogesima Adveniens* (1971) and
    Evangelii Nuntiandi (1975).

John Paul II's *Redemptor Hominis* (1979), *Laborem Exercens* (1981), *Sollicitudo Rei Socialis* (1987) and *Centesimus Annus* (1991).

Conciliar Documents:

Vatican II's *Gaudium et Spes* (1965) and *Dignitatis Humanae* (1965)

Synodal Documents:

Iustitia in Mundo (1971) and *The Final Report of the Extraordinary Synod* (1985)

Episcopal Statements:

U.S. Catholic Bishops: *The Pastoral Letter of 1919, The Challenge of Peace* (1983), *Economic Justice for All: Catholic Social Teaching and the U.S. Economy* (1986), and *A Century of Social Teaching: A Common Heritage, a Continuing Challenge* (1990).

Latin American Bishops: Medellín documents of the Second General Conference of Latin American Bishops (1968) and the Puebla documents of the Third General Conference of Latin American Bishops (1979).

I shall trace the ecclesiological evolution of these documents according to the following chronological order: (1) from *Rerum Novarum* to the Second Vatican Council, (2) the Second Vatican Council, and (3) the post-conciliar period.

From Rerum Novarum (1891) to Vatican II (1962)

Rerum Novarum (1891)

One has to keep in mind that, prior to the pontificate of Leo XIII, there was a very close and mutually beneficial alliance between the Catholic church and the most conservative forces in nineteenth-century society. The church, especially during the pontificates of Gregory XVI (1831–1846) and Pius IX (1846–1878), regarded the growing influence of secularism and anti-clericalism as a direct and dangerous threat to its own interests. The conservatives among the ruling classes and the aristocracy were delighted, in their turn, because the church's enemies were *their* enemies too—politically, socially and economically.

On the other hand, there were more progressive forces also at work in the church, which prepared the way for *Rerum Novarum*. In Germany Bishop von Kettler of Mainz denounced the exploitation of workers in his

The Labor Question and Christianity (1864). In England Cardinal Manning intervened in the London dock strike of 1889 on behalf of labor, and in the United States Cardinal Gibbons and Archbishop Ireland championed the fledgling labor union movement and prevented Rome from condemning the Knights of Labor. Although Leo XIII may have been relatively more liberal than his immediate predecessors in the papal office, he shared their concern for the interests of the church, i.e., for resisting the encroachments of its enemies and for restoring its power and influence in the secular world. It has been conjectured that Leo was inspired in the writing of *Rerum Novarum* as much, perhaps even more, by the loss of the working classes to the church as by their exploited condition in the new industrial society.[9]

When he did intervene, however, his initiative directly attacked one of the most basic tenets of nineteenth-century liberal thought, namely, that the church has neither the competence nor the right to intervene in the social, political and economic orders.

"We approach the subject with confidence, and in the exercise of the rights which manifestly appertain to us," Leo XIII wrote in *Rerum Novarum*, "for no practical solution of this question will be found apart from the intervention of religion and of the Church" (no. 16). The proximate purpose of this intervention, he insisted, was the improvement and betterment of the condition of working people. But a more fundamental concern, rooted directly in the Gospel, was the reconciliation of human beings with one another: of upper classes with lower classes, of rich with poor, of property owners with workers, in bonds of friendship and love (nos. 19–20). A tearing apart of the social fabric through revolutionary means had to be avoided at all costs.

Leo made it clear, going against some of his own contemporaries (and our own as well), that the church has the right and the duty not only to teach, but also to *apply* the teaching to the temporal order, i.e., "to point out the remedy" (no. 26). Indeed, the church is not "so preoccupied with the spiritual concerns of her children as to neglect their temporal and earthly interests" (no. 28). Consequently, the church "intervenes directly in behalf of the poor, by setting on foot and maintaining many associations which she knows to be efficient for the relief of poverty" (no. 29).

The church's intervention, however, was not to be limited to the activities of the hierarchy and clergy. There was an important and indispensable place for the laity as well (nos. 54–55), to whom he had referred, however, as "children" (see above). At the same time, Leo conceded that the state has its own proper role to play, independently of the church but bound by its teachings pertaining to justice and human rights (nos. 32–49). The church, for its part, always stands ready to cooperate and "will intervene with all the greater effort in proportion as her liberty of action is the more unfettered" (no. 63).

On these and other points, Leo XIII anticipated some of the ecclesiological breakthroughs of Vatican II's *Gaudium et Spes*. At the same time, it must be said that the ecclesiological content of *Rerum Novarum* was exceedingly thin in comparison with that of the council's Pastoral Constitution.

U.S. Catholic Bishops: *The Pastoral Letter of 1919*

One has to read the U.S. Catholic bishops' Pastoral Letter of 1919 in historical context. Only twenty years earlier, in 1899, "Americanism" had been condemned in a papal rescript. Eleven years earlier, in 1908, the church in the United States, heretofore considered mission territory, had been accorded full canonical status. And two years earlier, in 1917, the United States had entered the First World War on the side of the allies.

It is not surprising, in view of their recent ecclesiastical experience and of the anemic state of ecclesiology at the time, that the bishops' pastoral letter should have reflected such a strong Roman and papal bias.[10] Neither is it surprising that, in view of their ardent desire to underscore the loyalty of Catholic citizens to their country (so bitterly challenged by anti-Catholic organizations), the bishops should have pointed with pride to the service of Catholic soldiers and chaplains in the war and, at the same time, emphasized the war's moral justification.[11]

On the other hand, the bishops reaffirmed one of the most basic ecclesiological themes to be found in Leo XIII's *Rerum Novarum*, namely, the right and responsibility of the church to intervene in the temporal order to advance the cause of justice, peace, and the reconciliation of classes: "The Church which Christ established has continued His work, upholding the dignity of man, defending the rights of the people, relieving distress, consecrating sacrifice and binding all classes together in the love of the Saviour."[12] Although the bishops acknowledged the proper role of the state, they urged it not to reject "the assistance which Christianity offers for the maintenance of peace and order."[13]

It should be noted that the bishops seemed implicitly to acknowledge some linkage between the inner life of the church and its capacity to shape and influence the temporal order: "The combination of authority and reasonable freedom, which is the principal element in the organization of the Church, is also indispensable in our social relations. Without it, there can be neither order nor law nor genuine freedom."[14] I shall return to this point in due course.

Quadragesimo Anno (1931)

What is striking about Pope Pius XI's encyclical letter marking the fortieth anniversary of *Rerum Novarum* is its taken-for-granted papal triumphalism. In the midst of the conflicts and confusion of the late nineteenth century, Pius XI wrote, "all eyes as often before turned to the Chair of Peter, to that sacred depository of all truth whence words of salvation pour forth to all the world." Economists, employers, and workers alike were flocking "to the feet of Christ's Vicar . . . begging him with one voice to point out, finally, the safe road to them (no. 7). Everyone greeted the encyclical, we are told, with "marvelling admiration" and hailed it "with the greatest applause" (no. 12), while Catholic workers received it "with special joy" (no. 13). It also rivetted the attention of the world's leaders "after the Apostolic voice had sounded from the Chair of Peter" (no. 26).

Pius XI, like Leo XIII before him, mounted a vigorous defense of the church's right and duty to speak out and to intervene in matters of social and economic consequence. Moral issues are at stake, he argued, because the economic order has to do with the just distribution and use of goods provided for us by our Creator, with a view to the attainment of our last end (nos. 41–43, 136–137).

Among the moral principles articulated in the encyclical was the right of workers to form unions. At the same time, Pius XI was wary of workers' associations not directly under the supervision of the hierarchy. Where there was no real alternative to a secular union, there should always be, side by side with it, "associations zealously engaged in imbuing and forming their members in the teaching of religion and morality" (no. 35). In the pope's mind, this followed from the principle, heralded in the Catholic Action movement, that the lay apostolate is, at root, a participation in the apostolate of the hierarchy and is carried on always in subordination to it (no. 96). Pius XI recognized the proper role of the laity—in this case, the workers—in the temporal order, serving as apostles to their fellow workers. But he described those lay "apostles" as "auxiliary soldiers of the Church" (no. 141). "The Church" here was clearly the hierarchy.

The most important ecclesiological item in the encyclical, however, had nothing directly to do with any of the above. It was *Quadragesimo Anno* which gave us the "fixed and unchangeable" principle of subsidiarity, namely, that "it is an injustice and at the same time a grave evil and disturbance of right order to assign to a greater and higher association what lesser and subordinate organizations can do" (no. 79). "For *every* [my emphasis] social activity," the encyclical continued, "ought of its very nature to furnish help to the members of the body social, and never destroy and absorb them." Although Pius XI applied this principle immediately to the state and to economic life, it has applications beyond the state and the economic order, even to the "social activity" we know as the church.

Mater et Magistra (1961)

Pope John XXIII drew explicit attention to the principle of subsidiarity in his own *Mater et Magistra*, although he, too, limited its application to the political and economic order (no. 53). His encyclical also seemed to take for granted the right and duty of the church, both its hierarchy and its laity, to speak out and intervene in the temporal order (nos. 1–6, 178–184, 218–241, where the emphasis on lay involvement is especially strong and detailed). It is clear, however, that even John XXIII continued to identify "Church" with "hierarchy." To achieve the goal of implementing its social teachings, he wrote, "the Church especially asks the cooperation of the laity" (no. 256).

John XXIII was particularly emphatic about the right and duty of the church "not only to safeguard principles relating to the integrity of religion and morals, but also to pronounce authoritatively when it is a matter of putting these principles into effect" (no. 239). Because he anticipated some disagreement, even among Catholics, over the most effective or appropriate ways to implement this teaching, he urged that "they should take care to have and to show mutual esteem and regard, and to explore the extent to which they can work in cooperation among themselves" (no. 238). Dialogue and cooperation, which so characterized the council he would soon convene, were hereafter to be the hallmarks of ecclesiastical activity in the temporal order.

Pacem in Terris (1963)

Although *Pacem in Terris* was published between the first and second sessions of the council, it was less a product of the council than an influence upon it.

One of the most ecclesiologically significant aspects of this encyclical was its opening greeting. A papal document was addressed for the first time "to all men [and women] of good will," and not just to the usual assortment of patriarchs, primates, archbishops, bishops, other local ordinaries, and the clergy and faithful of the whole church. Consequently, if the audience for the church's social teachings is to be wider than the church, the teachings' content, language, and supporting arguments must be formulated in such a way as to be intelligible and persuasive for those outside as well as inside the church. This principle would be especially highlighted by the U.S. Catholic bishops in their pastoral letter, *The Challenge of Peace.*

As in *Mater et Magistra* two years earlier, John XXIII referred in *Pacem in Terris* to Pius XI's principle of subsidiarity, and again seemed to leave no room for its application to the church itself. Or did he? "Just as within each political community the relations between individuals, families, *intermediate associations* [my emphasis] and public authority are governed by the principle of subsidiarity," he wrote, "so too the relations between the public authority of the world community must be regulated by the light of the same principle" (no. 140). The church is surely one of society's "intermediate associations."

John XXIII also repeated his call for dialogue and cooperation in the implementing of Catholic social teaching, insisting that "one must never confuse error and the person who errs" (no. 158). The encyclical thereby anticipated Vatican II's ecumenical orientation as well as its defense of the principle of religious freedom. *Pacem in Terris* also anticipated the council's affirmation of the laity's proper sovereignty in the temporal order because they "live and work in the specific sectors of human society in which those problems arise" (no. 160). At the same time, the encyclical reaffirmed the teaching that "the Church has the right and the duty not only to safeguard the principles of ethics and religion, but also to intervene authoritatively with her *children* [my emphasis] in the temporal sphere, when there is a question of judging about the application of those principles to concrete cases" (no. 160). Even an encyclical as forward-looking as *Pacem in Terris* was not without the same paternalistic overtones found in earlier papal statements, including Leo XIII's *Rerum Novarum.*

Vatican II (1962–1965)

Gaudium et Spes (1965)

Two major concerns pervaded the Pastoral Constitution on the Church in the Modern World: first, to reaffirm the traditional distinction between the sacred and the temporal orders, as well as the transcendence of the church to the temporal order; and, secondly, to insist upon the active role of the church in the world, so that "the earthly and heavenly city penetrate each other" (no. 40).

Regarding the first concern, the Pastoral Constitution insisted that the church has "no proper mission in the political, economic, or social order. The purpose which [Christ] set before it is a religious one. . . . Moreover, in virtue of its mission and nature, it is bound to no particular form of human culture, nor to any political, economic, or social system." The church asks only that, "in pursuit of the welfare of all, it may be able to develop itself freely under any kind of government which grants recognition to the basic rights of person and family and to the demands of the common good" (no. 42).

Regarding the second concern, *Gaudium et Spes* restated the traditional paradox of a church existing for a spiritual purpose and yet situated in, and committed to serve, a temporal world. The Pastoral Constitution pointed to a resolution of the paradox in its notion of the church as "a leaven and as a kind of soul for human society as it is to be renewed in Christ and transformed into God's family." The relationship between the two realms is captured in the word "compenetration," but it is a reality that is "accessible to faith alone" (no. 40).

The church not only "communicates divine life" to men and women, but also contributes toward making the human family and its history more human, "by its healing and elevating impact on the dignity of the person, [and] by the way in which it strengthens the seams of human society and imbues the everyday activity of people with a deeper meaning and importance" (no. 40). Everything is anchored now in the dignity of the human person. Indeed, "by virtue of the gospel committed to it, the Church proclaims the rights of man" (no. 41).

If one were looking for a single formulation by which to resolve the problem addressed in *Gaudium et Spes*, namely, the relationship of church and world, that formulation might be found in article 76: "For [the church] is at once a sign and a safeguard of the transcendence of the human person." The text suggests that "the Church may neither be enclosed within the political order nor be denied its own mode of spiritual entrance into the political order. It indirectly asserts the rightful secularity of the secular order, at the same time that it asserts the necessary openness of the secular order to the transcendent values whose pursuit is proper to the human person."[15]

Indeed, the cooperation of church and state in the service of the human person is here stated *as* a principle:

> In their proper spheres, the political community and the Church are mutually independent and self-governing. Yet, by a different title, each serves the personal and social vocation of the same human beings. This service can be more effectively rendered for the good of all, if each works better for wholesome mutual cooperation, depending on the circumstances of time and place. (No. 76)

The council acknowledged here that there are no ideal forms of church-state arrangements. The contingencies of history, and not some abstract theory (or "thesis"), must determine the institutional forms of church-state cooperation. Furthermore, the cooperation between the two is not required by the need of the church, but by the dual nature of the person: "For the human person is not restricted to the temporal sphere. While living in history, he or she fully maintain their eternal vocation" (no. 76).

To fulfill its role in society, the church asks only the freedom to preach and to teach, and to pass moral judgment even on matters that belong to the political order "whenever basic personal rights or the salvation of souls make such judgments necessary." On the other hand, the church "does not lodge its hope in privileges conferred by civil authority," and is even ready to renounce those which have been granted already if they raise any doubts about the sincerity of the church's witness (no. 76).

In addition to this particular formulation of the role of the church in the temporal order, the Pastoral Constitution's ecclesiology includes the following important elements:

1) In its public preaching and teaching the church draws not only upon the primary sources of Scripture and tradition, but also upon its reading of "the signs of the times," which are to be interpreted "in the light of the gospel (no. 4).

2) In this task, the church must be prepared to learn from the world as well as to teach it, i.e., to draw upon the resources of men and women "of every rank and condition" (no. 44).

3) The "single intention" of the church is "that God's kingdom may come" (no. 45) a kingdom of "justice, love, and peace" (no. 39).

4) The church is "on earth the initial budding forth of that kingdom" (*Lumen Gentium*, no. 5), "a sign of that solidarity [*fraternitatis*] which allows honest dialogue and invigorates it" (*GS*, no. 92).

With this document, therefore, Catholic social teachings take a decisive ecclesiological turn.

Dignitatis Humanae (1965)

The Declaration on Religious Freedom has been described as another landmark document because it acknowledged the fact of the religiously pluralist society as the necessary historical context of the whole discussion concerning religious liberty; secondly, because it defined the role of government as constitutional and limited in function (namely, the protection and promotion of the rights of persons and the facilitation of the performance of civic duties), and at the same time disavowed any sacral function of government; and, thirdly, because it affirmed the freedom of the church as "the fundamental principle in what concerns the relations between the Church and governments and the whole civil order" (no. 13).

The entire teaching contained in the document is based on two principles: (1) the dignity of the human person (no. 1), and (2) the freedom of the act of faith (nos. 9–12). Inherent in both principles is the demand that people should act on their own initiative and responsibility, not under coercion.

J. Bryan Hehir has detected in this Declaration an "explicit shift in Catholicism's public posture—from a claim to favoritism to a claim for freedom." It thereby guaranteed "the transcendence of the Church in the face of any and all political regimes" and, at the same time, depoliticized the church's social role because it withdrew the church "from dependence upon or alliance with any specific civil power."

Hehir continued:

> By itself, depoliticization could result in the church's withdrawal from the public arena, creating the image and reality of a "sacristy church." The conciliar vision of Catholicism, however, particularly as embodied in *Gaudium et Spes*, moved in precisely the opposite direction. It called the church into the public order—to a concern for the human dimension of politics, economics, and international relations—as an expression of the gospel.[16]

If there is a problem with the Declaration's ecclesiology, it is its failure to apply the principle of religious freedom to the life of the church itself. Even the document's principal architect, John Courtney Murray, acknowledged that during an international theological conference held at the University of Notre Dame in March 1966. Murray observed in a discussion following his formal presentation on the document:

> Having declared religious freedom in the civil and social order, we've got simply to face up to the problem of freedom within the Church. I see no reason why, *mutatis mutandis*, the principles of the Declaration itself—notably the dignity of man and that there be as much freedom as possible and only as much restriction as necessary—should not also be valid within the Church as well as within civil and social society.[17]

As ecclesiologically advanced as Vatican II was, it was not *that* advanced.

The Post-Conciliar Period

Pope Paul VI

Populorum Progressio (1967)

This encyclical begins as all others do, situating itself in the line of previous papal documents and reaffirming the church's right and duty of "shedding the light of the Gospel on the social questions of their times" (no. 2). Paul VI's distinctive contribution to the development of Catholic social teachings was his insistence that the social question had become global and political in character.

Populorum Progressio situated itself clearly in the line of Vatican II's *Gaudium et Spes*, underscoring the distinction between the two realms, ecclesiastical and civil, reminding the church of its duty "to scrutinize the signs of the times and interpret them in the light of the Gospel," and eschewing all the while any political advantage for itself (no. 13).

The encyclical repeated yet another point found in previous papal and conciliar documents, namely, that lay persons have their own proper place in the proclaiming and implementing of Catholic social teachings. They are to do so "without waiting passively for orders and directives" (a point repeated in *Octogesima Adveniens*, no. 48). Indeed, they should "take the initiative freely" at all levels: national and international, official and private, civil and religious (no. 81). And in keeping with the example set by John XXIII's *Pacem in Terris*, Paul VI directed his words not only to Catholics but to all people of goodwill (no. 83).

Octogesima Adveniens (1971)

This document is called an apostolic letter rather than an encyclical, although it is indistinguishable from an encyclical in content and form. Because of the startlingly negative reception accorded his encyclical on birth control, *Humanae Vitae* (1968), Paul VI designated none of his subsequent documents as encyclicals. "Call to Action," therefore, was in the form of a letter to Cardinal Maurice Roy, president of the Council of the Laity and of the Pontifical Commission for Justice and Peace.

The apostolic letter acknowledged more explicitly than previous papal documents the diversity and complexity of the world order and the corresponding difficulty of formulating a unified message and of putting forth a solution with a claim to universal validity. Each Christian community, therefore, has to apply the Gospel and the social teachings of the church to its own particular situation. And it must do so not only in communion with the bishops but also "in dialogue with other Christian brethren and all men [and women] of good will" (no. 4). Increasingly, the application will occur within the context of political activity: "The Christian has the duty to take part in this search and in the organization and life of political society" (nos. 24, 46), but without falling prey to political ideologies (nos. 26–29).

Paul VI repeated what he had written in *Populorum Progressio* regarding the distinctive contribution of the church to the bettering of the human condition, namely, its offering of "a global vision of man and of the human race" (no. 40). The church offers not a ready-made set of practical solutions, but a framework of values, a "vision." This places the teaching of the church *in medio*, where *virtus* is to be found: "If it does not intervene to authenticate a given structure or to propose a ready-made model, it does not thereby limit itself to recalling general principles" (no. 42). What it does, it does with "a disinterested will to serve and by attention to the poorest" (no. 46).

In the social sphere, therefore, the church serves a double function: "first, to enlighten minds in order to assist them to discover the truth and to find the right path to follow amid the different teachings that call for their attention; and, secondly, to take part in action and to spread, with a real care for service and effectiveness, the energies of the Gospel" (no. 48). It is "a double task of inspiring and of innovating, in order to make structures evolve, so as to adapt them to the real needs of today" (no. 50).

This "passing to the political dimension" also underscores today's demand, which he called a "legitimate aspiration," that people share in responsibility and decision making (no. 47). Citing John XXIII's *Mater et Magistra*, Paul VI insisted that "the admittance to responsibility is a basic demand of man's nature, a concrete exercise of his freedom and a path to his development" (*idem*), all of which can be applied as well to the inner life of the church. But Paul VI, like all other popes before and after him, did not draw this implication.

Evangelii Nuntiandi (1975)

This document, perhaps the most impressive of Pope Paul VI's fifteen-year pontificate, is called an Apostolic Exhortation, given in the aftermath of the Third General Assembly of the Synod of Bishops, held the previous year to discuss the subject of evangelization. *Evangelii Nuntiandi* ("On Evangelization in the Modern World") linked the process of evangelization with the church's abiding concern for the social question. Evangelization proclaims the coming of the Kingdom of God as a form of liberation ("from sin and the Evil One"), and liberation is also the purpose of the church's social teaching—liberation from every form of economic, social, and political oppression (nos. 9, 29).

"The Church . . . has the duty to proclaim the liberation of millions of human beings, many of whom are her own children—the duty of assisting the birth of this liberation, of giving witness to it, of ensuring that it is complete. This is not foreign to evangelization" (no. 30). On the other hand, the church's mission cannot be reduced "to the dimensions of a simply temporal project" (no. 32). Indeed, we see here the antecedents of John Paul II's later insistence on the depoliticization of the church's activities in the temporal order. Should the church become captive to political parties or political ideologies, Paul VI argued, it would lose its credibility and effectiveness as a moral teacher and witness.

Paul VI also took care to mark out a middle position, as did Vatican II's *Gaudium et Spes* (no. 39), on the relationship between human progress and the coming of God's Kingdom. "The Church links human liberation and salvation in Jesus Christ," he wrote, "but it never identifies them, because . . . not every notion of liberation is necessarily consistent and compatible with an evangelical vision of humanity, of things and of events" (no. 35).

The specific contribution of the church, therefore, is "to encourage large numbers of Christians to devote themselves to the liberation of people"—to inspire and to motivate them to "translate [the church's social teachings] concretely into forms of action, participation and commitment" (no. 38). This would normally be done from within the context of ordinary parish and diocesan life, and always in communion with the local bishop and the bishops of the universal church (nos. 60–64). However, this Apostolic Exhortation also allowed for apostolic activities within specialized communities such as the *comunidades de base* of Latin America, but with reservations (no. 58), as well as within the family unit (no. 71). This effort, however, should not be limited to Catholics, but should be extended to all Christians and even to non-Christians (nos. 53–55, 77).

Paul VI also warned against the dangers of exaggerating the importance of the local churches over the universal church and of neglecting the central importance of the teaching office of the pope and the other bishops (nos. 67–68). Although he acknowledged readily the role of the laity in the process of evangelization within the temporal order of politics, economics, society, culture, science, the arts, international life, and the mass media, he reminded them that their "primary and immediate task is not to establish and develop the ecclesial community—this is the specific role of the pastors—but to put to use every Christian and evangelical possibility latent but already present and active in the affairs of the world" (no. 70). He tended thereby to perpetuate the false dichotomy between the ecclesiastical and the temporal spheres, leaving the affairs of the church largely, if not exclusively, in the hands of the clergy and the affairs of the world mostly, although not exclusively, in the hands of the laity.

Nevertheless, Paul VI *did* concede that the laity have a ministerial role in the life of the church itself, "in the service of the ecclesial community" (no. 73).

It is the essence of the church's mission to evangelize, he wrote, but it must begin "by being evangelized itself" (no. 15), for the church, as "the visible sacrament of salvation" (no. 23), must give witness to it (nos. 30, 41). He continued: "Modern man listens more willingly to witnesses than to teachers, and if he does listen to teachers, it is because they are witnesses" (no. 41). But, again, Paul VI did not draw from the principle of sacramentality any practical implications for the life of the church itself. He insisted only that the task of "ensuring fundamental human rights cannot be separated from this just liberation which is bound up with evangelization and which endeavors to secure structures safeguarding human freedoms" (no. 39). But structures must "safeguard human freedom" inside as well as outside the church.

Synodal Documents

Iustitia in Mundo (1971)

The Second General Assembly of the Synod of Bishops produced two documents: one on "The Ministerial Priesthood" and the other on "Justice in the World." The latter, also known by its Latin title as *Iustitia in Mundo*, was especially significant because (1) it is the only Vatican document, in one hundred years of Catholic social teachings, which applied the social teachings of the church to the church itself; and (2) it stated, more explicitly than any other comparable document, that the social apostolate of the church is a "constitutive dimension" of the church's mission.

"While the Church is bound to give witness to justice," the synodal document declared in its crucial third chapter, "it recognizes that anyone who ventures to speak to people about justice must first be just in their eyes. Hence we must undertake an examination of the modes of acting and of the possessions and life-style found within the Church itself" (III, para. 2). It is "a witness to be carried out in Church institutions themselves and in the lives of Christians" (II, para. 8).

The bishops applied this principle across the board to all those employed in the service of the church—laity, religious and clergy alike. The bishops also applied the principle beyond economic matters (e.g., wages and the right to unionize) to "freedom of expression and thought" in the church (III, para. 6), due process (III, para. 7), and the right to participate in decision making in the church (III, para. 8). The document also insisted that Catholic social teachings must permeate Catholic education so that it will become an "education for justice" (III, para. 13).

"Action on behalf of justice and participation in the transformation of the world," the synodal document also taught, "fully appear to us as a constitutive dimension of the preaching of the Gospel, or, in other words, of the Church's mission for the redemption of the human race and its liberation from every oppressive situation" (Intro. para. 6).

Otherwise, *Iustitia in Mundo* repeats familiar, albeit important, ecclesiological themes, namely, that the church has the right and duty to proclaim justice and denounce injustice at every level (II, para. 8); that the church has "a proper and specific responsibility" in this realm (II, para. 8); that this responsibility devolves upon laity as well as the hierarchy (II, para. 10); that the church has no specific political or economic programs to offer (II, para. 9); and that the church's efforts on behalf of justice must be global and ecumenical in character (III, paras. 21, 23–24).

The Final Report (1985)

The Extraordinary Synod of Bishops, meeting in Rome in late 1985 to commemorate the twentieth anniversary of the close of the Second Vatican Council, recapitulated the principal ecclesiological themes found in previous Catholic social teachings: the church as sacrament of salvation of the world; its need to read and interpret the signs of the times (including "hunger, oppression, injustice and war, sufferings, terrorism, and other forms of violence of every sort") in the light of the Gospel; its need for dialogue with non-Catholic Christians, non-Christians, and non-believers; its preferential option for the poor; and its need to put aside any false and useless opposition between the church's spiritual mission and its service of the world (II, D., paras. 1–6).

Latin American Bishops

Medellín (1968)

The Second General Conference of Latin American Bishops (CELAM) met in Medellín, Colombia, in 1968. For the most part, the Medellín documents reaffirmed and reinforced the teachings of the Second Vatican Council, especially *Gaudium et Spes*, on the social mission of the church. The documents ranged widely: justice, peace, family and demography, education, youth, pastoral care, catechesis, liturgy, lay movements, priests, religious, poverty of the church, pastoral planning, and mass media.[18]

The documents reflected and generally supported the newly emerging liberation theology (4, nos. 8–9), called upon the church to exercise its authority as a form of service "exempt from authoritarianism" (5, no. 15c), insisted that the church itself must practice what it preaches, and that it must make a preferential option for the poor in its evangelization and social ministry (see document 14, "Poverty of the Church").

Puebla (1979)

The Third General Conference of Latin American Bishops met in Puebla, Mexico, in early 1979. Although there had been some conservative reaction and resistance to the Medellín documents and to the subsequent pastoral development of the church in Latin America, and although the newly elected Pope John Paul II was beginning already to mark out a more conservative course for the papacy, Puebla did not substantially modify, much less repudiate, Medellín. On the contrary, in its Final Document, entitled "Evangelization in Latin America's Present and Future," Puebla reiterated Medellín's summons to the church to make the Gospel "a leaven of transformation" and itself a champion of the poor. Furthermore, the church must carry on its social mission independently of "the powers in this world," lest it be compromised by a too close association with them (nos. 142–149). Puebla was more concerned about this danger than was Medellín (nos. 558–561).

The ecclesiology of the Final Document was generally well balanced. It was careful, for example, to warn against triumphalism but it also cautioned against placing too much emphasis on the church's failings (no. 231). Although it underscored the council's teaching that the church is the People of God, it also expressed a concern about the so-called "people's church" *(iglesia popular)* which can degenerate into a "sectarian elitism" (nos. 261–263). Otherwise, the ecclesiological themes in the Final Document were identical with those of Vatican II: the church as the universal sacrament of salvation, the church as a servant community, the church as a communion, and so forth (see nos. 270–281). Given the importance of Marian piety in the church of Latin America, the Final Document understandably reserved a large place for Mary as Mother and Model of the Church (nos. 282–303).

Because of the excessive length of the Final Document, it is impossible to provide a detailed ecclesiological analysis here.[19] Jon Sobrino has cited four "major *lacunae*": (1) a failure to acknowledge the church's own "mistakes, errors, and sins"; (2) a failure to acknowledge "the internal tensions and divisions within the Church and within the hierarchy"; (3) its silence about "that area of ecclesial reality that lies between the specifically evangelical and the concrete historical task that is necessarily bound up with political and ideological factors"; and (4) its silence about martyrdom in the Latin American church.[20]

Pope John Paul II

Redemptor Hominis (1979)

In his first encyclical, *Redemptor Hominis*, John Paul II declared that the very core of the Gospel is the proclamation of our "worth and dignity," and that this affirmation "determines the Church's mission in the world and, perhaps more so, 'in the modern world'" (no. 10, paras. 1–2). The document is, in large part, an extended essay on Christian humanism.

The encyclical, however, contained nothing new ecclesiologically. Where it touched upon the mystery and mission of the church, it tended to favor a transcendental ecclesiology, emphasizing the spiritual and eschatological dimensions of the church's existence rather than its servanthood and its sociopolitical role in the world (no. 18).

Laborem Exercens (1981)

Laborem Exercens was much less the kind of personal statement that John Paul II provided in *Redemptor Hominis* and much more in the tradition of the major social encyclicals of the past.

The pope drew the same careful distinction his immediate predecessors had made about the church's role in the modern world, namely, that it does not presume "to analyze scientifically" the consequences that technological, political and economic changes have wrought, but only "to call attention to the dignity and rights of those who work, to condemn situations in which that dignity and those rights are violated, and to help to guide the above-mentioned changes so as to ensure authentic progress by man and society" (no. 1, para. 4; no. 24, para. 3). In other words, the church's role is to provide a moral framework within which these practical problems can be addressed by those technically competent to address them.

Sollicitudo Rei Socialis (1988)

Sollicitudo Rei Socialis ("On the Social Concern of the Church") is the most explicitly ecclesiological of John Paul II's social encyclicals.

John Paul II reiterated and embraced several of the ecclesiological themes found in *Populorum Progressio*. The role of the church, he declared, is "to lead people to respond . . . to their vocation as responsible builders of earthly society" (no. 1). It must apply the word of God "to people's lives and the life of society, as well as to the earthly realities connected with them, offering 'principles for reflection,' 'criteria of judgment,' and 'directives for action'." However, in the church's concern with the "development of peoples" it is not "going outside its own specific field of competence and, still less, outside the mandate received from the Lord" (nos. 8, 41). Indeed, by virtue of its own evangelical duty, the church is "called to take its stand beside the poor, to discern the justice of their requests, and to help satisfy them, without losing sight of the good of groups in the context of the common good" (no. 39).

But the church has no economic or political systems and programs to promote, nor does it show any preference for one or another. Its only concerns are that "human dignity is properly respected and promoted," and that the church's own freedom "to exercise its ministry in the world" is safeguarded (no. 41).

John Paul II, following the principle laid down already in *Redemptor Hominis*, pointed out that the church's mission to evangelize overlaps with its social teachings. Both have to do with proclaiming human dignity in the context of the mystery of the redemption. "The teaching and spreading of its social doctrine are part of the church's evangelizing mission" (no. 41) and its condemnation of evils and injustices is an aspect of its prophetic role. John Paul II also echoed Paul VI's insistence on the global character of Catholic social teachings as well as the church's preferential option for the poor (no. 42).

Perhaps the most newsworthy item in *Sollicitudo Rei Socialis* was John Paul II's declaration that the church not only calls upon others to alleviate the suffering of the poor, but is itself also "obliged by its vocation" to relieve their misery out of its own abundance and necessities alike, including even "Church ornaments and costly furnishings for divine worship." He noted that "it could be obligatory to sell these goods in order to provide food, drink, clothing and shelter for those who lack these things" (no. 31). Elsewhere he made a brief reference to the sacramental nature of the church and its call, linked with its solidarity with the human race, to be a sign and instrument of unity (no. 40). But the encyclical did not develop the point.

Centesimus Annus (1991)

Centesimus Annus ("The Hundredth Year") essentially reiterated and carried forward the ecclesiological perspective of the Second Vatican Council and of various post-conciliar documents, including John Paul II's own previous social encyclicals.

Following *Sollicitudo Rei Socialis*, the encyclical insisted that the church's social teaching "pertains to the church's evangelizing mission and is an essential part of the Christian message, since this doctrine points out the direct consequences of that message in the life of society and situates daily work and struggles for justice in the context of bearing witness to Christ the savior" (no. 5, 54).

That teaching, however, is not an ideology. It "recognizes that human life is realized in history in conditions that are diverse and imperfect. Furthermore, in constantly reaffirming the transcendent dignity of the person, the Church's method is always that of respect for freedom" (no. 46). Accordingly, in addressing issues which are always laden with historical and circumstantial contingencies, the church "has no models to present." Instead, the church "offers her social teaching as an indispensable and ideal orientation" (no. 43). Its "analysis is not meant to pass definitive judgments, since this does not fall per se within the magisterium's specific domain" (no. 3).

On the other hand, the church's analysis does not stop at theoretical reflection. "The Church, in fact, has something to say about specific human situations, both individual and communal, national and international. She formulates a genuine doctrine for these situations, a corpus which enables her to analyze social realities, to make judgments about them and to indicate directions to be taken for the just resolution of the problems involved" (no. 5).

"As far as the Church is concerned," the encyclical continued, "the social message of the Gospel must not be considered a theory, but above all else a basis and motivation for action" (no. 57). And at the center of this social message is always the dignity of the person: "This, and this alone, is the principle which inspires the Church's social doctrine" (no. 47, 53, 54–56). John Paul II had made the same point in his first encyclical, *Redemptor Hominis.*

Centesimus Annus reaffirmed the church's "preferential option for the poor" (nos. 11, 57), as well as the principle of subsidiarity (no. 48), but without applying the latter to the life of the church itself. There was a similar failure of application when the encyclical acknowledged, as did Paul VI's *Evangelii Nuntiandi*, that a credible teacher must be a witness to what is taught. "Today more than ever," John Paul II observed, "the Church is aware that her social message will gain credibility more immediately from the witness of actions than as a result of its internal logic and consistency" (no. 57).

U.S. Catholic Bishops

The Challenge of Peace (1983)

Long after the ethical content of this pastoral letter is out of date and forgotten, the ecclesiological significance of *The Challenge of Peace* will endure. Indeed, the process by which it was formulated should serve for many decades as a model of official teaching in the church: open to all points of view, eager to draw upon the expertise of competent and experienced resources, public in its manner of seeking this advice and input and in revising and amending its various drafts, careful to distinguish levels of authority within its magisterial pronouncements, and attentive to the wider audience beyond the church.

Thus, the pastoral letter was careful to insist at the very outset that "not every statement in this letter has the same authority" (no. 9). Some statements, the bishops pointed out, simply reassert universally binding moral principles; other statements reaffirm recent papal and conciliar teachings; still others apply principles and teachings to specific cases where prudential judgments are employed. Prudential judgments, in turn, are "based on specific circumstances which can change or which can be interpreted differently by people of good will" (no. 9). The bishops asked only that these prudential judgments be given "serious attention and consideration" in the formation of conscience (no. 10).

The pastoral letter also emphasized that Catholic social teaching has more than one audience. In addition to the community of faith, for which appeals to Scripture and tradition are always appropriate, there is the wider civil community, for which such appeals are usually inappropriate. "The conviction, rooted in Catholic ecclesiology, that both the community of the faithful and the civil community should be addressed on peace and war has produced two complementary but distinct styles of teaching" (no. 17).

The ecclesiological model preferred in this pastoral letter is that of a community of disciples, which the bishops suggest is derived from John Paul II's first encyclical, *Redemptor Hominis* (no. 21). Actually, it is only hinted at there. The bishops' real source is Avery Dulles' *A Church to Believe in: Discipleship and the Dynamics of Freedom.*[21] Given the minority status of the church, the Christian community is called upon ever more to be a witnessing community, standing over against a world that is "increasingly estranged from Christian values" (no. 277). The church must be detached from worldly comforts and become not only hearers but doers of the word of God. In the wrong hands, however, the community-of-disciples model can degenerate into a form of Catholic sectarianism.

The bishops left some pertinent and controverted ecclesiological questions untouched, for example, the right of a national episcopal conference to teach (*mandatum docendi*) in the name of a whole national community of Catholics, and the proper role of the bishops in the temporal order.

Economic Justice for All (1986)

The ecclesiology of this second pastoral letter on the U.S. economy (subtitled, "Catholic Social Teaching and the U.S. Economy") overlapped in many ways with *The Challenge of Peace*. It was formulated according to the same open and diversified process, and it underscored the church's nature as a community of disciples (nos. 45–47) and its mission as one of solidarity with the poor (no. 55).

On the other hand, it also contained a remarkably extensive recapitulation of *Iustitia in Mundo's* insistence that the church must practice what it preaches about justice: *"All the moral principles that govern the just operation of any economic endeavor apply to the Church and its agencies and institutions; indeed the Church should be exemplary"* (no. 347). Taking this principle as their starting point, the bishops insisted that it is the church's responsibility to respect its own employees' right to form unions in Catholic institutions (no. 353), its need to be "particularly alert to the continuing discrimination against women throughout Church and society" (*idem*), and its need to be sensitive to the image it projects through its properties, investments and the like (no. 354–355). But neither here nor in any other official expression of Catholic social teachings has the principle of sacramentality been invoked as the ecclesiological foundation of the argument.

Synthesis and Prospectus

It should be evident by now that no consistent and coherent ecclesiology has shaped and directed this century-long evolution of Catholic social teachings. Indeed, it would be astonishing if it were otherwise, given the extraordinary changes in theology and in the life of the church since the pontificate of Leo XIII, and especially those brought about by the Second Vatican Council. This final section of the paper attempts simply to bring some ecclesiological order out of these one hundred years of Catholic social teachings.

I shall offer herein a brief synthesis of the ecclesiology, stated or implied, in Catholic social teachings and then suggest what remains to be developed as the church approaches the threshold of a new century and a new Christian millennium. The individual elements of the synthesis include the following: mission, ministry, structure, the right and duty of the church to teach, the mode of such teaching, church-and-state, the witness of the church, and, finally, the principle of subsidiarity. It should be clear already that the Second Vatican Council is the turning point in the century-long ecclesiological development.

Mission

For Vatican II's *Gaudium et Spes* and John Paul II's *Sollicitudo Rei Socialis*, the church is a servant church with "a single intention: that God's kingdom may come" (*GS*, no. 45; *Lumen Gentium*, no. 5). This kingdom, however, is a kingdom not only "of truth and life, of holiness and grace, [but also] of justice, love, and peace" (*GS*, no. 39).

Both *Gaudium et Spes* and *The Final Report* of the 1985 Extraordinary Synod of Bishops insisted that there is no opposition between the spiritual mission of the church and its concern for justice and peace. There is a *distinction* between the two, to be sure, but no *separation.* "This duality is not a dualism" *The Final Report* pointed out (II, D., 6). Indeed, the church's "action on behalf of justice and participation in the transformation of the world . . . [are] a constitutive dimension . . . of the Church's mission for the redemption of the human race and its liberation from every oppressive situation" (*Iustitia in Mundo*, Intro., para. 6).

As noted above, it was not until the Second Vatican Council that this formally ecclesiological turn occurred in Catholic social teachings. Before that time, any formal consideration of Catholic social teachings was usually confined within moral theology, where these teachings were treated under the cardinal virtue of justice, and not within ecclesiology. After the council, Catholic social teachings have been included within both moral theology and ecclesiology. In other words, they are now perceived to be concerned not only with Christian moral behavior, but also with the very mission of the church.

Ministry

Until the pontificate of John XXIII the ministry of the church was generally defined in a narrowly clerical manner. Only the ordained were regarded as ministers in any formal sense of the word. On the other hand, the laity have been acknowledged from the time of Leo XIII himself to have an important role to play in the implementing of Catholic social teachings. That role tended to be interpreted, however, according to the model of Catholic Action, traditionally defined as the participation of the laity in the work of the hierarchy. Pope Pius XI, in fact, had referred to the laity in *Quadragesimo Anno* as "auxiliary soldiers of the Church" (and "the Church" in that context clearly meant the hierarchy).

But it was John XXIII, in both *Mater et Magistra* and in *Pacem in Terris*, who placed strong emphasis on lay social ministry, and it was Paul VI who went a step further and insisted that the laity may often have to take the initiative in the social apostolate, "without waiting passively for orders and directives" from the hierarchy (*Populorum Progressio*, no. 81). Moreover, they should be given some meaningful share in the responsibility for making decisions in this area (*Octogesima Adveniens*, no. 47).

Although the strongest affirmation of the laity's role in the mission of the church is to be found in the synodal document *Iustitia in Mundo* (III, paras. 3–8), it was the council which provided the ecclesiological turning point. In its Dogmatic Constitution on the church (*Lumen Gentium*), the laity were accorded full membership in, and missionary responsibility for, the church. Everything the Dogmatic Constitution had said about the People of God's sharing in the prophetic, priestly, and kingly functions of Christ was explicitly applied "equally to the laity, religious, and clergy" (no. 30). Indeed, the council described the lay apostolate as "a participation in the saving mission of the Church itself" (no. 33). This participation was not something granted juridically, i.e., by hierarchical power (as in Catholic Action), but sacramentally, i.e., by baptism, confirmation, and the Eucharist in particular.

Structure

Here, too, the Second Vatican Council provided the turning point in the ecclesiological development. Before the council, it was simply taken for granted in Catholic social teachings that "the Church" meant the hierarchy, and that the pope was at once a part of the hierarchy and above it. Even John XXIII's *Mater et Magistra* reflected this hierarchical approach, but it was nowhere more strikingly evident than in Pius XI's *Quadragesimo Anno*. As recently as 1962, the very year Vatican II opened, even the best of the Latin manuals of theology were still speaking of the church in monarchical terms.[22]

The council set Catholic ecclesiology on a different course with its teaching on the collegial nature of the church (*Lumen Gentium*, chapter III). Nevertheless, some subsequent papal statements have continued to warn against an exaggerated emphasis on the role of the local church and have, at the same time, underscored the importance of the universal church and of the papal office which is responsible for maintaining its unity (*Evangelii Nuntiandi*, nos. 67–68). This concern has been especially evident in the Vatican's generally negative assessment of the "popular church" movement in Latin American countries such as Nicaragua.

The Church's Right and Duty to Teach

No assertion appears more frequently or more forcefully in Catholic social teachings—from Leo XIII to John Paul II—than the insistence that the church has the right and the duty to teach officially on matters pertaining to social justice and peace. In essence, the argument has been that the issues, although also economic and political in content, are laden with moral concerns. In fact, so central are these concerns to the Gospel (especially the dignity of the person) that the church's social teachings can be regarded as a constitutive part of its evangelizing mission (*Iustitia in Mundo*, Intro., para. 6; *Redemptor Hominis*, no. 10, paras. 1–2; *Sollicitudo Rei Socialis*, nos. 41, 47; *Centesimus Annus*, nos. 5, 54). One would think the argument self-evident, or almost nearly so. However, many Catholics who otherwise regard loyalty to the pope as the principal criterion of Catholic orthodoxy continue to resist it.

According to Paul VI, the church's teaching responsibility is a double one: "first, to enlighten minds in order to assist them to discover the truth . . . ; and, secondly, to take part in action and to spread, with a real care for service and effectiveness, the energies of the Gospel" (*Octogesima Adveniens*, no. 48). It is "a double task of inspiring and of innovating, in order to make structures evolve, so as to adapt them to the real needs of today" (no. 50). In other words, the church is not limited to enunciating principles; it also has the right and duty to suggest courses of action and to pass judgment on practical solutions proposed by others. Even Leo XIII insisted on that point. The church is also called upon "to point out the remedy," he declared in *Rerum Novarum*.

Mode of Teaching

Here the dividing line comes slightly earlier than the council. It is John XXIII. With his pontificate, Catholic social teaching became more tentative, more sensitive to the complexities of social problems, more modest in suggesting concrete solutions, and more ecumenical, i.e., more open to dialogue with others, even if those others should disagree with the church's positions.

Increasingly, the official teachers see their task now as one of providing a moral framework and of proclaiming a moral vision within which particular problems can be analyzed and addressed (*Octogesima Adveniens*, no. 42). In matters of social justice and peace, prudential judgments are at issue. People of good will can, with a clear and informed conscience, find themselves at times in disagreement with the church's official teachers, not over the basic moral principles, but over their application to concrete circumstances (*The Challenge of Peace*, no. 10). Hereafter, the official teachers have to take care to distinguish among the various levels of authority which their teachings are intended to have (no. 9). Not everything in a papal, episcopal, synodal, or even conciliar document is of equal doctrinal weight.

The teaching church must be a learning church as well. It must be prepared to read the "signs of the times" and to interpret them in light of the Gospel (*Gaudium et Spes*, no. 4), and it must first listen to those whom it would presume to teach (note, again, the process employed by the U.S. Catholic bishops in the formulation of their two major pastoral letters).

Following the precedent set by John XXIII in *Pacem in Terris*, the teaching church must also be aware of the wider audience it is addressing on issues of justice and peace: not only fellow Catholics or even fellow Christians, but the whole civil community, including non-Christians and non-believers (*The Challenge of Peace*, nos. 16–17). And that wider community is now a global one as well (*Populorum Progressio*, no. 3; *Sollicitudo Rei Socialis*, no. 42; *Centesimus Annus, passim*).

Finally, the church's teaching must demonstrate a preferential option for the poor. This is evident already not only in the Medellín and Puebla documents of the Conference of Latin American Bishops, in Paul VI's *Evangelii Nuntiandi* (no. 29), and in *The Final Document* of the 1985 Extraordinary Synod of Bishops (II, D., 6), but also in John Paul II's *Sollicitudo Rei Socialis* (no. 42) and *Centesimus Annus* (nos. 11 and 57).

Church and State

One of the most significant ecclesiological elements in Catholic social teachings has been their consistent affirmation of the autonomy of the church and the state in their respective spheres of responsibility. Before Leo XIII's pontificate, however, this was not the case. One finds the Leonine position developed most fully (and most authoritatively) in Vatican II's *Gaudium et Spes*.

Catholic social teachings, as expressed in the council, in Paul VI's *Evangelii Nuntiandi*, and in the synodal document *Iustitia in Mundo*, call upon the church to free itself from entangling political alliances to provide even more effective and credible moral witness on the great social issues of the day. It involves a dual process which Bryan Hehir has referred to as depoliticization and resocialization. The church is more active than ever before in the social order, but more independent of partisan political movements, parties and officials.

The relationship between church and state, therefore, is neither one of union nor of separation. It is a relationship of cooperation. Members of the church are also citizens of the state. And all human beings, Catholic or not, are created by God and called by God to their one common destiny in the Kingdom of God.

Because the great public policy issues of our day are at the same time great moral issues, the church has both the right and the duty to participate in the public debates surrounding those issues. But upon entering the public forum, the church can no longer demand or expect any special privileges. It must make its case, not on the basis of its spiritual authority alone, but on the basis of arguments that are accessible and compelling to all people of good will (*Gaudium et Spes*, no. 76).

The Witness of the Church

There are only two places in the entire corpus of Catholic social teachings where these teachings are explicitly applied to the church itself: *Iustitia in Mundo* (chapter III) and the U.S. Catholic bishops' pastoral letter, *Economic Justice for All* (no. 347). Significantly, neither document grounds its argument properly, namely, in the principle of sacramentality. It is because the church itself is a sacrament, a visible sign of the invisible presence of God, that it has a missionary responsibility to practice what it preaches and teaches (see *Lumen Gentium*, no. 1). There are other documents in which a connection is made, at least indirectly, between the church's social teachings and the life of the church itself: Paul VI's *Evangelii Nuntiandi* (nos. 15, 23, 30, 41), and John Paul II's *Sollicitudo Rei Socialis* (nos. 31, 40). Elsewhere, when the sacramentality of the church is explicitly referred to, no practical application is made to the inner life and structures of the church (e.g., *Lumen Gentium*, no. 1; *Gaudium et Spes*, no. 92).

The Principle of Subsidiarity

The principle of subsidiarity was first enunciated in Pius XI's *Quadragesimo Anno* (no. 79), then reaffirmed by John XXIII in both *Mater et Magistra* (no. 53) and *Pacem in Terris* (no. 140), and by John Paul II in *Centesimus Annus* (no. 48). The reference in *Pacem in Terris* is particularly intriguing because, although John XXIII did not apply the principle directly to the church, he did indicate that "within each political community the relations between individuals, families, *intermediate associations* [my emphasis] and public authority are governed by the principle of subsidiarity." Since the church is one of those "intermediate associations," it would seem that the principle does, or at least should, apply to it as well as to the state and to economic institutions.

The Unfinished Agenda

As Catholic social teaching continues to develop over the next century, it will have to be shaped even more directly than it has thus far by the ecclesiology of the Second Vatican Council. That will require underscoring, even more than it has, the reality of the church as the People of God. "The church" is not simply the hierarchy, and the laity are not simply helpers, or "auxiliary soldiers," of the hierarchy, much less "children." The hierarchy and the so-called lower clergy will continue to assume important leadership roles in the proclamation and even in the application of Catholic social teachings, but the social apostolate itself will have to become increasingly less clerical in character.

Secondly, Catholic social teachings will have to recognize and respect the legitimate diversity and pluralism which characterize the universal church, and especially the autonomy of the local churches. The most difficult social problems today are shaped by the particular cultural, political and economic circumstances of the region; very few, if any, yield to universal solutions based on universal principles. Papal, synodal, and conciliar teaching still will be important, but the social teaching of national episcopal conferences will have to assume an increasingly significant role, the anxieties and opposition of certain people in the Curia and of politically conservative Catholics notwithstanding.

Thirdly, the church at the international level and in the individual countries of the world will have to take its lead from the example set by the U.S. Catholic bishops in the formulation of their two pastoral letters on peace and the economy. The U.S. bishops have given the church a new mode of teaching, one that is open, dialogical, tentative and competent. Catholic social teachings have embarked already on that course, beginning with John XXIII. Perhaps that model could be adopted more broadly to include the church's official teachings on sexual ethics as well.

Fourthly, the church's social teachings have yet to apply directly the principle of subsidiarity to the inner life and structures of the church. No initiatives should be taken at higher levels (the universal church, administratively centered in the Vatican) that more properly belong to lower levels in the church (the local churches at national, regional or diocesan levels). Initiatives undertaken by the church's central administration should be in the category of "last resort," as in the criteria for a just war.

One should note here that the principle of subsidiarity is linked closely with the doctrine of collegiality. The church is not one large parish, with the pope as its universal pastor. The church is a communion, or college, of local churches, all of which together constitute the universal church. Just as the doctrine of collegiality requires the church to acknowledge the autonomy of each local church, without prejudice to its bond of communion with all of the other local churches in the Body of Christ, so the principle of subsidiarity requires the church to respect the particular pastoral experiences, insights and judgments of the local churches as they strive to fulfill their missionary responsibilities in the world.

Finally, and most importantly, the social teachings of the church must establish and then continually emphasize the point that these teachings apply not only to the world outside the church but also to the inner life and structures of the church itself, and these teachings must ground this argument explicitly in the principle of sacramentality. Because the church itself is a sacrament, it has a missionary obligation to practice what it preaches and teaches, especially on matters pertaining to social justice, human rights and peace.

Thus far, only two documents in one hundred years of Catholic social teachings have made this point, although without explicit reference to the sacramentality of the church. The correction of this deficiency remains the great unfinished business of Catholic social teachings for the decade of the 1990s and beyond.

"While the Church is bound to give witness to justice," the 1971 Synod of Bishops declared, "it recognizes that anyone who ventures to speak to people about justice must first be just in their eyes" (III, para. 2).

It is time these one hundred years of Catholic social teachings should begin to make some real, practical difference inside the church as well as outside.

Notes

1. Donal Dorr, *Option for the Poor: A Hundred Years of Vatican Social Teaching* (Maryknoll, N.Y.: Orbis Books, 1983), p. 9, and Liam Ryan, "The Modern Popes as Social Reformers," *The Furrow*, 42, February 1991, p. 89.

2. Ryan, *op. cit.*, p. 89.

3. Dorr, *op. cit.*, p. 9.

4. John Eagleson and Philip Scharper, eds., *Puebla and Beyond: Documentation and Commentary* (Maryknoll, N.Y.: Orbis Books, 1979), p. 69.

5. *Laborem Exercens* (Washington, D.C.: United States Catholic Conference, 1981), I,2, pp. 4–6; *Sollicitudo Rei Socialis* (Vatican City: Libreria Editrice Vaticana, 1988), nos. 1–3, pp. 3–6; and *Centesimus Annus*, nos. 2, 43, 53, 54, 59 (full English-language text in *Origins*, 21/1 [May 16, 1991], pp. 1, 3–24).

6. The pastoral message is entitled, "A Century of Social Teaching: A Common Heritage, a Continuing Challenge," November 13, 1990. See *"Rerum Novarum*'s Centenary," *Origins*, 20/24, November 22, 1990, pp. 394–395 (my emphasis).

7. *Op. cit.*, I, 2, pp. 4–6.

8. *Op. cit.*, p. 395.

9. Ryan, *op. cit.*, p. 87.

10. "The Pastoral Letter of 1919" in *The National Pastorals of the American Hierarchy* (Washington, D.C.: National Catholic Welfare Conference, 1923), pp. 269–270. Note their praise of "the unbroken tradition of the Papacy with respect to international peace" (p. 331). It is remarkable, too, that the bishops should have pointed with pride to the church's dominant presence and influence during the later Middle Ages (p. 323).

11. *Ibid.*, pp. 294–296, 298.

12. *Ibid.*, p. 301.

13. *Ibid.*, p. 308.

14. *Ibid.*, pp. 301–302.

15. John Courtney Murray, "The Issue of Church and State at Vatican Council II," *Theological Studies*, 27, December 1966, pp. 602–603.

16. "The Church in the World: Where Social & Pastoral Ministry Meet," *Church*, 6, Winter 1990, p. 18.

17. John H. Miller, ed., *Vatican II: An Interfaith Appraisal* (Notre Dame, Ind.: University of Notre Dame Press, 1966), pp. 581–582.

18. Second General Conference of Latin American Bishops, *The Church in the Present-Day Transformation of Latin America in the Light of the Council: Conclusions* (Washington, D.C.: United States Catholic Conference, 1973), vol. II.

19. For a fuller critique, see Jon Sobrino, "The Significance of Puebla for the Catholic Church in Latin America," *Puebla and Beyond*, pp. 289–309.

20. *Ibid.*, pp. 298–299.

21. (New York: Crossroad, 1982), chap. 1.

22. Joachim Salaverri, *"De Ecclesia Christi," Sacrae Theologiae Summa* (Madrid: Biblioteca de Autores Cristianos, 1962), vol. 1, pp. 544–585.

Eleven

New World, New Church: Political, Pastoral, or Prophetic

Joan Chittister, O.S.B.

There are several ancient tales, I think, that indicate with particular poignancy the problems connected with attempting to treat the role of the church in any society.

The first comes from the sayings of the desert monastics whose spiritual direction consisted of aphorisms designed to lead the disciple to new levels of insight:

> "*Duc verbum*" ("Give me a word"), the seeker said, and the elder responded to the disciple with a wisdom saying meant to be explored in all its ramifications, "Go into your cell and your cell will teach you everything."

The implications of this story for the role of the church in society are, on one level at least, relatively clear: an immersion in the immanent, a touch of the transcendent, the meeting with mystery, the meaning of the mysterious, a confrontation with the self, an encounter with the mystical deep within each person, alone with the alone. These are the ends, the beginnings, the fruits, and the measure of the spiritual life. The role of the church in society is to "Give us a word," to lead us into the mysteries where we cannot go, to show us where we have not been, to deliver us from the body of this death. This is surely the church of penances and manuals and disciplines and private exercises and incense and organs and candles and chant. And it is a good church.

The problem is that the stories do not end there. The desert monastics themselves, in fact, began to call for that kind of church to deal with the questions that authentic contemplation brings.

"Whose feet shall the hermit wash?" the holy father Basil asked.

Benedict of Nursia directed the communities he had formed in the face of the desert tradition to "Say 'Benedicite' ['Thanks be to God'] when someone comes to your door." In other words, embrace the stranger. Protect the pilgrim. Treat the guest as Christ. The cell is not enough, in other words. Bring peace. Bring stability. Bring community to the world around you. Care for the goods of the earth, the Benedictine vision required far beyond the bidding of the anchorite. That is the vision of church that saved Europe when civil structures collapsed and the economy collapsed and the empire failed.

But there are two other stories that perhaps highlight best what happens once you learn as a church to say "Benedicite." In the second piece of ancient wisdom literature, the struggle between visions of church dawns more clearly:

> Once upon a time, the story says, a group of disciples asked the elder, "Holy One, give us the answer to the greatest spiritual question of them all: Is there life after death?"
>
> And the elder smiled.
>
> "Ah, my friends," the elder said, "the question you ask is an interesting one but it is not the greatest spiritual question of them all. The greatest spiritual question of them all is not, 'Is there life after death?' The greatest spiritual question of them all is, 'Is there life before death?'"

The implications in this are also clear: Life is for the living. Life is more than breathing. Life itself is a spiritual quest.

From such a perspective the function of the church is to be the fulcrum because of which we can choose life—in all its fullness, in all its fervor.

Finally, from the tales of the Hasidim comes what may be the hardest tale of all:

> Once upon a time a rabbi returned to his home from the service in the synagogue, obviously tired, clearly disheartened.
>
> "And how was your sermon?" his wife asked.
>
> "Oh, my sermon was half good," the rabbi said and sighed.
>
> "And what was missing?" his wife asked.
>
> "Well," the rabbi said, "I now have the poor willing to take. But I am not sure that I have the rich as willing to give."

If contemplation is coming to see as God sees, then contemplation without confrontation with the self about the world and our place in it is not enough. Life hereafter without life here is not enough. Encouragement of the poor without the commitment of the rich is not enough.

These are the challenges that confront the church in the modern world. These are the questions we are struggling to answer. These are the gauntlets before which we stand and on which we shall be judged.

In every era the church has wrestled with the questions of life—life in this world and life in the next; life in the body and life in the soul; life for the elect and life for the many. And in every era the church has had to make a choice: to accommodate to the world and its governments, to attend to its miseries, or to pronounce its good news in the face of bad news aplenty. The question is, what does a new world demand of a new church?

A world in search of a church is struggling for models, and a church intent on being in the world is surrounded by models for the taking. The models come from multiple places. The church can choose its role from tempting historical paradigms, from a variety of scriptural demonstrations, or from the very clear, decisive Jesus moments that dare us and confront us and challenge us to this day. What the church chooses to do depends only on what the church chooses to be and whom the church chooses to serve. Now. In our time. Today.

It is sometimes easier to understand one thing by comparing it to another. In the United States where pluralism has encouraged, endorsed, and innervated the rise of multiple religious traditions, it may be particularly enlightening to gauge how we see church by examining how other churches see themselves. Thomas Sanders, in his now classic, *Protestant Concepts of Church and State*,[1] draws from specific denominational perspectives to demonstrate the relationship of church to world. But the Catholic experience is equally clear that these are also strands in our own approach to the role of the church in society.

There are, Sanders says, five main postures to consider in the eternal dance between church and state: the Lutheran, the Anabaptist, the Quaker, the separationist and the transformationist. The strains in each as they struggle to discover the relationship of church to world are eerily familiar to our own.

Pope Gelasius wrote to the emperor Anastasius in the late fifth century:

"Two there are, August Emperor, by which this world is ruled, on title of original and sovereign right—the consecrated authority of the priesthood and the royal power. . . . You are permitted rightly to rule the human race, yet in things divine you devoutly bow your head before the principal clergy and ask of them the means of your salvation."[2]

It is this continuing thought of two kingdoms that has played itself out in various forms, Sanders contends.

Luther, centuries later, in the same vein as Pope Gelasius, posited two kingdoms, one distinct from the other, one not to interfere with the other, one the monitor of the other. "The Church's front line," Luther also declared, "is wherever there are those who suffer unjustly."[3] But, for the most part, the record shows that the churches of two kingdoms embraced quiet as the price of public protection, and personal pietism as the cardinal product of the church.

The Anabaptists, according to Sanders, stressed discipleship. They saw themselves as creators of the perfect Christian community, distinct from the world around them, distant from its corruption, far from its sins. They fashioned themselves as light to the world, not leaven, as pure witnesses rather than instruments of righteousness. But if the history of the Anabaptists is any clue, churches that choose iconographic witness without public presence as their project are often, the chronicles show, persecuted but seldom appreciated. A spiritual profile they may indeed be in their ethnic ghettoes, in their parishes and in their cultic clubs but they are scarcely a public presence and almost never a spark, a social notary, perhaps, but not a social force.

Or, Sanders points out, historically there is another approach to the question of the role of the church that is embedded in the Quaker tradition. Where Anabaptists, in favor of creating, protecting and maintaining the perfect community, rejected the idea of any role for government in the attainment of the ideals of the church, the Quakers, Sanders argues, saw government as an instrument for the achievement of God's will in specific, defined and limited areas. A Quaker approach to the role of the church in society limits the church to single issues and leaves the rest of the human agenda to the government itself. If the government is interested. If the government cares.

Unlike the Lutherans who see themselves as citizens of two worlds, or the Anabaptists who see themselves as creators of a perfect one independent of the one around them, or the Quakers who respond to the government only to promote a persistent but predictable agenda, a fourth group, the separationists, Sanders concludes, want a "wall" of "absolute separation" between church and state. To the separationist, religion is designed to be a purely private affair, allowed to exist unhampered by the state so long as it does not as a body, as a voice, or as a public person, interfere in the affairs of the state. To the separationist, religion belongs in the individual mind but not in the marketplace, in the individual heart but not in the heat of the public's day.

Finally, Sanders points out, the fifth stream in the Protestant flood of answers to the role of the church in society was the rising tide of transformationism, the notion that churches as churches have the right to seek to influence public policy in response to their understanding of the will of God, to bring the foolish standards of the gospel to bear on the issues of the times.

As denominationally defined as the attitudes Sanders describes may or may not be, the fact is that as Catholics we have been a bit of all of them; at some times and in some ways we have fostered a touch of every germ.

Like the Lutherans who learned from Gelasius, we have lived our lives as "citizens of two worlds" and plied our Catholic action with more regard for the building of the church than for the coming of the reign of God. We set out to save souls, but not necessarily to save their lives as well. With a purism not unlike the Anabaptist vision of the perfection of discipleship, we sank into our ghettoes and fled the corruption of the world but came in our cells to see nothing but our own small image of the God we had reduced to our own small likenesses.

Like the Quakers, we have all made peace at times with a single issue religion that, good as it may be, often comforts us more than it challenges us to be beyond ourselves.

Like the separationists, we have built a wall between prayer and action, between the gospel and the government, between the private and the public, between civil religion and social sin.

And, like the transformationists, we have all wondered to what degree we should bring our values to what claims, in the name of pluralism, to be a value-free world.

The question is, who are we choosing to be as church now, in our time, and what does the choosing imply for the masses waiting to see what Christians say being Christian today is all about?

The last hundred years of Catholic life have brought us face-to-face with questions the scale of which never before have we faced. As a global church we have seen the globe in all its grandeur, all its grief and, too often, traced the cause of the grief of one part of us to the reasons for the grandeur of another part of us. What does a church say to its own in one part of the world whose boots rest heavy on the backs of its own in another part of the world?

As an ecumenical church we have seen the role that one religion can play against the peoples of another church. What does an ecumenical church say on behalf of those whose truths are scorned and whose people are reduced to non-persons in the name of the God of the other?

What is the answer to the unanswerable? Is the role of the church political, pastoral or prophetic? Is the function of the church in our time to support the system because, bad as it is, it is better than most? Or is the function of the church to minister to those wracked by the system and hope that the system will eventually right itself? Or is the function of the church to walk like Jonah from one end of the city to the other crying, "Repent and begin again," until someone finally listens, or to go like Esther to the king and plead for the people, at the risk of every institution and every privilege and every brick we have ever counted to measure our success? Or is the function of the church to insist like Jeremiah on change and, as a result, be driven from the pedestals of power, and the banquets of the boards, and the viewing stands of presidents?

Modern social science is full of the struggle to find the way we should go. Gallup polls mark drifts and swells in both interest and intent among "believers" in the last fifty years.[4] Church membership and church attendance have held relatively steady over the years, true, but the notion that religion is an important factor in people's lives has shown considerable decline among respondents, from 75 percent in 1952 to 55 percent in 1989. Now, too, the military has replaced the church as the nation's most trusted institution, and confidence in organized religion has dropped from 66 percent to 52 percent—a full 14 percent—in just four years, from 1985 to 1989. In twenty years, 20 percent fewer people think that religion can answer all or even most of today's problems and half of the surveyed population said that religion was losing its influence on American life. Then in a survey taken in May 1990 only 3.4 percent of the population said that church leaders were believable sources of truth and over 42 percent of the group said they trusted most their own experience when seeking direction in life decisions.[5]

This is a public that goes to church and finds no answers. This is a public that seeks direction and finds the military more sure than the church. This is a public that is seeking but says that we have lost our way.

In *Faith and Ferment*,[6] an in-depth study of contemporary religious belief conducted throughout the churches of Minnesota by the Ecumenical and Cultural Research Center at St. John's University in Collegeville by survey, interview and structural analysis, people saw little or no relationship at all between what they learned in the churches and what they were faced with in life.

They saw little or no relationship between religion and ecology. So much for the Garden of Eden.

They found little or no relationship between religion and business ethics. So much for the cleansing of the temple.

They realized little or no relationship between Christianity and their standard of living. So much for the rich young man.

They felt little or no relationship between religion and their ideas on war. So much for Peter and his sword.

"The churches are unclear," they said.

Perhaps there has never been a time in history when the churches have been so aware of the social questions and so remote from the social answers.

The question indeed is, Which model is proper for our time—the political, the pastoral or the prophetic—and how shall we know?

Scripture is full of possible models, each of them part of our past, each of them a possibility for our present. We can, for instance, look to Rahab and Simon of Cyrene as examples of the political character of religion.

Rahab, the prostitute, lived in the city walls on the edge of the city, not altogether part of it but not completely distinct from it either. She may not have been accepted totally by the system, true, but she was certainly not rejected by it as a whole. When the spies sent by Joshua to determine the military vulnerability of the Canaanites became trapped in that enemy city, Rahab hid them in her own house and lowered the Israelites down the city walls to safety. Rahab performed a political service that secured the state for the chosen people and also confirmed her own place in it. Rahab was honored for her support of the establishment, although she had certainly not chosen one over the other on principle. Rahab did not become part of the Jewish people by saving its spies but Rahab did save herself, her family and the future of Israel.

Rahab was a masterpiece of the political face of religion. She did whatever the dominant system said was necessary to preserve her own place in it, no questions asked, no protest entered, no cost to social position.

The political face of religion was also Simon of Cyrene who, when pressed into service for the state, never so much as questioned the nature of the service. Simon never demanded to know why the condemned prisoner was condemned. Simon never asked whether the condemned prisoner should be condemned. Simon simply went along, satisfied apparently that the state had the undoubtable right to command him to cooperate, whoever the person, whatever the crime.

The political face of religion is an alluring one. After all, what is to be gained by making enemies in the state? It is the political face of religion that puts the flag of the country in its sanctuaries. It is the political face of religion that inscribes the names of its war dead on bronze plaques in the vestibules of its churches to prove the quality of its citizenship—as Catholics did after World War II—rather than on a memorial in the city park—as Protestants did after World War II. It is the political face of religion that cooperates with requiring I-9 forms from its employees as proofs of citizenship and so makes it impossible for refugees to earn a living, all scriptural mandates to the contrary. And all in the name of good citizenship.

It is the political face of religion that says nothing about Nazism to spare a church that was bred by the blood of martyrs, and nothing about militarism because that would be unpatriotic, and nothing about segregation in the sixties because that would upset the social "order." It is the political face of religion that saves the church for the sake of the church. It is the political face of religion that gives homage to the civil religion and blesses bombs and gives invocations and, like Rahab and Simon of

Cyrene, questions nothing until the state is invested with a legitimacy far beyond its merit.

Robert Bellah,[7] following Rousseau, argues that the civil religion "provides a transcendent goal for the political process." More than that, however, it is established religion that provides a transcendent meaning for the tasks of the state. Every law that goes unanalyzed by the church is affirmed by the church. Every injustice of the system that goes unresponded to by the church cedes the value formation role of the church. Every war that goes unquestioned by the church is blessed by the church. Every act of religion that gives uncritical confirmation to the destructive policies of the state reduces the role of religion.

From the thrones won by Theodosius to the colonies of Spain, from the courts of the Papal States to the chaplaincies of the modern military, the church has been a political figure. Never more political, ironically, than when it claimed not to be but bought its security at the price laid down by the state. The political church is the church that was made privileged and struck dumb at the same time, separated from the state and identified with it by that very distance.

The problem, of course, is that a covenant of separation can become a covenant of silence that puts the reign of God outside of history, that teaches the gospel but cedes its application, that abandons the poor to those who made them poor. The situation is not an easy one. It pits the public against the private definition of religion. It pits Jesus in the desert against Jesus in the court of Herod, it pits Richelieu against Romero.

It is true that Rahab saved the Jewish spies, but she went on, apparently, being Rahab, independent, unmoved, unconverted. Simon of Cyrene supported Jesus, yes—in fact saved him for the state to execute. But Simon of Cyrene did nothing to wrest away the cross.

There is, of course, another option. To the notion of church as silent observer in a corrupt world can be added the image of the church as healer and servant. This is the church of Veronica, the helper, and Joseph of Arimathea, the faithful one.

Veronica was a simple, sincere and concerned woman who walks across the pages of scripture with compassion and quiet. She did not set out to change the system, she set out to repair the wreckage that the system had made. She stepped out of the shocked and jeering and careless crowd and performed an act of comfort. She held Jesus up at a time of breakdown. She cared.

Joseph of Arimathea, all four evangelists agreed, appeared after both religion and government had done their damage to the body of Christ, to treat tenderly its abuse.

Joseph and Veronica performed the pastoral work of the church. They gave witness to the love of God in a system that needed justice as well. They performed the corporal works of mercy but it seems they seldom, if ever, asked why the body was being battered. They proclaimed a faith and a love and a presence that was steadfast and true and even courageous. They went where others would not go. They brought a sense of the sacred to what would otherwise have been sacrilege. They did it at a cost. But little or nothing changed because of it.

They were a church for the poor but they were not a church with the poor. They wanted the church to be healed and taught and fed and housed and bathed and dressed and comforted. But when did they ask, Who did this to you and why? They looked for cures that would enable people to take part in the very system that was crushing them. They sought conversion of the system through the enlightenment of the crushers and the assimilation of the crushed.

This church has built, operated and designed one of the largest alternative human service institutions in the history of the world. In the United States alone, according to the 1990 Kenedy Directory,[8] there are 821 Catholic hospitals and dispensaries, 742 special care homes, 876 child welfare centers and nurseries, 1,666 protective institutions, 1,771 special care centers, and over 2,500 grade schools, high schools and colleges or universities.

The list is not simply impressive, the list is overwhelming. The list is awesome.

The people in these institutions wipe the faces and tend the bodies of the forgotten day after day after day and stand as silent observers of a society that lets the bleeding bleed or makes the bleeding bleed. This church models a type of care. It does not necessarily model the charism of indignation. This church cares for those who die from malnutrition but says little if anything about a government whose policies deny food to the hungry. This church walks with soldiers to the gallows but says little, if anything, about the morality of capital punishment in a country that rates itself among the most civilized in history but kills with the impunity of few. This church educates women but says little, if anything, about the morality of the fact that educated women are not sought out to be hired in leadership positions or granted equal pay or seen as dispensers of grace. This pastoral church goes everywhere in the world with the poorest of the poor, to the richest of the rich, binding wounds but seldom decrying them, teaching the coming of the reign of God but only rarely, and on limited single issues, judging its presence. This church brings balm, perhaps, to rich and poor alike, but not a new world view to either. This church brings relief but not truth. This church pastors in the face of great odds but does not confront the social sin that underlies the wounds.

Veronica's church, Joseph of Arimathea's church, is a necessary solace but not necessarily a discomforting challenge to a world that has gotten more comfortable with welfare than with justice.

Finally, there is a third model of church equally scriptural, equally apparent, greatly admired, little understood: There is the church of John the Baptist and Mary of Magdala. Herod slew him and the Pharisees scorned her. They both made fools of themselves. He shouted in the streets and she invaded parties of the rich to show Jesus' commitment to the poor. They were changers, these two. They were trouble. Neither state nor church wanted the two of them around.

The woman, the outcast, really thought she had a right to a seat at the tables with the well-placed men. She ministered to Jesus' needs in embarrassingly public ways. She washed his unwashed feet with her tears and dried them with her hair. After his death, it was she who proclaimed, beyond all the religious protocol of it, the new kind of presence that would change the world. And she proclaimed it to his big, brave, consecrated and cowering apostles who were ominously quiet, socially subdued, sickeningly safe, and hiding somewhere in a locked room.

He, John, announced his coming to the winds and denounced the kingdom that obstructed it; he was plagued by doubt for the doing of it and was destroyed for that faith as a result. And, the scripture says, many believed because of him.

Certainly, Mary Magdalen and John traced the outline of the prophetic church in broad, bold strokes for all to see.

The prophetic church is a church that cares for something beyond its place in society, and something beyond the system itself. The prophetic church cares for the coming reign of God and its obligation to be it and bring it and build it up. A prophetic church does not temporize with neo-colonialism and industrial slavery while the poor in Haiti are paid thirteen cents apiece to make baseballs that sell in the United States for over ten dollars each. A prophetic church does not cede the articulation of the just-war theory to its president while the innocent die and the powerful refuse to negotiate. A prophetic church does not stand by silently and watch the moving of manufacturing plants from Tennessee to Costa Rica so the rich can get richer at the expense of the poor in both countries. A prophetic church asks what form of government is better for the poor, not what form of government is better for the church.

John and Mary Magdalen's church speaks the truth in the light. While millions beg and millions starve and millions die and millions are exploited and millions are kept in subhuman conditions by the trade policies and the budgets and the banks of the mightiest, richest, most powerful, best dressed people on earth who eat fresh strawberries in the winter and Australian lobster tails in the North American desert, a prophetic church does not simply beg for charity for the poor. It also demands justice for them. It calls the poor to dignity and the rich to repentance. It shows Lazarus to Dives.

A prophetic church rises above nationalism to world citizenship. It rises above capitalism to humanity. It rises above pious privatism to religion. It rises above devotions to the kind of contemplation that, with Mechtilde of Magdeburg, sees God in all things and all things in God. It rises above the intimidated silence of the political and the necessary, but enabling, services of the pastoral church to the hot, hard, blistering critique of the prophetic. Come what may. At whatever cost. To bring light to the eyes of the poor about the kind of life God really wills for them, and to support those rich and powerful and mighty who really want to leave behind a better world for suffering people.

A prophetic church says clearly, "It is easier for a camel to pass through the eye of a needle." A prophetic church learns in its cell to see as God sees. A prophetic church comes to bring life before death as Jesus did. A prophetic church preaches a whole homily.

The question is, of course, to which of those models is the church calling us now and what must be done about it.

For one hundred years the church has been in the throes of sloughing off the claims of government to inherent goodness and right, for the proclamation of the gospel to those for whom "the good news" is more rumor than fact. It has been a slow process and often a somewhat tentative one but, nevertheless, the progress has been steady and inexorable.

When Leo XIII in *Rerum Novarum*[9] chose to speak at all about the major social issue of the day and then, in a world fresh from kings and kingdoms and divine rights and class distinctions, called for parity between capital and labor, between the worker and the owner, between the serf and the lord, between the haves and the have-nots, the church was not calling for political alliances or pastoral presence. On the contrary, the church was issuing a moral warning to all the sweatshops in New York, to all the U.S. machiladores in Tijuana, to all the U.S. baseball plants in Haiti, to all the U.S. nonunion, nonpaying assembly plants in the Philippines, and to all the U.S. Catholics—priests, nuns, bishops, and laity—who reap the profits but who see no sin at all.

"After all," they say, "aren't those people better off with our factories than without them?" Which translated means: Aren't those people better off with our injustice than without it?

When Pius XI's *Quadragesimo Anno*[10] denounced economic dictatorships that control investment and credit, when *Quadragesimo Anno* began to recognize that governments run by the rich have a bias for the rich and seek to reward the rich for their riches, and when *Quadragesimo Anno* began the critique of capitalism as well as the denunciation of socialism, the right of the West to the resources of the East for the sake of the West at the expense of the East began to wane and, with it, the legitimacy of wars for resources that parade as wars for liberation.

When Pius XII insisted again, in the encyclical *Sertum Laetitiae*,[11] and repeated in his radio broadcasts to the world that the right of private property was a less primary right than the rights of all people to the goods of the garden, the concepts of land reform and welfare and even the idea of "development" itself came to be moral issues in an era more fearful of communism than critical of capitalism.

When John XXIII in *Mater et Magistra* and *Pacem in Terris*[12] called for "interior unity" between what we say we believe about the will of God for humanity and what we do in the world because of what we believe, when he pointed to specific realities—the arms race and the wasteful use of resources—and condemned them, when he proclaimed the obligation of the state to the economic well-being of the world poor in the face of "free enterprise," beyond "free enterprise," the church simply ceased to be the legitimators of the *status quo*, the sanctifiers of the *status quo*, the catechetical bulwark of the *status quo*.

When *Gaudium et Spes*[13] embraced the idea that the role of the church is to make the human family more truly human and relinquished its own privileges for the sake of its witness, the church began a whole new chapter of gospel presence.

When Paul VI in *Populorum Progressio* and *Octogesima Adveniens* and *Evangelii Nuntiandi*[14] stretched beyond and above *Rerum Novarum* to speak for the rights of poor nations as well as poor people and the moral trust of rich nations as well as the charity of rich people, then the universal church finally became universal, then "bold transformations" were called for, then change was summoned because reform had failed, then the new world order strove to be born, then confrontation became compatible with faith, then resistance became a moral responsibility, then the church of Veronica and Joseph gave way decisively to the church of Mary Magdalen and John.

When the 1971 Synod of Bishops issued the statement, "Justice in the World,"[15] and formally recognized social sin as perfidious, as real and as heinous as personal sin and called itself to justice, then the prophets rose again.

When John Paul II at Puebla declared that "the church opts solely for the human being,"[16] the church announced its freedom from any and every ideological system. The bad would never be good enough again simply because something else could be worse, if the lives of people should be better and could be better.

In *Laborem Exercens* and *Redemptor Hominis*[17] when the pope called not only for "conversion of the heart" but also for "transformation of structures"[18] and the "strong commitment of peoples. . .who are in solidarity with one another," the way was laid for global change and global citizenship, for a real "concern for human beings" which John Paul II said is "inextricably linked to the church's own mission and an essential element of it."[19]

And he said it in the barrios. And he said it in the favelas. And he said it to the urban poor. And he said it to the exploited farm workers. And he said it to bishops.

The question is, when will the bishops say it to the government and say it to the businesses and say it to this generation's children and say it to their poor and say it to the sisters and say it to their priests to say it in their pulpits?

No doubt about it. History is a patchwork quilt of the church as citizen of another world, of the church as model of the perfect world, of the church as single issue presence, of the church as silent separationist, of the church as transformer. And the record is a motley one. It is true that we have seen the church involved in colonialism and slavery and suppression of conscience and the Inquisition and on every single national side in the very same war. But we have also seen the church as the vanguard of the labor movement, as the basis of the social reconstruction of medieval Europe and as the architects of the "just-war theory," however inadequate that theory is in a technological world in which bomb is "apocalyptic" and able to reduce both combatants and noncombatants alike to "the pre-industrial age."[20] We have seen the church squarely on the side of the unborn and deeply, totally, financially invested in the sufferings of the born but unwanted, the born but uncared for, and the born but illiterate, all great ventures, all costly ventures, and all important human ventures.

For one hundred years, with the rise of the global village, the international economic system, the multinational employer, and the concentration of capital, the call has been getting clearer and clearer. The call is to global solidarity and planned global economy with a new theology of development and planetary protection and structural change on behalf of the masses of the poor. The call is to think again, to think newly, to think right about the sins built into the system. The call is to speak for those who are never asked to speak in such grand places as this, and to become one with those whom no one wants to be, and to cry out to everyone—congress person and corporate tycoon, president and Pentagon general, the wealthy and the secure—who benefit from the system and who hold the power to change that system, and to go on crying out until the brutally poor, the living dead are raised from their graves of injustice.

There are three arguments most commonly advanced to discourage the voice of the gospel in the midst of the government.[21] It is precisely these arguments that contribute to the appeasement of evil in society: the national commitment to the separation of church and state, the teaching of the church on the involvement of religious in politics, and the words of Jesus, "Render unto Caesar the things that are Caesar's." All of them are important and all of them are being misused to chloroform the Christian community into compliance with the unthinkable.

The notion of the "separation of church and state" has been used repeatedly to justify the silence of the churches in the face of evil. "When I go to church, I don't want to hear about politics," people say. "I want to hear about religion." And so the separation of church and state becomes the separation of religion and life. What was intended by the early formers of U.S. political culture to guard the country against the imposition of any single state religion so that all religions could function freely has become a gag order on the human soul. Religion has become a social club to which people go for the sake of personal satisfaction or a cocoon into which people enter to escape the realities of life rather than an arena of public struggle to find the will of God for all people and to walk in it.

Consequently, it is no longer acceptable in this country for the prophet to call the conscience of the king. As a result, we live in a country where multiple theories of finance, business, profit, and social theory are all admissible concerns in the debate on public policy but where the notion that an action should be questioned, let alone rejected, because it may disturb the created order or principles of human decency is met with embarrassment and resistance.

We have not been able, therefore, to raise the question in Congress— or in our churches either, for that matter—of whether or not a nuclear strike force with first strike capability is a posture the morality of which we can abide. We have not been able to consider whether or not abortion is against human rights or women's rights. What we do discuss is how our national actions will or will not make us number one, not whether it is conscionable to even think of being number one in a world where starvation has become the number one national reality around the globe.

The concept of the separation of church and state clearly never was meant to suppress human morality. On the contrary. It was meant to unleash it, from all sectors, in all places, at all levels so that truth could be heard and truth rather than expediency could prevail.[22]

The second argument used against the raising of religious voices on behalf of the poor is that the pope has told the church to stay out of politics. It is a fair concern. But staying out of politics and staying out of the political debate are two entirely different matters. The fact is that history is replete with churchmen who held power in both the political system and the ecclesiastical system, to the detriment of each. Too many a medieval bishop or corrupt cleric tried to serve two masters and wound up burning Joan of Arc or manipulating the czar or preaching the gospel of national chauvinism. But for every church politician who has attempted to function in both offices, there has been a prophetic voice to call the lawgivers to a higher law: Martin of Tours, Martin Luther King, Thomas Merton, Jerry Popuzelski, Dorothy Day, Barbara Ward, the Berrigans.

In our own day, John Paul II, the latest in the one-hundred-year-long line of papal teachers of Catholic social thought, has spoken clearly, not simply against atheistic communism but also against ruthless capitalism, about the political situation in Poland and the economic condition of the Vatican. He is proof positive that religion is a potent force in any state, with or without an official place in the political structure of the system itself.

There are those, of course, lay and cleric alike, who want the gospel silenced so that government can proceed without the critique that flows from love of neighbor and care for the world as a whole. Like the prophets of the court in ancient Israel, they want a religion, not separate from the state, but devoted to advancing its causes or at least not obstructing them. They want a quiet church in Hitler's Germany, a comatose church in Botha's South Africa and a simpering church in a United States that is nuclear, engorged and thirsty for cheap oil. It is a far cry from the Christ who took on the money changers in the temple and the interrogators in the crowds.

Finally, the argument goes, Jesus himself said that we are to submit to the state in matters of state. "Render to Caesar the things that are Caesar's and to God the things that are God's," the gospel says in answer to whether or not Jews should pay taxes to the Romans. The conscientious read the passage to mean that obedience is owed to civil rulers in civil affairs, no questions asked, no grief given. But the Jesus who rendered a place to civil authority is also the Jesus who did not hesitate to question Pilate, or to resist his demands, or to argue with his premises. To the end he contested with the powers of darkness in both church and state.

And why? Because, surely, in rendering to Caesar what is Caesar's, no one must render more. If we are at the same time to "render unto God what is God's," we can never render uncritical obedience to Caesar. There is a law above the law which binds us more and calls out of the unconscious state of religion for its own sake to the religion of the Jesus who came "that they may have life and have it more abundantly." It calls us to follow the Jesus who answered the question, "Are you the one who is to come or should we wait for another?" not by saying, "I am tradition, I am orthodoxy, I am the law, I am the mystical, I am silent, I am the separatist," but by saying, "I am the one on account of whom the blind see and the deaf hear and the poor have the gospel preached to them."

The choice we make now as church in our time to be political, pastoral or prophetic is made in the face of the Jesus who raised a woman from death to life—a useless, unwanted, and inferior woman of all things—as a sign of his total commitment to the poor. The choice we make now as church to be political, pastoral or prophetic is made in the face of the Jesus who hangs everywhere on a cross for us as a sign that he failed in the state. The choice we make now as church to be political, pastoral or prophetic is made in the face of the Jesus whose resurrection message was, "Tell Peter and the others that I have risen and I go before you into Galilee." The message, note, was not, "Tell Peter and the others that I have gone before you to Jerusalem," to the center of power and prestige where they could impress the public and get established in the system and settle down in the country, secure. No, the message was, "I have gone before you to the Galilee"—to the backwaters, to the Appalachia, to the squatter's areas of Israel where the poor waited for the waters to stir and the spittle to work and the Sabbath to be subdued in their favor.

"He has gone before us to the Galilee," the scripture says. He has, in other words, gone before us to the poor as a sign of the contemplative who sees as God sees. He has gone before us to the poor as a living sign of the gift of life before death. He has gone before us to the poor as a prophetic sign of a whole homily, to the rich as well as to the needy, to the West as well as to the East, to the churches of the First World as well as to the people of the Third.

He has gone before us to the Galilee. He has, indeed, gone before us to the Galilee. And, clearly, it is in the Galilee that he expects to meet us.

Notes

1. Thomas G. Sanders, *Protestant Concepts of Church and State* (New York: Holt, Rinehart and Winston, 1964), p. 6.

2. Pope Gelasius, as quoted in Sanders, p. xx.

3. Martin Luther, as quoted in Dean M. Kelly, "Protestant Perspectives on Church and State," *The World and I,* January 1991, p. 479.

4. George Gallup, Jr., *Religion in America* (New Jersey: The Princeton Research Center, 1990), p. xx.

5. George Gallup, Jr., *Lake Shore Visitor Register* (Erie, Penna.: March 10, 1991), p. 1.

6. Joan Chittister and Martin Marty, *Faith and Ferment: An Interdisciplinary Study of Contemporary Christian Belief* (Collegeville, Minn.: Liturgical Press, 1983), p. xx.

7. Robert N. Bellah, "Civil Religion in America," in Russell E. Richey and Donald G. Jones, *American Civil Religion* (New York: Harper and Row, 1974), p. 25.

8. "General Summary," *The Official Catholic Directory* (Wilmette, Ill.: P. J. Kenedy and Sons, 1990), pp. 1–40.

9. Donal Dorr, *Option for the Poor: A Hundred Years of Vatican Social Teaching* (New York: Orbis Books, 1983) pp. 11–28.

10. Dorr, pp. 57–75.

11. Dorr, pp. 78–84.

12. Dorr, pp. 105–115.

13. Dorr, pp. 120–124.

14. Dorr, pp. 139–142, 162–170, 190–196.

15. Dorr, pp. 178–182.

16. Dorr, p. 217.

17. Dorr, pp. 233–251, 217–222.

18. Dorr, p. 221.

19. Dorr, p. 218.

20. United Nations Survey, "Iraq's War Damage Near Apocalyptic," *New York Times*, Vol. CXL, No. 48537, March 22, 1991, p. 1.

21. Joan Chittister, "Religion and Politics: Siamese Twins Untimely Separated," *New Catholic World*, May–June 1991.

22. William Lee Miller, "On Meddling," *The Churches and the Public* (California: Center for the Study of Democratic Institutions, 1960), pp. 20–28.

Bibliography

Bainton, Roland H., *Christendom, A Short History of Christianity and Its Impact on Western Civilization, Vol. I, II* (New York: Harper and Row, 1966).

Balasuriya, Tissaw, *Planetary Theology* (Maryknoll, New York: Orbis, 1984).

Boff, Leonardo, *Church: Charism and Power, Liberation Theology and the Institutional Church* (New York: Crossroad, 1986).

Charles, Rodger, *Theology Today: The Christian Social Conscience*, Edward Yarnold, ed. (Notre Dame, Indiana: Fides Publishers Inc., 1970).

Chittister, Joan, "Religion and Politics: Siamese Twins Untimely Separated," *New Catholic World*, May-June, 1991.

Chittister, Joan, and Martin Marty, *Faith and Ferment: A Study in Contemporary Christian Belief* (Collegeville, Minnesota: Liturgical Press, 1983).

Cone, James, *God of the Oppressed* (New York: The Seabury Press, 1975).

Dawson, Christopher, *Religion and World History,* James Oliver and Christina Scott, eds. (Garden City, New York: Image Books, Doubleday and Company, Inc., 1975).

Dawson, Christopher, *The Dynamics of World History*, John J. Mulloy, ed. (New York: Sheed and Ward, 1956).

Dorr, Donal, *Option for the Poor: A Hundred Years of Vatican Social Teaching* (Maryknoll, New York: Orbis, 1983).

Dwyer, John C., *Church History: Twenty Centuries of Catholic Christianity* (New York: Paulist Press, 1985).

Franzen, August, and John P. Dolan, *A History of the Church*, Peter Becker, trans. (New York: Herder and Herder, 1969).

Gallup, Jr., George, *Religion in American* (The Princeton Religion Research Center, Princeton, N.J., 1990).

Gardner, E. Clinton, *The Church as a Prophetic Community* (Philadelphia: Westminster, 1967).

Glock, Charles Y., and Robert N. Bellah, eds., *The New Religious Consciousness* (Los Angeles: University of California Press, 1976).

Granberg-Michaelson, Wesley, *A Worldly Spirituality: The Call to Redeem Life on Earth* (San Francisco: Harper and Row, 1984).

Greeley, Andrew M., *Religion in the Year 2000* (New York: Sheed and Ward, 1969).

Greenawalt, Kent, *Religious Convictions and Political Choice* (New York: Oxford University Press, 1988).

Haughey, John C., ed., *The Faith that Does Justice, Examining the Christian Sources for Social Change* (New York: Paulist Press, 1977).

Hutchison, John A., ed., *Christian Faith and Social Action* (New York: Charles Scribner's Sons, 1953).

Jay, Eric G., *The Church: Its Changing Image Through Twenty Centuries* (Atlanta: John Knox Press, 1978).

Kelley, Dean M., "Protestant Perspectives on Church and State," *The World and I*, January 1991.

Kenedy, P.J., and Sons, *The Official Catholic Directory* (Wilmette, Ill.: 1990).

Neal, Marie Augusta, *A Socio-Theology of Letting Go: The Role of a First World Church Facing Third World Peoples* (New York: Paulist Press, 1977).

Nichols, James Hastings, *Democracy and the Churches* (Philadelphia: Westminster, 1951).

O'Donnell, Charles, ed., *The Church in the World* (Milwaukee: Bruce Publishing Company, 1967).

Lekachman, Robert, William Lee Miller, Arthur Cohen, William Clancy and Mark DeWolfe Howe, *The Churches and the Public* (California: The Center for the Study of Democratic Institutions, 1960).

Morgan, Elizabeth, Van Weigel and Erie DeBaufre, *Global Poverty and Personal Responsibility* (New York: Paulist Press, 1989).

Richey, Russell E., and Donald G. Jones, eds., *American Civil Religion* (New York: Harper and Row, 1974).

Reuther, Rosemary Radford, *Disputed Questions: On Being A Christian* (Maryknoll, New York: Orbis, 1989).

Sanders, Thomas G., *Protestant Concepts of Church and State* (New York: Holt, Rinehart and Winston, 1964).

Smith, Donald Eugene, ed., *Religion, Politics, and Social Change in the Third World* (New York: The Free Press, Macmillan, 1971).

Steidlmeier, Paul, *Social Justice Ministry: Foundations and Concerns* (New York: Le Jacq, 1984).

Weigel, George, "Catholicism and Liberal Democracy, The 'Other Twentieth-Century Revolution,'" *The World and I*, January 1991.

Part IV

The New World Order and the Plight of Developing Countries

Movement toward a new world order poses special concerns for developing countries. Part four offers three perspectives, one from a pastor-scholar and two from major church leaders in the developing world.

Chapter twelve is by a priest-scholar schooled in social analysis, who has spent the last several years working for the church in Zambia. Peter Henriot, S.J., is concerned that the development crisis in Africa might be exacerbated by the economic and political power shifts associated with the demise of the old world order. Public policy in the United States and other world powers can have a profound effect on the development possibilities in Africa. Catholic social teaching offers a vision of "integral development" and Henriot presents ten "theses" about the requirements of integral development which can serve as criteria for judging the present state of affairs as well as for envisioning the tasks yet to be accomplished. He is especially concerned that structural and ideological issues that may be inhibiting development be addressed.

Henriot is not naive about the problems in Africa and notes that the social role of the church has a significant challenge regarding such issues as poverty, low health standards, corruption, poor productivity, weak physical infrastructure, deteriorating social services, serious environmental problems and population explosion.

The author of chapter thirteen, the Archbishop of Panama, Marcos McGrath, C.S.C., provides an overview of Catholic social teaching in Latin America. With 40 percent of the world's Catholics living in Latin America, this area always has had a special place in the teachings of the church. McGrath notes that the emerging order in Latin America has been marked by the collapse of military dictatorships and the rebirth of civil democratic countries.

The major challenge for the church in Latin America is to communicate the social teaching of the encyclicals and the Latin American bishops' conference in such a way that it can be heard. McGrath sees the need for a new Catholic action-like movement that can effectively reach the family, the marketplace and the political leaders with the vision and principles of the social teaching.

Chapter fourteen is by the long-time president of the National Conference of Catholic Bishops of Southern Africa, Archbishop Denis E. Hurley, O.M.I. Hurley was the architect of many anti-apartheid pastoral letters issued in South Africa, well before the issue was fashionable. He is known as a man of character who never hesitates to confront political authorities when issues of justice are at stake.

The hallmark of the new world order is the move toward democratic politics, and Africa is no exception. Recent elections in Ghana and Kenya, however, point out that often leaders and the people are not fully prepared for political freedoms. Archbishop Hurley chose to focus his essay on the need for Catholic social teaching and practice to address the formation of peoples who value and understand freedom and democracy. He notes that the church always has underestimated the challenge of changing attitudes that conversion to Catholic social thought entails and urges that the church move aggressively to group or community formation using the best research. In his own diocese in Durban, South Africa, Hurley has initiated the Renew process, first developed in the archdiocese of Newark, New Jersey. He writes, "Imagine all the parishes of a diocese bristling with small communities and developing, as an essential dimension of the spiritual life of their members, a good dose of social awareness and concern."

Encouraging people to love and understand freedom is surely a major task for Catholic social teaching and practice in the developing world today, and Hurley's essay should alert many to the task ahead.

Twelve

Who Cares about Africa? Development Guidelines from the Church's Social Teaching

Peter J. Henriot, S.J.

Introduction

An exercise that is very popular in the "development education" program in which I worked in villages in southern Zambia during 1989 is called "photo language." Twenty or thirty pictures from magazines or newspapers are laid out in front of a group. The pictures are scenes of people and projects, urban and rural, in Africa and in Europe. The villagers are asked to look over the pictures and then each person has to pick the picture which for her or him best symbolizes the "development" they would like to have in their local area. In small groups, each person uses the picture to talk about what she or he wants and why. The groups then report back and a lively discussion follows about what "development" means for these villagers.

I describe this "photo language" exercise because, through it, the local Zambian villagers taught me a lot about the topic I want to address. To my initial surprise, the people overlooked the pictures of nice suburban homes and high-rise office buildings, of modern kitchen conveniences and high-technology industries. Instead, they chose pictures of mothers and children visiting a well-equipped rural health clinic, of fields of tall maize or herds of fat cattle, of children learning in a local school, of families eating meals together. As they explained it, "development" was for them the chance to meet the basic needs of food, health, economic well-being, education, and so forth. Moreover, they also picked pictures which showed how the people were working with each other—family, friends, neighbors—to bring about improvement.

For these local villagers—as "grassroots" as you could ever be!— "development" simply meant people cooperating together to meet their basic needs. Watching these conclusions come spontaneously from the people themselves, I recalled what my good friend Denis Goulet, of the

University of Notre Dame, repeatedly has said of development, that it is both a means and an end—a *means*: people cooperating with each other; an *end*: improvement in basic livelihood.

A simple exercise to learn a simple lesson. But the experience of a wealth of wisdom which has influenced profoundly what I now share with you. And it is wisdom which I believe could make a difference in our wider world if we really paid attention to it.

Purpose

"Who cares about Africa?" A shocking question? A meaningless question? No, in my opinion, a necessary and disturbing question. There are many reasons to ask that question today. Three global events have diverted the attention—affective and effective—of the countries of the North away from Africa and its 480 million people:[1] the political liberalization of Eastern Europe, the economic unification of Western Europe, and the military confrontation of the Gulf War. Indeed, in the light of these events—encouraging, challenging, frightening—"Who cares about Africa?"

Because I care about Africa, and because I want my church to care about Africa, my purpose in this chapter is (1) to describe the current situation of "maldevelopment" in the sub–Saharan countries of Africa, (2) to present the understanding of "integral development" found in the church's social teaching (CST), and (3) to suggest what the social role of the church might be in addressing the development crisis in Africa today.

The Problem of "Maldevelopment"

Negative Images

It is not easy for me to describe the situation in Africa today. I say that quite honestly because you may have images of Africa as I speak, images which I do not wish to reinforce. Let me explain what I mean. A young African friend of mine recently wrote to me that he felt very depressed when he listened to the litany of woes that people tend to recite regarding Africa:

The white man's grave..Africa
Origins of AIDS ....Africa
The dark continent..Africa
Hunger-ridden land ....Africa
Poverty-stricken ....Africa
Land of refugees...Africa

Tribal fighting...Africa
Cannot decide for themselves ....Africa

My friend was further depressed when he saw some of the literature put out by agencies seeking funds for Africa: "Help the millions dying in Africa!" "Save a black child who has no food!" And always the pictures: mothers in rags; children with sad faces, swollen bellies; scenes of deserts and destitution and desolation. And he asked me quite poignantly, "If you were an African, how would you feel and what would you do, seeing and hearing all that is so negative being communicated about your people and your land?"

I want to respect my friend, and all other Africans, and not simply reinforce those totally negative images of the continent of Africa. It is an astonishingly beautiful land, inhabited by ancient peoples of striking diversity and ingenuity. It is a vast land, potentially very rich with abundant minerals, wildlife and vegetation. It is a land of wonderful culture, fascinating history and inspiring struggle.

Yet the sad but true story is that today it is a land of immense suffering in human terms. Natural disasters of drought and human-made disasters of war have caused millions of deaths in recent years and, even at this very moment, put millions more at risk of death. But the human tragedy on the continent stands most starkly revealed when we look at the seeming inability of African countries to "develop" (and I purposely put that word in quotes) in terms of providing an environment of decent living standards for the majority of their people. The decade of the 1980s has been called "The Lost Decade" for Africa. By almost any measure of economic and social improvement, most African countries are worse off at the start of the 1990s than they were at the start of the 1980s.[2]

What does this mean? I list here a summary of the problems, but I do so with hesitancy. I hesitate not simply because it is so painful and possibly so offensive to my friends. But it is also so dulling. Not dull, for it surely is not that, but dulling, numbing, deadening to our sensitivities because it is so overwhelming, so seemingly hopeless. But we must hear these problems and analyze their roots if we are to understand to what point the "maldevelopment" of orthodox economics has brought us, and if we are to appreciate what a challenge it is to work for "integral development."

Problems

1. Africa is poor. The economic performance for the region as a whole in the 1980s recorded an average annual growth rate in gross domestic product (GDP) of only 0.4 percent, while the average annual

population growth rate was 3 percent. The average growth rate in per capita income declined during the past decade by about 2.6 percent per annum, that is, a negative growth rate. This has meant a sharp decline in the standard of living for most Africans, especially the most vulnerable groups in the population—women, youth, the disabled and the aged.

2. As a result, Africa is unhealthy. Malnutrition rose in the 1980s as the average daily calorie supply per capita dropped. For comparison, that figure today for all of Africa is 2,097, only 60 percent of the 3,645 figure for the United States. Infant mortality rates continue to be high, and in many areas have stopped declining and have begun again to rise in the past few years. Average life expectancy in sub-Saharan Africa is just over 50 years, compared with 76 years in the United States. And the spectre of AIDS grows increasingly frightening—with, you may not immediately realize, a direct link to poverty. I know in Zambia and in many other places that many women resort to prostitution to gain money to feed their children or provide school fees.

3. In Africa, overall production has declined. Agricultural output and particularly food production has been reduced substantially; food production now rises annually more slowly than the population growth rate, about 1.5 percent average compared with 3 percent. Deindustrialization appears to have set in across the continent, with most of Africa's industries operating much below their installed capacities. (The most vibrant economic sector in many parts of Africa is the informal sector, which accounts for 20 percent of the total output and 20 percent of the total labor force.) Africa's share in the world markets has fallen almost half since 1970. Commodity prices fell by 50 percent in the 1980s.

4. One result of a faltering economy is that the physical infrastructure of African countries has experienced significant collapse, due to poor maintenance and lack of renovation. Communications and power systems are weak, paved highways are disintegrating, railway lines are operating poorly, water and sanitation systems are non-functioning. This has consequences not only on personal convenience and health but also, in a major way, on the possibility of effective economic activity.

5. A second result is the growing evidence of rapid deterioration in social services, especially education, public health, housing and transportation. Government spending per capita in the social sectors fell dramatically in the 1980s. School enrollments have actually begun to decline in the primary grades, in spite of an increasing number of children, as parents see no tangible results coming from the overcrowded classrooms devoid of basic materials such as books, chalk, paper and pencils. Hospitals and clinics experience chronic shortages of medicines and instruments. The all-important drive to provide primary health care is thwarted.

6. Africa is a land of refugees. By official estimates, there are over five million refugees today on the continent. If internal refugees and those displaced by conflicts are included in the count, the number rises to more than twenty million. They are driven from their homes by drought, famine, economic deprivation, political oppression and war. These refugees and displaced people put immense strains on the already fragile systems of neighboring regions which receive them. Although international assistance comes to the aid of many refugees, in Africa it is a striking case of the poor welcoming the poor.

7. Finally, Africa faces serious environmental degradation. Population growth rates of over 3 percent means a doubling of population every 20 to 25 years. The pressure from this growing population is accelerating decertification as people and their livestock move farther onto marginal grasslands. Fuel wood (still the primary energy for 80 percent of the people) is increasingly scarce, and the resulting deforestation causes soil erosion and may reduce rainfall further in arid areas. Soil fertility is damaged by overgrazing, erosion, shorter rotations and over-use of fertilizers. Water pollution affects not only drinking sources but fish resources. Unplanned and uncontrolled migrations from rural to urban areas is creating megacities with immense environmental problems.

But, you might ask, is it all that bad? Surely there are bright spots in Africa, pockets of prosperity, stories of economic success, circumstances of notable improvement? True, there are some bright spots, largely due to the extremely hard work of Africans, especially African women. But what is important to grasp here is that the "development" promoted by so many non-Africans and pursued by so many Africans, has not in fact achieved its goal of human improvement.

Reasons

Why has Africa, with such potential in human and natural resources, not "developed"? I want to mention briefly several of the best known reasons—more or less accepted in the development literature about Africa—which are given for the current state of "maldevelopment" in Africa.

1. To begin with, the colonial legacy simply cannot be ignored as a major causal factor. It surely is not the *only* factor, but it is a *major* factor. To ignore its influence is even more dangerous, I believe, than to exaggerate it. The artificial boundaries drawn by the Europeans have been the source of many conflicts. Agricultural and industrial development skewed primarily for the benefit of the colonial power did not adapt easily to a new world of political independence. Commercial, transportation and communication infrastructure likewise was designed for colonial

advantage. With the bulk of the African population denied educational opportunities by the colonialists, the lack of well–trained personnel to take over key political, economic and social responsibilities has had bad consequences from the start.

2. Internal factors certainly account for many of the current problems. Unskilled management has made mistakes; corrupt management has compounded them. Civil wars—frequently along tribal lines—have drained resources. (But who drew the maps which frequently are the cause of such conflicts?) Military spending has diverted scarce funds from more productive areas. (But who sells the sophisticated armaments?) Expenditures on grandiose projects by self-aggrandizing rulers have wasted millions and millions of needed foreign exchange. (But who has advised the investments, supported the dictators, attended the imperial crownings, and blessed the basilicas?)

Moreover, the public economic policies chosen by many African governments were often neither adequately conceived nor efficiently managed. Investments and operating costs are markedly higher in Africa than in other developing countries. Efforts to "socialize" the economy—however laudable in pursuit of greater equity—in most instances have had the opposite consequence of creating a greater gap between rich and poor. For the politicization of the administrative apparatus has caused increased inefficiency and failure to deliver the goods and services.

3. External factors, or the international environment, also figure heavily in causing the current problems and deserve more in-depth analysis here. During recent years, there have been sharp falls in the world price of key commodities. (Zambia, for example, has been hard hit by the precipitous decline in copper prices—close to 40 percent in real terms since Independence in 1964.) This has been accompanied by the rising prices of imports and, most particularly, the dramatic rise in oil prices. With all but a few African countries being oil importers, the terms of trade have declined sharply over the continent.

This situation has led to the well-known and widely experienced "debt crisis," as African countries began borrowing heavily to keep up the levels of expenditures—e.g., on subsidies—which had been possible in earlier, more prosperous years. Total debt increased from $6 billion in 1960 to $134 billion in 1988, a sum about equal to the region's gross national product (GNP) and three-and-a-half times its export earnings. Africa's debt is small in comparison to total developing country debt (only 10 percent), and poses no major threat to the international banking system. But it causes a heavy burden on the nations of Africa, especially the lower-income nations. Debt service obligations—$29 billion in 1988—

amount to almost 50 percent of export revenues, though actual payment on debt service averaged about 27 percent.

This is not the place for a lengthy discussion of African debt.[3] But a few remarks are necessary to see what debt has done to development and, even worse, what debt-management programs have done.

To meet their debt crisis, African countries have entered into the structural adjustment programs mandated by the International Monetary Fund (IMF) and the World Bank. These programs apply across the board the classical instruments of control of the money supply, credit squeeze, adjustments in exchange rates and interests rates, trade liberalization, privatization, curtailment of social services, etc. As demonstrated in recent studies by the United Nations International Children's Emergency Fund (UNICEF), these programs have had very harsh consequences on the majority of the population, the poor.[4] I agree with the judgment of Adebayo Adedeji, United Nations Under Secretary-General and Executive Secretary of the Economic Commission for Africa, that

> in many cases sustained economic growth has not materialized, the rate of investment rather than improve has tended to decrease, budget and balance of payments deficits have tended to widen after some temporary relief and debt service obligations have become unbearable.[5]

Why is this so? What is the reason for the failure of the structural adjustment programs? Again, in the words of Adedeji:

> The overall assessment of orthodox adjustment programs has led to the conclusion that, although these programs aim at restoring growth, generally through the achievement of fiscal and external balances and the free play of market forces, these objectives cannot be achieved without addressing the fundamental structural bottlenecks of African economies.[6]

These structural bottlenecks include the predominance of subsistence and commercial activities in the African economy rather than domestic production, dualistic development patterns, fragmentation of the overall African economy, neglect of the informal sector, excessive dependence on external inputs, and weak, institutional capacities.

There is urgent need to address effectively these harmful structures of the African economy through long-term objectives of social and economic transformation and not merely through a focus on short-term objectives of re-establishing financial balances. In an effort to do that, the United Nations Economic Commission for Africa proposed in 1988 the *African Alternative Framework to Structural Adjustment Programs.* While not being able here to discuss further this framework, I will simply remark that I find its vision to be more in accord with the "integral development" which is the goal of CST.

4. Finally, one root of the problems Africa faces today is a combination of external and internal factors, and is evident in much of what already has been stated. The prevailing influence of Western models, frequently very little suited for the African scene, has had unfortunate consequences. In the sober judgment of the World Bank report:

> The post-independence development efforts failed because the strategy was misconceived. Governments made a dash for "modernization," copying, not adapting, Western models. The result was poorly designed public investments in industry; too little attention to peasant agriculture; too much intervention—in areas in which the state lacked managerial, technical, and entrepreneurial skills; and too little effort to foster grassroots development. This top-down approach demotivated ordinary people, whose energies most needed to be mobilized in the development effort.[7]

To be honest, this influence of inappropriate Western models was a result of the eagerness of African politicians and economists (often Western-trained) and of the persuasion of outside funders and consultants (frequently associated with the World Bank). Moreover, it was not just inappropriate Western models which did not serve well the African people, but also, and in many instances even more so, inappropriate Eastern models. Politics in the past made many African countries look to European and Asian communist states for guidance and assistance. But present economics has made it clear that much of that guidance and assistance has been far from beneficial to the people. Centralized state capitalism within one-party political structures has worked no better in Zambia than it did in Romania.

These, then, are some of the reasons—historical, structural, ideological—which have contributed to the current state of "maldevelopment" in Africa. Of course, it is always easy to look back and see the mistakes of the past. It is much more difficult to propose alternative approaches for the future. Because I am aware of that difficulty, I do not intend to offer any overall plan to move Africa out of its dire situation. But we can be helped greatly by analyzing the concept of "integral development" proposed in CST and so draw some guidelines for correcting the mistakes of the past and evaluating proposals for the future.

The Challenge of "Integral Development"

The use of the word "development" stirs mixed reactions in many scholarly and political circles and is usually seen as both a goal and a process, an end and a means. Depending on the values aimed at and the steps taken to achieve them, different models of development abound. In the 1960s, largely influenced by the thinking of economists such as Rostow, development was viewed as a linear process marked by various "stages" through which a nation progressed, as measured primarily by economic growth rates. At a certain stage of progress, the economy "took off" and became fully "developed" (i.e., structured and functioning like the nations of the industrialized world).[8]

More radical economists, many from the Third World, challenged this narrow notion of development—they called it "developmentalism"--as being inadequate and misleading.[9] It was said to be inadequate because it failed to take sufficient account of the structures of power which determined national progress, and it was misleading because it proposed as a model something which only a few nations could, or should, attain. An ethical critique of developmentalism put forward by some liberation theologians in Latin America[10] and by some Christian humanist thinkers in Europe,[11] challenged the absence of basic human values and moral criteria in the guidance and evaluation of what was being promoted as true development.

It is against this background that we need to review the concept of development espoused in CST.[12] In my opinion, what is presented in CST is more a vision than a program, more a set of principles than a blueprint. There is not a fully coherent and formally delineated theory of development in the various documents of CST. But there is a fairly complete statement of the elements which should go into any approach to development that respects the dignity of a person in the setting of true human community.

Like other components of the social wisdom of the church, the teaching on development rests upon an understanding of human nature and society, an understanding based on biblical revelation, philosophical reasoning, scientific research, and practical experience. It offers us "principles of reflection, norms of judgment, and directives for action" (OA 4) highly relevant to current discussions about human progress across the globe and particularly in Africa.

Drawing upon the major documents of recent CST, I want to propose ten "theses" about development which I believe can serve as guidelines for evaluating what has taken place in recent years in Africa, and will be helpful in suggesting the social role the church might play in improving the human condition in Africa. The development I describe as proposed in CST is frequently styled "integral development," emphasizing from the start of the discussion that it takes into account the whole person in the context of the entire social setting of human community and creation.

The most complete statement in CST of this integral development is found in Paul VI's *The Development of Peoples* (*Populorum Progressio*, 1967). This teaching is updated and elaborated in John Paul II's *The Social Concern of the Church* (*Sollicitudo Rei Socialis*, 1987). These are the two major CST documents on development. But various other aspects of integral development are emphasized in all the recent documents of CST, including John XXIII's *Christianity and Social Progress* (*Mater et Magistra*, 1961) and *Peace on Earth* (*Pacem in Terris*, 1963); the Second Vatican Council's document *The Church in the Modern World* (*Gaudium et Spes*, 1965); the Synod of Bishops' statement, *Justice in the World* (1971); Paul VI's *A Call to Action* (*Octogesima Adveniens*, 1971) and *Evangelization Today* (*Evangelii Nuntiandi*, 1975); and John Paul II's *On Human Work* (*Laborem Exercens*, 1981) and *Christians and the Ecological Crisis* (1990). Significant background to the teaching is to be found also in the earlier statements of Leo XIII, *The Condition of Labor* (*Rerum Novarum*, 1891), and Pius XI, *The Reconstruction of the Social Order* (*Quadragesimo Anno*, 1931).

Well emphasized in studies of CST is the articulation of the church's social wisdom that goes on within the dynamic context of global change—political, economic, social, cultural and religious. CST is necessarily historically influenced which, of course, has consequences for its specific judgments on contemporary events and trends.

As regards development, for example, this point is clearly illustrated in the contrasting evaluations made by John XXIII and John Paul II in documents spanning three decades of crisis and change. Reflecting early in the 1960s, John XXIII makes an *optimistic* judgment about the response to his earlier appeal to rich nations to come to the aid of poor nations:

> We are greatly consoled to see how widely that appeal has been favorably received. And We are confident that even more so in the future it will contribute to the end that the poorer countries, in as short a time as possible, will arrive at that degree of economic development which will enable every citizen to live in conditions more in keeping with their human dignity. (PT 122)

Contrast this with the *pessimistic* appraisal made in the late 1980s by John Paul II of what has actually occurred since the late 1960s: "the hopes for development, at that time so lively, today appear very far from being realized" (SRS 12, 13); "there has been no development—or little, irregular, or even contradictory development" (SRS 35).

Ten Theses

Thesis 1: Integral Development Is at the Service of All Humans

The first thesis on integral development can be the briefest because it is the simplest to understand. Yet, however brief and simple, it is profound in its meaning and its consequences. The greatest document of the Second Vatican Council, *The Church in the Modern World*, presents the core of this thesis: "For the human person is the source, the center, and the purpose of all socioeconomic life" (GS 63). The major orientation of CST is human-centered, a truth which needs strong emphasis in a world of ever increasing technological sophistication. (That truth needs also to be balanced by the truth of a creation-centered outlook, to be discussed in Thesis 9.)

The development possibilities which are now within our grasp are recognized by CST, but equally recognized is the central purpose of all these endeavors: the service of all humans. Again, the Council states:

> Today, more than ever before, progress in the production of agricultural and industrial goods and in the rendering of services is rightly aimed at making provision for the growth of a people and at meeting the rising expectations of the human race. . . . The fundamental purpose of this productivity must not be the mere multiplication of products. It must not be profit or domination. Rather, it must be the service of the human person, and indeed of the whole human person, viewed in terms of their material needs and the demands of their intellectual, moral, spiritual, and religious life. And when we say human person, we mean every human person whatsoever and every group of human persons, of whatever race and from whatever part of the world. Consequently, economic activity is to be carried out according to its own method and laws but within the limits of morality, so that God's plan for humankind can be realized. (GS 64)

As a result of this centrality of the person, the other theses about integral development unfold with a clear logic. Recent CST, however, has indicated that within the focus on the human there must be special focus on the *poor*. This is the now well-known "preferential but non-exclusive option for the poor": preferential because priority is given to the economically disadvantaged; non-exclusive because it does not mean a complete rejection of the non-poor. This option, deeply rooted in scripture and the church's tradition, was articulated in recent decades in the Latin American church but now finds universal expression in CST through the influence of John Paul II. In *On the Social Concern of the Church*, he states that the option is "a special form of primacy in the exercise of Christian charity" and that it applies "to our social responsibilities and hence to our manner of living, and to the logical decisions to be made concerning the ownership and use of goods" (SRS 42).[13]

That this focus on human service is simply not pious words but an expression of political significance is seen when we recall the earlier description given of Africa's "maldevelopment." What has gone on for the past several decades under guise of "development" has not in fact served the people in Africa in any way congruent with this basic thesis. Under colonial rule, the "progress in the production of agricultural and industrial goods and in the rendering of services" was only secondarily directed to the service of Africans. It was mainly for the profit of the colonial powers. All too frequently, such neglect of the people goes on in a politically independent Africa, as a result both of continued economic dependence and also of distorted political priorities favoring those in power.

Thesis 2: Integral Development Is "Being More" Rather than "Having More"

Given the "service of all humans" as the goal of integral development, we should then expect a *human-centered* definition of development. In fact, there has been for several years a generally universal dissatisfaction with the standard *economic-centered* definition of development. This is obvious in the numerous reports, studies and manifestos coming from institutions of the established order (e.g., the World Bank)[14] and of the dissenting ranks (e.g., the South Commission).[15] Something clearly has gone radically wrong in the thinking and action around development when we look back and evaluate three "decades of development" in which billions of dollars have been spent on projects and plans that have resulted in today's "maldevelopment" on a global scale, experienced so profoundly in Africa. In this light, John Paul II's question in *The Social Concern of the Church* is highly challenging: "Hence at this point we have to ask ourselves if the sad reality of today might not be, at least in part, the result of a too narrow idea of development, that is, a mainly economic one" (SRS 15).

To move beyond such a narrow idea of development is to move toward a more complete understanding of what it means to be human. As we saw in Thesis 1, people are conceptually and normatively central to the thrust of CST. For this reason, there is a strong rejection of a merely economic emphasis in the understanding of development. John Paul II has criticized what he terms a "materialistic economism" which gives priority to the products of economic activity rather than to the producer, i.e., a person (LX 7). In *The Development of Peoples*, Paul VI made his position very clear when he wrote: "Development cannot be limited to mere economic growth. In order to be authentic, it must be complete: integral, that is, it has to promote the good of every person and of the whole person" (PP 14). The good of every person requires a *communitarian* vision; the good of the whole person demands a *humanistic* vision.

Stressing the originality of this concept of development, John Paul II stated in *The Social Concern of the Church*:

> True development cannot consist in the simple accumulation of wealth and in the greater availability of goods and services, if this is gained at the expense of the development of the masses, and without due consideration for the social, cultural and spiritual dimensions of the human being. (SRS 9)

What is emphasized here is the simple truth stated by the Second Vatican Council: "The human person is more precious for what she or he is than for what she or he has" (GS 35). "Being" takes priority over "having." "To 'have' objects and goods does not in itself perfect the human subject, unless it contributes to the maturing and enriching of that subject's 'being,' that is to say unless it contributes to the realization of the human vocation as such" (SRS 28).

It may at times be true that the accumulation of more and more material things can be a sign of growth in terms of the strictly economic measurements of GNP per capita. Indeed, it may be a sign of overall improvement in the material quality of life within the human community—a very important goal. Yet it falls short of providing a truly accurate picture of the integral development envisioned by CST. Not only does it not tell us how these material benefits are *distributed* throughout society, but of itself it does not tell us how women and men are progressing in becoming fully human: creative, responsible, loving individuals within a social setting.

It is important to note, however, that the vision of integral development found within CST is not "spiritualistic" in the sense of denying the importance of material growth. Paul VI's classic statement of the meaning of authentic development said: "It is a development which is for each and all the transition from less human conditions to those which are more human" (PP 20). In his list of "less human conditions," he expressly mentions "the lack of material necessities for those who are without the minimum essential for life" and under "conditions that are more human": "the passage from misery towards the possession of necessities" (PP 21).

Because of the importance of meeting the needs of material survival, CST denounces the growing gap between rich and poor, calling the unequal distribution of material resources "one of the greatest injustices in the contemporary world" (SRS 28). But CST does emphasize that the whole person must be considered in any authentic development process. This emphasis on the *integral* character of development is the foundation for the other theses regarding respect for the spiritual, cultural, and communitarian dimensions of development.

In Africa, as in so many other parts of the South, governments fell under the influence of narrow Western models of "development" (and, in many instances, equally narrow Eastern models), in which "modernization" was viewed primarily in economic terms. While leaders professed concern for the people, they spent more financial and intellectual resources on things. A "trickle-down" distributive theory did not, in fact, improve the lot of the poor, by far the majority of the population.

Thesis 3: Integral Development Is a Religious Task, the Work of on-going Creation

Because of its full vision of people, CST has a perspective on development which could be called decidedly religious, i.e., a faith perspective. I believe that this perspective is rooted in the clear rejection by CST of any sort of *dualism*. Christians simply deny their faith in the Incarnation when they make artificial and unnecessary splits or dichotomies between this world and the next, between the material and the spiritual, between the temporal and the eternal, between the secular and the sacred, between body and soul.

Surely there are distinctions to be drawn between promotion of the Kingdom of God and the work for human progress, yet their integral connection is more to be emphasized than their distinction (EN 31). In the view of CST, the values of the Kingdom are already present here in the works of love and justice, community and freedom, cooperation and enterprise, liberation and development. These are works which people endeavor to achieve in community and which Christians recognize as works of the Kingdom. One of the most powerful statements of this view is found in the careful nuances of the justly famous Paragraph 39 of *The Church in the Modern World*, which concludes: "On this earth that kingdom is already present in mystery. When the Lord returns, it will be brought into full flower" (GS 39).

This emphasis opens up a way of viewing integral development as fundamentally a religious task, "a moment in the story which began at creation" (SRS 30). It is the participation by people, made in the image and likeness of the Creator, in the on-going work of creation.

> God who has endowed men and women with intelligence, imagination and sensitivity, has also given them the means of completing

God's work in a certain way: whether she or he be artist or crafts person, engaged in management, industry or agriculture, everyone who works is a creator. (PP 27)

Improving the human condition is the will of God the Creator and the vocation of every person (GS 57, 72).

In *On Human Work*, John Paul II develops this understanding in his reflections on the Genesis story. He stresses that we are all given the vocation to work to "subdue the earth," a task which embraces "every phase of economic and cultural development" (LX 20). It is important to note here that John Paul's Genesis reflection is nuanced much further in the direction of *respect* rather than *domination* of the earth in both *The Social Concern of the Church* (SRS 34) and the 1990 World Day of Peace Message, *Christians and the Ecological Crisis* (CEC 3-5). This point will be addressed under Thesis 9.

Because of this link in CST between development and creation, the task of promoting integral development is not to be seen merely as "lay" or "profane," simply secular work with no ultimate religious value. The use of these categories is a result of highly dualistic thinking, something broken down by a faith vision rooted in scripture. Thus, there is a dignity to the task of promotion of integral development, a dignity intimately related to the Genesis revelation that women and men are made in the image of God the Creator.

Indeed, John Paul offers yet another faith vision of development by moving beyond his Genesis reflections to reflect on a series of Pauline texts which emphasize that the divine plan orders all things to the fullness that dwells in Christ (SRS 31). He sees as a result of this faith vision the "reasons which impel the Church to concern itself with the problems of development, to consider them a duty of its pastoral ministry, and to urge all to think about the nature and characteristics of authentic human development" (SRS 31).

Why is it important to emphasize here this religious dimension to integral development? In evaluating the African situation of "maldevelopment," I consider it yet another reason for viewing the *urgency* of the task of integral development. A Christian simply cannot walk away from the sad state of the globe today, marked as it is with the lack of progress in making "for each and all the transition from less human conditions to those which are more human" (PP 20). God's creative plan is violated in the "maldevelopment" afflicting Africa and many other parts of the world today, a result of human selfishness and apathy. As Paul VI says quite forthrightly: "We must make haste: too many are suffering, and the distance is growing that separates the progress of some and the stagnation, not to say regression, of others" (PP 29).

Thesis 4: Integral Development Requires Respect for All Human Rights and Is Itself a Human Right

The movement from less human conditions to more human conditions—i.e., conditions more in keeping with full human dignity—is the goal to which every person aspires. This accounts for the drive which has been referred to as "the revolution of rising expectations," something that has marked the struggle for development and liberation so dramatically in recent years. In the perspective of CST, this movement is seen not simply as a desirable consequence of human progress but as a fundamental human right. Furthermore, it is seen as intimately related to the hopes and forces spurred on by the dynamism of the Gospel and the power of the Holy Spirit (JW 5; GS 4, 9).

Because it gives such primary emphasis to human dignity, CST places great importance on the understanding and practice of human rights. To be human is to have, by nature and not by social arrangement, certain basic rights, rights which are "universal, inviolable and inalienable" (PT 9). The clearest enunciation of these rights can be found in the opening paragraphs of John XXIII's *Peace on Earth*. Here a fairly complete list of rights is given, covering both what are called political and civil rights, and social and economic rights (PT 11-27). Such rights are central to the movement from less human to more human conditions, i.e., integral development. John clearly echoes the listing of the United Nations Universal Declaration of Human Rights. He states that all rights have reciprocal duties, (1) to exercise them responsibly and (2) to acknowledge and respect the rights of others (PT 28-32).

But John goes further and stresses what is surely a key element in CST: that political society is to be organized to facilitate the recognition and fulfillment of the mutual rights and duties of people. It is a requirement of human society that "all collaborate in the many enterprises that modern civilization either allows or encourages or even demands" (PT 33). Surely, one of the most important "enterprises" demanded by modern civilization today is the task of promoting integral development. To be effective, however, this task requires in many nations a reform of unjust political structures and a movement to more democratic and participatory ones. According to John Paul II:

> The "health" of a political community—as expressed in the free and responsible participation of all citizens in public affairs, in the rule of law and in respect for and promotion of human rights—is the *necessary condition and sure guarantee* of the development of "the whole individual and of all people." (SRS 44)

Some social commentators have criticized the inclusion of "economic and social" rights under the concept of basic human rights. They see it as a dangerous step toward reinforcing the powers of the state, leading to a totalitarian government.[16] In my opinion, this critique has been answered adequately both by other scholars[17] and by John Paul II himself in his treatment of rights in *The Social Concern of the Church*. His broad sketch of the rights which integral development must encompass explicitly lists both legal/political rights and social/economic rights (SRS 15, 34).

With this understanding of human rights as being central to integral development, it is easy to appreciate the teaching of the 1971 Synod of Bishops that development itself is a basic human right. "The right to development must be seen as a dynamic interpretation of all those fundamental human rights upon which the aspirations of individuals and nations are based" (JW 15). Furthermore, "The right to development is above all a right to hope according to the concrete measure of contemporary humanity" (JW 16). To strive to move from less human to more human conditions is a right and a duty to be faced by every person and every society. The national and international structures of society—products of human ingenuity and desires—must make possible the achievement of this right and duty.

The current movement throughout Africa toward more democratic politics can be seen as a step toward implementation of the rights central to integral development. Of course, multi-party systems of participatory democracy do not of themselves assure more development than do one-party systems. But it seems clear from the experience of the past three decades that one-party systems have lacked the political *accountability* which would make them more oriented to serving the people. Any real evaluation of Africa's progress thus must take measure of the full range of human rights, social and economic as well as legal and political.

Thesis 5: Integral Development Recognizes that the Goods of the Earth Are for All People

This is surely the most radical thesis of CST about development, once its full implications are realized, for it states that the common purpose of all created things is to be for the benefit of all people, not simply for the benefit of those who acquired them by wit or wile, labor or luck. According to the Second Vatican Council: "God intended the earth and all that it contains for the use of every human being and people" (GS 69). John Paul II has called this "a faithful echo of the centuries-old tradition of the Church" (SRS 7).

The immediate consequence of this emphasis becomes evident when we see how Paul VI applied the principle in *The Development of Peoples*:

> All other rights whatsoever, including those of property and free commerce, are to be subordinated to this principle. They should not hinder but on the contrary favor its application. It is a grave and urgent social duty to redirect them to their primary finality. (PP 22)

In effect, this principle qualifies two important economic rights which CST also puts forth: (1) the right of private property, expressed throughout the tradition of CST; and (2) the right of economic initiative, explained more recently in *The Social Concern of the Church* (SRS 15). Since, in some circles today, these two rights are extolled without sufficient recognition of this social qualification, I feel that it is important to be more explicit about this thesis.

As is well known, the idea of the right to private property has been central in the tradition of CST. In the face of Marxist denial of this right, Leo XIII proclaimed it clearly in the first modern social encyclical, *The Condition of Labor* (RN 9). It has been repeated in almost every document of CST since that time. But why such an emphasis on private property? Because, in the words of John XXIII in *Christianity and Social Progress*, "in the right of property, the exercise of liberty finds both a safeguard and a stimulus" (MM 109). Ownership of property, even of the means of production, protects individuals from both material deprivations and political oppressions. It also encourages the socially necessary and advantageous virtues of entrepreneurship.

But as strong as has been the support of CST for the right of private property, equally strong has been the assertion that this right is not absolute but carries with it a very serious social obligation. According to Paul VI: "Private property does not constitute for anyone an absolute and unconditioned right. No one is justified in keeping for their exclusive use what they do not need, when others lack necessities" (PP 23). In other words, the right of an individual to hold private property is always limited by the social setting.

It appears that one reason why Paul's 1967 encyclical was banned in some Latin American countries was that he followed up that statement with a specific reference to the large landed estates (*"latifundia"*) which impede general prosperity because of their poor use and the hardships they inflict on people. "The common good," stated Paul, "sometimes demands their expropriation" (PP 23). Such a forthright rejection of an absolute right to private property would have been viewed by many wealthy landowners as an outright call for revolution.

But it is John Paul II who has made even clearer the CST position on private property in light of the thesis that the goods of the earth are for all people. In *On Human Work*, he rejects the understanding of property put forth by both Marxist collectivism and liberal capitalism. According to him, property is acquired through work to serve work. Legitimate title to possession of the means of production, whether owned privately or through public or collective ownership, is only "that they should serve labor, and thus, by serving labor, that they should make possible the achievement of the first principle of this order, namely, the universal destination of goods and the right to the common use of them" (LX 14). John Paul repeats this teaching in *The Social Concern of the Church*, with the felicitous expression: "Private property, in fact, is under a 'social mortgage,' which means that it has an intrinsically social function, based upon and justified precisely by the principle of the universal destination of goods" (SRS 42).

This point is especially important in the discussion of integral development in Africa today. In the wake of the collapse of states in Eastern Europe, there is much talk today about the efficiency of the market and the need for privatization (a position reinforced by the imposition of IMF conditionalities). Capitalism is said to have conquered socialism. Rhetoric may have its appeal, especially in the rich countries of the North, but reality needs to be examined critically. Any such talk needs to be subjected to the principle that the goods of the earth belong to all. It can be stated very clearly, I believe, that economic structures which do not specifically promote that principle—e.g., if they protect private property that does not truly serve the common good—do not have the approval of CST.

Thesis 6: Integral Development Anywhere Requires Integral Development Everywhere

The unevenness throughout the world of the transition from less human conditions to more human conditions is painfully evident. One can take the statistical charts of the World Bank and note infant mortality rates ranging from 172 in Mozambique to 7 in Sweden; or life expectancy ranging from 46 years in Chad to 78 years in Japan; or adult illiteracy rates ranging from 83 percent in Mali to less than 5 percent in Europe. Or one can walk the streets of Lagos or Calcutta or Lima; then stand in line in the markets of Bucharest or Moscow or Hanoi; then tour the shopping malls of New York or Paris or Tokyo. The various parts of the world are increasingly separated by a widening gap, measured in terms of a variety of economic and social indicators. As a consequence, we readily speak today of different worlds within our one world: First, Second, Third, even Fourth

World. "Such expressions," says John Paul II, "are significant: they are a sign of a widespread sense that the *unity of the world*, that is, *the unity of the human race*, is seriously compromised" (SRS 14).

This gap is described in *The Church in the Modern World* in terms of social inequalities present both among nations and within nations:

> While an enormous mass of people still lack the absolute necessities of life, some, even in less advanced countries, live sumptuously or squander wealth. Luxury and misery rub shoulders. While the few enjoy very great freedom of choice, the many are deprived of almost all possibility of acting on their own initiative and responsibility, and often subsist in living and working conditions unworthy of human beings. (GS 63)

This unequal distribution of the means of subsistence meant for everyone and of the benefits deriving therefrom is not, according to John Paul II, the fault of the needy or the inevitable outcome of the natural order of things. It is the consequence of personal decisions and decisions of governments, all of which much be critically analyzed and morally evaluated (SRS 9).

What consequence does this division caused by the gap have on the human community worldwide? Here the message of CST is very clear. In the blunt words of *The Development of Peoples*: "The world is sick" (PP 66). Paul VI expands his judgment further by explaining: "There can be no progress towards the complete development of humans without the simultaneous development of all humanity in the spirit of solidarity" (PP 43). In Paul's analysis, he sees an eroding of true humanity in the excessive accumulation of the goods of the earth by a small minority of the human family while the majority of the family lacks basic essentials. John Paul II gives as an example of this the "consumerism" which marks a distorted "superdevelopment" in the rich countries (SRS 28).

Such an integral link among nations is not always recognized or accepted in the politics and economics of today. *Peace on Earth* had stressed earlier the structural relationships between nations: "At the present time no political community is able to pursue its own interests and develop itself in isolation, because its prosperity and development are both a reflection and a component part of the prosperity and development of all the other political communities" (PT 131). John Paul II analyzes this link further, using the category of *interdependence*, for he sees negative consequences coming to the rich countries when they ignore the objective situation of the poor countries:

> Thus it should be obvious that development either becomes shared in common by every part of the world or it undergoes a process of

regression even in zones marked by constant progress. This tells us a great deal about the nature of authentic development: either all the nations of the world participate, or it will not be true development. (SRS 17)

What can bring about more effective and uniform development worldwide? According to Paul VI and John Paul II, *solidarity*—both as a moral virtue and as a political act—is essential. The term is particularly associated with the Polish pope. Having developed it *On Human Work* in the context of "solidarity of workers and with the workers" (LX 8), John Paul goes on to apply it more systematically to the world scene in *The Social Concern of the Church*. He sees this solidarity demanding (1) on the part of the more influential, a responsibility and a readiness to share; (2) on the part of the weaker, an active claiming of their legitimate rights; and (3) on the part of intermediate groups, a respect for the interests of others (SRS 39). While I believe that this "class analysis" of John Paul needs much further clarification, particularly relating to the power relationships inherent in the structures of interdependence and solidarity,[18] his emphasis has value in highlighting the significance of the common sharing of integral development.

Two practical consequences of this solidarity between rich and poor are (1) the provision of foreign assistance in the form of grants, loans, technical aid, etc., and (2) the design of equitable structures of trade, investment and monetary arrangements. *The Church in the Modern World* states that "the advanced nations . . . have a very heavy obligation to help the developing peoples" (GS 86). Paul VI, in his 1967 letter, outlined in detail the duty of the rich nations to provide aid to the poor (PP 45-55) and to redress unjust patterns of trade (PT 56-61). In speaking of the responsibility to provide aid, CST has emphasized strongly the need to avoid any manipulation or domination. The possibility of neo-colonialism under the guise of assistance is especially singled out as a serious danger (MM 171-174; PT 125; PP 52; JW 16). It is significant that in *The Social Concern of the Church*, John Paul II says little about aid but spends considerable time addressing the need to correct the imbalance in the international systems of trade, monetary relationships and finance, technical transfer and international organizations (SRS 43).

Today, Africa experiences serious problems regarding both these aspects of solidarity. Overall aid levels have fallen dramatically in recent years. Commodity prices in real terms are the lowest since the 1940s. It is true that worldwide response to the disasters of famine and refugees has been periodically very generous. But long-term, sustained solidarity at a structural level—central to integral development worldwide—has been weakened in recent years.

Thesis 7: Integral Development Is Linked to Peace

Surely one of the most celebrated phrases in recent CST is from Paul VI's *The Development of Peoples*: "Development is the new name for peace" (PP 76). In this phrase, Paul recognizes the link between promotion of integral development and the work for peace. It is a two-fold link: (1) a world filled with poor and oppressed people will not be a peaceful world; and (2) a world preparing for war or actually waging war will not be a world wherein people move from less human to more human conditions.

Peace and the conditions necessary for peace have been central to the tradition of CST. The popes and the Second Vatican Council have endorsed strongly the building of a world order in which peoples and nations could live in harmony. But the emphasis always has been on the reality that peace is not simply the absence of conflict. Rather, it is the presence of a structured order of national and international society within which justice and development occur. This emphasis is made clear in a unique fashion in the only encyclical which would seem, at least by title, to be addressed specifically to the topic of peace, John XXIII's "last will and testament," *Peace on Earth*. In this letter of 173 numbered paragraphs, only eleven paragraphs explicitly deal with the topic of war, and here only under the heading of disarmament (109-119). The remainder of the document treats quite thoroughly human rights, political authority and international relationships. What John makes clear is that justice in both the national and international orders is necessary for the genuine promotion of a lasting peace.

This point was clearly made by Paul VI:

> Peace cannot be limited to a mere absence of war, the result of an ever more precarious balance of forces. No, peace is something that is built up day after day, in the pursuit of an order intended by God, which implies a more perfect form of justice among humans. (PP 76)

The wisdom of this emphasis in CST has become more and more evident in recent years as conflicts have flared in many parts of the world because of the struggle for justice. Faced with the oppressive structures of an entrenched and privileged elite, many popular movements have resorted to violence. In the words of John Paul II, "Peoples excluded from the fair distribution of the goods originally destined for all could ask themselves: why not respond with violence to those who first treat us with violence?" (SRS 10). There can be no peace in the full sense when the inhuman situations of hunger, poverty, and the lack of basics afflict the majority of the population. Conditions of true development are necessary for true peace.

But the other side of the thesis is equally true. Preparations for war and the actual waging of war destroy precious resources, divert immediate assistance, distract urgent attention, and distort realistic priorities. It is obvious today that "war and military preparations are the major enemy of the integral development of peoples" (SPS 10). The gross distortion of priorities is surely fresh in our minds when we reflect on the immense cost of the recent Gulf War, estimated roughly at one billion dollars a day.[19] Highly sophisticated war technology is extremely expensive. For example, the Patriot antimissile missile costs $1.1 million (5200 were available for use in the Middle East); the Tomahawk computer-guided cruise missile fired from the USS Wisconsin battleship costs $1.35 billion; and the F-15 E attack-fighter jet, equipped for precision bombing, costs $50.43 million.[20]

The authoritative report on social and military expenditures prepared annually by Ruth Sivard makes abundantly clear the consequences of the arms race, as rich nations and poor nations alike spend more on instruments of mass destruction than on investments in human progress.[21] The judgment of *The Church in the Modern World* in 1965 is all the more true today: "The arms race is an utterly treacherous trap for humanity, and one which injures the poor to an intolerable degree" (GS 81). And *Justice in the World* states: "The arms race is a threat to the human's highest good, which is life; it makes poor peoples and individuals yet more miserable, while making richer those already powerful" (JW 9).

John Paul II makes a critique of arms production and the arms race central to his analysis of the reasons for underdevelopment in the world today. In a world of restricted general trade, he notes a disturbing phenomenon: "While economic aid and development plans meet with the obstacle of insuperable ideological barriers, and with tariff and trade barriers, arms of whatever origin circulate with almost total freedom all over the world" (SRS 24). Given the gross distortions of military spending and the frightening stockpiling of destructive weapons, "The prevailing picture is one destined to lead us more quickly toward death rather than one of concern for true development which would lead all towards a 'more human' life" (SRS 10).

Wars in Africa have caused extensive damage to populations, environment, and the basic infrastructures of economic growth. We need only to look to the Horn of Africa to see the effects over the years of the ravages of war compounded by arms sales from both East and West. Development of any sort—integral or otherwise—is out of the question while cruel civil wars rage on in Ethiopia, the Sudan and Somalia.[22] The other most notable instance of the effects of war is in Southern Africa, where the destabilization policy of the Pretoria government has been devastating for its neighbors. The World Bank reports studies which indicate the quantifiable costs to nations in Southern Africa of this policy approach 25 to 40 percent of GDP annually.[23]

The intimate link between integral development and respect for the environment, a point to be taken in Thesis 9, also has bearing on the link between peace and development. This is brought out in the 1990 World Day of Peace Message, in which John Paul II warns against the dangerous menace posed by the severe environmental damage inflicted during modern warfare. In words poignantly prophetic of what would actually occur one year later in the Gulf War, the pope warns that wars

> not only destroy human life and social structures, but also damage the land, ruining crops and vegetation as well as poisoning the soil and water. The survivors of war are forced to begin a new life in very difficult environmental situations of extreme social unrest, with further negative consequences for the environment. (CEC 12)

Thesis 8: Integral Development Puts High Priority on Agriculture

During the First Development Decade of the 1960s, under the influence of an economic model of development which emphasized industrialization as central to "take off" in the countries of the South, the agricultural sector was sorely neglected. Adequate attention was not given to provision of rural services and inputs for farmers, such as equipment, credit and marketing, transport, extension training, and so forth. Urban dwellers were favored, with a consequent movement, especially among young people, to the cities. But the agricultural sector is still a key factor in any future development, accounting as it does for 33 percent of Africa's GDP, 66 percent of its labor force, and 40 percent of its exports.

Early CST had focused primarily on industrial problems. But with John XXIII, who was himself raised on a farm, agricultural issues came to the fore in CST. In *Christianity and Social Progress*, John speaks strongly about the need to address the serious problems of agriculture (MM 123-156). He points to the fact that "rural dwellers leave the fields because nearly everywhere they see their affairs in a state of depression, both as regards labor productivity and the level of living of farm populations" (MM 123). In eloquent words, he speaks of the dignity of the vocation of farmers:

To them it should be quite evident that their work is most noble, because it is undertaken, as it were, in the majestic temple of creation; because it often concerns the life of plants and animals, a life inexhaustible in its expression, inflexible in its laws, rich in allusions to God, Creator and Provider. (MM 144)

John Paul II refers to agriculture as being of "fundamental importance" and "the basis for a healthy economy" (LX 21).

A central issue in agricultural development is agrarian reform, or reform in land tenure. As we have seen in discussing private property, this issue has been returned to repeatedly in CST in recent years with a bluntness which has not failed to create controversy. Both the Second Vatican Council (GS 71) and Paul VI (PP 24) criticized the large landed estates that were not used properly to serve the populations. The common good can demand their expropriation. *On Human Work* also pointed to this serious problem: "In certain developing countries, millions of people are forced to cultivate the land belonging to others and are exploited by the big landowners, without any hope of ever being able to gain possession of even a small piece of land of their own" (LX 21).

In most of Africa, the chief agricultural problem is not large estates and landless workers, but low productivity. Integral development demands much greater attention to the needs of the rural sector, recognizing it as the primary source of healthy national growth. In particular, the challenge of providing food security to the nations of Africa must be met. Too many people are undernourished, too much food must be imported, and too little agricultural potential is used. In further development of agriculture, however, environmental issues must be taken seriously and sustainable agricultural techniques fostered.

Thesis 9: Integral Development Is Ecologically Responsible

Concern for the environment is a relatively new concept in CST. Indeed, some ecological writers have blamed religious thinking for promoting an anthropocentric worldview which has accounted for a disregard for nature. In 1971, one year prior to the United Nations Conference of Environment in Stockholm, two CST documents did point to the dangers of pollution and exploitation of resources. Paul VI warns in *A Call to Action* that humans risk destroying nature and, in turn, becoming the victim of nature's degradation (OA 21). The Synod statement on *Justice in the World* speaks of natural resources as the "unique patrimony belonging to all humankind," which should not be treated as infinite but should be saved and preserved (JW 8).[24] Furthermore, it criticizes the high rates of consumption and pollution that mark the economic patterns of the richer nations, having damaging consequences for the whole of humanity (JW 11).

But it is *The Social Concern of the Church* that presents the first full CST statement on the respect due to nature. According to John Paul, "Nor can the moral character of development exclude respect for beings which constitute the natural world, which the ancient Greeks—alluding precisely to the order which distinguishes it—call the 'cosmos'" (SRS 34). Besides repeating the standard concern for limited resources and unhealthy pollution, the pope goes on to add a third consideration, namely, the intimate links which all created things—including humans—have with each other. Therefore, "one must take into account the nature of each being and of its mutual connection in an ordered system, which is precisely the 'cosmos'" (SRS 34).

This third consideration is sometimes referred to as "ecological consciousness," as distinct from the "environmental concern" shown regarding resources and pollution. Ecological consciousness recognizes that humans belong to the community of creation and, as such, have certain duties to respect the inherent structure of the natural order, "the need to respect the integrity and the cycles of nature" (SRS 26). The implications for integral development are made explicit by John Paul: "A true concept of development cannot ignore the use of the elements of nature, the renewability of resources and the consequences of haphazard industrialization—three considerations which alert our consciences to the moral dimension of development" (SRS 34).

Just how central to CST this ecological consciousness is to become in the future is evident in the 1990 World Day of Peace Message, *Christians and the Ecological Crisis.* Here, John Paul II goes much more into depth on the moral responsibility of all humans to respect the "integrity of creation" (a significant phrase used by the World Council of Churches). He builds his case for this responsibility on two concepts. (1) There is "a harmonious universe . . . a 'cosmos' endowed with its own integrity, its own internal, dynamic balance. This order must be respected." (2) Furthermore, "the earth is ultimately a common heritage, the fruits of which are for the benefit of all" (CEC 8). Any effort at development which ignores these two concepts can lead only to disaster.

So important for integral development is this respect for the environment that we can even speak of a "right to a safe environment," one which should be included in an updated Charter of Human Rights (CEC 9). This right is dangerously threatened in Africa by unchecked demographic factors, rural poverty and urban congestion, and curtailment of environmental protection activities because of serious financial constraints.

Furthermore, some desperately poor African countries are negotiating with industrial countries in the North to sell sites for toxic waste disposal—certainly a threat to the "right to a safe environment" today and in the future.

John Paul sees the global ecological situation revealing the urgent need for a new solidarity, especially in relationships between rich countries and poor countries. Echoing many of the concerns of the poor countries, the pope argues that these countries cannot be asked to apply strict environmental standards to their emerging industries if the rich countries do not first do the same within their own boundaries. Nevertheless, the poor countries must not repeat the errors made in the past by the rich and cause reckless damage to the environment through pollution, deforestation, and exhaustion of non-renewable resources. The ecological crisis faced on a global scale demands an approach to development marked by solidarity (CEC 10).

Thesis 10: Integral Development Respects Cultural Values

Precisely because of the emphasis in Thesis 2 that integral development involves "being more" rather than "having more," cultural values assume a central importance. In his list of conditions that are "more human," and hence whose attainment signify greater development, Paul VI lists "the acquisition of culture" (PP 21). He goes on to caution poorer nations to protect their culture, especially against temptations coming from wealthier nations, lest they lose the best of their "patrimony" (PP 40-41).

Thus, the concern of CST about culture as it relates to integral development can be said to be two-fold: to *foster* and to *protect*. The need to foster arises from the recognition that people have a right to culture, a right exercised, for example, in pursuing a basic education (PT 13; GS 60). No true development is possible without commitment to the growth in people's innate potentials. But there is also a need to protect what is good in one's own culture, resisting influences which erode the values proper and precious in a society. Nations should respect each others' peculiar "moral heritage and ethnic characteristics," avoiding domination of any sort (PT 125).

But what are we speaking about when we refer to "culture"? Sociologists and anthropologists come up with many definitions, most of which refer to both (1) the beliefs, values, attitudes and customs of society, especially religious and ethnic traditions and symbols; and (2) the activities in society which express, enrich and transform these elements, such as music, art, literature and the media.[25] Culture is the deep "soul" of a people and a nation. Hence the importance of the question put by the Second Vatican Council in its extensive treatment of human culture: "How can the vitality and growth of a new culture be fostered without the loss of living fidelity to the heritage of tradition?" (GS 56; 53-62).

Recognition of the damage done to culture by pursuit of a purely economic model of development is now commonplace in most development circles. Even the World Bank has hired anthropologists to help understand the cultural dimensions of new projects and avoid the numerous mistakes of the past. It is increasingly recognized that the process of development is not a "value-free" process, but brings with it a whole series of cultural values: rationality, efficiency, mastery of nature, reliance on technology, growth, consumption, and so forth. That these values frequently clash with the more traditional—and higher—values of many in the poor world is emphasized in CST (MM 175-177).

An increasing number of development analysts and practitioners are placing great emphasis on the link between culture and development. What John Paul II emphasized in *The Social Concern of the Church* about "the ethical and cultural character of the problems connected with development" (SRS 8) is the subject of numerous publications[26] and, recently, of an international network of scholars.[27] There is significance in the fact that we are now into another "United Nations Decade," but this time not of "Development" but of "Culture." Integral development demands this attention to culture in all aspects of planning and implementation.

Recognition of the specific role cultural values should play in the task of integral development in Africa is given in the 1985 statement of the Symposium of Episcopal Conferences of Africa and Madagascar (SECAM). The bishops call for a clear look at the "values on which we must count in building an Africa where everyone will blossom in self-fulfillment in becoming more human."[28] Among these values they list human relations put above economic relations, a sense of celebration and sharing, communal solidarity, hospitality, a sense of family, and an appreciation of the sacred. According to the bishops, "It is this cultural vitality which is the greatest support of the African peoples in their struggle for total liberation and the building of a society capable of facing the problems of our time."[29]

Difficulties

Before concluding this section on the CST vision of integral development, I want to mention three difficulties or deficiencies which I see in the teaching. While global in character, they have special meaning in Africa. They relate to (1) the role of women, (2) the issue of demographics, and (3) the strategy of change.

1. CST has been woefully negligent of attending to the role of women in the process of development. This point has immense importance in

Africa, where 70-80 percent of the food production is done by women. Within the past decade it has been obvious that no adequate description of the problems of development and no effective prescription of solutions to be taken is possible without specific attention begin paid to what is referred to as the "gender dimensions of development." The South Commission states the issue as follows:

> Women account for more than half of the South's population. They participate in the development process in a myriad of ways, but their contribution to economic and social change continues to be inadequately recognized and greatly undervalued, because male-dominated cultures have given them an inferior position in society, and custom, taboo, and the sexual division of labor keep them subordinate to men.[30]

It is unfortunate that in its otherwise comprehensive analysis of the elements of integral development, CST gives the impression that women's contributions are "inadequately recognized and greatly undervalued." It is true that CST has strong statements rejecting discrimination based on sex (GS 29, 60) and that John XXIII names as a "sign of the times" the struggle by women to claim in every sphere of life "the rights and duties that befit a human person" (PT 41). Yet, when women are discussed at length in CST it is generally in the context of marriage and family. As several feminist scholars have pointed out, this may be the result of an emphasis on the "proper nature" and "proper role" of the woman— seeming to imply that women have a "nature" distinct from men's.[31] As a result, insufficient attention is paid both to the massive contributions made by women to economic development (e.g., food production and health care) and social development (e.g., education), and to the massive obstacles they face (e.g., suffering disproportionately from poverty, illiteracy and malnutrition).

This neglect to deal with the gender issue is painfully obvious in both Paul VI's and John Paul II's very thorough treatments of development in their 1967 and 1987 letters. It is all the more striking in John Paul's case, since his letter was published after the topic had been exhaustively examined in development circles throughout the world. Such neglect surely prompts those of us committed to CST to examine the influence of, in the words from the South Commission, "male-dominated cultures" and "custom, taboo, and the sexual division of labor."

2. A second difficulty in CST's perspective on integral development relates to the demographic issue. This is a sensitive issue for the church because it is linked to doctrine on the morality of family planning methods. As a result, it has not always been treated as forthrightly as it deserves.

It is my opinion that the very important values which CST proposes regarding the family and the rights of parents to determine the number of their children, as well as its strong emphasis on social justice in dealing with population questions, is sometimes overshadowed by the insistence on adherence to its strict teaching on artificial contraception. Promotion of "natural family planning" is important for psychological, health and moral reasons. But can it be and should it be the *only* approved method?

The seriousness of demographic growth rates is downplayed by John XXIII in his treatment of the relationships between population and development in *Christianity and Social Progress* (MM 185-192). He questions the statistical reasoning that argues that a crisis is in the offing if the population outstrips food resources, and he relies on technological breakthroughs and greater sharing through international cooperation. Ultimately, he relies on Divine Providence, as he reiterates that no methods and means to limit population growth can be used which are contrary to human dignity. This ruling out of any population planning which incorporates artificial contraception is repeated by the Council (GS 51), by *The Development of Peoples* (PP37), and by Paul VI's 1967 encyclical *On the Regulation of Birth* (*Humanae Vitae*). It is true that *The Development of Peoples* does acknowledge the role of the government in meeting the demographic challenge by "favoring the availability of appropriate information and by adopting suitable measures" but always within conformity to the moral law against artificial contraception (PP 37).

John Paul II has reiterated strongly many times the teaching on birth control. But in his *The Social Concern of the Church*, he limits his remarks to criticizing most sharply the "systematic campaigns against birth," the "result of pressure and financing coming from abroad," and "an absolute lack of respect" for the freedom of the parents (SRS 25). He does acknowledge the existence of "a demographic problem which creates difficulties for development" (SRS 25).

What seems to be the heart of the difficulty here in CST is, I believe, the failure to come to grips realistically with the rapid population growth in the South. Africa's growth rate of over 3 percent annually means a doubling of the population every 20 to 25 years—with staggering consequences on the size of cities and the demand for jobs, services and resources. This growth rate may, of course, be tragically affected by the deadly path of AIDS. But for now, the church needs to support planning for dealing more effectively with the issue—planning which does indeed respect human dignity and morality but which also acknowledges serious differences of opinion—medical, sociological, cultural, theological and pastoral—on the application of the traditional teaching against artificial contraception. Promotion of "natural family planning" is important for psychological, health and moral reasons. But can it be and should it be the only approved method?

3. I believe CST is weak analytically in its view of the process for bringing about change. It is true that CST does take seriously the power of social structures. In his account of "less human conditions," Paul VI refers to "oppressive social structures, whether due to abuses of ownership or to the abuses of power, to the exploitation of workers or to unjust transactions" (PP 21). The 1971 Synod statement, *Justice in the World*, highlights the influence of social structures, speaking of the "systematic barriers and vicious circles" which block true development. *The Social Concern of the Church* presents John Paul II's sophisticated analysis of the power of ideologies and structures to perpetuate the suffering of the poor world. He adds to his sociopolitical analysis of the superpower blocs a theological analysis of the "structures of sin" which today can be found in the attitudes and actions that flow from the "all-consuming desire for profit, and . . . the thirst for power" (SRS 36-37).

But CST does not seem to have a correspondingly in-depth analysis of how structural change can be effected. What is desired is not a set of plans for organized change, for that would be beyond the competence of CST. But we might expect at least a recognition of the conflict of interests among various actors, the significance of power arrangements, the interconnections between economic and political structures, and the challenge of organizing coalitions which effectively empower the poor and oppressed. Without such an analysis, there is danger of recommendations being dismissed as mere moralisms. What seems to be endorsed as a strategy for change is in effect a call more to personal conversion to solidarity than to structural change to justice.[32]

Africa today is at the crossroads of a set of power relationships— economic and political—which are shifting dramatically as a result of shifts in other parts of the world. The future of the continent depends not only on the struggles of Africans themselves but also on the actions of key actors in the North. Consequently, CST has to probe more deeply the structural influences as well as ideological stances which determine the direction of that future.

The Social Role of the Church

We have analyzed the situation of "maldevelopment" which afflicts Africa today, and have summarized the vision of "integral development" which CST proposes. What can we say now about the task of the church in efforts to transform the present situation? What is the social role the church could and should play in participating in the development drama occurring today in Africa?

At the outset, it is important to recall both the proper activity in which the church can engage and the proper limit to its competence. At the beginning of *The Social Concern of the Church*, John Paul II makes clear why the church considers it fitting to involve itself in matters of development. Precisely because of the "ethical and cultural character of problems connected with development," there is a "legitimacy and necessity" in such involvement (SRS 8). Yet, it is not for the church to get into specific details about different approaches to development. This is a point CST has always made clear, as in this statement from the 1971 Synod of Bishops:

> Of itself it does not belong to the church, insofar as it is a religious and hierarchical community, to offer concrete solutions in the social, economic and political spheres for justice in the world. Its mission involves defending and promoting the dignity and fundamental rights of the human person. (JW 37)

Within its proper competence, then, the social role of the church has wide scope. This is particularly true when we take the "church" in its fullest sense as the "People of God," and do not think in narrow terms only of bishops and other church officials.

In Africa

The Catholic church in Africa is one of the fastest growing Christian communities in the world. "Five years ago, African Catholics numbered about 64 million (12 percent of the whole population); today they are 73 million (12.5 percent). In no other continent do we witness a similar growth."[33] Although in most of the continent the church has been established for only about one hundred years, today it is strong in personnel, institutions, and pastoral practice. There are, of course, many difficulties. One is the serious shortage of priests to serve the fast-growing population. Every Sunday, more and more Catholics throughout Africa attend non-Eucharistic services.

At the present moment, the church in Africa is preparing for the African Synod (officially known as "The Special Assembly for Africa of the Synod of Bishops), to be held sometime in 1993. The focus for the Synod is "The Church in Africa toward the Third Millennium," and one major theme area is "Justice and Peace." It is important to note that the preliminary study guide (*"lineamenta"*) for raising issues to be considered by the Synod speaks directly to the link between evangelization and development. It states that the Synod itself should be "the occasion to present clearly to all the Christians of Africa their duty and responsibility to transform society in its economic, social, political and cultural aspects" (no. 84).

For a variety of reasons, the church in Africa has not been as outspoken on social issues as has been the church in other parts of the world, for example, in Latin America. Some of these reasons may be: the church is still young; in many places its ministers are still disproportionately expatriate; it operates in a cultural milieu which shows deference to those in political authority; and in general it lacks many resources for social analysis and teaching about social issues.

Nevertheless, an increasing number of church social statements have come out in recent years from individual bishops, national conferences, and regional gatherings. These statements have addressed a variety of economic and social crises, political challenges and cultural issues. At least in a few instances, the statements have been made at great risk, when a courageous stance has been taken in the face of strong governmental opposition. Two recent examples of this occurred in 1990 in Kenya and Zambia.[34]

I believe the primary social role of the church as regards development in Africa is to keep in front of the public—political leadership as well as ordinary citizens—the vision of a model of development which puts people first. The integral development CST proposes needs constant emphasis these days, especially in light of the serious economic problems being faced throughout Africa. The structural adjustment programs being designed by the IMF and World Bank place priority on getting an efficiently operating economy able to restore fiscal balance. Efficiency is measured in strict economic terms of reduced budgets, increased imports, greater productivity and, of course, regular servicing of debts. The social consequences of such efficiency is treated as a problem to be dealt with only by remedial "social action programs" designed as a buffer to the harsh impact on the poor majority of the restructuring.

Government officials, political parties, international agencies, banks and businesses both national and international, all need to be reminded that the economy is at the service of the people and not vice versa. But what institution has the moral influence of the church to speak out this truth? As mentioned previously, reports from UNICEF and the UN Economic Commission for Africa have made abundantly clear the facts about the social consequences of current economic policies in Africa. In the promotion of integral development, then, the church through its leadership and its laity involved in public affairs plays an important social role in keeping these facts in front of decision makers and the general public.

In speaking about the consequences in people's lives of certain economic policies, the church is supporting the cause of social justice by promoting *human rights*. It is important to remind authorities that *economic and social rights* are also central to the United Nations Universal Declaration of Human Rights and, very relevantly, to the "African Charter on Human and Peoples' Rights" of the Organization of African Unity (1981). An authority—national or international—which dictates a development policy resulting, for example, in the increased malnutrition of children or a curtailment of basic health services, is just as guilty of violating human rights as is an authority which unjustly imprisons its citizens or restricts their right of free speech. The church has an obligation to speak out about this injustice and to promote effective action to counter it.

Moreover, the church in Africa should make its voice heard also in the rich countries of the North. This voice should not speak only of the need for *charity* in the current desperate situation but also, and especially, for *justice*. True solidarity, in the sense in which CST proposes it, demands addressing the international structures that block development in Africa. These are the "structures of sin" condemned by John Paul II (SRS 39). Instances of this social role being played have been visits in recent years by African church leaders to Europe and the United States to put the case of their people before both political officials and the general public.

Another major social role the church can play in Africa is to promote integral development itself through its many institutions and projects. It does this already in many significant ways in most countries. Besides pastoral programs of catechesis and sacraments, the church sponsors schools, hospitals and numerous social projects. Starting from the earliest missionaries, the church in Africa has worked to promote human development through agricultural projects, employment schemes, cooperatives and credit unions, youth technical training, and so forth. This is in accord with the understanding of evangelization Paul VI articulated in *Evangelization Today*, stressing the link between evangelization and development/liberation (EN 30).

In exercising this social role which promotes integral development, the church needs to pay special attention to two things. First, it should try to involve the people as much as possible in identifying the problems, planning the solutions, and implementing the projects. Participation is the key if the people are to be *subjects* of development and not simply *objects* of development. One program widely used in several parts of Africa that promotes this development participation is *Training for Transformation*, which puts into practice the Paulo Freire approach of "conscientization."[35]

Second, the church should strongly promote self-reliance in all its development programs. A "hand out" approach should be avoided. This is not always easy to do. On the part of some church personnel, there is a sense of generosity which occasionally militates against asking the people to help themselves. And on the part of many participants in the programs, there is frequently a mentality (conditioned by previous experiences) which expects something for nothing. But if integral development is to be promoted, self-help and self-reliance is essential.

Finally, the church has a role to play in witnessing in its own manner of living and decision making to the values essential for true human development. What the 1971 Synod of Bishops said about the promotion of justice in general has relevance to the promotion of integral development: "While the church is bound to give witness to justice, it recognizes that anyone who ventures to speak to people about justice must first be just in their eyes" (JW 40). Many of the values of integral development we analyzed in thesis form in the second part of this paper have application within the life of the church: service of the whole person, option for the poor, respect for human rights, genuine solidarity, respect for culture, and so forth.

Within Africa, the church should witness to a life-style that does not separate it from the people, the vast majority of whom are quite poor. As recognized in several places in recent CST, this has implications for such things as church buildings and ornamentations. John Paul II makes this point explicitly in *The Social Concern of the Church* when he reminds us that in the face of the urgent needs of the poor, "one cannot ignore them in favor of superfluous church ornaments and costly furnishings for divine worship" (SRS 31). Those who would argue that it is right and proper for the African church to have as grand a style of church as does Europe must deal with the even sharper critique offered by Paul VI in speaking of wasteful expenditures which result from pride:

> When so many people are hungry, when so many families suffer from destitution, when so many remain steeped in ignorance, when so many schools, hospitals and homes worthy of the name remain to be built, all public or private squandering of wealth, all expenditure prompted by motives of national or personal ostentation . . . becomes an intolerable scandal. We are conscious of our duty to denounce it. Would that those in authority listened to our words before it is too late! (PP 53)

In North America

There is also a social role for the church outside Africa in confronting the challenge of integral development within Africa. With due modification, the message of the social role of the church in the United States can be applied to other churches within the rich world.

As was highlighted in the discussion of Thesis 6, a necessary inter-connection exists between development in one part of the world and development in other parts. John Paul II has pointed to that in his stress on the fact of "interdependence" and his insistence that this interdependence "must be transformed into solidarity" (SRS 39). On the part of a rich nation like the United States, that solidarity translates into specific obligations regarding poorer nations such as in Africa.

> Surmounting every type of imperialism and determination to pre-serve their own hegemony, the stronger and richer nations must have a sense of moral responsibility for the other nations, so that a real international system may be established which will rest on the foundation of the equality of all peoples and on the necessary respect for their legitimate differences. (SRS 39)

While many people in the United States may not be comfortable to hear their nation's international activity characterized by the words "imperial-ism" and "hegemony," the fact is that many people in Africa feel that these words are quite fitting descriptions of what they experience.

Given this challenge to foster a "sense of moral responsibility" as relates to the international order, the church in the United States can act to promote global integral development. In recent years, the National Conference of Catholic Bishops in the United States has exercised an impressive role in speaking out on important issues of social order. Most noteworthy are the pastoral letters on peace (1983) and on economic justice (1987). In both of these letters, the issues of international development are significantly treated, both in themselves and as they are related to domestic issues and policies.

What can the church in the United States do regarding the challenge of integral development in Africa? First and foremost, the church should remind the people insistently of the struggle in which their sisters and brothers in Africa are engaged, a struggle for survival in human dignity. This reminder is all the more important as public interest is attracted increasingly away from the countries in the South to focus on events in Europe. To be honest, concern for Africa is no longer the "fashionable" pastime it was only a few years ago.

Keeping African issues before the public is a task for "development education" by church schools, parishes, organizations and media. This education should be guided by the principles of CST. Furthermore, it should be sensitive also to the images and messages it conveys and should avoid presenting Africa simply as a place of immense suffering. What a non-governmental group (NGO) in Europe recently said regarding the role of NGOs has direct bearing also on the role of the church:

The information in our daily news too often presents the Third World in a way that is incomplete and biased—starving people portrayed as the helpless victims of their own fate. This fatalistic approach can be overcome with the provision of more realistic and complete information, thereby increasing awareness of the intrinsic value of all civilizations, of the limitations of our own society and of the need for a more universal development which respects justice, peace and the environment. It is the duty of NGOs to provide the public with truthful and objective information which respects not only the human dignity of the people in question but the intelligence of the public at large.[36]

A second social role of the church in the United States is to raise the issue of the justice of the international structures which block integral development in Africa. This is being done in a variety of ways by groups such as the Africa Faith and Justice Network, Bread for the World, and the Coalition for Peace in the Horn of Africa. The Office of International Justice and Peace of the United States Catholic Conference (USCC)—an arm of the Bishops' Conference—also addresses African issues.

Because of its wide-ranging consequences, one obvious issue deserving of continuing attention is the support the United States government has offered and/or continues to offer to regimes and movements in Africa which violate basic justice. By backing Mobutu of Zaire, Savimbi of the National Union for the Total Independence of Angola (UNITA), Barre of Somalia, and other such leaders, the United States has seriously compromised its position in Africa. And for years it undercut its commitment to justice and peace by remaining almost silent in the face of the destructive policies of destabilization practiced by South Africa. Such U.S. government policies deserve constant monitoring and challenging by church agencies and individuals.

But, in my opinion, the major challenge to be made by the church to the structures of injustice should be to the issue of debt. The possibility of integral development in Africa is seriously in doubt so long as debt and the management of debt continue to be such a problem. The structural adjustment programs are wreaking social havoc, while the projected economic gains remain as yet uncertain. In 1987, the Justice and Peace Commission of the Vatican spoke out on the ethical aspects of the question of debt.[37] Following up this lead and its own pastoral letter on the economy, the administrative board of the USCC in 1989 issued a statement calling for considerations of justice, solidarity and human rights in meeting the debt issue.[38]

I believe that the church in the United States should go still further and call for *complete forgiveness* of all African debt. There is a strong moral case which can be argued for this position.[39] Granted, there may be many complications with this approach, but one feature that recommends it is its directness. It would not solve all the problems blocking integral development, but it would remove the major economic distraction to addressing the very serious human and structural issues Africa faces today. So long as progress in development is cast mainly in terms of securing fiscal balance and servicing of debts, no long-term integral development will occur. The only "conditions" I feel should be placed on governments whose debts are forgiven are to demand full respect of political and economic rights of the citizens.

Opponents to forgiveness of African debt will be quick to point to the financial cost of such a sweeping action. But the United States already has joined other industrialized countries in selectively forgiving debts in many African countries. It has forgiven the $6.8 billion debt of Egypt (as a reward for its joining in the Allied anti-Iraq coalition), and more than $5 billion of Poland's debt (as a support for its movement to a market economy). Furthermore, it should not be forgotten that it was possible to spend one billion dollars a day during the Gulf War!

Finally, the church in the United States has a social role to play by continuing to offer a generous hand of relief and development assistance to the people of Africa. This can be done—is already being done—through pressuring the U.S. government to keep up programs of foreign assistance and through church programs such as those sponsored by Catholic Relief Services. I am aware of the many difficulties associated with all aid programs. Therefore, I hasten to add that all such programs need careful monitoring and evaluation to assure that they really do promote integral development and do not contribute to serious problems of dependency, displacement of local resources, corruption, political exploitation, etc. Indeed, there may be times when the church's social role in this matter is better played by slowing down or halting foreign assistance than by promoting it.

Conclusion

In the vision of CST, the church has an important role to play in the promotion of integral development in Africa. It is a role of education and training, of mobilization and monitoring, of witnessing and pressuring, of sharing and supporting. But above all, it is a role of offering hope.

Throughout Africa today, people are painfully aware of immense problems to be faced simply to survive. In the face of natural and human-made disasters which daily confront millions, the temptation is great to succumb to resignation, fatalism, despair. An ethic of individualism, tribalism, or nationalism, fostered in a climate of economic, political and social chaos, can easily undercut traditional communitarian values. In such a situation, purely technical solutions are of no great help.

The church has a role of going beyond technical solutions. In my opinion, its greatest contribution comes in its ability to counter the present situation of maldevelopment with a vision of integral development. "Without vision, the people perish." By offering that vision, the church continually emphasizes that a person in community with others and with all of creation is the source, subject and goal of all development activities. As such, people have rights and responsibilities which must be protected and fostered by every social arrangement, local, national and international.

For the church to raise its voice and its hands in promotion of integral development in Africa today is to fulfill its mission in a particularly effective fashion. The "Good News" especially needed in Africa now is hope—hope experienced in concrete acts of solidarity and justice. Promoting integral development according to the guidelines of CST is playing a social role which builds hope. *The Church in the Modern World* states: "We can justly consider that the future of humanity lies in the hands of those who are strong enough to provide coming generations with reasons for living and hoping" (GS 31).

Who cares about Africa? Those who give hope . . .

Notes

1. Throughout this chapter, "Africa" refers only to sub-Saharan Africa. Because I use World Bank data, South Africa and Namibia are not included. Extremely rich diversity marks the region, as summarized in a recent World Bank publication:

> The region contains a multiplicity of ethnic groups, languages, and religions. Almost no country is culturally or socially homogeneous. Governments vary from working democracies that encourage debate and dialogue to authoritarian regimes that trample dissent. Some economies are tightly controlled, while others operate largely on market principles. The climatic zones span the whole spectrum from temperate, well-watered highlands to arid deserts and from dry savannah to tropical rain forests. Countries vary from tiny to vast. Five alone account for more than half the inhabitants of the region. The population of Nigeria is more than 100 million, while nine countries have less than 1 million. Population densities are very uneven,

with more than 246 persons per square kilometer around Lake Victoria to less than 1 in Mauritania. Fifteen countries are landlocked, and six are islands. Income per capita vary by a factor of 20. Some countries have considerable mineral or oil wealth, while others have almost none.

World Bank, *Sub-Saharan Africa: From Crisis to Sustainable Growth* (Washington, D.C.: The World Bank, 1989), p. 17.

2. Unless indicated otherwise, the statistical data used in this paper are all drawn from three main sources: World Bank, *Sub-Saharan Africa, op cit.*; World Bank, *World Development Report* (New York: Oxford University Press, 1990); and United Nations Economic Commission for Africa, *African Alternative Framework to Structural Adjustment Programs for Socioeconomic Recovery and Transformation (AAF-SAP)* (New York: United Nations, 1989).

3. For a more detailed analysis of global debt, see George Ann Potter, *Dialogue on Debt: Alternative Analyses and Solutions* (Washington, D.C.: Center of Concern, 1988).

4. See UNICEF, *The State of the World's Children* (New York: Oxford University Press, 1989).

5. United Nations Economic Commission for Africa, *op. cit.*, p. i.

6. *Ibid.*, p. ii.

7. World Bank, *Sub-Saharan Africa, op. cit.*, p. 3.

8. Walt W. Rostow, *The Stages of Economic Growth: A Non-Communist Manifesto* (New York: Cambridge University Press, 1960).

9. See especially the writers of the *"dependentia"* school in Latin America.

10. See, for example, Gustavo Gutierrez, *A Theology of Liberation* (Maryknoll, N.Y.: Orbis Books, 1973).

11. See, for example, L. L. Lebret, *Dynamique concrete du development* (Paris: Economie et Humanisme, Les Editions Ouvrieres, 1961). See also Denis Goulet, *The Cruel Choice* (New York: Atheneum, 1971).

12. In referring to the documents of the church's social teaching (CST), I use the following abbreviations in the text:

CEC *Christians and the Ecological Crisis*
EN *Evangelization Today*
GS *The Church in the Modern World*
JW *Justice in the World*
LX *On Human Work*
MM *Christianity and Social Progress*
OA *A Call to Action*
PP *The Development of Peoples*
PT *Peace on Earth*

QA   *The Reconstruction of the Social Order*
RN   *The Condition of Labor*
SRS   *The Social Concern of the Church*

A collection of CST during the time of John XXIII and Paul VI, with a very helpful introductory essay, is Joseph Gremillion, ed., *The Gospel of Justice and Peace* (New York: Orbis Books, 1976). A more recent study guide is Peter J. Henriot, Edward P. DeBerri and Michael J. Schultheis, *Catholic Social Teaching: Our Best Kept Secret* (New York: Orbis Books, and Washington, D.C.: Center of Concern, 1988).

13. For a fuller discussion, see Peter J. Henriot, *Opting for the Poor: A Challenge for North Americans* (Washington, D.C.: Center of Concern, 1990).

14. *The World Development Report 1990, op. cit.*, is devoted to a special study of global poverty, and attempts to give a wider-than-economic picture of development. For a thorough discussion of measuring real development, see UNICEF, *op. cit.*, pp. 73–87. See also the new efforts to develop social indicators by the United Nations Development Program.

15. The South Commission, *The Challenge to the South* (New York: Oxford University Press, 1990). The Commission was chaired by Julius Nyerere of Tanzania.

16. See, for example, the critiques by Michael Novak.

17. See, for example, David Hollenbach, *Claims in Conflict: Retrieving and Renewing the Catholic Human Rights Tradition* (New York: Paulist Press, 1979).

18. See Peter J. Henriot, "Interdependence and Solidarity in *Sollicitudo Rei Socialis*," *National Catholic Reporter*, May 1988.

19. The magnitude of this expenditure on the Gulf War is portrayed dramatically in the following comparison:

A comparison of the costs of this war and the financial resources available to development cooperation reveals a discrepancy almost beyond imagination: according to official statements, an amount of up to one billion US dollars per day is being spent on the war on the side of the coalition forces, which means that during the first week alone, more money was used to finance this war than Misereor had at its disposal to fund development and peace work in the countries of the so-called Third World in the whole period of 32 years since its foundation.

"Statement on the Effects of the Gulf War on Development Aid," German Catholic Bishops' Organization for Development Cooperation, Misereor; Aachen, Germany, January 25, 1991.

20. See Robert J. Samuelson, "Don't Worry about the Cost," *Newsweek*, February 4, 1991, pp. 44–45.

21. Ruth Leger Sivard, *World Military and Social Expenditures* (Washington, D.C.: World Priorities, 1990).

22. See the reports from the Coalition for Peace in the Horn of Africa, c/o Center of Concern, 3700 13th Street, N.E., Washington, D.C., 20017, U.S.A.

23. *Sub-Saharan Africa, op. cit.*, p. 23.

24. This emphasis on humanity's patrimony echoes the "common heritage of humankind" concept put forward in the Law of the Seas Treaty of the United Nations, drafted in the 1970s.

25. See, for example, the discussion in *The Challenge to the South, op. cit.*, p. 21.

26. See, for example, Thierry Verhelst, *No Life without Roots: Culture and Development* (London: ZED Books, 1990).

27. The South-North Network on Cultures and Development, rue Joseph II 172, 1040 Bruxelles, Belgium.

28. Symposium of the Episcopal Conferences of Africa and Madagascar (SECAM), *The Church and Human Promotion in Africa* Today (Kinshasa, Zaire: SECAM Secretariat, 1985), p. 7.

29. *Ibid.*, p. 14.

30. *The Challenge to the South, op. cit.*, p. 129.

31. See Maria Riley, *Transforming Feminism* (Kansas City, Mo.: Sheed and Ward, 1989), pp. 81–87. See also Maria Riley, "Feminist Analysis: A Missing Perspective," in Gregory Baum and Robert Ellsberg, eds., *The Logic of Solidarity: Commentaries on Pope John Paul II's Encyclical "On Social Concern"* (Maryknoll, N.Y.: Orbis Books, 1989), pp. 186–201.

32. Commenting on this section of *The Social Concern of the Church*, Donal Dorr writes:

> This account seems somewhat bland. It could have benefitted from a
> social analysis that would take more seriously the causes of the class
> structure of society and an examination of ways in which tensions
> between the different classes can be lessened. Furthermore, the
> account given here seems to lack a certain theological dimension:
> there is no great emphasis on the special role that God has given to
> those who are weak and poor in bringing liberation to all.

"Solidarity and Integral Human Development," *The Logic of Solidarity, op. cit.*, p. 149.

33. "The Catholic Church in Africa: Toward the Year 2000," *New People*, July 1989, pp. 16–17.

34. "On the Present Situation in Our Country," Pastoral Letter of the Catholic Bishops of Kenya, Nairobi, June 20, 1990. "Economics, Politics and

Justice," Pastoral Statement of the Catholic Bishops of Zambia, Lusaka, July 23, 1990.

35. Ann Hope and Sally Timmel, *Training for Transformation: A Handbook for Community Workers*, 3 vols. (Gweru, Zimbabwe: Mambo Press, 1984).

36. "Code of Conduct: Images and Messages Relating to the Third World," brochure published by NGO-EC Liaison Committee, 62 Avenue de Cortenbergh, B-1040 Bruxelles, Belgium, 1989.

37. Pontifical Commission *Justia et Pax, At the Service of the Human Community: An Ethical Approach to the International Debt Question*, 1987.

38. United States Catholic Conference Administration Board, *Relieving Third World Debt: A Call for Co-responsibility, Justice, and Solidarity* (Washington, D.C.: United States Catholic Conference, 1989).

39. See Peter J. Henriot, "Forgive Us Our Debts . . . "*America*, December 9, 1989, pp. 420–424.

Thirteen

Catholic Social Thought in Latin America: A Brief Overview from Pope Leo XIII to the Present

Marcos McGrath, C.S.C.

The theme for this volume is the influence of religion on economic, social and political institutions—in a word, on society—specifically from *Rerum Novarum*[1] to the present day. Emphasis has been upon the United States, Europe and European origins, with some reference to Africa, the international order and the Third World.

According to a recent poll, 90 percent of the population in the United States identify with a religion: 60.2 percent of them non-Catholic Christian, 26.2 percent Roman Catholic, and 2 percent Jews. Obviously, "Religious Social Thought" in the United States is of prime concern, especially "Catholic Social Thought."

Population tendencies and shifts since the publication of *Rerum Novarum* have resulted in a large majority of Christians, particularly Catholics, to be found in the South—in Africa, and especially in Latin America which has more than 40 percent of the Roman Catholics of the world today—rather than in the North, in Europe and North America.

Historians tell us that some liberal governments in Latin America forbade the printing or distribution of *Rerum Novarum* after its publication. Christian readers had to smuggle copies across the Argentinean border. This fact illustrates the low-point, the nadir, to which Catholic church life in Latin America had sunk by the end of the last century. After three hundred years of conquest and colonization, the church was buffeted back and forth between the political factions that evolved into the conservative (clericals), the liberals and, later, radicals (anti-clericals). Bishops were exiled, priests jailed, and seminaries closed for decades. Churches that had been strong, with large numbers of native clergy, were prostrate by the end of the century.

Rerum Novarum signified the beginnings of modern Catholic social thought for the Church of Latin America, but in a broader context. Pope Leo XIII presided over the first (and only) Latin American synod in Rome in 1899, attended by all the bishops of the continent, and this was the start of the recovery. His pontificate was significant also from its beginning in 1879, through pre-Vatican Council II, and the take-off and development of so many church factors that were European in origin but which had a strong impact in Latin America. It pointed, however unconsciously, to the second Vatican Council, the greatest religious event of our time that would have such a profound impact upon the church and upon Catholic social thought in Latin America.

From the time of Leo XIII, with the synod of 1899, to Pius XII, the conciliar popes—John XXIII and Paul VI—and the post-conciliar John Paul II, the Holy See took a direct and active role in promoting the renewal of the church in Latin America. After the Second World War, 10 percent of the clergy and religious from Europe and North America were sent to Latin America, with lay volunteers and substantial monetary collections that continue to this day.

To be historically complete, we would have to trace the beginnings of lay action (named "Catholic Action" by Pius X) and liturgical participation, the catechetical reforms, biblical study and promotion, social thought and action, and a number of ecumenical endeavors. Some European countries and movements had a more significant impact on the Church of Latin America: the early stages of the four traditional groupings of Catholic Action in Italy; subsequently, the specialized form of Catholic Action in Belgium and France, and the "new theology" that accompanied it and which would so affect the Council.

Beginning in the twenties, the official linkage of church and state was broken in one Latin American country after another. Today, except for Mexico and Cuba which officially do not sanction any church, the Spanish- and Portugese-American states typically recognize in their constitution that the majority of their citizens are Roman Catholic, and provide for that religion in the schools; however, these governments normally do not afford further privileges.

The thirties saw the beginnings of more centers of Catholic social teaching and action: Young Christian Workers (YCW), Young Christian Farmers (YCF), Young Christian Students (YCS), Young Christian University Students (YCU), Young Christian Independents (YCI)—and the see-judge-act "inquiry" method which they employed.[2] This growth was due partly to *Quadragesimo Anno*[3] and to the new emphasis, since Pius XI, on the like-by-like specialized forms of Catholic Action. Young men and women emerging from these movements gave impulse to Christian groups in their media or milieux—labor unions, student associations, business groups, and academics.

The Second World War brought instant prosperity in Latin America to many who were called upon to supply the allied nations with food and raw materials. But the country people who had come to the cities to work were left high and dry, poor and uprooted, when the market collapsed after the war. Swelling shanty towns had grown up around the urban areas—"belts of misery," as they were called. The new and intense social problems gave rise to a more ardent attempt by the church to apply Catholic social teaching, an effort which launched active Catholics into the political arena and created Christian Democratic parties, or groups similar in intent, in many nations. By this time Catholic social teaching, basically through papal documents and encyclicals, was becoming part of seminary and Catholic university curricula. In many countries a strong conservative block, composed mostly of business and industrial leaders, many of them traditional Catholics, opposed this as a dangerously radical movement and sought (and often found) alliances with bishops and clergy. This *integrist* attitude evolved into the movement for "family-tradition and property," based in Brazil and given to violent verbal and even physical attacks upon the more progressive new Christian social leaders such as Eduardo Frei of Chile.

In 1961 the Alliance for Progress was born, backed by President John F. Kennedy who was then inordinately popular in Latin America because of Castro's Cuba. Hope was bright. The alliance was based upon social reform in Latin American countries, to be legislated and applied, for instance, in (1) fairer tax and land reforms and more ample social welfare, and (2) upon generous annual financial aid from abroad in three equal parts—from the United States, Europe, and from international financial institutions (IFI). As the years rolled by and none of the sectors involved even remotely fulfilled their commitments, the vision faded, hope declined, and some bitterness became apparent. The key word of the decade had become "development." Bishop Manuel Larrain of Chile coined an expression which Paul VI would borrow in his encyclical *Populorum Progressio*:[4] "Development is the new name for peace."

Meanwhile, the Council convened. When announced by John XXIII in January 1959, it stirred interest in Latin America but not much expectation. The image of the Council was that of Vatican I during 1869–1870, highly centralized around Pius IX and dealing with ecclesiastical problems of jurisdiction and magisterium. It was felt, in curias, seminaries and among theological faculties, that the new Council simply would complete those questions left unfinished when Garibaldi interrupted Vatican I. This was also the impression given by the commissions that prepared the Council. Not until the election of new commissions, spontaneously promoted from the floor in the first days of the Council, did this mood and agenda change.

Even then, the agenda continued to consist of matters *intra ecclesiam*—internal church matters, from magisterium to liturgy and ministry. But under the impact of John XXIII's opening discourse that was so

sympathetic and open to the modern world, and the atmosphere generated in and around the Council, as well as the mounting interest among
official "observers," including the international press (especially the
Western press), the stage was set for the decisive intervention of Cardinal
Suenens in the waning days of the first session. He called for the Council
to divide its work into two areas of consideration: *ecclesia ad intra* and
ecclesia ad extra. Seconded the following day by Cardinal Montini who
was known to be speaking for Pope John, the proposal carried and the
Council, not aware yet of the consequences, altered its course substantially and undertook to discuss matters of temporal concern which no
Council in the twenty centuries of church history had thought to touch.

This was a qualitative difference of which we should take due note in
our reflection upon "Catholic Social Thought, 1891–1991." It was the turning point. First, that the Council, in announcing the current papal social
teaching, decided to speak and expand on these areas. Secondly, that in
so doing it marked many clear advances, a kind of doctrinal watershed, in
matters of social teaching, specifically regarding the Council's dynamic
view of the church and the church in the world.

The Council, under the pope, was exercising the supreme teaching
authority of the church but, at the same time, the bishops were learning. A
clear and strong majority, led and encouraged by Pope John and then
Pope Paul, took to heart the task of renovation—that double movement of
return to the sources and going out into the world—and, with the Council
fathers and their many advisors, set themselves enthusiastically to the
task. Carefully, step-by-step, line-by-line, a renewed vision of church and
church in the world evolved. There is certainly evolution of dogma here,
of doctrine, and of Catholic social thought, a fact which has not been duly
attended, with the danger that Vatican II simply will take its place after
Vatican I on our bookshelves and cease to guide and energize the universal church as it is called to do.

The Council had provoked strong enthusiasm among the Latin
American bishops and their *periti*—experts, official and unofficial. During
the four sessions they had frequent, almost daily meetings, grouped principally around the Chilean and Brazilian delegations and in the office of
the Council of Latin American Bishops (CELAM), the president of which
was Bishop Larrain.

CELAM set up new episcopal commissions that corresponded to the
key pastoral areas, and charged each president to arrange meetings for
bishops and experts to discuss the application of the Council's edicts in
Latin America. These meetings had begun already in early 1964, before
the third session of the Council. The second general conference of Latin

American bishops in Medellín, entitled "The Church in the Present Transformation of Latin America in the Light of the Council," grew out of these meetings. Inaugurated in Colombia in August 1968 by Paul VI, its sixteen conclusions, following the inquiry method of see-judge-act, were surprisingly fresh, strong and concrete. They spoke of and from a church in search of renewal, the double renewal of the Council. Its title and content assumed for the Church of Latin America the double challenge of *ecclesia ad intra* and *ad extra.*

The Medellín conclusions were not uniformly accepted. One major Latin American hierarchy did not authorize an official text until preparing for the third general conference in Puebla ten years later. The decade after Medellín witnessed "contestatory" groups, including priests and nuns, which called for more rapid change; a decline in the number of seminaries and religious vocations; and a call to suppress "development" in favor of liberation that would or should bring about more than a cosmetic social change.

All this history is too long and embattled to treat here. Many other nations and areas went through similar experiences but we are most intent in this chapter upon the aspect of Catholic social thought in Latin America. Several factors helped to ratify, confirm and clarify the Council teaching and the Medellín document: (1) the papal magisterium, especially *Populorum Progressio* and *Octogesima Adveniens*,[5] (2) the Vatican synods, in particular the synod on "Justice in the World";[6] (3) the papal exhortation *Evangelii Nuntiandi* after the synod of 1977; (4) the ordinary and extraordinary meetings of CELAM, for example, during 1967 in Mar del Plata, Argentina, on "The Church in the Development and Integration of Latin America"; and (5) the activity of the individual and sub-regional conference of bishops.

The preparation of the third general conference of Latin American bishops lent itself to ardent public debate between the integrists and the advocates of the still newly expressed liberation theology. In fact, the real preparation took place in all the communities, churches and diocese of Latin America, a vast consultation which inspired and guided the bishops at Puebla to a fuller development of the Medellín conclusions and their application to the many faceted task of evangelization in Latin America. This is the confirmation of a new and conciliar church, confirmed by the people of God and their pastors.

The debate on liberation continued, fanned by the expression of "popular church" versus hierarchy in some few cases. Eventually, for most, liberation theology was given full right of citizenship in the church by John Paul II who wrote to the bishops of Brazil that we *need* liberation theology; the correction was pointed out earlier by the Vatican Doctoral Congregation.

There were two marked tendencies during the 1970s and 1980s, related to each other, that greatly affect Catholic social thought in Latin America at the present time: the military takeovers in so many of the countries, and the churches' focus, in most areas, upon more religious and spiritual functions.

Regarding the first point, it is important to recall the Nelson Rockefeller Report, prepared at the end of 1968 at the request of President-Elect Richard Nixon. The report brushed off the influence of the Catholic church as immature, similar to that of university students, but advised support for the military as the more stable element in those countries. We can, charitably, explain this egregious historical miscalculation by supposing that the reporter considered the military to be as observant of civil order in Latin America as it is in the U.S.A. Because this is not the case and since the United States, principally through its military "schools" in the Canal Zone, trained the leaders of the *coups d'état* that took place in many of the Latin American countries during the 1970s and 1980s, we simply mention the point here. In some cases, as in Panama, the military dictator had actually been in the secret employ of the United States for some time. This kind of martial thinking also affected the Kissinger Committee and Report a decade later. After prolonged conversations with leaders from all areas in the countries of Central America, the report proposed an interesting project of economic recovery with strong U.S. financial aid for the entire area, but made it subject to a previous military victory for the U.S. side in every country. Shortly before, we bishops of the area had insisted that the basic problem was the requirement for military solutions which cost so many lives, considerable social division, destruction and money, and profoundly complicated the social, economic and political problems, especially for the poor. In fact, the proposals of the Kissinger Report were never put into operation.

Until recently, the prolonged situation of repressive military dictatorship in so many of the Latin American countries during this period had other effects. The church expanded one aspect of the social pastoral task: the defense of human civil rights by legal means, including the investigation of many cases of abuse, through material assistance to the oppressed and their families; and to the poor in general through declarations and pastoral letters in defense of human rights. Hundreds of these declarations, from Mexico to Chile, make up a practical compendium on human rights in our times. They also placed the church solidly with the oppressed and poor, a fact that has given the church strong moral strength today.

It is worth noting that in most cases it was the bishops who spoke out, in statements read in all the parish pulpits, but very seldom the laity or any civic or religious lay groups. However, there was little opportunity to discuss or present other equally important aspects of social doctrine such as work, wages, security, income, local problems, etc.

With the collapse of most of the military dictatorships and the return to civil democratic regimes we find:

1. We must come out of our defensive shell, look about more broadly, and address positive solutions in the wide realm of social, economic and political problems facing the people of Latin America.
2. We must, in a certain sense, learn what democracy is and train for it, even set up centers and schools for the teaching of values and leadership.
3. We pastors must encourage dialogues such as ours at Notre Dame, and stimulate the laity to act and assume their responsibilities for promoting Christian social values; and to go beyond, into more specific decisions in the political and economic spheres, as the document of Puebla points out:

Taking their inspiration from the contents of Christian anthropology, there is an indispensable need for the commitment of Christians in the elaboration of historical projects which respond to the needs of every moment and every culture.[7]

The pontificate of John Paul II has given guidelines for social thought and action in Latin America, especially in labor and economic matters, and regarding Third World problems (for example, foreign debt). The great task before us is to bring all this effort into the family, the marketplace and the arenas of political action.

The Vatican synod of 1987 brought out clearly the fact that laity are much more active in church structures and tasks than they are as apostles in the secular sphere. This is true of Latin America where we experience daily the strong commitment of millions of laity to prayer and to spiritual or religious action, along with a remarkable upsurge of religious and priestly vocations. But at the same time, we find much less noticeable lay commitment in the social order than in the forties and fifties, when the specialized movements of Catholic Action trained in designated environments.

As a church, with *Gaudium et Spes*,[8] we have learned to use the inquiry technique. We must all, clerics and laity, learn to apply it more concretely and effectively in the secular world around us. The Fourth

General Conference of Latin American Bishops, held in 1992 on the fifth centenary of the first proclamation of the Gospel in the New World,[9] called on all of us to look and work for a new evangelization in our lives and communities. In this process Catholic social thought will be a *faro en el camino*—a light to guide our way.

Notes

1. Pope Leo XIII, encyclical, *Rerum Novarum*, May 15, 1891.

2. The original group, the YCW, was founded after the First World War in Belgium by Canon Cardijn (later a cardinal).

3. Pope Pius XI, encyclical, *Quadragesimo Anno*, May 15, 1931.

4. Pope Paul VI, encyclical, *Populorum Progressio*, March 16, 1967.

5. Pope Paul VI, apostolic letter, *Octogesima Adveniens*, May 14, 1971.

6. Synod of Bishops, Second General Assembly, "Justice in the World," November 30, 1971.

7. Latin American Bishops, Third General Conference, Puebla, January 28, 1979, no. 553.

8. Second Vatican Ecumenical Council, Pastoral Constitution on the Church in the Modern World, *Gaudium et Spes*, December 7, 1965.

9. The Fourth General Conference of the Latin American Bishops was held in Santo Domingo, Dominican Republic, from October 12–28, 1992. It was inaugurated by Pope John Paul II.

Fourteen

Catholic Public Opinion for Freedom and Political Institutions

Denis E. Hurley, O.M.I.

An Issue of Social Concern

Catholic public opinion for freedom and political institutions pertains to the field of social concern. By social concern I mean having an interest in the values and practices that constitute a human society in all its political, economic and cultural complexity. Obviously, freedom and political institutions are vital ingredients and public opinion about them is the very condition of their existence, if public opinion is taken to mean the network of thoughts, feelings and attitudes that constitute the soul of a society. My topic therefore falls under the umbrella of social concern. I feel that I cannot treat it without saying something about our experience of social concern in the Catholic church.

It is a hundred years since *Rerum Novarum* was published and inaugurated an era in which social concern should have been an issue of consuming interest in the church.

That this should have happened seems a logical conclusion from what social concern implies: all the major torments of the human family, from the industrial injustices that were the immediate theme of *Rerum Novarum*, through widespread experience of poverty, unemployment, colonial abuses and racial oppression, warfare, ideological tyrannies, the threat of nuclear disaster of cosmic proportions and the AIDS pandemic. Social concern embraces all the worst sins of the human race and all its worst sufferings.

Social Concern a Slow Developer

Yet social concern in the hundred years since *Rerum Novarum* has not become the compelling issue that by its very nature it should be.

There are many reasons for this, among them the difficulty of introducing a new concern into the church with a long history of traditional priorities, the sheer size and multiplicity and complexity of social concerns and, perhaps most important of all, the failure to realize that new concerns require new methods of communication and education.

Looking back with the wisdom of hindsight, we realize that when Pope Leo XIII published *Rerum Novarum* he was calling for an attitudinal revolution, a huge social conversion, but gave little thought as to how this was to be achieved. We cannot blame him. It was a big enough achievement to call for the social conversion. It would have required at the time and in the circumstances a colossal stroke of genius to foresee that the achievement of conversion needed new pastoral and educational methods as yet undreamed of and totally alien to the accepted practices of the time. If any are to blame, it is those of us who have lived through whole decades of the hundred years since *Rerum Novarum* without realising the need for the revolutionary methods necessary to achieve a revolutionary result. But, then, perhaps we too cannot be blamed, for one cannot blame people for not being geniuses. Besides, a change in so vast a body as the Catholic church is like a cultural change in society. It does not happen overnight. It develops slowly as multitudes of individuals in a succession of generations make their contributions.

Social Concern and Lay Participation

We thank God for the contributions made by those who responded to the call of Leo XIII and who embarked on the trial and error process of moving the church into social concern. One cannot comment on these contributions without referring at the same time to the evolution of lay participation in the church. Social concern and lay participation have been linked inseparably. A little reflection indicates that it could not have been otherwise. Social concern could not have developed without the laity playing a major role. The overwhelming majority of the church is lay and this majority in many countries is an important segment of society and, in some countries, the dominant religious segment. If social concern is to be a reality it must be so through the laity; there can be no promotion of social concern without them. Therefore, I shall endeavour to trace the development of lay participation up to and beyond the Second Vatican Council.

Already in the time of Leo XIII, wherever there were significant numbers of Catholics, Catholic associations were in full flower: some promoted by the clergy, some founded and promoted by leading lay persons, some concerned with piety and devotion, some with social issues, including the major issues of poverty and work, and some concerned with politics. This blossoming of associations was the church's response to what were seen as the two major threats to Catholicism in the nineteenth century: liberalism and socialism.

Pope Saint Pius X who succeeded Leo XIII in 1903 is well known for his liturgical reforms in the matter of church music and early and frequent communion. He drove hard also for the reform of seminary education and the promotion of catechetical instruction. But the issue raised by Leo XIII in *Rerum Novarum* was not one of his priorities. In the matter of lay participation, Pius X's concern focused on what was starting to be called Catholic Action. As Pius X understood it, the group aimed at organising and harnessing the apostolic efforts of lay people in close union with and in strict subordination to the clergy. The lay forces of Catholic Action were to be a spiritual and apostolic extension of hierarchical and clerical evangelization.

Pope Pius XI (1922–1939) pushed the idea of Catholic Action very vigorously. He envisaged dioceses and parishes extending the drive and influence of the bishop and clergy through the four sections of organised Catholic Action: Catholic Action of men and women and of the youth of both sexes. Other associations of lay apostolate were not excluded but Catholic Action was the apple of the eye of Pius XI. I remember from my days as a seminarian in Rome in the 1930s how he loved to repeat the definition of Catholic Action as "the participation of the laity in the apostolic mission of the hierarchy." If I remember rightly he maintained that this definition of Catholic Action was inspired by the Holy Spirit. Thank God Pius XI did not promulgate *ex cathedra* that Catholic Action, as he understood it, is lay participation *par excellence.* We would be having a difficult time now explaining that he did not quite mean that. As Pius XI was proclaiming it, two events were happening that would soon relativize its value.

One was the appearance of Joseph Cardijn. In the early 1920s he founded the Young Christian Workers, organised them into cells and sections and gave them a method of formation enshrined in the trilogy, *See, Judge and Act.* This new method became the most effective way of training young laity. It soon spread far beyond the world of young workers and was taken up by a variety of Catholic organizations. These continued to be called Catholic Action but with a qualification—Specialised Catholic Action. The new method, emphasizing experience and Bible, in due course revolutionized catechetics, inspired liberation theology, the emergence of Christian-base communities in Latin America and other parts of the world and became responsible for one of the most important documents of the Second Vatican Council, namely, *Gaudium et Spes*, the Pastoral Constitution on the church in the Modern World.

The other event was the growth of the realization that the apostolate of the laity was not just an extension of the apostolic mission of the hierarchy. The laity had their own job to do, in close association with the hierarchy, obviously, but with a certain autonomy of their own. The role of the laity does not depend on the invitation to help the hierarchy do its job. It flows from baptism. During the time of Pope Pius XII (1939–1958), the term "lay apostolate" grew in popularity. It emphasized the role of the laity in "consecrating" the world—a concept that was to have revolutionary consequences under Pope John XXIII.

Pope John XXIII and Catholic Reappraisal of the World

John XXIII became pope in October 1958 and died in June 1963. In just over four years, as one disgruntled ecclesiastic is supposed to have remarked, he did more damage than can be repaired in four hundred years. Part of the "damage" he perpetrated was to give the papal blessing to a new, more appreciative, more optimistic view of the world. This he did by just being the person he was and by publishing two encyclicals, *Mater et Magistra* in 1961 and *Pacem in Terris* in 1963. The Council he called crowned his work in this respect by its *Gaudium et Spes*, and crowned the slow and painful growth since Leo's *Rerum Novarum*.

Catholics under forty years of age may find it difficult to realize the extent of the revolution in the church's attitude to the world. For 1900 years the church had been ill at ease in its assessment of the world, appreciating it as the work of God's creation but apprehensive of the evil that lurked in it. The very term "world" was ambiguous in the gospel, in catechesis and in the theology of the priesthood and religious life. For religious there was a certain satisfaction in having "renounced the world," and priests were exhorted to be "in the world but not of it." Theology had little idea of how this world was related to the true and lasting values of the next. At best, this world looked like a testing ground where Christians proved whether or not they were worthy of eternal happiness. Apart from this, what they actually did in the world was of scant importance; what counted was the "right intention."

The Catholic theological reappraisal of the world was a tremendous boost for the laity. The great majority of laity spend most of their waking time at work in the world. Having to do this within a situation of ambiguity is not very encouraging. *Gaudium et Spes* did a splendid hatchet job on the ambiguity view.

Vatican II and the Role of the Laity

The Second Vatican Council also produced a specific document dedicated to the role of the laity, the Decree on the Apostolate of the Laity. The Council in this document, as well as in its Dogmatic Constitution on the Church (*Lumen Gentium*, nos. 2 and 4), gave powerful and comprehensive expression to the fuller understanding of the laity that had been developing since the time of Leo XIII. The treatment in *Lumen Gentium* of the people of God before the hierarchy, emphasized that membership of the church was more important than ordained ministry. The laity had arrived—at least on paper. The dignity, importance and place in the church of the laity was formulated clearly and, much more than that, in many passages of Council documents some of the consequences were spelled out—consequences such as these:

- The laity share fully in the mystery of the Church, that is, in the communion of the Father, the Son and the Holy Spirit.
- They are expected to live out the extension of this communion in the communion of the Church, the Body of Christ, the People of God.
- They share in and are expected to give expression in their lives to the threefold function of Jesus: prophet, priest and shepherd king.
- They do this in the world and through their Christian influence on the world they play the major role in bringing about what is so beautifully described in *Gaudium et Spes* 39.

Therefore while we are warned that it profits a man nothing if he gain the whole world and lose himself, the expectation of a new earth must not weaken but rather stimulate our concern for cultivating this one. For here grows the body of a new human family, a body which even now is able to give some kind of foreshadowing of the new age.

Earthly progress must be carefully distinguished from the growth of Christ's kingdom. Nevertheless, to the extent that the former can contribute to the better ordering of human society, it is of vital concern to the kingdom of God.

For after we have obeyed the Lord, and in His Spirit nurtured on earth the values of human dignity, brotherhood and freedom, and indeed all the good fruits of our nature and enterprise, we will find them again, but freed of stain, burnished and transfigured. This will be so when Christ hands over to the Father a kingdom eternal and universal: "a kingdom of truth and life, of holiness and grace, of justice, love and peace." On this earth that kingdom is already present in mystery. When the Lord returns, it will be brought into full flower.

In light of these considerations when one is talking about the church one should have the laity principally in mind. It should be easy enough to use the terms "clergy" and "religious" when these are specifically intended. Such usage would accord perfectly with the definition of the laity in *Lumen Gentium* 31: "The term laity is here understood to mean all the faithful except those in holy orders and those in a religious state sanctioned by the Church." In this definition the laity are the ordinary members of the church; clergy and religious are the exceptions.

It will no doubt take us some time to get round to this use of the word church, which historically has been so much identified with clergy and religious. So I continue to speak of the role of the laity as I do now in quoting from the *Lumen Gentium* description of the secular quality that is proper and special to lay people.

> The laity, by their very vocation, seek the kingdom of God by engaging in temporal affairs and by ordering them according to the plan of God. They live in the world, that is, in each and in all of the secular professions and occupations. They live in the ordinary circumstances of family and social life, from which the very web of their existence is woven. They are called there by God so that by exercising their proper function and being led by the Spirit of the gospel they can work for the sanctification of the world from within, in the manner of leaven. (LG 81)

If this is the particular role of the laity, they carry most of the burden of responsibility for evangelization as described by Paul VI in *Evangelization in the Modern World*:

> For the Church evangelizing means bringing the Good News into all the strata of humanity and through its influence transforming humanity from within and making it new. . . . all this could be expressed in the following words: What matters is to evangelize human culture and cultures (not in a purely decorative way as it were by applying a veneer, but in a vital way, in depth and right to their very roots) in the wide and rich sense which these terms have in *Gaudium et Spes*, always taking the person as one's starting point and always coming back to the relationships of people among themselves and with God. (EMW 18, 20)

A very large segment of that colossal job is the work of justice, of eradicating all the discrimination, unfairness, oppression and tyranny that abound in this world and substituting for them the justice of Jesus, inspired by his love.

If we think about this too long we will throw our hands up in utter despair. It sounds tantamount to shifting the Rocky Mountains with a tea-spoon. Fortunately, the Lord does not expect us to achieve all this in our lifetime. The transformation of the world will be accomplished ultimately only at the Second Coming. In the meantime, we are expected to plug away at our little share of the work. If all of us shovel away with our tea-spoons over a sufficiently long period of cosmic time we can handle the Rocky Mountains.

The Example of Latin America

Since the Second Vatican Council, one part of the church that has been setting an example in this respect is Latin America. Better than most areas of the church, Latin America, particularly Brazil, has been putting into effect the image of the church that emerged from the Council and is beautifully summed up in a trilogy which has fascinated me since I came across it. My source is literature associated with the 1990 Synod of Bishops on the training of candidates for the priesthood and the trilogy is: mystery, communion, mission.

The Latin American church has been giving the lead through its liberation theology and its Christian-base communities. These seem to have evolved after the Council, from earlier experiences of the lay apostolate tracing their origin fairly obviously back to Joseph Cardijn's *See, Judge and Act.* Cardijn, the supreme Christian educator of the twentieth century, had formulated the basic values which were to give rise to both liberation theology and the base communities: group or community, reflection on life experience in light of the scriptures, action flowing from reflection and the training of leaders.

Relevance to Catholic Public Opinion for Freedom and Political Institutions

Has the experience of Latin America a lesson for the rest of us? Has it, in particular, a relevance to the topic I am endeavouring to deal with, namely, Catholic public opinion for freedom and political institutions? To seek answers to these questions it is necessary to explain what the topic means. It is about freedom, that most precious of human attributes, often suppressed and easily abused. There are many aspects of freedom: personal freedom, family freedom, national freedom. Freedom and rights go hand-in-hand. Human rights are usually described in terms of freedom: freedom of speech, of association, of religion, of movement and so on. What is less emphasized is the obligations that go hand-in-hand with freedom. Freedom is a noble thing but, as the French say, *noblesse oblige*, nobility obligates. In a way, the greatest human right is freedom to serve others.

Personal and domestic freedom are forms of freedom within a nation or state. National freedom is the freedom of a society to pursue its own political economic and cultural welfare. Denial of this freedom and the drive to recover it have been the greatest sources of conflict among human beings. The strongest guarantees of freedom, whether personal, domestic or national, are human conviction, human attitude, human conscience, social conscience. When freedom is a value in the culture of a country, that is, in the ways of thinking and feeling of that country, it has a hope of surviving and flourishing. Obviously, the thinking and feeling of the culture have to be expressed in institutions that give concrete expression, protection and promotion to the value of freedom: the courts of law, the legislative and executive functions of government.

It took the Catholic church a long time to come to terms with the modern understanding of freedom and its expression in political democracy. Among the problems that the church experienced were its long historical association with political monarchies and its difficulty in working out a theology of religious freedom. The Catholic church of Europe had grown up with monarchies, sometimes friendly with them, sometimes fighting them. The long association of throne and altar seemed as binding as the law of gravity. When the democratic revolutions of the United States and France started the fashion of toppling monarchies, what did this mean for the Catholic church? The disappearance of a familiar social order. For a conservative body such as church this was disturbing. Besides, the papacy itself was a political monarchy until 1870. In time the church came to terms with the change and finally, at Christmas 1944, as the Second World War was drawing to an end, Pius XII expressed in a radio broadcast his preference for democracy.

The theology of religious freedom took longer. The Catholic church saw itself and still sees itself as the true church of Christ. For a long time it had appeared to church people, and in particular to church authorities, that the acceptance of religious freedom would be tantamount to saying that error has the same right as truth. Finally, under the intellectual leadership of two great thinkers with their fingers on the pulse of the time and their sharp minds cutting through the confusion, Jacques Maritain, a French layman, and John Courtney Murray, an American Jesuit, the church found its way out of the mental block. It realized that an abstraction, like truth, is not the subject of rights. The subject of rights is the human being, and human dignity demands that every person have the right to pursue the truth freely. The full theological appreciation of religious freedom had to wait until the last period of the Second Vatican Council. It was gratifying that Jacques Maritain and John Courtney Murray were in Rome when the Declaration on Religious Freedom was promulgated in Saint Peter's Square on December 7, 1965.

Having achieved this, the Catholic church has no further inhibitions about promoting the full value of freedom as an integral part of its social doctrine. It falls under the umbrella of that celebrated statement from the document on justice that emanated from the Synod of Bishops in 1971:

> Action on behalf of justice and participation in the transformation of the world fully appear to us as a constitutive dimension of the preaching of the gospel; or in other words, of the church's mission for the redemption of the human race and its liberation from every oppressive situation.

We have come to realize the value of freedom in human society and the necessity of promoting it with all the means at our command, of which the most important is building up a powerful Catholic public opinion in its favour. Inevitably, this is going to have repercussions on the church itself. The church in the United States has been experiencing this for some considerable time, starting with the endeavours in the nineteenth century to get Rome to understand the advantages of a democratic political system with built-in provision for religious freedom. That battle has been won. With John Courtney Murray in the van, the United States made the most of its opportunities in the Second Vatican Council. Now the issues we face concern the church itself: collegiality, decentralization, ecclesial subsidiarity—and the big one: theological research and debate. I am happy to presume that I am not expected to deal with these issues in this chapter.

Two Centenary Lessons

Looking back over the hundred years of Catholic social teaching and involvement since *Rerum Novarum*, I think we have learned two valuable lessons. The first is a negative one, namely, that social concern does not flourish spontaneously in the church; it has to be painstakingly cultivated. Catholics in general do not wait with bated breath for the publication of a new papal encyclical on social issues, nor do they set about vigorously implementing its teaching. If, six months after its publication, the great majority even knows it exists, it would be a miracle. The second lesson is positive. When success has been achieved in communicating and applying Catholic social teaching, this has been achieved usually through group or community methods.

I do not wish in any way to detract from the success achieved by the Episcopal Conference of the United States in involving great numbers throughout the country in the drafting of important joint pastoral letters. This certainly has helped to create a considerable segment of public opinion. I wish I were wrong, but I doubt the practice is sufficient to create the kind of public opinion that is needed in matters of social concern. Besides, it would be difficult for Third World countries to imitate the example of the United States—they would not have the personnel resources nor a sufficiently high average standard of education among their populations.

The Community Approach

The lesson of the community approach comes through loud and clear from the associations at the time of Leo XIII, Catholic Action groups promoted by Pius X and Pius XI, movements that owe their origin to Joseph Cardijn, the lay apostolate in all its variety, and the Christian-base communities of Latin America and their counterparts in other countries. Since Joseph Cardijn, few would dare to promote any socially oriented educational project that does not include the elements of group or community organization, experience and Bible-based reflection, individual or corporate action and training in leadership.

At the beginning of this chapter I remarked, "Looking back with the wisdom of hindsight we realize that when Pope Leo XIII published *Rerum Novarum* he was calling for an attitudinal revolution, a huge social conversion, but gave little thought as to how this was to be achieved." Presumably, it was expected that the contents of *Rerum Novarum* would be taken up at all levels in the church and become a regular feature of its preaching and catechising. That expectation would have been typical of the Catholic attitude as it was in the liberal attitude of the day: All that was required was to launch the Catholic or liberal idea into the atmosphere and the fallout would take care of itself, as people hungry for truth absorbed its message and propagated it. Now we know it is not as easy as that. Experience has taught us that in matters of social concern an immense amount of hard work is necessary to communicate, disseminate and educate, and that the best methods so far discovered are those associated with groups and communities that owe much to Joseph Cardijn and the practices he inaugurated. Of course, there have been additions and refinements to what Joseph Cardijn initiated, such as Paulo Freire's literacy method with its generative themes, the psychosocial approach, action/reflection and exposure/immersion, but they all owe much to the emphasis on experience popularized by Joseph Cardijn.

The promotion of communities in which people, inspired by the Bible, meet, pray, discuss, reflect and, wherever possible, involve themselves in corporate action must be as important an element of church life as preaching, catechising and celebrating the liturgy. There seems no other way of building up real religious awareness related to the circumstances of life and geared to the challenge of secularism. So long as we omit to promote these kinds of communities we shall be neglecting one of the most powerful means that God, through our human nature, places at our disposal.

We are social beings. We cannot survive outside society, we cannot grow or develop. As the force of gravity holds the universe together, community instinct holds human society together. It is the most powerful instinct in us, more powerful than sex or the instinct for individual survival. An able leader can get people to do anything, suffer anything, dare anything for the sake of social survival. Every war and revolution tells us that.

Community instinct is an extraordinary force. I remember a British priest of Scots extraction who came to South Africa to live out the last years of his life with lungs damaged by gas in the First World War. He once said to me, "I feel somewhat ashamed of saying this but the happiest years of my life were those spent in the Royal Artillery in France." He had not been a priest then, but he never forgot the camaraderie, the *esprit de corps* that made life bearable and more than bearable at the battlefront. Remember, too, how people speak of times in their lives marked by some intense experience of community. They talk of the wonderful spirit. Remember, too, what makes a sporting group rise to unsuspected heights of achievement: the team spirit. If we are neglecting this as a means of formation and evangelization in the church we are neglecting one of the greatest forces given to us by God.

In March 1991, in Durban, we held the first of a series of meetings of our Diocesan Pastoral Council to debate what we should do to carry on the good work of the process called Renew which we borrowed from the archdiocese of Newark, New Jersey. Renew has been a fresh and invigorating breeze affecting the life of the archdiocese of Durban. We cannot imagine the archdiocese without it. We are into the third year of Renew, so we have to work hard to formulate, launch, promote and sustain a pastoral practice grown out of Renew as we build on the experience of community it has given us. We shall be turning to another American source to help us, Father Arthur R. Baranowski of Detroit, a dedicated promoter of the community principle.

I do not know how, without an intense practice of community, Catholic public opinion can be created and maintained. Imagine all the parishes of a diocese bristling with small communities and developing, as an essential dimension of the spiritual life of their members, a good dose of social awareness and concern. What a dynamo that would be for creating Catholic public opinion, not imposed, not straight-jacketed, but emerging spontaneously and freely from the multitude of communications in faith fermenting all over the diocese, or the country for that matter. We have had an experience of what small communities can do in Durban and we are determined, with the help of God, not to let the impetus die down but to make the most of it in our future pastoral growth.

The understanding and practice of small communities should become a mandatory course in the training of lay leaders and ministers, in the curricula of seminaries and houses of religious formation and the training of permanent deacons. The future dynamism of the church depends to a large extent on how we express the divine communion of Father, Son and Holy Spirit in human and Christian terms among ourselves.

Only through a recognizable practice of community can we give credible witness to our reality as the body of Christ and to the will of God "to make people holy and save them not merely as individuals without any mutual bonds, but by uniting them into a single people, a people which acknowledges him in truth and serves him in holiness" (*Lumen Gentium* 9). Only through such practice of community can we give evidence that the prayer of Jesus is being heard: "That they may be one as we are one. With me in them and you in me, may they be so completely one that the world will realize that it was you who sent me and that I have loved them as much as you loved me" (John 17: 22–23).

It is, therefore, a sound conclusion that only through the widespread and genuine practice of community can Catholic public opinion be fostered in regard to social concern in general, and to freedom and political institutions in particular.

Part V

The New World Order: Shaping a Just Community

The over-arching theme of the fifth and final section of this volume is that the advent of a new world order has not diminished many of the pressing concerns that dominated the old world order. The search for social justice and community in a new world order highlights the need to empower all for responsible citizenship.

Chapter fifteen is a very thoughtful essay by a prolific writer who is no stranger to the task of promoting the merits of a market economy. In this study, however, Michael Novak takes on the challenge of defending the term "social justice" against conservative critics who might claim that it "is an empty and mischievous term" (F. A. Hayek).

The term "social justice" gained prominence with the publication of the 1931 encyclical *Quadragesimo Anno* by Pope Pius XI, where it was used ten times. Novak maintains that social justice is that virtue "by which humans join with others to change the institutions of their society for the common good of the *civitas*." People seek structural changes so that society might be more just. To be sure, Novak is critical of those who seek major changes in the market system in the name of social justice because, for all its flaws, it is superior to "any known alternative mechanism." Yet he is a champion of "a carefully thought out virtue of social justice," and he gives a vision of what that might mean, including "some version of the welfare state."

While chapter one argued the merits of a communitarian democratic capitalism, the author of chapter sixteen, Amitai Etzioni, skillfully makes the case that a democratic polity requires shared virtues (communitarian values) for its health and survival. Etzioni is well known for his important work on communitarianism and is the editor of the communitarian journal, *The Responsive Community*.

There is a growing consensus that there are limits to interest-group pluralism and the stress on individual rights. Etzioni proposes that we need to cultivate the language of virtue as well as rights when we discuss and plan our common life. With a communitarian focus and its core of shared values, problems of pluralism and multiculturalism are seen in a new light. Many have noted that the political rhetoric of President Bill Clinton and Vice President Al Gore, with the themes of common purpose and community service, echoes the communitarian perspective.

Chapter seventeen is authored by a distinguished social ethicist, Peter J. Paris. Paris is concerned about the role of Catholic social thought in the struggle for racial justice in the United States. He notes that the Catholic church has had some success: "A 1966 *Newsweek* poll found that 58 percent of blacks viewed Roman Catholics as more helpful to the cause of civil rights than white Protestants." However, Catholic social teaching, similar to most other public policy, is basically flawed because it does not give sufficient attention to structural racism. Economic justice for African-Americans will be realized only when structural racism is confronted.

While noting that U.S. bishops have issued a 1979 pastoral letter on racism and have established a National Office for Black Catholics, Paris argues that there is still a need for more African-American clergy and laity on the staff of the National Conference of Catholic Bishops.

Echoing the theme of Joan Chittister in chapter eleven, Paris finds little prophetic idealism demonstrated in the Catholic role in the civil rights movement. While sympathetic to the goals of church teaching, he challenges all who will listen to focus on improving structural racism.

Chapter eighteen is an insightful analysis of how the classical notion of the common good might be retrieved for our times. Authored by M. Shawn Copeland, O.P., professor of theology and black studies at Yale University Divinity School, the study focuses on two pastoral letters of the U.S. bishops, one on racism and the other on the poor and the land of Appalachia.

Copeland traces the idea of the common good from its development in classical thought to its appropriation by Thomas Aquinas and later Catholic social teaching. She outlines opposing philosophic views to help the reader understand how "what had been in classical philosophy among the most noble of human pursuits, the common good," evolved under the influence of new intellectual currents to a conception where the role of the state is to protect individual freedom, thus, in the words of Thrasymachus in the *Republic*, "giving the strong full freedom to oppress the weak."

By analyzing two recent pastoral letters of the U.S. bishops, *Brothers and Sisters to Us* (on racism) and *This Land Is Home to Me* (on Appalachia), Copeland shows how Catholic social thought continues to assume and promote the classical understanding of the common good. The reader is challenged: "Are we willing to confront sin and evil within the Christian community?" The essay concludes by considering some of the important implications of the retrieval of the notion of the common good for Catholic social thought.

Dennis P. McCann is a theologian who has written extensively on Catholic social teaching and its import for the business world. In chapter nineteen, McCann argues that, as we enter this New World Order, the major challenge is to show clearly how business is a true calling and how the business system actually fulfills God's purpose in history.

McCann takes as his own the thesis of Robert B. Reich's 1991 book, *The Work of Nations: Preparing Ourselves for 21st Century Capitalism,* and presents an insightful, constructive proposal to advance religious social thought in our new global situation. McCann writes: "The good news . . . is that the internationalist vision that has always informed Catholic social teaching as a tradition . . . may now come into its own as uniquely relevant for creating a system of international accountability for the capitalism of the twenty-first century."

The final chapter is by "Mr. Labor" in U.S. Catholic circles, Monsignor George Higgins. He offers some most valuable personal reflections on church teaching and the labor movement. Higgins argues that trade unions must be valued not only for their negative role, "as indispensable bulwarks against statism," but also for their positive role, "the proper ordering of economic life." He is deeply concerned that the decline of trade unions in the U.S. is not a banner issue with the scholarly or business communities. Higgins takes some hope in the new spirit of cooperation between business and union leaders in their search for solutions to health care costs. Putting aside outdated ideological battles over capitalism and socialism, leaders are exhibiting a new spirit of collaboration that gives hope for the New World Order.

Fifteen

Liberty and Social Justice: Rescuing a Virtue

Michael Novak

F. A. Hayek's powerful criticisms of the concept of "social justice" in *The Mirage of Social Justice*, the second volume of his highly acclaimed trilogy,[1] have persuaded a surprising number of scholars that "social justice" is an empty and mischievous term. Clearly, this attack succeeds against some vague and woolly usages of the term; and most people who use it, inspection shows, do use it rather loosely. Such loose usage becomes vulnerable when it employs the term "social justice" simultaneously to describe some particular social condition ("a violation of social justice") and as the name of a moral virtue. For if the subject of "social justice" is society, it is not a person and only the latter can practice a moral virtue. Besides, modern societies are so complex that no authority controls their outcome. To attribute intention or control to all social outcomes is simple-minded. Consequently, say the objectors, to claim to be speaking for "social justice" can only be an ideological claim. Those who claim it merely foreclose arguments concerning means and ends by defining those who contest their own plans for society as "unjust." In brief, the objection runs, use of the term "social justice" is a sign of moral imperialism.

My aim is to rescue the term "social justice" from such accusations: My strategy for doing so is to concentrate on the term's *locus classicus*, Pius XI's *Quadragesimo Anno*, since all later papal references take this usage as authoritative. Further, Pius XI's usage is morally sound and highly useful in the analysis of public policy, and it is capable of true development. According to Cardinal Newman's criteria for the development of doctrine, the capacity of an idea slowly to align itself with other solid teachings, and to shed new light on old perplexities elsewhere in the system, is a clear sign of a true development. Thus, I want to show how the germinal idea of "social justice" fertilizes several lines of thought that connect with other teachings of the church, notably on religious and civic liberty in democratic societies, and on the Christian idea of liberty in general.

Finally, I want to show that, once stated in a way that cleanses it of woolly misunderstandings, social justice denotes a virtue especially appropriate to modern free societies: a personal virtue concerned with improving the institutional structures of the *civitas*, in line with the responsibilities of free persons in modern societies. It is a virtue especially necessary for lay persons in the modern world, since it requires them to work with others cooperatively and freely for aims shared in common. It allows for pluralism among competing organizations of activists who may not, in fact, agree with one another in their prudential judgments about what needs to be done or how to do it. Social justice includes, therefore, a concept of solidarity that is compatible with freedom of conscience and diversity of purpose. In a word, the virtue of social justice is fully compatible with life in the free society, and perfectly suited to its necessities. That special compatibility may explain why this particular concept has become explicit and flourished precisely in our time.

The notion "social justice" has a special history worth recording. It skips across history like a rock skipping across a pond, not breaking the surface for centuries at a time, but then for some years creating large ripples. In its classical appearances, the root idea was referred to as "legal justice" (Aristotle) or "general justice" (Aquinas). During the nineteenth century, the term "legal justice" came to be used by German jurists in ways ("the letter of the law," "state laws") that brought that term into disrepute. Finally, in 1931, Pope Pius XI made an intensive effort to recover the idea that Thomas Aquinas had intended by the name "general justice." He did this by placing this term in a context of rapid social change, and giving it a more precise meaning and a new name, "social justice."[2]

Pius XI used this new term ten times in his encyclical "On the Reconstruction of the Social Order" (*Quadragesimo Anno*, 1931); this was its first official use, its *locus classicus*. In the religious world (not only the Catholic world) this name has since become canonical. The pope did not invent the term "social justice"; it had begun to be used (in various senses) from about 1840 on by theologians in Sicily, France and Germany. But where there had been considerable confusion and vagueness about the three terms "legal justice," "general justice," and "social justice," Pius XI established a rather precise concept, raising and answering questions no one had asked before with such clarity. Let me briefly recapitulate this historical record.

In the fifth book of the *Nicomachean Ethics*, Aristotle needed a term to express two insights: first, that there seems to be a habit or virtue required for keeping the law, something like law-abidingness; and, second, that it is better for the whole city if there are many law-abiding citizens.[3] These observations suggested new moral territory, something necessary for moral life, which Aristotle designated "legal justice." Still, Aristotle was not willing to call "legal justice" a separate virtue. He thought of it, rather, as a general name for all the virtues without whose practice the law would go unobserved. He did not think of "legal justice" or "law-obeying justice" as requiring any new type of human act or habit. But he did sense the presence of some larger concept, involving society and law, beyond the individual virtues taken singly. For this he invented the special name.

Aquinas thought about this matter a little more deeply. He saw that one's moral life is radically affected by the condition of the city in which one resides. Like Aristotle, Aquinas had vivid personal experiences of civil war, flight, and exile (Aristotle as a young man, Aquinas as a child). When the accustomed order falls, the worst in people often comes out, and virtuous practice is rendered exceedingly difficult. Therefore, if the existing order is reasonably just (there is no paradise on earth), to defend it against an unjust order is a very great moral good. Thus, a soldier who defends his city is practicing not simply the virtue of bravery but also the virtue of acting for the common good of the city. So Aquinas took Aristotle's insight and made it sharper. There is a type of act that is drawn into exercise specifically for the sake of the *civitas* as a whole, i.e., for the common good that surrounds and supports the good of individuals. Aquinas saw this virtue as a habit of justice whose direct object is not some other individual or discrete group, but the whole social order—as it were, the general good or the common good.[4] He called this specific virtue "general justice," and noted that it differs from other habits of justice by its object. He did not press the matter further. He did not ask whether this newly identified habit would be exercised through any special and direct acts of its own or whether it would always be simply an accompaniment of some other virtue such as the bravery of the soldier or the law-abidingness of the citizen.

I am going to skip the German controversy and the rise of the slogan "social justice" in the mid-nineteenth century and go directly to the clarifications added by Pius XI in 1931. Writing in the depth of the worldwide Depression (and an especially severe banking crisis in Germany), and drawing on a team of German social theorists led by Oswald von Nell-Breuning, the pope began with the great modern fact: social instability. As he worked on his text, Stalin was beginning to terrorize the Ukraine, Hitler was on the rise in Germany, Mussolini was already arrogantly exercising in Italy what he described as "the totalitarian will," and Japan's warlords were on the rise. Already forty years earlier in 1891, Pope Leo XIII had spoken of "the spirit of revolutionary change" that was even then undercutting the institutions of the past. The widening dimensions of the "social question," Leo saw, had passed from politics into practical economics, yet it was at bottom a profound moral and religious crisis.

Pius XI grasped the moral challenge implicit in this generations-long social change, and wondered what claims justice makes upon humans in unstable times. "There is an instability from which no single thing can escape, for that, precisely, is the essence of created things," he had written in 1926, for the thirty-fifth anniversary of *Rerum Novarum*. "Precisely in those social elements which seem fundamental, and most exempt from change, such as property, capital, labor, a constant change. . . is not only possible, but is real, and an accomplished fact." He looked at each of these "fundamental social elements" in turn, and it will prove useful to cite one of his discussions in full:

> It is the same with labor. From the primitive work of the man of the stone age, to the great organization of production of our day, how many transitions, ascensions, complications, diversities!. . . What an enormous difference! It is therefore necessary to take such changes into account, and to prepare oneself, by an enlightened foresight and with complete resignation, to this instability of things and of human institutions, which are not all perfect, but necessarily imperfect and susceptible of changes.[5]

This is the context in which, five years later, Pius XI takes up the term "social justice" as his solution to the moral problems inherent in social change. In most of the ten passages in which he introduces this term in *Quadragesimo Anno* (paragraph 71, for example), the pope begins with a concrete problem—in this case that fathers of families are not receiving wages adequate to support their children. The pope has already seen that social systems are in flux and that social change is quite natural. What he sees also is that human beings have a responsibility to shape these changes in a moral way. If fathers are not receiving wages sufficient to support their families "under existing circumstances," he writes, "social justice demands that changes be introduced into the system as soon as possible, whereby such a wage will be assured to every adult working-man." A society that would allow children to starve, and individual fathers to be helpless in improving their family's condition, is in his view neither a good nor a stable nor a fully legitimate society. Humans must not simply wring their hands about this. They should "introduce changes into the system as soon as possible." This, indeed, is the object of the virtue of social justice.[6] Three points are worth stressing here.

First, humans are required by the morality written into their own nature (as Aristotle and Aquinas had discerned) to accept responsibility for the shape of the institutions of their society. Second, they should fix their eyes on changes in the *system*, that is, in those institutions and organizations that in their ensemble constitute society. Third, they should be realistic, fixing their aim on what is "possible," not on utopian visions.

These three characteristics help clarify the nature of the new virtue for whose development Pius XI calls. During past ages, common people were relatively passive "subjects" rather than responsible "citizens." In the new circumstances, they need to exercise new responsibilities, whose object and methods are social and whose exercise requires prudence and practicality. Social justice is that specification of the virtue of justice by which humans join with others to change the institutions of their society for the common good of the *civitas*. Through active association, they try to change the system for the better in one or another practical respect.

In a sense, this formulation recovers Aristotle's sense of the impact that the political structure has on ethos, i.e., that the life of the city has on the life of the individual. What the pope adds to Aristotle is an emphasis, first, on the citizen's responsibility for the shape of economic institutions and, second, on the need for voluntary organizations and associations to bring individuals out of isolation and to empower them. The pope sees that free men and women in modern times can join together, organize, and make changes in the institutions of the societies in which they live. To do this requires of them vigilance, farsightedness, courage, realism, organizational skills, and perseverance. All these requirements are signs that social justice is a demanding virtue.

To my own way of thinking, this discussion by Pius XI justifies (against Hayek, for example) the validity of the term "social justice."[7] There is room in the free society for individuals to work in association for goals they deem enhancing of the common good, particularly but not only when they show concern for the least fortunate. Both democracy and capitalism need citizens to be civic-minded, to take the larger view, to apply their temporal energies to alleviating pressing social ills, and to remedy obvious social deficiencies. We want citizens to practice the virtue of acting freely, and in concert with others, for the many social goods—political, economic, cultural—that, in a free society, individuals must have the enterprise to imagine and to achieve for themselves.

Nonetheless, there are several undeveloped elements in the theory of social justice set forth by Pius XI. First, he fails to mention the social conditions that would seem to be required for its exercise. Second, perhaps by accident, the concrete setting in which he introduced his new term in *Quadragesimo Anno* has led to a misunderstanding, viz., that the virtue of social justice is to be exercised solely (or mostly) in connection with distributive justice, whereas the needs of the *civitas* (and the object of the virtue of social justice too) are much broader than that. Third, while the pope speaks well of capitalism, and quite strongly of the importance of private property, it is plain that he has not thoroughly considered the ways in which liberty, particularly in economic matters, is necessary to social justice and the best available servant of the common good. Let us examine briefly each of these weaknesses in the pope's argument.

It would seem heroically difficult to exercise the virtue of social justice within a totalitarian society, in which no room is allowed either for personal initiative or for free association. Similarly, an oppressive dictatorship in a less than totalitarian society might also prevent reformist initiatives from coming to fruition. However, many prison memoirs make plain that, even in the bleakest circumstances, those individuals who think and act as members of a community survive best, trying by whatever slender means are available to better the lives of their fellows and to render more humane, by whatever tiny increments, the inhumanity of their surroundings. There is never reason to despair; we are required always to be faithful, even if not always to succeed. Thus, many survivors testify in their memoirs as to the practice of social justice even in the concentration camps.[8] Nonetheless, full civic space is plainly required for the completely free exercise of social justice.

Thus, it is a suppressed premise of the argument of Pius XI that social justice is most readily practiced in a democratic society or, at least, in a society that allows considerable civic space, with full rights of free association and civic initiative, and perhaps also a free press. Moreover, if citizens are to have economic resources for "changing the system," they will almost certainly have to be living under a regime of private property, so that they may have dominion over the material goods necessary for their project.

On the second point, Ernest Fortin has remarked on how thoroughly, both before and after Pius XI, the term "social justice" has been thrown into confusion, as though it consisted mainly of concern for the distribution of income. The concrete examples given by Pius XI, as we have seen, lend themselves to this vulgarization. Fortin summarizes the way in which most people speak of "social justice"—what might be called "the vulgar view of social justice"—in these words:

> As nearly as I can make out, social justice, in contradistinction to either legal or distributive justice, does not refer to any special disposition of the soul and hence cannot properly be regarded as a virtue. Its subject is not the individual human being but a mysterious "X" named society, which is said to be unintentionally responsible for the condition of its members and in particular for the lot of the poor among them. It makes complete sense only within the context of the new political theories of the seventeenth century, the thrust of which was to shift the focus of attention from virtue or moral character to the reordering of our social structures in such a way as to insure the

security and freedom of the autonomic individuals who choose to enter into society or accept to remain in it for that reason and that reason alone. As such, it is of a piece with the modern rights theory, which is concerned only with the perfection of the social order as distinguished from that of the individual. Yet it goes beyond the early modern view in that it seeks to equalize social conditions.[9]

Like Calvez, Fortin notes that the first author to use the term "social justice" was the Sicilian priest, Taparelli d'Azeglio, in his *Theoretical Essay on Natural Right Based on Facts* (1840). However, it was Rousseau's radical critique of civil society as corrupting the pure individual that really laid the groundwork for this new concept of social justice. Rousseau reformulated virtually all human problems in terms of the distinction between nature and history, as opposed to the classical distinction between body and soul. Fortin summarizes the vulgarized consequences:

> If society and its accidental structures are the primary cause of the corruption of human beings and the evils attendant upon it, they must be changed. Social reform takes precedence over personal reform; it constitutes the first and perhaps the only moral imperative. Better institutions will give us better human beings and not vice versa. Under such circumstances, the premodern emphasis on education and moral character as the true causes of the happiness of both the individual and the community could safely be laid aside. The only true evil is social evil, just as the only sin is social sin.[10]

There is no doubt that Fortin is correct in describing the wild and woolly sloganizing to which "social justice" has become prey. Even the communists find it useful for their propaganda, and socialists use it unabashedly as the generic name for their own purposes. To rescue the term from such ideological misuse is no easy task.

Still, I have given evidence above that Pius XI, at least, did describe social justice as a disposition (habit) of the soul that is specified by a distinctive object (the changing of the system that structures the common life of the *civitas*). Social justice, in *his* sense at least, is a virtue exercised by individuals. Its subject is not a mysterious "X," the state.

Nonetheless, even though Pius XI's concept of "social justice" meets one test that the more vulgar notions do not, it still faces many difficulties. In paragraph 88, for example, *Quadragesimo Anno* gives to social justice the task of correcting the market system:

> Just as the unity of human society cannot be founded upon an opposition of classes, so also the right ordering of economic life cannot be

left to a free competition of forces . . . a truth which the outcome of
the practical application of the tenets of this evil individualistic spirit
has more than sufficiently demonstrated. Therefore, it is most necessary that economic life be again subjected to and governed by a true
and effective directing principle.

This invocation of a "directing principle" to which the market must be
"subjected" and by which it must be "governed" raises three difficult
moral questions that the pope does not face.

First, will not such governing of the market bring back the poverty of
the pre-capitalist or of the communist era? At the very least, will it not
inflict serious costs on the common good?

Second, *cui bono?* Who will interfere with the market and steer it, and
to whose benefit and whose loss?

Third, what guarantee is there that the "governors" of the free market
either know or truly care about the full effects of the distortions their activities cause in the signalling function of prices? It often happens that even
interventions made with the best of intentions defeat their own purposes,
and there is no guarantee that actual interventions will even be well
intended. If the pope assumes that individual actors in their freedom will
sin, why should he not assume the same of "governors" or "directors"?
Interventions in markets in Catholic countries such as those of Latin
America and the Philippines, for example, are reported by Hernando de
Soto and others to be devastating to the poor, despite many flowery
remonstrations to the contrary.[11]

Pius XI was indeed worried about excessive power in the hands of
those who claimed to be "directing" society to utopian purposes; he was
forthrightly anti-socialist. In paragraph 120, he states openly that
"'Religious socialism', 'Christian socialism' are expressions implying a
contradiction in terms," and adds: "No one can be at the same time a sincere Catholic and a true socialist."

By contrast, the pope is by no means an anti-capitalist. His views of
capitalism and of socialism are not symmetrical. For example, in paragraph 101, he writes:

With all his energy, Leo XIII sought to adjust this (capitalistic) economic system according to the norms of right order; hence it is evident that this system is not to be condemned in itself. And assuredly
it is not of its own nature vicious. But it does violate right order when
capital hires workers, that is the non-owning class, with a view to
and under such terms that it directs business and even the whole
economic system according to its own will and advantage, scorning

the human dignity of the workers, the social character of economic activity, Social Justice itself, and the Common Good.

As Ferree explains, in the interpretation I have been making my own, the pope condemns the abuse of a system that is "not of its own nature vicious." The pope condemns only a deliberate manipulation of that system "with a view to and under such terms as" to capture the system itself for selfish ends. That such a deliberate abuse shows scorn for human dignity and for the other members of the economic team is obvious. When the pope says that such manipulation shows scorn for "social justice itself," he means that it formally denies that the system *should be so organized* as to benefit all.[12] Doing so, it announces to the world its own illegitimacy.

The central difficulty with the pope's new concept is its reliance on the "mirror-effect" of the concept *bonum commune*, the common good. As Calvez and Perrin write in their magisterial chapter on social justice, "The concept of the common good is at the center of its definition."[13] But to those who use it, the concept *bonum commune* turns out to be more comforting than illuminating. True, the absence of the common good is obvious enough; there are situations so bad that almost everybody can say, "The country's in a mess, we need a change." But when it comes to remedies or to schemes of action for the resurrection of the common good out of the ruins, four large difficulties loom into view.

First, in projecting upon an empty mirror what they think the common good of the future ought to look like, most observers see an image of themselves and their own aspirations. Among these many projections, naturally, there is great variety and internal contrariety.

Second, when they claim to speak for the common good and not merely for themselves, people often deceive themselves about their true purposes. The Tammany Hall saying catches this as nicely as Adam Smith once did: "When a fella says, 'Tain't the money, it's the principle,' it's the money."

Third, while the term common good suggests to some a firm sense that they know what they are talking about, on actual inspection it becomes clear that they cannot easily gain consensus on the practical changes in institutions and arrangements that they are hiding behind that rosy phrase.

Fourth, and in particular when they are speaking about the distribution of income or the supplying of concrete needs, it is quite literally impossible for them to know the full consequences of any particular arrangements or institutional changes they would like to effect. Experience shows that their best laid plans for improvements often go awry.

Moreover, schemes to "direct" income distributions usually reflect the political power of already organized groups, and thus thwart economic dynamism and mobility. They are a recipe for reaction and fixity, not for change.

Therefore, a good arrangement can be defeated if it is headed by the wrong people. Good people can be frustrated by an ill-conceived or untimely arrangement. The ways of failing are numerous, and the details necessary to master for regularly successful outcomes are nearly infinite, far beyond the mental powers of a single set of social engineers, however brilliant. In brief, it is far easier to imagine that one is serving the common good than actually to achieve the common good or even to know for sure and in advance, concretely and materially, which among possible institutional arrangements will work out best, even for one's own best purposes.

Plainly missing at this early stage in the thinking of Pius XI is the crucial distinction between the common good as a *formal* and as a material concept.[14] The formal concept works as a principle of social progress, like a searchlight fixing on those benefits yet to be achieved or those institutional improvements yet to be made, which operate as "benchmarks" in whose light current inadequacies are discerned. The material concept is constituted by those particular concrete arrangements and practical institutions that do achieve a higher level of well-being for the community. It is much easier to conceptualize a formal concept of the common good— a more or less realistic "wish list"—than to put in place the many elements of material content that actually improve the common life of the city by some measurable degree.

It was quite clear to Pius XI and to the Catholic tradition that there is no perfect attainment of the common good on earth; sinful humans, with the help of divine grace, can but approximate it. Perhaps, too, Pius XI suspected the practical difficulties inherent in the early stage of the discussion in which he initiated the official use of the term "social justice." If social justice is the virtue through which the "common good" is to be progressively approximated, the very idea of the common good would require a great deal more clarity and practical purchase than he had at his disposal in 1931.

In many ways, the condition of the working classes in Europe in 1931 was at a far higher level than in 1891, and a considerable number of the lower classes had moved up into the middle classes (or higher). True, the sufferings brought on by the Depression were cruel, and the stranglehold ("dictatorship," the pope called it) the bankers in Germany held in those inflation-wracked years horrified the public (and prepared the way for Adolf Hitler). Nonetheless, the free market of the nineteenth century had impressed the public mind with a visible sense of "progress," and in many

ways had served the common good better than any earlier social arrangement. During that century, slavery was abolished and serfdom ended;
longevity increased; medicine began to be scientific; and living standards
had improved visibly. Moreover, among the chief causes of the Depression (and of the "dictatorship" of the German central bankers) were mis-
guided attempts to "govern," to "direct" and to "control" the free market.
So, at least, many economists have argued.

Nonetheless, the popes (even until today) have devoted exceedingly
little space to analyzing how and to what degree free markets serve, or do
not serve, the common good. Nearly all the brief comments of Pius XI on
market freedoms have a pejorative ring. Is this meant to suggest that freedom is antithetical to social justice? A qualification instantly suggests itself:
In speaking of markets, the pope is objecting to "untrammeled" freedom
or "unrestrained" freedom (the adjectives normally used), but not to
"ordered" freedom. As Hayek and others have pointed out, markets can
exist only within the framework of law, custom and tacit moral practice.
In those respects, far from being "untrammeled," it is because of such
restraints that markets are such powerful instruments of intelligible order.

Still, what we miss in the pope's discussion of these issues is greater
skepticism concerning the mere declaration by officials or private citizens
that it is their intention to act for the common good. Have the popes really
known much actual material good to follow merely from such declarations? On the other hand, what we miss is lack of reflection on the internal
dynamics of a market system *qua* system. Before free markets slowly
became the (partial) practice of certain leading political economies, moral
arguments were made on their behalf. It was argued that they would serve
the general welfare better than mercantilist, highly regulated, land-based,
agrarian economies. Pius XI recognized that this argument is subject
to empirical testing, because in asserting that "the right ordering of economic life cannot be left to a free competition of forces," he appeals precisely to an empirical proof "which the outcome of the practical
application of the tenets of this evil individualistic spirit has more than sufficiently demonstrated."

This empirical principle should be more thoroughly deployed. No
doubt, in certain matters of the general welfare "the free competition of
forces" in the market is not a sufficient guide. For example, those too old,
too young, too ill or too disabled to fend for themselves in markets need
special care. Adam Smith argued further that education and many other
public goods, which would be unlikely to be practicable for private
efforts, should be provided by governments. Indeed, the neoclassical
tradition—the tradition called "liberal" precisely because of its leadership
in urging freer markets—has recognized a rather large panoply of social

purposes better met by other social mechanisms than the free market. The market is an indispensable tool of the free society; but it is a limited instrument. It is not designed to establish truth or moral principles, for example. Yet, in giving rise to a dynamic economic order, it is unsurpassed.

In brief, moralists have insisted that the free market is a *social* mechanism that serves the economic welfare of the whole society (especially the poor) better than any known alternative mechanism. They insist also that the chief merit of the market system is the number of moral advantages it maintains over other systems. A free market teaches social cooperation better than any alternative system, since transactions in markets are those of free, consenting adults. Again, markets tend to promote positive-sum outcomes. They orient their participants, for reasons of self-interest if not for reasons of generosity and sympathy, to the needs of other participants because, in markets, each participant benefits more if others are well pleased. The social energies of markets are centripetal; they draw individuals toward a study of each other's needs, and they draw them together. (Even "window shopping" is a way of gathering information and getting out in public.)

Furthermore, markets depend upon law, tradition and tacit knowledge—upon all those skills of finger, sense, instinct, practice and experience that craftsmen learn and pass along across the generations. Markets are conservators of human capital, and also the teachers and carriers of human capital from one population to another. Through rapid international interchange, they stimulate the further development of human capital and prompt social improvements of all sorts. It is no accident that the term "progress" has so often found its empirical grounding in the rapid diffusion of new discoveries to the broad and general public through open, efficient and responsive free markets, or that progress has been slowed by both traditionalist and communist forms of economic organization.

In a word, the papal tradition on free-market economics, of which we are using Pius XI as a watershed illustration, has often spoken disparagingly to free markets, but without presenting a full-dress and detailed argument or analyzing the deficiencies of the alternatives. This is true not only of the Catholic tradition, but also of those many anti-free market tendencies in various Protestant traditions. It is almost as if the clergy, having their roots in the aristocratic era, when bishops were "princes" in more than metaphor, are deeply biased against the central economic institution by which so many hundreds of millions of the world's poor have been pulled up into the middle class and higher. Dislike for the market seems more visceral than reasoned.

By contrast, the popes have always been outspoken in defending a social regime of private property as indispensable to the common good.

(This right was always important to the landed aristocracy, as markets were not.) For example, Pius XI quotes Leo XIII in defense of private property: "However the earth may be apportioned among private owners, it does not cease to serve the common good of all." Then Pius XI repeats once more his own defense of property:

> This same doctrine We Ourselves also taught just above in declaring that the division of goods which results from private ownership was established by nature itself in order that created things may serve the needs of mankind in a fixed and stable order. Lest one wander from the right path of truth, this is something which must be continually kept in mind. (Paragraph 56)

In paragraph 57, the pope notes that "not every distribution among human beings of property or wealth is of a character to attain . . . with a satisfactory degree of perfection, the ends which God intended." Like Leo XIII, Pius XI has already made plain that God certainly did not intend absolute equality. There is pitifully little evidence in nature that God is an egalitarian, except the fact of death for all. On the contrary, diversity of kind and degree appears to be His chief delight. Nonetheless, Pius XI does hold that a just system must safeguard "the common advantage of all." He calls this "the law of social justice" and the very definition of the common good. Compared, then, to other alternatives, does the market system "safeguard the common advantage"? It seems to do so better than either the traditionalist (Third World) or socialist systems. Objectively, although plainly not in his eyes, it seems to meet the standard set by Pius XI.

Still, it is not surprising that Pius XI did not analyze more fully both the internal and external controls built into market systems. Indeed, some of the best neoclassical writing on these themes—by Mises and Hayek, for example—did not appear until after 1931. When markets are described as "free," this does not mean they are unrestrained by law, morals, custom, tradition, peer pressure, competition and state regulators. Nonetheless, if Catholic social thought had had a more detailed grasp both of what is wrong and what is right about market systems—both of the moral gains they have registered in the common good of societies, and of their limitations and specific temptations—the church would have been in a far better position to prepare for, and to predict, the "economic miracles" that followed World War II. It would also have been in a better position to help set the Third World upon a much more productive route than that taken by most new nations since that time. (In a certain sense, Germany's postwar "social market economy" represents the sort of blend of Austrian economics and Catholic social thought for which I am arguing. For various reasons too complex to enter into here, I believe that the American model of "democratic capitalism" is a better example of what used to be called "the middle way.")

It was characteristic of Third World countries after independence that their economies were all too thoroughly "directed" and "governed" in the name of the common good, but in fact in the interests of tiny, wealthy (and heavily armed) elites. In such contexts, to preach solely in favor of "directed" and "governed" markets was to strengthen enormously the hand of tyrants and to destroy the openness of economic systems to opportunity for the poor. Given such an interpretation, the cry of social justice may be used to injure, not to achieve, the common good. Indeed, it was in observing the empirical fact that those who spoke much about the common good actually achieved very little of it that Adam Smith awakened himself from traditional modes of thought. This led him to hypothesize that, in economic matters, the principle of ordered liberty would serve better than past alternatives what the popes would later call social justice and the common good.

Unless I am mistaken, most thinkers who approach "the social question" while having uppermost in their minds the principle of liberty are quite aware, these days, that the free society is in need of energetic, associative efforts of self-reform. Liberty is too easily lost; vigilance must be constant. In addition, certain constraints are necessary even to practice liberty. The needs of the unfortunate who cannot help themselves must also be met. Some version of the welfare state (no doubt much reformed) is necessary for the stability and legitimacy of the free society, but also for its moral self-respect. In these ways, the partisans of liberty make room for a carefully thought out virtue of social justice—yet correctly fear the vulgar versions of social justice as leading to tyranny.

From those whose primary principle is "social justice" or "the common good," however, these days there seems also to be greater willingness to look again at the fecundity of the principle of liberty. Certainly, the prospect of Third World and Second World societies that lack liberty has not been encouraging.

It seems there is considerable room in the social thought of the popes for expanding the role of ordered liberty in economic matters for achieving a higher level of the common good on a universal planetary basis. This means giving ordered liberty greater place within the concept of social justice. Indeed, liberty and responsibility are the rock upon which human dignity is built. It does not seem possible to attain social justice without them. A society that defaces or undermines that rock can never serve human dignity.

Were the Catholic church more vigorously to incorporate the principle of ordered liberty in its concept of social justice, much good would be done for the poor of the Third World, particularly in such Catholic territories as those of Latin America and the Philippines. Properly understood, the two concepts of social justice and ordered liberty need each other. It is much to our disadvantage that they have been allowed to remain separated for so many years.

Notes

1. F. A. Hayek, *Law, Legislation, and Liberty* (Chicago: University of Chicago Press, 1973, 1976, 1979); vol. 1: *Rules and Order,* vol. 2: *The Mirage of Social Justice;* vol. 3: *The Political Order of a Free People.* A crisp summary of this critique is found in John Gray, "Social Injustice," *Crisis* (September 1990).

2. The best discussion of social justice I have encountered is the booklet, *Introduction to Social Justice*, by William J. Ferree (Dayton, Ohio: Marianist Publications, 1948); there is also a good chapter given to the question in Jean Yves Calvez and Jacques Perrin, "Justice," *The Social Teaching of the Church* (London: Burns & Oates, 1961). There is a brief discussion in Messner, *Social Ethics: Natural Law in the Western World* (St. Louis: B. Herder Book Company, 1965), pp. 320–321. Curiously, there is no entry under this topic in the theological dictionary produced after Vatican II, *Sacramentum Mundi* (New York: Herder and Herder, 1970), even though Oswald Von Nell-Breuning, the reputed author of *Quadragesimo Anno* and of the concept of "Social Justice," wrote the long entry under the title "Social Movements" (vol. 6, pp. 98–116). For a brief discussion of the concept of "General Justice" in St. Thomas, see Thomas Gilby, *Between Community and Society* (London: Longmans, Green and Company, 1953), pp. 208–211.

3. Aristotle, *Nicomachean Ethics*, book V.i.8,12–13. Note especially (V.i.13):

> Now all the various pronouncements of the law aim either at the common interest of all, or at the interest of a ruling class determined either by excellence or in some other similar way; so that in one of its senses the term "just" is applied to anything that produces and preserves the happiness, or the component parts of the happiness, of the political community.

4. Aquinas, *Summa Theologica*, IIa–IIae, q. 58, art. 5–6. For a fuller discussion, see Calvez and Perrin, pp. 139–145.

5. Ferree, p. 7.

6. *Ibid.*, p. 11.

7. See Friedrich A. Hayek's objections in "Social or Distributive Justice," *Law, Legislation, and Liberty*, vol. 2: *The Mirage of Social Justice* (Chicago: University of Chicago Press, 1976), ch. 9, pp. 62–100.

8. I am thinking of Anatoly Scharansky, Aleksandr Solzhenitsyn, and Mihailov; also Admiral James Stockdale, etc.

9. Ernest Fortin, "Natural Law and Social Justice," *The American Journal of Jurisprudence*, 1985, vol. 30 (Natural Law Institute at Notre Dame Law School), pp. 1–20. Quotation from pp. 14–15.

10. *Ibid.*, pp. 15–16.

11. See Hernando de Soto, *The Other Path: The Invisible Revolution in the Third World* (New York: Harper & Row, 1989).

12. Ferree, p. 18.

13. Calvez and Perrin, p. 152.

14. Yves R. Simon introduced the distinction in *The Philosophy of Democratic Government* (Chicago: University of Chicago Press, 1951), p. 42. For a fuller discussion, see Michael Novak, *Free Persons and the Common Good* (New York: Madison Books, 1989), pp. 82–98, 176–187. Jacques Maritain gives a particularly vivid description of the complexity of the material content of the common good: What constitutes the common good of political society is not only

> the collection of public commodities and services—the roads, ports, schools, etc., which the organization of common life presupposes; a sound fiscal condition of the state and its military power; the body of just laws, good customs and wise institutions, which provide the nation with its structure; the heritage of its great historical remembrances, its symbols and its glories, its living traditions and cultural treasures. The common good includes all of these and something much more besides—something more profound, more concrete and more human. For it includes also, and above all, the whole sum itself of these; a sum which is quite different from a simple collection of juxtaposed units. . . . It includes the sum or sociological integration of all the civic conscience, political virtues and sense of right and liberty, of all the activity, material prosperity and spiritual riches, of unconsciously operative hereditary wisdom, of moral rectitude, justice, friendship, happiness, virtue and heroism in the individual lives of its members. For these things all are, in a certain measure, *communicable* and so revert to each member, helping him [or her] to perfect his [or her] life and liberty of person. They all constitute the good human life of the multitude.

> (*The Person and the Common Good*; Notre Dame, Indiana: University of Notre Dame Press, 1966; pp. 52–53.)

Sixteen

Virtues in a Democracy*

Amitai Etzioni

When one points to the merits of the language of virtue over that of rights or interests, one faces the charge that the position is dogmatic, undemocratic or majoritarian. After briefly stating the issue, I endeavor to show that while these criticisms merit moral and social attention, they can be accommodated without yielding on the basic point: the virtue of virtues. To put it differently, the language of virtues and democratic polities can be reconciled; indeed, we shall see, they may thrive together, and whither apart.

Proliferation of Rights

Over the last decades there has been a strong and well-documented tendency to extend the language of rights. While once only a rather short list of what sometimes is referred to as basic or fundamental rights was recognized, the trend has been to expand and multiply moral claims expressed in the form of rights. Many of the rights initially added to the list are associated with the addressing of major social ills and building up the civil rights of minorities. However, over the years rights also were added that are less widely legitimated, more controversial, or outright dubious. These include the rights of children to sue their parents for "wrongful" life (in some cases children claim that, given their predictable afflictions, their parents should not have brought them into the world), the rights of animals, the right of handicapped individuals to sit at emergency exits on airplanes, and even of brooks and trees:

> It is no answer to say that streams and forests cannot speak. Corporations cannot speak either; nor can states, estates, infants, incompetents, municipalities, or universities. Lawyers speak for

---

*The author is indebted to Sharon Pressner for research assistance.

them, as they customarily do for the ordinary citizen with legal problems. . . . On a parity of reasoning, we should have a system in
which, when a friend of a natural object perceives it to be endan-
gered, he [or she] can apply to a court for the creation of a guardian-
ship. (Stone, 1974, p. 17)

In reaction to this trend, opposition has risen to specific rights by
those who favor the *status quo* and are affected adversely by the new
rights. For example, homeowners opposed the rights of homeless to shelter in Washington, D.C., once the shelters were put into their neighborhoods. Conservatives in general oppose the proliferation of rights either
because they curb the freedom of businesses to conduct their business
(and eat into their profits). For example, unpaid parental leaves, a newly
won right in many companies, exacts some costs by having to find substi-
tutes for people on leave. Moreover, they write critically of a "rights revolution" or "industry":

The "rights revolution" refers to the tendency to define nearly every
public issue in terms of legally protected rights of individuals. Rights
of the handicapped,. . . workers,. . . students, . . . women,. . . consumers, the right of a hearing, the right to know—these have become
the stock and trade of American political discourse. (Melnick, 1989,
p. 188)

Conservatives often prefer to refer to the new rights as "entitlements"
and argue that they are either claims without merit, as part of self-aggran-
dizement of undeserving claimants (e.g., welfare rights) or unnecessary in
view of existing laws (e.g., a reason given for opposing ERA). According
to Bell (1975, p. 97), "the promise of equality has been transformed into a
revolution of rising 'entitlements'—claims on government to implement
an array of newly defined and vastly expanded social rights." MacIntyre
(1984, p. 69) put it most strongly: "There are no such rights [natural and
human], and belief in them is one with belief in witches and unicorns."

Inflationary, Contentious and Litigious

There is more to the opposition to the "rights industry" and "explosion of entitlements" than efforts to maintain the *status quo* and reserve
previously established claims. The proliferation of rights has social and
moral consequences that should concern even those who are favorably

disposed to many of the specific new rights advanced in the last decades. These include a self-defeating feature: The more rights are generated in a community and the more they are validated, the weaker the appeal of additional rights that are newly minted; indeed, the appeal of old ones also tends to be diluted. The same with currency; the more that is issued, especially if printed quite freely, the lower its value. While there seems to be no precise zero-sum condition, there is no precisely limited moral stock of claims, so that as one exhausts it—no moral stock to be issued is left—there is nevertheless some dilution effect that is readily discernable. Rights that are fought for today seem not to have nearly the punch that such claims had in previous eras, although the inflation of rights is only one reason. (Another, which we do not deal with here, is major value changes in society.) It follows, as a law of the socioeconomics of rights, that *those who care about moral claims—whether these are the new ones, old ones, or both—would be wise to favor a sparing use*, to ensure that these claims will have the required standing.

A second concern is the confrontational and litigious nature of rights. It is often stated that rights are "absolute." If one means by that their claims are unlimited or do not require qualifications or have an unquestionable standing, this is hardly the case. All rights are limited by some other rights and other concerns. The limit on the right to free speech by the well-known dictum about not being allowed to shout fire in a crowded theater, illustrates the much more general point. Rights of children are curbed by those of parents, as are those of parents—by rights of their children. The freedom of the press is limited by genuine national security needs, and so on.

The references to rights being "absolute," therefore, should be understood best as a sociological observation that those who advance them are often "true believers" (or act as if they were, for tactical reasons) and lay them on others as if they were incontestable. It is this quality of rights that tends to make them contentious, difficult to reconcile and, as they proliferate, strain the ability of democratic communities to form consensus and shared public policies. Hence, the alarm with which "single issue groups," groups that are ideologically committed unlike "typical" interest groups, are viewed by many students of democratic polities. Pro-life groups are an example that is frequently cited.

The "absolute" feature of rights also tends to lead parties to courts as the place to settle conflicting claims, rather than through the more compromise prone political give and take, labor negotiation, or mediation. This is probably one of the reasons our society is so much more litigious than other democracies such as in Europe and especially in Japan.

The Language of Interests

Critics of the rights "industry" have suggested that instead of validating ever more rights (in the sense of accepting as morally compelling, as legitimate claims of those who proffer them), we should treat them as interests. As Lomasky (1987, p. 7) put it, "Problems tractable if formulated in terms of contending *interests* or *preferences* become rigidified when transformed into disputes over basic *rights.*" It seems that to characterize a right as an interest defangs it, diminishes its moral fervor, and makes compromise more likely between groups with divergent interests (e.g., by splitting differences). However, such an approach avoids the moral issues of which claims are just and which are without merit; all claims are treated as someone's "interests." We are left with the socioeconomic need to cope with the surfeit or claims, even if they are viewed as "merely" expressing interests rather than rights. This is all too evident in the fact that we have great difficulties in curbing the federal deficit, caused only in part by rising entitlements, much driven by a proliferation of interest groups (for details see Etzioni, 1984).

In addition, the language of interests instead of rights (or at least instead of all but basic rights) has problems of its own. It is basically ·diminishing and dismissive, deconstructive if not cynical. It treats moral claims as if they were positions parties adopt in cold blood, and are ready to trade as if the claims had no normative standing or affective power.

Environmentalists and polluters, welfare mothers and country club members, the National Rifle Association and the Peace movement, are all framed as mere "interest groups" (Etzioni, 1988, p. 201). Justice is not so much denied as not considered; moral dialogues and ruling are replaced with marketplaces. Such an approach *may* make a society more manageable, but hardly sustain the legitimacy of its policies and institutions or its moral fabric.

The Virtue of Virtues

The language of virtues avoids many of the difficulties entailed in the proliferation of rights and its reduction to interests. If a community recognizes a set of moral values and commitments as compelling, as virtues, these become the foundations of moral discourse in that community (Williams, 1990, p. 9). Other statements and new moral claims—so long as they are not absorbed into the set of shared virtues—have no or little standing. While there are frequently differences in interpreting the meanings and indications of prevailing virtues—e.g., how much is due to charity?—virtues do provide sound and shared foundations for consensus formation, shared endeavors, public policies and moral standing. For example, in the traditional European Jewish *shtetl*, studying the scriptures was accorded high virtue. It left little doubt as to which activities were to be extolled and merited the seat nearest the preferred Eastern (oriented to Jerusalem) wall of the synagogue. It was not a question of the rights of one subgroup versus those of others but a community-wide recognition of the virtue of commitments to the scriptures.

Also, in communities with shared virtues (or communitarian values), contentiousness and litigiousness are curbed because relatively clear and shared criteria are available to resolve differences. Finally, the cynicism of "anything goes as long as it satisfies a deal among the interpreted parties" is avoided.

The Fear of Consensual Morality

Despite all these apparent merits, the language of virtues troubles many who are committed to democratic values. While some of their misgivings are misplaced or overstated, they point to considerations and measures that those who wish to embrace the language of virtue best heed. One frequently raised objection to the notion of virtues (as well as to communitarian values), is that they are "majoritarian" ("communitarian really means majoritarian," Glasser, 1990). That is, once a community comes to share a set of values, these will be used to suppress dissent and minorities, to violate individual and civil rights. (The lack of a secure place for individual and minority rights is a criticism levelled against Alasdair MacIntyre, one of the champions of the language of virtues [Thigpen and Downing, 1987, p. 643].) While, historically, this fear grows out of the roots of the American existence, a society fashioned by dissenters escaping dogma, it is a legitimate concern for all democracies.

Actually, there are two versions of the concern that are often intertwined and mutually reinforcing but should be kept apart for both diagnostic and therapeutic purposes. One concerns the polity; the other—the community. Within the polity, it is feared that a government will follow a simplistic notion of democracy: it will impose public policies and rules that the majority favor without regard to other rights (e.g., imposing prayers in schools). While this is not a problem necessarily or exclusively caused by the language of virtues, it can be exacerbated by the elevation of shared consensus to the status of virtues. Historically this happened in the United States when abortion and divorce were morally condemned and difficult to obtain legally.

Even when the government is not involved, and when there are no votes and hence no "majoritarian" positions or threat, a parallel concern is raised and not without reason. It is argued that when a community shares one set of virtues that are strongly endorsed and urged upon the members, even without the power of law, only through the community mechanisms of social pressure and ostracism, these can exert great pressures on those who deviate, whether these are gay or conscientious objectors or individuals who refuse to join a strike or boycott. (Salem during the witch trials, Geneva during the heyday of Calvinism provide historical cases in point.) Libertarians and *laissez-faire* conservatives, therefore, tend to favor a community without a set of overarching values, and build instead of the social (not merely economic!) merits of a world in which individuals are the only judges of their own conduct, each choosing what is best and hence personally right for them, from how much to work, to whether or not to have a family, to ride a motorbike without a helmet, and even to use addictive substances. At most, these libertarians and *laissez-faire* conservatives are willing to change social incentives to affect the calculations of free individuals, but not to try to influence their "preferences" or the courses of conduct they value. While it is rarely put in the following terms, in effect this approach holds that we are better off without an established set of virtues and community-wide consensus on what is of value.

As I see it, we should not scrap the quest for shared virtues and communitarian values, and the social mechanisms to affirm them, because nothing makes for more government and ultimate coercion (that is, the demon libertarian and *laissez-faire* conservatives properly fear) than the absence of shared morals, backed by strong commitments. Once virtues are eroded, social and civic order must by default rest more and more on government regulation, controls and police force. Thus, if a community ceases to define drug abuse and alcohol abuse, violence or greed as unacceptable behavior, it is left solely to the state to protect citizens from these abuses and from one another, an often untenable task. Communities require moral foundations to minimize the role of the government and make those roles it must play possible and properly circumscribed.

Moreover, a community without value commitments is a jungle of warring or selfish parties, indeed no community at all. Ballfield depicted such a village in his *The Moral Basis of a Backward Society* (1958). In this village, the poverty and backwardness, he concluded, is largely explained by the villagers inability to act together for their common good, or for any end transcending the immediate interest of each family (*ibid.*, p. 10).

In short, *clearly what is needed is a political and moral conception that accommodates the protection of minority and individual rights without giving up the language of virtues.*

Virtue and Democracy

U.S. institutions already reflect an ingenious answer to the need to combine consensus making and the moral power of virtues with a democratic polity. Instead of allowing unrestrained sway to policies that reflect majorities, we have the well-known "balancing" institutions whose task is not only to curb one another to limit the general power of each, but specifically to protect the rights of individuals and minorities. The same protection is, of course, accorded by the courts, above all the Supreme Court, and the Constitution itself, not only as a force that directs law enforcement, regulatory, administrative and other agencies but also as a moral/social, normative factor. (The moral/social role of the Constitution is highlighted by the finding that the majority of Americans do not agree with much of the Bill of Rights if it is presented to them without indication that the various statements are from the Constitution, for example, that a person often previously convicted and newly indicted is nevertheless innocent until proven guilty, and that communists are to be allowed to speak at colleges. Nevertheless, they subscribe to these norms, and find them legitimate once they are told or reminded that these statements are part of the Constitution). In short, the U.S. political system is far from a simple democratic government if by that one means, as it is all too often put, the rule of the majority, or of the people by the people for the people. Constitutional democracy is, of course, characterized in part by defining areas over which "the people" or the majority may not set policies, whatever its size.

Historically, the U.S. political system did not always work quite the way it was designed to work, say, in the McCarthy era, and there is a constant and proper debate where the lines should be drawn between the majority rule and other rights. But there can be no doubt that the American practice, not just design, shows that at least some virtues can be institutionalized without undermining individual and minority rights, without turning majoritarian.

The Limits of Pluralism

The question arises what sociological forces sustain the delicate balance between the will of the majority and consensual virtues, and the constitutional safeguards? The key concept that is often advanced in response to this cardinal question, as both a political and moral/social remedy to the dangers of majoritarian virtues, is pluralism.

On the community level, it is argued, if there is no one orthodoxy but several competing truths, the fervor of each will be restrained and people of different moral persuasions and commitments will each find their own set of virtues (various religions, or set of secular moral values). And, regarding the polity, it is often suggested that if various politically active groups advance different sets of values, no one majoritarian position will arise. Policies then would reflect compromises among the various positions advanced.

However, pluralism and virtues do not accommodate each other readily because pluralism mitigates commitments and provides no moral foundations for community-wide consensus *per se*, no overarching values and criteria for working out differences other than such mechanical and uncommitting notions as splitting the differences and nose-count. On the contrary, when there are a number of value commitments, all of which are considered legitimate, all commitments become relative and weak, and there remains only practical, no principled, grounds for community-building, shared values and policies. In effect, this "deideologizing" is precisely what the opponents of virtues and proponents of pluralism seek.

It might be argued that in a society in which little is done on a shared basis, as in a frontier society in which everyone who seeks change can go and find their individual ways in unsettled territories, there is no need for community values, consensus and virtues. (Actually, an historical study of the United States, we suggest, would show the existence of a rather strong consensus despite the low volume of shared projects and activities.) However, there can be little doubt that for a society like contemporary America that (a) has a long list of matters to which it must attend collectively such as defense, public safety (crime), the environment, and global competitiveness, and (b) has lost the basic moral/social foundations of a shared social and civic order, pluralism *per se* will not suffice.

Pluralism-within-Unity; Virtues with Rights

The answer lies in the concept of pluralism-within-unity which recognizes that the legitimation of diversity is not unlimited, that some ultimate values must be shared for the diversity to be contained, share policies to be based on firm grounds and criteria for settling conflicting claims to be provided. These virtues include, first of all, a set of ultimate values such as compassion for the poor, concern for the viability of the family, and concern for the environment. (The fact that these values are fuzzy at the edges it is not necessarily detrimental, because so long as the basic commitments stand, societies have various ways to work out the specific meanings of such values; this ceases to be the case, when the values are directly challenged or their basic meaning is contested.)

Second, the shared values or virtues are to include a legitimation of democracy and tolerance of diversity within the shared framework, and of individual standings and hence certain basic rights (Langan, 1990). This point should be stressed: Individual rights do not rest on individuals, somehow born endowed with them, but on a community-shared morality that legitimates and otherwise sustains them. In the polity, community values and virtues take the form of recognizing a public interest or interests above and beyond the plurality of special ones. Both these points deserve some elaboration.

The first issue is frequently raised in discussions of bicultural education. Pluralists stress the merits of allowing, even encouraging, people of different ethnic, cultural, and racial backgrounds, especially immigrants, not only to learn in their language and tradition, say Spanish, rather than be forced to shift right away and learn all subjects in English, but also to maintain separate traditions and learning (e.g., black English) and to maintain parallel tracks of values and commitments, without a commitment to a shared, overarching, educational program. Thus, in Miami, a Cuban-American can complete twelve years of school in a Spanish program without ever mingling with other Americans or learning about American core values, at least not without a strong Hispanic orientation. These educational programs are compatible with the concept of a "rainbow" society, in which a variety of equally legitimate "colors" with different traditions and virtues, are to coexist next to one another.

We suggest that such unbounded pluralism that cuts into ultimate values and shared virtues is not compatible with maintaining a moral, social and civic order, nor with providing a community with a set of criteria to sort out differences and form a consensus; hence, it is incompatible with the democratic process. Pluralism is compatible with community and virtue so long as it is limited to maintaining *sub*-traditions, so long as they all recognize areas of *communalities that frame the community* as well as mutual tolerance and respect of the various plural traditions. Thus, no sociopolitical difficulties arise if various groups adhere to different folk dances, songs, food tastes, religious beliefs, and social manners (say, at weddings and funerals). No melting pot is needed here. However, when these groups cease to share a commitment to one community, society or nation, the unity that needs to contain pluralism is strained.

For example, in a debate with a representative of a major Hispanic group on William F. Buckley, Jr.'s show "Firing Line," I suggested that while it is fine for various ethnic groups in the United States to maintain their languages as a second language (from Hebrew to Japanese), they all need to learn English. The Hispanic representative argued that we all live in an Hispanic hemisphere and hence we should all first learn Spanish and then those who wish may learn English on the side. This notion cuts into the bonds of unity. (Language often has this power—it still divides Belgium and Canada; while the Swiss make do with several, it is only following a thousand years of warfare among the various language loyal cantons; one of the bitterest fights in the history of the Jewish community that preceded Israel was over the question whether Hebrew should be the uniting language [Etzioni, 1959].)

In the same vein, and later in the same debate on "Firing Line," the representative of the Hispanic group declared that should the United States engage in war in Latin America, say, in Nicaragua (this program took place before the United States' intervention in Panama), Hispanic-Americans should refuse to fight. Similarly, some black Americans opposed participating in the war in the Persian Gulf because they saw it as a black-against-black confrontation. At a Harlem rally, the Reverend Al Sharpton proclaimed, "We will not fight our brothers in the Middle East" (*The New Yorker*, March 18, 1991).

Typically, communities cannot tolerate pluralism on these issues when sizable groups are involved (they can and do tolerate a few conscientious objectors). Ravitch (1991, p. 36) put it well:

> If there is no overall community, if all we have is a motley collection of racial and ethnic cultures, there will be no sense of the common good. Each group will fight for its own particular interests, and we could easily disintegrate as a nation, becoming instead embroiled in the kinds of ethnic conflicts that often dominate the foreign news each night.

There is no clear established list of what belongs in the shared framework versus in which areas pluralism is welcome or essential. Indeed, the specific list may differ from one community to another (e.g., many European countries include good samaritan laws, we do not [Glendon, 1990–1991, p. 10]) so long as the realm of virtues is sufficiently powerful to provide a containing capsule to the centrifugal forces of the various plural parts. A shared set of basic moral values, a language, some shared national symbols and values, a commitment of mutual tolerance and to democracy as a "good" and not merely as a procedural devise, seems to be essential and found in most if not all functioning democracies. These shared values are noticeably absent in other societies as different as the USSR is from Nigeria. The jury is out about India, where the weak set of share virtues is reflected in massive intergroup violence and frequent violations of individual rights.

In the polity, the same issue arises with reference to the concept of the public interest. Unbounded pluralists have argued that there is no need for a concept of public interest and that none is possible (Truman, 1964, p. 50). Politics, they argue, is an extension to society from a market concept, as special interest groups vie with one another over the direction of public policies (Key, 1958, p. 166). The state is merely a point that reflects the results of the relative power of the various special inputs (Milbrath, 1963, p. 345). While it is true that the notion of public interest is often raised, unbounded pluralists argue that these statements are mere ideological ones each special interest groups mouth to advance its particular cause (Horowitz, 1979, p. 4); that public interest cannot even be defined.

In contrast, we argue that a concept of public interest, recognizing that some virtues rest in the commons, is needed to correct and balance the political centrifugal forces because it is necessary in the community to balance the moral/social effects of pluralism there. Moreover, one can determine when a group advances the needs of its members and when it serves the public at large according to who benefits from the action. Thus, the Sierra Club, a leading environmentalist group, on the basis of its stated goals, is clearly a public-interest group. On the other hand, if it really dedicates itself, as Tucker (1982) argues, to gaining privileges for its upper-middle-class members, say untrammeled mountains on which to ski, it clearly is a special-interest group.

In Historical Perspective

If one starts with the conception of a balance between community-wide shared virtues (including commitment to tolerance and democracy, individual and minority rights) and a range of different moral and other values and commitments, the question arises at each point in historical time: What is the state of the balance? Societies constantly shift and change; as a result, frequently one force or another is gaining in disproportional weight. In some periods and societies, shared virtues come to predominate and intrude into areas in which pluralism ought to dominate (e.g., when states seek to set religions). In others, the power of tribal commitments and conflicting moral values are so strong they destroy the moral social order, tear societies apart and cause civil wars and massive strife as in recent years in Lebanon (once the Switzerland of the Middle East).

Those committed to both virtues and democracy must throw their weight on whatever side the balance is lacking. Hence, in periods and places in which collective fanaticism holds sway, say, in China, they must champion pluralism and tolerance. And in periods and places, as in contemporary America, where radical individualism, championed by libertarians and *laissez-faire* conservatives, undermines the foundations of the community, of both the moral and the civil fabric, the time has come to flag the merits of shared virtues, keeping in mind at all times that communities flourish when pluralism is sustained but also bounded by a firm set of communitarian values and shared virtues.

Bibliography

Ballfield, Edward, *The Moral Basis to a Backward Society* (Glencoe, Ill.: Free Press, 1958).

Bell, Daniel, "The Revolution of Rising Entitlements," *Fortune*, April 1975.

Etzioni, Amitai, *Capital Corruption: The New Attack on American Democracy* (New Brunswick, N.J.: Transaction, Inc., 1984).

Etzioni, "Alternative Ways to Democracy: The Example of Israel," *Political Science Quarterly*, 4:1, June 1959.

Glasser, Ira, cf. *Businessweek*, September 3, 1990, p. 56.

Glendon, Mary Ann, "Does the United States Need 'Good Samaritan' Laws?" *The Responsive Community: Rights and Responsibilities*, 1:2, Winter 1990/1991.

Horowitz, Irving Louis, "Interest Groups and the Patriotic Gore," *The Humanist*, September/October 1979.

Key, V.O., Jr., *Politics, Parties, and Pressure Groups*, 4th ed. (New York: Thomas Y. Cromwell, 1958).

Langan, John, "The Moral Dimension—One or Many?" paper presented at the Association for Social Economics, Washington, D.C., 1990.

Lomasky, Loren E., *Persons, Rights, and the Moral Community* (New York: Oxford University Press, 1987).

MacIntyre, Alasdair, *After Virtue: A Study in Moral Theory*, 2nd ed. (Notre Dame: Notre Dame University Press, 1983).

Melnick, R. Shep, "The Courts, Congress, and Programmatic Rights," in *Remaking American Politics*, Richard Harris and Sidney Milkis, eds. (Boulder, Colo.: Westview Press, 1989).

Milbrath, Lester W., *The Washington Lobbyists* (Chicago: Rand McNally, 1963).

Ravitch, Diane, "Pluralism vs. Particularism in American Education," *The Responsive Community: Rights and Responsibilities*, 1:2, Spring 1991.

Stone, Christopher D., *Should Trees Have Standing?* (Los Altos, Calif.: William Kaufman Inc., 1974).

Thigpen, Robert B., and Lyle A. Downing, "Liberalism and the Communitarian Critique," *American Journal of Political Science*, 31:637–55, 1987.

Truman, David B., *The Governmental Process: Political Interests and Public Opinion*, (New York: Knopf, 1964).

Tucker, William, *Progress and Privilege: America in the Age of Environmentalism*, (New York: Anchor Press, 1982).

Williams, Oliver F., "Life On a Fault Line: The Challenge for SIM," paper delivered at the Academy of Management, Social Issues Department, Conference in San Francisco, Fall 1990.

Seventeen

Catholic Social Teaching and the African-American Struggle for Economic Justice

Peter J. Paris

Since racial injustice has been the paramount reality for African-American existence for over four centuries, no adequate evaluation of the Christian churches in general, or the Catholic church in particular, can be undertaken apart from that fact. That is to say, the ubiquity of structural racism in the American society has constituted a fundamental condition for the whole of public policy in the nation. Thus, assuming the primacy of structural racism over every other social issue, I have chosen to look at Catholic social thought from that perspective: In what respect and to what extent has the social teaching of the Catholic church been a helpful moral resource in the struggle for racial justice in the United States?

According to the best estimates, African-American Catholics numbered approximately 100,000 at the end of the Civil War.[1] Raboteau tells us they were concentrated mainly in the Catholic states of Louisiana and Maryland. Interestingly, the first black priest to be ordained in the United States was the Josephite Charles Randolph Uncles who was ordained by Cardinal Gibbons in Baltimore in 1891, the same year *Rerum Novarum* was published. Previously, however, four blacks born in the south of mixed racial parents had been ordained to the priesthood in Europe and one, James Augustine Healy, was installed as bishop of the diocese of Portland, Maine, in 1875. Not until 1977, however, was a second black appointed to head a Roman Catholic diocese in the United States—the Most Reverend Joseph L. Howze, bishop of the diocese of Biloxi.[2] Clearly, the Catholic practice of excluding blacks from positions of ecclesiastical authority was not unlike that which prevailed in white Protestant churches. Also like Protestants, Catholics owned slaves but, unlike Protestants, it was not a universal practice among Roman Catholic churches to practice segregation in worship even though many churches did so right up to the middle of the twentieth century. Similarly, Catholic schools in the south often showed a measure of disdain for racial segregation by its frequent practice of racially integrated education.

The second Vatican Council clearly and unmistakably condemned racism in its various forms as an offense against human dignity, "foreign to the mind of Christ and contrary to God's intent."[3]

Pope John XXIII condemned racism in his *Pacem in Terris* (43–44, 86, 89) as did Pope Paul VI in his *Populorum Progressio* (63) and his *Octogesima Adveniens* (16). The general impact of Vatican II was evidenced clearly in the increased participation of priests and nuns in the civil rights demonstrations of Martin Luther King, Jr., who, on several occasions, spoke favorably of the Roman Catholic church's opposition to racial discrimination. Following his 1964 audience with Pope Paul VI, Dr. King praised the Holy Father for his stand on civil rights.[4] Similarly, he applauded Cardinal Francis Spellman's call for the acceleration of the church's activity in the quest for racial justice and Cardinal Richard Cushing's decision to name eleven priests to represent him at the 1963 March on Washington.[5] Further, when he marched through hostile neighborhoods in Chicago, King was encouraged by the presence of Archbishop Cody at his side. For these and other reasons, a 1966 *Newsweek* poll found that 58 percent of blacks viewed Roman Catholics as being more helpful to the cause of civil rights than white Protestants.[6]

In spite of these significant facts, the Roman Catholic church failed to gain notable distinction as a significant agent in the civil rights movement of the mid-twentieth century. This may be attributed to a number of causes, among which are the following:

First, the exclusive use of the natural law method in Catholic social teaching prior to Vatican II implied little attention to sin and redemption relative to societal structures. As a result, the church has tended to assume an uncritical stance *vis à vis* sociopolitical structures of law and order, believing that the function of the state is to serve the common good. Second, (and closely related to the first), the church's traditional commitment to a teleological ethic implied a preference for social and political effectiveness over the moral judgments of prophetic idealism. This contributed to the church's relatively easy disposition towards making compromises with various formal and informal structures of societal power. Third, the church's pre-Vatican II dialectical understanding of nature and grace implied a dichotomy between the spiritual and temporal welfare of its people, as evidenced in the church's disinclination towards empowering various African-American social reform groups within the church. Fourth, the general social and ecclesial insularity of the Catholic church prior to Vatican II may have served the church's Euro-American immigrant populations rather well in their cultural assimilationist processes which, unwittingly perhaps, included the inculcation of racist attitudes and practices towards African-Americans. In many urban areas, black ghettos and working-class immigrant neighborhoods (many of which were Irish, Polish and Italian Catholic) shared mutually hostile borders that constantly were vulnerable to explosive outbreaks of violence, due to the natural processes of ghetto expansionism on the one hand and to the characteristic resentment and strong resistance of the white immigrant property owners on the other.

Yet, in various and sundry ways, African-American Catholics have struggled to keep the issue of racial justice alive within the church, relying, in large part, on the universal nature of the church and its inclusive teaching. Unfortunately, the church's teaching on racial justice prior to Vatican II was more implicit than explicit and that was a hindrance to the civil rights struggle. Happily, that constraint was removed by the new ethos ushered in by Vatican II. Under the inspiration of the African-American Catholic Congresses of the early 1890s and the Federated Colored Catholics organization formed after World War 1, the National Black Sisters Conference was founded in 1968 and this, in turn, became a stimulus for the calling of the recent national African-American Congress. Under the pressure of African-American bishops, the National Conference of Catholic Bishops issued its pastoral letter on racism in 1979, "Brothers and Sisters to Us" and later authorized the establishment of the National Office for Black Catholics. All these events have been enormously important for the well-being of African-American Catholics in particular and to the church as a whole, to say nothing of their collective impact on the struggle for racial justice within the nation at large.

Social Teaching and Social Practice

Various theological claims of the Catholic church would seem to imply that the church enjoys a high measure of independence from culture. In fact, the Catholic church makes the following theological claims: (a) a position of transcendence over culture on all matters of faith and morals; (b) apostolic authority relative to the proclamation of the faith and the universal governance of the church. Let us look more closely at these claims to assess their import for our subject matter.

Assuming the non-racist character of the church's social teaching, one would have expected the church to have had a history of non-compliance with the cultural practice of racism in the United States. On the contrary, however, and as already indicated, one finds little difference between the Catholic and Protestant churches relative to this matter. Scholars have documented the church's many and varied compromises with slavery and its aftermath of racial segregation and discrimination. Yet, in spite of that history, some have argued that the Catholic church played a more constructive role in race relations than the Protestant churches. The African-American political scientist Frederick Wright has modified that viewpoint:

> Still, when compared to Protestant denominations, the Catholic church (whether in the eighteenth or the twentieth century) was a moderating influence. The church "sought to ameliorate the lot of the bondsman; but it made no frontal attack on slavery as an institution, nor did it assert itself against social injustice to which free Negroes later became subjected."[7]

Prior to the Civil War the Catholic church appears to have adhered to its canon law which stipulated that all Catholics in a parish were under the jurisdiction of one bishop and, hence, were expected to worship together, regardless of race. Clearly, however, when the entire South succumbed to the dictates of racial segregation after the fall of Reconstruction, the Catholic church was no exception. The first black Catholic priest in the United States was ordained in 1891 in Baltimore, and Wright quotes the historian, Dolores Egger Labbe, in support of the claim that the first black Catholic church was formed in 1895. By the end of World War I the majority of blacks had been assigned to black parishes. Unlike the formation of black Protestant churches, however, the initiative for the formation of black Catholic churches did not arise from blacks but from white bishops who were motivated not by a moral disposition to oppose the assault of racism on humanity but acted in compliance with the culture of racism.

A further contrast with the black churches was the issue of leadership. Black Catholic churches were under the leadership of white priests who could in no way guide blacks in using their cultural traditions as expressive means of worshipping God—that process had to await the initiative of black Catholic leadership in the 1970s. Clearly, the long history of black Catholic churches led by white priests served to alienate black Catholics from their cultural traditions which were rendered invisible in the celebratory dimensions of the church's liturgical life. In this respect, black Catholics experienced even greater cultural alienation than black Protestants in predominantly white denominations because, at the congregational level, black pastors were usually in charge of the liturgy and of church governance. Hence, it is not surprising that as soon as black Catholics felt free enough in the post-Vatican era to express their desires for ecclesiological change, they wasted no time in pressing the church to give greater consideration to African-American culture in all dimensions of its institutional life and mission.[8] Accordingly, they called quickly for the installation of black diocesan bishops and the institutionalization of their voice in the National Office of Black Catholics.

One of the ambiguous blessings that accrued to black Catholics, however, was easy access to the Catholic parochial educational system. This contributed to the production of a black, middle-class Catholic elite, of which more study is needed to discern its distinctive function in the struggle for racial justice in the United States. Clearly, Catholic schools provided a welcome alternative to the segregated public school education available to blacks in large parts of the south.

The extent to which the Catholic church was able to remain faithful in practice to its own teaching on race relations depended solely on the degree of moral commitment and courageous leadership of specific diocesan bishops. Some of them carried on a constant struggle within the jurisdiction of their own parishes. They refused to succumb to the social demands of their white parishioners to hold segregated membership classes, to serve whites before blacks at the mass, to disallow black priests to celebrate mass in white churches and to prohibit racial integration in Catholic schools. In many circumstances, bishops often were forced to use their power to excommunicate those who stubbornly resisted their instruction; sometimes they were forced to close churches. Under these conditions, and especially in Louisiana, Wright refers to the Catholic church as "a moral sentry"[9] in the struggle for racial justice, even though it did not have the capacity to effect an end to racial injustice in the society at large. In short, the church had the moral and theological authority to police its own domain and, seemingly, little institutional capacity to raise its voice in public criticism against the customary practices of societal racism.

Interestingly, the historic march on Washington by Martin Luther King, Jr., in 1963 illustrates the timidity of both Protestant and Catholic church leaders in their public support of the civil rights movement. The Catholic church was represented on the march's leadership team by the Catholic layman Matthew Ahmann, executive director of the National Catholic Conference for Interracial Justice.[10] Just as importantly, and certainly much more dramatic, was the day-long dispute relative to Cardinal Patrick O'Boyle's demand for a revision of the speech by John Lewis, president of the Student Non-violent Coordinating Council (SNCC), parts of which he and others considered inflammatory. If the speech were not revised, the Cardinal vowed he would not give the invocation as planned and that all official Catholic participation would be withdrawn. Minutes before commencement time, the speech was handed to him for approval and the program proceeded as planned.[11] Cardinal Boyle was one of many ecclesiastical sponsors of the march who exercised a veto on the content of Lewis's speech on that historic occasion. Many white church leaders were content to lend cautious support to the civil rights movement, while not identifying with so-called left-wing trends within the civil rights movement and especially those espoused by the SNCC. Further, they did not wish to give the impression that they were supporting the student side of a growing dispute within the Southern Christian Leadership Conference relative to the character of white liberals in general and to the U.S. government in particular. Thus, Lewis was forced to revise his speech to keep the many distinguished clerics on the platform. These diverse ecclesiastical leaders feared being accused of complicity with SNCC's philosophy by sharing a platform with that organization's president; they were prepared to undergo that criticism provided they approved Lewis's address. This episode typified the cautious attitude of most white church leaders (Protestant and Roman Catholic) in the struggle for racial justice.

Nevertheless, Ahmann integrated in his speech the principles of conscience, the U.S. constitution and the Christian faith, thus setting forth "the goals that the Catholic community shares with all other Americans." Under those principles, he set forth certain policies for which his group would work:

> We dedicate ourselves today to secure federal civil rights legislation which will guarantee every man a job based on his talents and training, legislation which will do away with the myth that the ownership of a public place of business carries the moral or legal right to reject a customer because of the color of his hair or of his skin. We dedicate ourselves to guarantee by legislation that all American citizens have integrated education and the right to vote on reaching legal age. We dedicate ourselves today to secure a minimum wage which will guarantee a man or a woman the resources for a vital and healthy family life, unencumbered by uncertainty and by racial discrimination. A good job for every man is a just demand and it becomes our motto.[12]

Ahmann's speech clearly exhibited not only the principles of the five-month-old *Pacem in Terris* encyclical but also the corresponding duties implied by the principles: duties that pointed individuals and the church to social action. Since *Pacem in Terris*, the moral goal "freedom" had received papal blessing, alongside truth, love and justice. Because "freedom" had always been the primary religious and political principle in the African-American struggle, solidarity with black Americans could be fully expressed only by an unequivocal affirmation of it, morally, religiously and politically. Ahmann's speech must have emboldened the many white Catholics whose presence was a demonstration of their solidarity with the goals of the civil rights movement and was a dress parade for the new spirit of Roman Catholicism *à la* Vatican II. All of this, and much more, strengthened the resolve for racial justice that had been born alone by African-Americans for centuries. This latter point cannot be overly emphasized. Up to now African-Americans had never succeeded in gaining the public support of the masses of white Americans for racial justice. Thus, the march itself marked the realization of a long-desired goal—the demonstrated public support of the religious and political establishment for the civil rights of black Americans. Until that moment, both the Protestant and Catholic white churches had maintained a very low profile. It should be noted, however, that a Catholic lay person had read the speech and the Cardinal had offered the prayer of invocation. Had the Cardinal read the speech it would have carried with it the full authority of the church, which was probably too much to expect.

The entire mainline political and religious establishment endorsed the march on Washington. In many ways it was a mass celebration of the goals of the civil rights movement which had, at long last, become legitimated. But the march did not focus attention on any particular public policy and, in that respect, it was not political. This is indicative of the way white churches (Catholic and Protestant) have lent their support to issues of racial justice—giving moral and theological support to broadly conceived goals in isolation from the means to the attainment of those goals. The latter is calculative, specific, practical and, more often than not, controversial. Both Catholic and Protestant churches carefully select those political issues with which they choose to become identified: issues that invariably are racially nonspecific. Given the specificity of structural racism to exclude a certain racial group from participation, there can be no effective opposition to it apart from specific policies.

Although the church condemns racism in general and the Catholic bishops have encouraged their members to work for the elimination of racial discrimination, and although the bishops have asked the government and the private sector to give special attention to education, jobs, housing and welfare, and although they have seemed to support affirmative action programs, they have advocated no specific public policies relative to the effective elimination of structural racism from the body politic. The economic policy statements of the U.S. Catholic bishops are impressive (e.g., their call for full employment guarantee, national health insurance policy, a national housing policy, and their support for labor unions) but there appears to be virtually no consciousness of the function of structural racism in each of those spheres. Thus, their analyses inevitably are limited when viewed from the perspective of structural racism—they fail to speak directly to the cause of unfair distribution of economic resources among African-Americans. In my judgment, the social teaching of the

Catholic church reveals a major deficiency, namely, its apparent lack of reliance on a more racially balanced staff of competent people, including lay persons, as advisors to the bishops. The bishops need the regular guidance of African-American clergy and laity so they can speak more effectively to the issue of structural racism and its impact on the economic condition of African-Americans.

The Church's Pastoral and Prophetic Functions

There are two reasons the Catholic church has difficulties with being prophetic while being much more easily disposed toward a pastoral style of ministry. The first reason derives from the Troeltschian and Niebuhrian ideal typification of Catholic social teaching as fitting into the "church" type of model, the logic of which is to synthesize the authority of Christ with that of culture, taking care not to run the risk of accommodating Christ to culture. The church type of orientation tends to focus its energy on discerning the continuities between Christ and culture rather than the discontinuities, thus enabling the church to give high priority to the question of social order and to view social disorder as dysfunctional in every respect. Hence, this model tends mainly to shun confrontational politics, even though it engages aggressively in confrontation on occasion (e.g., the issue of abortion). The church type of orientation aims at encouraging the culture to continue pursuing and improving upon those dimensions of its life that are commensurate with the theological and moral values of the church. In this way, the society may come to see that the goal of the church is also society's rightful goal. Clearly, this model of church-culture relationship rarely, if ever, issues in prophetic utterance *vis à vis* the society at large. Relative to the issue of structural racism, this may well signal the church's major deficiency, namely, its inability to bring prophetic criticism to bear on societal structures. Consequently, the church has no other alternative than to provide pastoral ministries to the victims of societal injustice. For the most part, Catholic social teaching throughout this century has assumed a non-racist world both within and outside the church. Therefore, its teaching inevitably fails to speak directly to the primary need of African-Americans to be liberated from structural racism which has a long history of preventing the exercise of justice in all dimensions of their common life.

The assumption of a non-racist world bypasses the real world of the United States. Accordingly, formal discussions of the common good and the just distribution of economic resources ignore African-Americans because a society organized under the principle of structural racism clearly will ensure that the common good and all forms of justice enhance the well-being of one race while threatening and denying that of the other. Thus, I conclude that a public policy that ignores the efficacious and pervasive breadth of structural racism cannot effect economic justice for African-Americans; the social teaching of the Catholic church is no exception. In spite of its good intentions, theological anthropology and moral principles regarding societal justice in general and economic justice in particular, the church's teaching generally neglects the most fundamental conditioning reality of African-Americans, namely, structural racism. It is to be hoped the church will recognize this neglect and seek to address it in constructive ways.

Notes

1. Albert J. Raboteau, *Slave Religion: The "Invisible Institution" in the Antebellum South* (New York: Oxford University Press, 1978), p. 271.

2. Kenneth K. Bailey, "The Post-Civil War Racial Separations in Southern Protestantism: Another Look," *Church History*, The American Society of Church History, vol. 46, no. 4 (December 1977), p. 462, no. 11.

3. Joseph Gremillion, *The Gospel of Peace and Justice: Catholic Social Teaching since Pope John* (Maryknoll, N.Y.: Orbis Books, 1976), p. 422.

4. John J. Ansbro, *Martin Luther King, Jr.: The Making of a Mind* (Maryknoll, N.Y.: Orbis Books, 1984), p. 180.

5. *Ibid.*, p. 316.

6. *Ibid.*

7. Frederick D. Wright, "Black Liberation and the Catholic Church: The Louisiana Experience," *The Journal of the Inter-Denominational Theological Center*, Atlanta, Ga., p. 64.

8. The leadership that black Catholics have given in adding their expressive cultural traits to the liturgy is described impressively in M. Shawn Copeland's "African-American Catholics and Black Theology: An Interpretation," *African-American Religious Studies*, Gayraud Wilmore, ed., (Durham, N.C.: Duke University Press, 1988), pp. 228–248.

9. Wright, *op. cit.*, p. 72.

10. David J. Garrow, *Bearing the Cross: Martin Luther King, Jr., and the Southern Christian Leadership Conference* (New York: William Morrow and Co., 1986), p. 280. Ahmann was one of four whites on the ten-person team. See also Taylor Branch, *Parting the Waters: America in the King Years 1954–63* (New York: Simon and Schuster, 1988), pp. 874ff.

11. *Ibid.*, pp. 282–283.

12. John Hope Franklin and Isidore Starr, eds., *The Negro in 20th Century America: A Reader on the Struggle for Civil Rights* (New York: Vintage Books, 1967), pp. 205–206.

Eighteen

Reconsidering the Idea of the Common Good[1]

M. Shawn Copeland, O.P.

In the discourse of classical Western political philosophy, the idea of the common good is central to interpretations of political life. The classical understanding is exemplified best in the political philosophy of Plato and Aristotle for whom the common good was the good of the *polis*, the Greek city-state. The common good was realized and manifested in the citizens' acceptance and fulfillment of those duties and obligations which defined membership and participation in the *polis*. It was the good of the whole, in and to which all its parts contributed. However, with the emergence of modern political philosophy, the philosophy of Niccolo Machiavelli and Thomas Hobbes, the classical idea of the common good underwent so decisive a reformulation that today we find ourselves alienated from its classical origins.[2]

The idea of the common good, possibly a key category in theology's effort to understand political life, has been rendered inaccessible by modernity, a term equally problematic.[3] This loss of the meaning of the idea of the common good signals the shift to a style of political thinking which devalues formation of character or education to virtue as the means of achieving a sound political order, and emphasizes institutional or structural change through such avenues as legislation.[4] Indeed, at the end of the nineteenth century, recognition of the idea of the common good as central to an interpretation of the political order had disappeared from nearly all but papal discourse. In *Rerum Novarum*, Pope Leo XIII attacked abuses bred by the industrial revolution and, in that context, attempted to redefine the meaning of the common good.[5] Yet, the idea seemed strangely out of place in a civil society conceived as contractual, as an aggregate of autonomous individuals or units cooperating only when the terms of that cooperation advanced the ends or advantage of the parties involved.

This inquiry is provoked by the cultural, social, and political consequences of the reduction and devaluation of the idea of the common good. More proximately, this essay comes from my concern for the idea of the common good in the context of the pluralist society that is the United

States of America.[6] Several large, disputed, and interrelated issues crop up in the attempt to speak about the common good in this context: How are we to name the artifacts and symbols through which women and men of different cultures and racial-ethnic heritages test, understand, conceptualize, express, and transmit cherished and contemporary meanings and values? How are we to respond authentically when those artifacts and symbols, meanings and values substantively and ferociously conflict? Why, on the cusp of the twenty-first century, in the United States of America, is our prevailing social order marked by intellectual escapism and decadence; by self-preservative morality; by plastic aesthetics; by massive poverty; by indifferent and xenophobic reactions to the human other; by suspicion of religion and a religion of suspicion; by virulent sexism, racism, anti-Semitism, and homophobia; by acquisitive individualism and hedonism; by disregard for common social duties, obligations, and responsibilities; by wanton destruction of nature; by crass and mindless living? How is Catholic social thought to meet the intellectual, moral, and religious challenges raised by this concrete existential situation? Or, to frame this last differently, What is the social role of the church in our time?

This essay brings together three strands: a general and brief historical study of the displacement of the classical idea of the common good; a review of the efforts of two pastoral letters by the bishops of the United States to address two egregious issues—racism and our destruction of the land; and some reflections on the functions of Catholic social thought in reconsidering the common good. What follows presumes the following: (1) that the common good is a rich and serious problem to be solved through concrete human living; (2) that the present concrete, social, and existential situation in which we live can be defined as a cycle of decline (i.e., a situation which is intellectually, morally, and religiously distorted);[7] (3) that the reversal of this cycle entails not only recognition that moral development or character formation has been ignored in the social order, but that new disciplines, new virtues, new values are required for ethical and moral thought and practice;[8] and (4) that religious faith is integral to the realization of the common human good; hence, the social role of the church in our time adheres to its promotion of the common good.[9]

The Common Good: A Conspectus

The phrase *common good* refers to one of the more troublesome and provocative notions in that cluster of problems and ideas which have preoccupied Western political thought from classical antiquity to the present. Once a normative feature in the discourse of classical-political philosophy, the idea of the common good is no longer available, neither lexically nor analogically, in most of contemporary political thought whether philosophical or theological. Cognate terms such as public good, public interest, social interest, or social welfare are used synonymously but arise from different philosophic parentage.[10] Ideas about the common good divide sharply along the intellectual boundary fixed, in the sixteenth and seventeenth centuries, by the political philosophy of Niccolo Machiavelli, Thomas Hobbes and John Locke. Their arguments concerning the common good differ rather substantially from those posed by that classical-political philosophy originating with Plato and Aristotle and carried into the Christian intellectual tradition by Augustine and Thomas Aquinas.

According to classical-political philosophy, "there is necessarily a common good, and the common good in its fullness is the good society and what is required for the good society."[11] In the classical tradition, the common good is identified with the virtuous life lived and perfected within a just political community, or at least a community which self-consciously and self-critically praises, desires, and seeks virtue. In this tradition, politics is the continuation of ethics and finds its highest expression in a good and just life. The *polis* is not founded on self-preservation or self-regard, but on self-sacrifice, courage, moderation, on attachment to the common good. On this view, there was no opposition between the common good and personal or individual good;[12] the citizen found his own good, his own end in the good of the *polis.*[13]

In the classical tradition, the common good was not a matter merely of accident; without deliberation and choice the common good could not be established. For the ancients, "politics was always directed toward the formation and cultivation of character; it proceeded pedagogically and not technically."[14] A life of virtue was paramount for the realization of the common good. Furthermore, the classical tradition taught that the human is by no means the highest thing in the universe; there are divine things. The philosophers of antiquity also taught the existence of a life higher than political activity; the theoretic or speculative life constituted happiness in the only true sense of the word.

The classical formulation of the common good continued, with modifications, in the work of Augustine and Aquinas. Their appropriation and transposition of the common good gave full weight to the dictates of divine revelation, thus extending the classical notion of the common good to encompass Christianity's promise of a supernatural destiny and end for the person. Despite differences and tensions, there was crucial agreement between classical-political philosophy and the Bible, between Athens and Jerusalem. Each acknowledged the limitations, the finiteness of human nature and human existence; each assented to a standard independent of human will which might direct human beings toward an end, toward the perfection for which humans yearned.[15]

Given the overwhelming influence of Aquinas on papal social teaching, it would not be out of place to summarize briefly his views on the common good. With Aristotle, Aquinas held that human beings were by nature social. Hence, in the treatise, *On Princely Government*,[16] Aquinas wrote: "When we consider all that is necessary for human life, it becomes clear that man is naturally a social and political animal, destined more than all other animals to live in community."[17] Considering all that is necessary for human life, no one individual alone is able to furnish himself or herself with all the necessary resources adequate for the fullness of human life. Nature has destined human beings to live in society; and, by dividing the labor among ourselves, we each devote ourselves to some branch of science, some interest, some occupation.[18] Social community is an end of the common good; personal relationships, such as associations, friendships, and marriage, contribute to this end (*ST* I-II, q. 152, a. 4; q. 153, a. 3; q. 154, a. 2).[19] This is a first approximation of the common good as the communal well-being of a group.

A second approximation of the common good is constituted by the welfare of the wider social community as a political body; this end is realized through legislation. Human law is a dictate of practical reason for the common good and framed either by the whole people or by the public official having this responsibility (*ST* I-II, q. 90, a. 2, resp.; a. 3, resp.). As the end of human living is happiness, law is ordered to the design of all things to achieve it (*ST* I-II, q. 90, a. 2, resp.), and this happiness finds its proximate fulfillment in virtue which is the end or purpose of human law (*ST* I-II, q. 92, a. 1, resp., ad. 1).

Aquinas's discussion of the common good also adverts to a notion of distributive justice and its relationship to the common good.[20] He appropriates Aristotle's definition of justice: "a habit whereby a man renders to each one his due by constant and perpetual will" (*ST* II-II, q. 58, a.1). As a general virtue, justice directs a person in his or her relationship with others and with the social whole. Justice is concrete rather than speculative; it governs actions. On Aquinas's account, injustice is a special vice; for it holds the common good in contempt and thus can lead to sin and the disruption of the equality between people (*ST* II-II, q. 59, a.1).

Aquinas further distinguished between legal justice which directs a person to the common good and particular justice which directs a person in his or her relationships to other people (*ST* II-II, q. 58, a. 6, a. 7, ad. 1, ad. 2). Two species of particular justice are detailed: commutative justice which is concerned with the mutual dealings of two persons, and distributive justice which is concerned with the proper and proportionate distribution of the common good (*ST* II-II, q. 61, a. 1).

Through legal justice, a man or woman strives to subordinate him- or herself to the common good, to participate in the social whole. The common good is neither this individual's good, nor is it a collection or an arithmetical sum of individual or private goods. Such an idea is divisive and disruptive, pitting one woman or man against another. The common good is of a higher order (*ST* II-II, q. 58, a. 7, ad. 2). Ultimately, for Aquinas, what undergirds an individual's participation in, claim upon, and duty to the common good is creatureliness, i.e., that human beings are created by God.

The *Summa Theologiae* charts the human departure from and return to that Ultimate Source in whom we rational creatures live and move and have our being. For Aquinas, the universe is not some self-contained, self-sufficient order: "the whole universe mounts by the inmost desires of every part to an end outside itself."[21] The end of the human scheme transcends sheer vital life and survival as well as what is merely human; the End of the scheme lies outside it.[22] Thus, the third approximation of the common good is found in the universal goodness of God who, while transcending the universe, nurtures, sustains, and embraces the whole and all its parts. The theological virtues open a person to a loving relationship with the perfect society of the Trinity, and the Aristotelian notion of perfect happiness as contemplation is transformed in light of the Beatific Vision.

Modern political philosophy was inaugurated by Machiavelli's rejection of the classical philosophic and theological tradition. Philosopher Leo Strauss explains that rejection on the basis of Machiavelli's contention that those traditional views lead to either of two consequences: "that the political things are not taken seriously (Epicureanism) or else that they are understood in the light of an imaginary perfection—of imagined commonwealths and principalities, the most famous of them being the kingdom of God."[23] Classical-political philosophy had taken its bearings from the ideal; the political philosophy inaugurated by Machiavelli took its bearings from the extreme. The standard by which human beings might orient their living was lowered considerably. Virtue was reinterpreted on the basis not of how men and women ought to live, but on the basis of how men and women actually do live.

On Machiavelli's view, human beings were "contemptible," "simpleminded" and so "dominated by their present needs that one who deceives will always find one who will allow himself to be deceived" (*Prince* xviii).[24] The wise ruler, Machiavelli observed, is one who knows the ways of the fox and the ways of the lion. The wise ruler cannot and should not uphold prior promises, if to do so meant his disadvantage. "If all men were good, this principle would not be good; but since men are a contemptible lot, and would not keep their promises to you, you too need not keep yours to them" (*Prince* xviiii). Further, Machiavelli counsels: "It is not necessary that a prince should have all of the [good] qualities, but it is certainly necessary that he appear to have them." He continues:

In fact, I would go so far as to say this, that having them and observing them at all times, they are harmful; and appearing to have them, they are useful; for example, appearing to be compassionate, faithful, humane, upright, religious, and being so; but his mind should be disposed in such a way that should it become necessary not to be so, he will be able and know how to change to the contrary. (*Prince* xviii)

Not only is this a profound departure from the classical understanding of the human, it is a profound departure from the classical understanding of virtue. Yet, this is what we have come to expect of politicians and of each other; we are more than surprised when some man or woman behaves otherwise.

Under the Florentine's tutelage, group self-interest now wraps itself in the cloak of the common good and puts on the crown of virtue. The state no longer exists to promote virtue or human flourishing of its citizens; rather, the flourishing of the citizen is identified with the well-being of the state. Political life is no longer subject to morality. The ancient connection between virtue as ethical action and custom and law was broken. Machiavelli continues:

It must be understood that a prince, and in particular a new prince, cannot observe all those things by which men are considered good, for it is often necessary, in order to maintain the state, to act against your word, against charity, against kindness, against religion. And so, he must have a mind ready to turn itself according as the winds of fortune and the fluctuation of things command him, and, as I said above, he must not separate himself from the good, if he is able, but he must know how to take up evil, should it be necessary. (*Prince* xviii)

Thus, Machiavelli levels what classical-political philosophy had so labored to inspire and obtain: the rule of the philosopher-king. Modern political philosophy proposes that the end justifies the means. Statescraft motivated by compassion, by fidelity to one's allies, by integrity, by the acceptance and endurance of fate, by kindness, by piety or religion is to be adhered to, but only if it achieves the desirable end. If necessary, might will make it right.

With the emergence of modern political philosophy, the classical idea of society as natural to human beings and crucial to our flourishing is displaced by a concept of society as contractual. The political teaching of virtue as the only fitting end of human living, of the primacy of the common good, was discounted by the new political philosophers,

Thomas Hobbes and John Locke, who argued that the individual by nature is complete, independent, prior to and above society. The moral fact of civil society was no longer duty, but rights. Instead of reasoned discernment of a hierarchy of inclinations, self-regarding passions rule self-interest. Moreover, these new political philosophers conceived of society as an aggregate of autonomous individuals or units cooperating only when the terms of that cooperation advanced the ends or advantage of the parties involved. The end or goal toward which the classical philosophers had exhorted us was lowered to self-regarding self-interest, to self-preservation. Under the powerful sway of the new political philosophers, what had been in classical-political philosophy among the most noble of human pursuits, the common good, now amounted to little more than what Thrasymachus described in the *Republic* as the "anarchistic conception of individualistic materialism in which the whole function of the city is to safeguard the liberty of each; thus giving the strong full freedom to oppress the weak."[25]

The complacency with which such ideas are entertained is reiterated in an essay by the noted economist Robert Heilbroner. Discussing the relationships of U.S. multinational corporations and an idea of the common good, Heilbroner asserts:

> A society working well is non-existent and absurd. As long as it is kept as the goal, it can only breed continuous and unwarranted feelings of disappointment and failed expectations. A realistic image to put in the place of this failed stereotype is: working well enough.[26]

A society working well enough aspires merely to maintain things as they are; a society working well enough is content with a lowered vision that guarantees and ensures success without disappointment, without frustration, without failed expectations. Yet it is a vulgar success, preferring image to substance, power to principle, measured security to passionate and daring sacrifice.

In our own time, politics has been reduced to the role of technical expertise in a utilitarian doctrine of prudence, the negotiation or adjudication of group or individual demands and rights.[27] The modern version of the common good is "surreptitiously reintroduce[d] in the form of 'those rules of the game' with which all conflicting groups are supposed to comply because those rules, reasonably fair to every group, can reasonably be admitted by every group."[28] The common good is manifest as an "identity of interests," virtues are lowered to "sentiments guided by corresponding moral principles" which bind persons together, and society is viewed as a "cooperative venture for mutual advantage."[29]

Modern political thought has blurred the distinction between just and unjust political orders, the distinction between the virtue and vice. It has severed the relationship between religion and politics, removing public or political conduct from the domain of religion and the criticisms of theology; it has swept away the premodern teaching that there exists an objective moral order knowable by human reason. Modern political thought has spawned an entirely new and amoral horizon. Indeed, as this review of the history of the devolution of the idea of the common good has illustrated, modern political philosophy and theory have brought into being "a kind of society wholly unknown to the classics, a kind of society to which the classical principles as stated and elaborated by the classics are not immediately applicable."[30] Now, it is neither reasonable nor accurate to expect to restore the classical understanding of the common good merely by linguistic usage. Neither is it reasonable, nor is it accurate to expect such usage to meet our social (i.e., technological, economic, and political) and cultural predicament; the idea of the common good as expressive of an organic, hierarchical order, contests our contemporary experience. However, a critical rather than nostalgic return to the classical understanding of the idea of the common good and its transmogrifications proves an indispensable starting-point for serious reflection on Catholic social thought—its role, its foundations, its possibilities, its future.

Race, Land, and the Common Good

From Leo XIII in *Rerum Novarum* to John Paul II in *Sollicitudo Rei Socialis*, Catholic social thought has sought to preserve the intent of the classical understanding of the common good. Two pastoral letters of the U.S. bishops, *Brothers and Sisters to Us* and *This Land Is Home to Me*, collaborate in this task, extending and concertizing the idea of the common good in the United States by taking up the issues of racism and destruction of the land. That these two letters have raised and addressed painful wrongs witnesses to the history we wish to heal and to the future we wish to create. That these letters have received so little public attention and discussion discloses just how ambivalent we are about that history and that future.

Racism is not a feature peculiar only to life in the United States, but it is a persistent and pernicious one.[31] Virulent and violent racism has attended every stage in the collective history of the peoples of the United States. Racism oversaw the European *discovery*, colonization, and creation of North America. Racism attended the United States' war for independence, its cultural and economic development, its industrial expansion. Racism has dogged its political infancy, adolescence, and maturation as well as its foreign and domestic policy. Today, racism retains its choke-hold on the most cherished institutions, cultural traditions, and mores of our national life. Even more poignantly and profoundly, racism taints our religion and contaminates our worship.

Racism may be defined as "the generalized and final assigning of values to real or imaginary differences, to the accuser's benefit and at [the] victim's expense, in order to justify the former's own privileges or aggression."[32] Albert Memmi's analysis unmasks four essential elements. First, this definition underscores the emphasis on difference, real or imaginary. Where difference is lacking, the racist supplies it; where difference is obvious, the racist interprets it to his or her own advantage, since the racist concentrates only on those differences that support or contribute to substantiating a racist argument. Second, this definition discloses the evaluative nature of racism. The racist evaluates this difference in such a way as to discredit the victim and to aggrandize self. This negative evaluation, explicitly or implicitly, is intended to prove the inferiority of the victim and the superiority of the racist. Third, this definition uncovers the totalizing and absolutizing character of difference. The victim's whole personality is determined by this difference and all members of his or her social-racial group are marked for the same accusation. Memmi's analysis lays bare just why and how biologically-based racism is so frightfully successful: the difference is inescapable, irrevocable, and visible in the flesh, penetrating the genes, transforming fate and destiny into heredity, hurling hopes and dreams into nightmare. Finally, this analysis discloses the *a priori* justificatory dimension of racism. With the absolute categorization of the victim, the racist explains and justifies attitudes, judgments, decisions, behavior. By exaggerated appeal to real or imaginary negatively determined difference, the racist justifies racism. The racist's experience, no matter how narrow, how limited or how skewed, is taken as normative.[33]

The pastoral letter, *Brothers and Sisters to Us*, is the third statement by the U.S. bishops.[34] This letter is provoked by a "mood of indifference" which has dulled society and church to the far-ranging economic, cultural, and educational consequences of racial discrimination (1). The bishops lament the tragic and brutal indignities suffered by "the Native Americans, the Mexicans, the Puerto Ricans, the Hispanics, the Asians, and the blacks." All these men, women and children "have suffered indignity; most have been uprooted, defrauded or dispossessed of their lands; and none have escaped one or another form of collective degradation" at the hands of a powerful majority" (5). The bishops celebrate the "distinctive and rich" contributions of each of these groups to the United States and to our national culture. And the bishops celebrate more the power and triumph of the human spirit over degradation and dehumanization. "The history of all gives a witness to a truth absorbed by now into the collective consciousness of Americans: their struggle has been a pledge of liberty and a challenge to future greatness" (6).

In *Brothers and Sisters to Us*, the bishops define racism in the context of theological anthropology:

> Racism is a sin: a sin that divides the human family, blots out the image of God among specific members of that family, and violates the fundamental human dignity of those called to be children of the same Father. Racism is the sin that says some human beings are inherently superior and others essentially inferior because of race. . . . Indeed, racism is more than a disregard for the words of Jesus; it is a denial of the truth of the dignity of each human being revealed by the mystery of the Incarnation. (3)

The bishops hold that racism is not merely "one sin among many," but a radical evil that divides the human family and denies the new creation of a redeemed world" (10). It is the church's mission

> to proclaim to all that the sin of racism defiles the image of God and degrades the sacred dignity of humankind which has been revealed by the mystery of the Incarnation. Let all know that it is a terrible sin that mocks the cross of Christ and ridicules the Incarnation. For the brother and sister of our Brother Jesus Christ are brother and sister to us. (9)

As a social construct, land marks a decisive moment in the modern history of the West: Spain and Portugal vie for land in Africa, Asia, and America; there is the discovery of a "new land" which comes to be known as the Americas; whole peoples are dispossessed of ancestral lands, because men in armor on horseback "discover" their land; children, men, and women are kidnapped and transported to other lands; millions of men and women will never see their ancestral homelands again; land is watered with blood; land is stolen; land is given; land is grabbed; land is sold; land is bought; land is fenced; land is farmed; land lies fallow; land becomes a reservation; land becomes an ideology.[35]

In *Brothers and Sisters to Us*, the bishops charge that many people of color have been "uprooted, defrauded or dispossessed of their lands" (5). Indeed, the ways in which laws have institutionalized land as property pose ethical and moral questions about the ways those same laws not only have dispossessed the native peoples of the United States but have plundered and ravaged the very source of their physical subsistence and callously disregarded their moral, religious, and psychic good.[36] Robert Allen Warrior, theologian and member of the Osage Nation, reminds us that theology—even liberation theology—has had a hand in stamping Native Americans as "Other."[37] Warrior recalls that many Puritan preachers frequently referred to Native Americans as Amelkites and Canaanites,

> people who, if they would not be converted, were worthy of annihilation. By examining such instances in theological and political writings, in sermons, and elsewhere, we can understand how America's self-image as a "chosen people" has provided a rhetoric to mystify domination."[38]

Warrior challenges us to read the Exodus narratives once again—this time, placing the Canaanites and Native Americans at the center. Given the slaughter of the Amelkites and Canaanites by the *oppressed* Hebrews, Warrior wonders:

> Is [the Exodus story] appropriate to the needs of indigenous people seeking justice and deliverance? If indeed the Canaanites were integral to Israel's early history, the Exodus narratives reflect a situation in which the indigenous people put their hope in a god from outside, were liberated from their oppressors, and then saw their story of oppression revised out of the new nation's history of salvation. They were assimilated into another people's identity and the history of their ancestors came to be regarded as suspect and a danger to the safety of Israel. In short, they were betrayed.[39]

We have not yet come to terms with the peoples who are indigenous to the land which gives us life and breath and nourishment. That we do so is a matter of justice intrinsic to the reconsideration of the common good.

In the pastoral letter, *This Land is Home to Me*, the bishops seek to ask and answer some of the questions around rural land and the powerlessness of the people who cling to it. In hauntingly poetical and simple language, the pastoral letter speaks to the hopes and fears, joys and griefs, struggles and anxieties of the people who live on the blighted, yet beautiful land extending from northern Georgia through western North Carolina, eastern Kentucky and Tennessee, and West Virginia, into western Pennsylvania, touching southern New York and regions of Alabama, Maryland, Mississippi, Ohio, South Carolina and Virginia. These women and men and their children are poor and suffer economic oppression. They toil and labor in the hills, farmlands, and hollows; "in industrial centers grown gray with smoke and smog, blaring with the clank and crash of heavy machinery and urban congestion." These women and men and their children are small "farmers and sharecroppers, day laborers and migrant workers, who help the earth yield its food to the hungry," and who battle to retain some measure of their dignity in the struggle for economic security (475). Mountains and coal bind rich and poor to the region, often pitting

> Indians, blacks, Mexican Americans, immigrants, Puerto Ricans, and poor whites. . .brothers and sisters in suffering, against one another for some meager piece of a pie, which, however big (the biggest the world had ever known) refused to feed all its children. (477)

Industrial development sustained by the resources of the land brought blessings for many, but for some it was like a "cancer eating away its own foundation. The system produced for production's sake, and it tried to train people to consume for consumption's sake" (480–81). To meet the artificially created demands of consumption and business, the land metaphorically and literally was turned into "an energy reservation or giant industrial park": Appalachia, a "field of powerlessness," its people used and discarded (483, 485).[40]

> The suffering of Appalachia's poor is a symbol of so much other suffering—in our land, in our world. It is also a symbol of the suffering which awaits the majority of plain people in our society—if they are laid off, if major illness occurs, if a wage earner dies, or if anything else goes wrong. In this land of ours, jobs are often scarce. Too many people are forced to accept unjust conditions or else lose their jobs. (485–86)

In Appalachia, like in so many other places in this land we call America,

> plain people work hard all their life, and their parents worked hard before them, yet they can't make ends meet. Food is too expensive. Taxes are too high for most. Sickness puts people into debt. College is out of reach for their children. Paychecks keep shrinking. And it's worse for those who can't work, especially the elderly. Meanwhile, corporate profits for the giant [coal and oil] conglomerates, who control our energy resources, keep skyrocketing. (490)

The bishops discern the presence of the Spirit of God in the gradual, fitful emergence of a changed and "new social order" (506–07). They exhort all men and women to authentic open-mindedness and open-heartedness, to prayerful and serious reflection on the nature and meaning of a just society, to active participation in bringing such a society to birth (507). In this creative process of growth and change, the bishops urge that the following three elements are to be balanced: (1) a closeness to the poor of the land, which entails active listening and creative reflection; (2) careful use of scientific resources; and (3) a "steeping in the presence of the Spirit" (507).

John XXIII in *Pacem in Terris* asserted that the common good is characterized in the following ways: (1) it concerns all people; (2) all members of the state must share in it; (3) attention must be given to the poor and marginalized members of a society; and (4) the state must assume the role of promoting the material and spiritual welfare of its citizens (no. 55–57). Society is an order between people and its end is the common good. *Brothers and Sisters to Us* and *This Land Is Home to Me* challenge that order's *status quo*. These letters offer critiques of racism and exploitation which extend and advance the meanings, values, and practices of our idea and realization of the common good. These critiques encourage concrete examination of our vision of the common good and, thus, increase the probabilities of its realization. These pastoral letters invite us to question, even discourse, about the common good: What do we mean by *common*? Who defines what is common and by what criteria? What values animate our vision? Can we articulate these clearly and distinctly? Are we willing to struggle and sacrifice for a new vision of the political order? *Brothers and Sisters to Us* and *This Land Is Home to Me* challenge us to an examination of our social conscience: Are we willing to confront sin and evil within the Christian community? Are we willing to open our lives to create a context for the coming Reign of God, and by what values and practices can we do so? How will we cooperate with the divine solution to the problem of evil? Can we allow the memory of the cross of Jesus to expose our pretense to personal innocence, to social neutrality?

Catholic Social Thought in Reconsidering the Common Good

Given flagrant abuses in the processes of technological, economic, political and cultural development of human societies and persons, the social role of the church adheres in the promotion of the common good. This is so, of course, for more than historical, philosophical, cultural or social reasons. The theological warrants for the church's intervention in cultural, social, political, and economic affairs have been argued substantially elsewhere; a summary statement is sufficient here.[41] There are four prevailing theological warrants for the church's intervention in the cultural, social, political, economic, and technological orders: (1) the mission of the church is grounded in a Trinitarian understanding of the Judeo-Christian God and in the purposes of and missions of each Person; (2) the church has no choice but "to discern and proclaim the presence and action of God" in every human activity; hence, politics and economics, at their depths, disclose a religious dimension; (3) the Gospel's message of unity of love of God and neighbor require the church to attend to cultural, social, political, economic, and technological issues; and (4) action on behalf of justice is a constitutive dimension in evangelization.[42] Yet, while the church is a leaven in the world, a unique agent of the divine mission and purpose, it is not identical with God's Reign of Justice; for, indeed, the Reign of God intends a gathering far larger than the church.

Catholic social teaching as an expression of the church teaching and learning may serve at least these four functions in a reconsideration of the common good. First, Catholic social thought exerts a *prophetic function*. It can give voice to the experiences of many people who have been ignored, overlooked, excluded and suppressed. It gives a voice to the victims of history and invites us to join in solidarity with them. In this way, Catholic social thought enlarges the self-understanding of the human community and celebrates the incarnate diversities of the image of God and publicly mourns its defacement. Catholic social thought also has a *didactic function*. Catholic social wisdom can teach us to apprehend, understand, judge, and evaluate the social matrix in light of the purposes of God. It identifies and opposes short-sighted solutions to many political, economic, and technological problems. Moreover, Catholic social thought can proclaim and teach a wider vision of humankind; it can champion many of the dimensions of human life that are not immediately or necessarily instrumental. Catholic social thought exercises a *critical function*, recognizing that no technological order or scheme, no economic program, no political platform or regime is so flawless as to be completely free from the taint of human sin and error. It recalls for us the deep poverty of any and all merely human solutions to the problem of evil. Finally, Catholic social thought has a *moral function*. The church has long understood that education is not only social, thereby transmitting culture; it is also moral, it purifies culture. Thus, the formation of character, the practice of virtue, is vital in any effort to realize the common good.

Expressed compactly, the transcendent solution to the problem of evil is the Passion, Death, and Resurrection of Jesus of Nazareth. What the church grasps and proclaims is the intimate and conditioning relationship between vital life (mere life), that which constitutes a virtuous life (a good life), and the enjoyment of the Beatific Vision (eternal life).[43] The realization of the complex common good is never achieved through the concrete transformation of the conditions of cultural, social, political or economic life alone. What is required is the development of the intellectual, psychic, and moral capacities of women and men to meet and to contest evil and social decline. The realization of the common good is dependent upon human evaluation, human choice, human decision; upon human acts of intelligence, of reasonableness, of responsibility. From the perspective of Catholic social thought, the realization of the common good is dependent upon our acceptance of and cooperation with God's gift of grace, by and through which we may speak, act, heal and create a society and history that conform to God's providence which is but God's great love for us.

Notes

1. The initial research for this paper was supported by a grant from the Bradley Foundation during my appointment as a Bradley Fellow at the Institute for the Study of Politics and Religion, Boston College, Chestnut Hill, Massachusetts. I thank Professor Ernest L. Fortin who made this opportunity possible.

2. We are alienated also from several corollary ideas which are central to an understanding of political life and philosophy as it has developed in our Western intellectual heritage. These include *phronesis* (prudence or practical wisdom), *proairesis* (deliberate choice), and *praxis*.

I rely here on philosopher Leo Strauss' argument of the "three waves of modernity" in his *Political Philsophy*, Hilal Gildin, ed. (Indianapolis, Ind.: Bobbs–Merrill, 1975), especially pp. 81–98, and his *Natural Right and History* (1950; Chicago: University of Chicago, 1953), especially pp. 35–119.

3. Three interdependent historical movements have contributed to shaping what is called modern society: the Enlightenment with its belief in reason and science; the French Revolution, with its pledge of equality, liberty, and fraternity; and the Industrial Revolution, with its increased production beyond previous expectation and imagination. The very term "modernity" has been invested with a "significance both normative and distortive" by the now failed myth of progress: normative because modernity has been apprehended as superior to whatsoever preceded it; distortive because such opinion inhibits modernity from being grasped as an historical phenomenon. Peter L. Berger, *Facing Up to Modernity: Excursions in Society, Politics, and Religion* (New York: Basic Books, 1977), p. 70.

4. J. Brian Benestad, *The Pursuit of a Just Social Order: Policy Statements of the United States Catholic Bishops, 1966–1980* (Washington, D.C.: Ethics and Public Policy Center, 1982), p. 129.

5. See paragraphs 7, 8, 34–35 in *The Social Teachings of the Church*, Anne Fremantle, ed. (New York: New American Library, 1963).

In the political, economic, and cultural aftermath of the Second World War, philosophers Jacques Maritain and Charles De Koninck sought to introduce the classical (Thomis) idea of the common good as a way to think about how to order the social context. But the vocabulary of rights eclipsed speech about the common good. Thus, until quite recently, other than Pope John XXIII's discussions of the idea of the common good in the encyclicals *Mater et Magistra* (1961) and *Pacem in Terris* (1963), the works of Maritain (*The Person and the Common Good*, John J. Fitzgerald, trans. [1947; Notre Dame, Ind.: University of Notre Dame Press, 1966]) and De Koninck (*Del la Primautè du Bien Commun Contre les Personnalistes* [Quebec: *Editions de l'Universitè Lavel*, Montreal: *Editions Fides*, 1943]) represented the last sustained effort on the part of Catholic theologians to engage the idea of the common good.

Recently, however, attempts at restoration seem afoot. In 1986, the U.S. Catholic bishops retrieved the idea of the common good in their pastoral letter on the U.S. economy and John Paul II has used the term frequently in speeches during his pastoral visits. Two volumes of essays engaging the common good and the economic order have appeared within the last few years: Robert B. Dickie and Leroy S. Rouner, eds., *Corporations and the Common Good* (Notre Dame, Ind.: University of Notre Dame Press/The School of Management, Boston University, 1986) and Oliver F. Williams and John Houck, eds., *The Common Good and U.S. Capitalism* (Lanham, Md.: University Press of America, 1987). Two recent explicit theological contributions are: Michael Novak, *Free Persons and the Common Good* (Lanham, New York, London: Madision Books, 1989) and Gary J. Dorrien, *Restructuring the Common Good: Theology and the Social Order* (Maryknoll: Orbis Books, 1990).

6. With the phrase *pluralist society*, I advert not only to the rich and exuberant racial–ethnic and cultural diversity of our citizenry, but also to clashing intellectual positions and practices that emerge as we wrestle with the basic questions of our common political life. See, John Courtney Murray, *We Hold These Truths: Catholic Reflections on the American Proposition* (1960; New York: Sheed & Ward, Inc., 1964), especially pp. 17–35.

For a critique of American individualism, see Robert N. Bellah, et al., *Habits of the Heart, Individualism and Commitment in American Life* (Berkeley: University of California, 1985) and the sequel, *The Good Society* (New York: Alfred A. Knopf, 1991).

7. Bernard Lonergan, *Insight: A Study of Human Understanding* (1957; New York: Philosophical Library, 1973), ch. 6 and 7.

8. Lonergan, *Method in Theology* (New York: Herder & Herder, 1972), especially pp. 27–55; *A Third Collection: Papers by Bernard J. F. Lonergan*, Frederick E. Crowe, ed. (London and Mahwah, N.J.: Geoffrey Chapman and Paulist Press, 1985), especially pp. 23–34 and 184–201; and *A Second Collection by Bernard J.F. Lonergan*, William J. F. Ryan and Bernard J. Tyrrell, eds. (Philadelphia: The Westminster Press, 1974), especially pp. 69–86 and 165–187.

9. Lonergan, *Method in Theology*, pp. 101–124.

10. Douglas Sturm, "On Meanings of Public Good: An Exploration," *Journal of Religion*, 58, January 1981, pp. 13–29.

11. Strauss, *Political Philosophy*, p. 123.

12. To be sure there was disagreement over how to articulate and ensure the common good of the *polis*. In this regard, the significance of rhetoric cannot be overestimated in Greek city-states like Athens, especially when immediate and direct democracy was the form of government. The capacity of rhetoric to persuade one's fellow citizens was a politician's most valuable asset. Indeed, Plato maintained rhetoric as "the instrument of persuasion for inducing belief" (David Grene, *Greek Political Theory* [= *Man in His Pride* 1950], Chicago & London: University of Chicago Press, 1965), p. 136.

13. The male possessive pronoun is used here intentionally, as women did not enjoy the rights, privileges, and responsibilities of citizenship in the Greek city-states.

14. Jurgen Habermas, *Theory and Practice* (Boston: Beacon Press, 1973), p. 42.

15. Strauss, *Political Philosophy*, pp. 85–86.

16. Thomas Aquinas, *On Princely Government in Aquinas: Selected Political Writings*, A. P. d'Entreves, ed., J. G. Dawson, trans. (Oxford: Basil Blackwell, 1959).

17. *Ibid.*, ch. I.

18. *Ibid.*

19. All references are taken from Thomas Aquinas, *Summa Theologiae*, Blackfriars, trans. (New York: McGraw-Hill, 1966). Citations from the *Summa Theologiae* are followed in the text in parentheses.

20. For a discussion of the paradigm of distributive justice which critiques a conceptualist apprehension of justice as well as the overextension and materialization of distributive justice, see Iris Marion Young, *Justice and the Politics of Difference* (Princeton: Princeton University Press, 1990), especially pp. 15–38; see also Stephen J. Pope, "Aquinas on Almsgiving, Justice and Charity: An Interpretation and Reassessment," *Heythrop Journal*, 32, 1991, pp. 167–191.

21. Thomas Gilby, *Between Community and Society, A Philosophy and Theology of the State* (London: Longmans, Green, 1953), p. 213.

22. *Ibid.*, pp. 211–12.

23. Strauss, *Political Philosophy*, p. 86.

24. Niccolo Machiavelli, *The Prince* [1513], Mark Musa, trans. ed. (New York: St. Martin's Press, 1964). Citations from *The Prince* are followed in the text in parentheses.

25. Maritain, *The Person and the Common Good*, p. 50; see also, Strauss, *The City and Man* (1964; Chicago: University of Chicago Press, 1978), p. 82.

26. Robert Heilbroner, "Realities and Appearances in Capitalism," *Corporations and the Common Good*, p. 41.

27. Habermas, *Theory and Practice*, pp. 42–81.

28. Strauss, *Political Philosophy*, p. 123.

29. John Rawls, *A Theory of Justice* (Cambridge, Mass.: Belknap Press, 1971), p. 11.

30. Strauss, *City and Man*, p. 11.

31. John L. Hodge, et al., *Cultural Bases of Racism and Group Oppression: An Examination of Traditional "Western" Concepts, Values and Institutional Structures which Support Racism, Sexism, and Elitism* (Berkeley, Calif.: Two Riders Press, 1975).

32. Albert Memmi, *Dominated Man* (Boston: Beacon Press, 1969), pp. 185–186.

33. *Ibid.*

34. See *Discrimination and Christian Conscience* (1958) and *National Race Crisis* (1968).

35. Francis Jennings, *The Invasion of America: Indians, Colonialism, and the Cant of Conquest* (1975; New York: W. W. Norton, 1976); Octavio Paz, *One Earth, Four or Five Worlds: Reflections on Contemporary History* (1983; New York: Harcourt Brace Jovanovich, 1985); Tzvetan Todorov, *The Conquest of America* (1982; New York: Harper & Row, 1984).

36. Charles A. Reich, "The New Property," *The Yale Law Review*, 73, 5, April 1964, pp. 733–787.

37. Robert Allen Warrior, "Canaanites, Cowboys, and Indians: Deliverance, Conquest, and Liberation Theology Today," *Christianity and Crisis*, 49, 12, September 11, 1989, pp. 261–265.

38. *Ibid.*, p. 264.

39. *Ibid.* See also Vine Deloria, Jr., *Custer Died for Your Sins: An Indian Manifesto* (New York: The Macmillian Company, 1969), and *God is Red* (New York: Grosset & Dunlap, 1973); Arnold Krupat, *The Voice in the Margin: Native American Literature and the Canon* (Berkeley: University of California Press, 1989).

40. The issue of ecology and abuse of the land is taken up in the pastoral letter; the focus here is on the relationship between the land and the people who cherish it and depend upon it for subsistence.

41. Among others see Donal Dorr, *Option for the Poor: A Hundred Years of Vatican Social Teaching* (Maryknoll: Orbis Books, 1983); Joseph Gremillion, *The Gospel of Peace and Justice: Catholic Social Teaching Since Pope John* (Maryknoll: Orbis Books, 1976), especially pp. 1–138; John C. Haughey, ed., *The Faith that Does Justice: Examining the Christian Source for Social Change* (New York: Paulist Press, 1977).

42. John A. Coleman, *An American Strategic Theology* (New York: Paulist Press, 1982), pp. 9–37, especially p. 10; see also Lonergan, *A Third Collection*, pp. 23–34.

43. Lonergan, *Collection: Papers by Bernard Lonergan*, Frederick E. Crowe, ed. (New York: Herder & Herder, 1967), pp. 16–53, especially 38–40.

Nineteen

Toward a Theology of the Corporation: A Second Chance for Catholic Social Teaching

Dennis P. McCann

The Roaring Eighties are history. Commentators may dispute when this, possibly the shortest of decades in U.S. history, actually passed away. Some may favor the Wall Street panic of October 19, 1987, which, if it did not result in the onslaught of another Great Depression, certainly yielded depression-like conditions within the investment industry. Others may argue that the eighties lasted until the current recession set in and, depending upon the astuteness of their economic analysis, may blame either Saddam Hussein or Alan Greenspan for putting an end to the Reagan prosperity. However the date for the demise is fixed, it is clear that the agenda for the nineties, its dominant styles in politics, business, and that bewildering monstrosity of conflicting signals that we regard as our civic culture, will not unfold simply as just more of the same.

One indication of just how much change we can expect is Robert B. Reich's attempt to redefine our agenda for "The REAL Economy" (*Atlantic Monthly*, February, 1991), in which he parts company with the conventional economic wisdom of both major political parties. Reich focuses instead on the need for major social investments in public education, research and development and material infrastructure to improve America's competitiveness in the emerging global economy. In exhorting us to make the sacrifices needed to fund these priorities for the nineties, he takes issue with President Bush's lament, "'We have more will than wallet.'" In Reich's view, "Bush has it backward: We have the wallet. What we lack is the will."

No little irony surrounds Reich's proposal, for it is reminiscent of precisely those diagnoses that were brusquely set aside by the apparent triumph of Reaganomics. It is as if the Roaring Eighties were merely a tranquilizing interlude, marked by a mercifully temporary paralysis in our capacity to recognize and address the structural problems in the U.S. economy. Reich's message is a throwback to Lester Thurow's *The Zero Sum Society* (1980). Although Thurow is much more emphatic about questions of distributive justice than Reich appears to be, both are seeking to mobilize a political and moral consensus on behalf of making the sacrifices necessary to stimulate genuine and socially useful economic development. Both are fighting the illusion that such a reordering of public priorities in this country need be a zero-sum game. Unfortunately, neither seems to have a clue as to how the case for sacrifice can be made except through conventional appeals to collective, long-term, and thus rational self-interest.

It would seem, then, that the Roaring Eighties—like a garish old merry-go-round at the county fair—merely took us for a ride. Have we come full circle only to find most of us back at the starting gate, now worth slightly or substantially less than when we started? Is the entire decade to be dismissed as a mindless distraction? I think not; and especially when considering the development of Catholic social teaching in the United States, I must insist not. Besides all the excesses that contributed to its demise, the eighties also witnessed the communications breakthrough effected by the pastoral letters of the National Conference of Catholic Bishops. The process that informed the drafting of *Economic Justice for All: Catholic Social Teaching and the U.S. Economy* (1986), especially the way in which it galvanized the debate between liberals and neoconservatives within the church as well as among those who influence public opinion generally, not only betokened a level of moral seriousness but also achieved certain insights into the nature of capitalist economic development that ought to be characteristic of Catholic social teaching for decades to come.

Some may be tempted to downplay the significance of the debate between Catholic liberals and neoconservatives, as if it were simply an echo of the stalemated irrelevancies that Reich has identified with the Democrats and Republicans. But did the Catholic liberalism, characteristic of those who drafted the pastoral letter, offer nothing more than a religious argument for expanding the Welfare State and increasing entitlements? Similarly, was the neoconservatism characteristic of its critics, simply a smokescreen for liberating the rich from their just tax liabilities and businesses from public accountability? The vociferous accusations hurled against each other by both sides, especially in the debate over Catholic social teaching's robust notion of economic rights, might support such suspicions. But amid the cacophony something new also was struggling to be born, a critical theological affirmation of capitalism's possibilities that would set the stage for a more discerning evaluation of the social practices of businessmen and women, and the institutional setting in which they seek to generate wealth.

My own attempt to take the measure of this sea change in Catholic social teaching deliberately takes its name from one of those groundbreaking essays by which Michael Novak tried to define the agenda for the eighties, "Toward a Theology of the Corporation" (1981). In hindsight, as we confront a similar moment with respect to the nineties, it is clear that Novak failed to develop such a theology, although he did outline several promising features for one. Because of the burden of public policy controversy, and the massive resistance of most theologians to his proposals, Novak delivered not a theological interpretation of life inside business organizations but a religious legitimation of the system sustaining them, namely, democratic capitalism. Despite the promise of Novak's systemic perspective, Catholic social teaching still lacks a credible theology of the corporation.

The end of the eighties, however, may provide us with a second chance to develop such a theology, one with a different set of priorities than Novak's might have allowed. For the debate, so dear to modern theologians, over the relative merits of systems of political economy as such, has been overtaken by the flow of recent events. Catholic social teaching needs to redeploy its resources beyond the narrow range of large abstractions rendered visible by that debate. For the most part, U.S. Catholics no longer need to be convinced of the merits of democratic capitalism, but need to make sense of their own vocation within this system, and its role in fulfilling God's purposes in history. Precisely because of our need for moral discernment regarding the social practices of business, the nineties challenge Catholic social teaching to provide a religious vision of the corporation, and its potential for both good and evil.

In the remarks that follow, I hope to renew the search for an adequate theology of the modern business corporation. The argument will proceed in four stages:

1. Because Michael Novak did make a pioneering attempt to develop a theology of the corporation, I must begin by offering a critical assessment of his effort. For while his admirers may need to be convinced that Novak's theology could stand some revision, his critics need to admit that his is a genuine contribution to the development of Catholic social teaching.

2. I will stake out a second chance for a theology of the corporation, developing further the themes outlined in a recent article Max Stackhouse and I published in *The Christian Century* (January 17, 1991), "Public Theology after the Collapse of Socialism: A Post-Communist Manifesto." Following the lead once given by James M. Gustafson and Elmer W. Johnson at the first of these symposia at the University of Notre Dame, I will outline a vision of business corporations as "aspects of the Divine governance of the world."

3. If such a vision of the corporation is to be anything more than a personal idiosyncracy, its continuity with the mainstream of Catholic social teaching must be established. Therefore, I will turn next to the tradition, to highlight its resources for understanding business. I will focus

on the principle of subsidiarity, especially as developed in the U.S. bishops' pastoral letter, *Economic Justice for All*, and its thematic discussions
of "solidarity" and "participation." I will assert that these ideas suggest a
robustly Trinitarian conception of the social order, which provides a substantively theological basis for assessing the patterns of organizational
development in business corporations as well as other human institutions.

4. Since the theology of the corporation I propose is meant to be practical, I will conclude this essay by trying to show what difference it can
make in helping to save Catholic social teaching from self-marginalization
in the emerging global economy. The repositioning of Catholic social
teaching I am hoping to achieve is informed significantly, but not exclusively, by Robert B. Reich's book, *The Work of Nations: Preparing
Ourselves for 21st Century Capitalism* (1991). The challenge he outlines, I
am convinced, will be met, not simply through a repetition of the church's
cry for social justice, but through a new understanding of the emerging
social order in which we must seek the common good. It is my hope that
a credible theology of the corporation will contribute to a renewal of
Catholic social teaching's perspective on the social order.

The Unfulfilled Promise of Michael Novak's Theology

When Michael Novak launched his defense of democratic capitalism
little over a decade ago, he did so knowing full well that his would be an
unpopular cause among theologians and ethicists. Indeed, the question
he took for his title, "Can a Christian Work for a Corporation?" accurately
reflected the consensus among religious intellectuals who held little hope
that anyone could preserve his or her integrity, let alone experience God's
favor, while pursuing a career in business. With characteristic boldness,
Novak lent his considerable rhetorical skills to the task of exposing this
prejudice and the web of distortions, half-truths, and hypocrisies that
informed it. His effort still is regarded as beneath notice by many whose
opinions it so devastatingly challenges. I am not suggesting, however, that
he be celebrated uncritically for pointing out the obvious. A more suitable
tribute to Novak's achievement, I think, is to show how to advance more
effectively along the path he opened up for us.

The question, "Can a Christian Work for a Corporation?" seems to beg
for an assessment of the internal dynamics of business organizations, and
the range, however limited, of moral values already operative in them.
Novak chose not to pursue this line of inquiry, but focused instead on "the
prior theology of democratic capitalism, which in turn depends on a prior
theology of economics" (1981, p. 2). Nevertheless, he anticipated the

outcome of these reflections, insisting that working for a corporation in principle ought to present no greater difficulty to a Christian sense of vocation than working for the state, within a university, or in high ecclesiastical office. Novak knew that in each of these institutions the exercise of responsibility would bring its own characteristic forms of moral ambiguity, but the ultimate challenge would always remain the same: "To grow in the holiness of Jesus Christ" (1981, p. 3).

Novak's outline of a theology of economics and his defense of democratic capitalism are, as he insisted, logically prior to theological reflections upon the morality of corporations. For if, in principle, democratic capitalism is fundamentally incompatible with a Christian commitment, the good intentions of entrepreneurs and business managers would count for little against the total depravity of the situation itself. The moral standing of the Christian in business would be analogous to that of the pious slaveholder. No amount of compassionate care could hope to make up for the affront to human dignity represented by the very existence of the institution of slavery. If capitalism, however democratic the societal infrastructure, is intrinsically immoral, then a Christian cannot work for a corporation. Because there seemed to be significant skepticism among theologians regarding the moral validity of capitalism as such, Novak focused with increasing intensity on this prior question.

Certain elements of Novak's theology of economics, however, are just as relevant for understanding the internal dynamics of corporations as they are for the system as a whole. His Notre Dame essay lists the following themes: Order, Emergent Probability, Sin, Practical Wisdom, The Individual, Community, Distribution, and Scarcity (1981, pp. 21–25). His purpose at that point was not to define them systematically, but to identify a program for further research and critical reflection. They receive more extended, though still sketchy treatment in *The Spirit of Democratic Capitalism* (1982), appearing first in a preliminary description of this political economy in its "ideal" form, and later as reflected in "six theological doctrines" common to most forms of traditional Christianity: The Trinity, The Incarnation, Competition, Original Sin, The Separation of Realms, and Caritas or Love (1982, pp. 333–360). Novak's theological reflections clearly were meant to suggest what David Tracy advocates as a "critical correlation" (1975, pp. 32–34) between Christian faith and contemporary experience, except that the experience he wished to emphasize was of persons and groups serving each other's needs in a market economy regulated by the policies of a constitutional democracy.

Such a correlation between the ideal of democratic capitalism and the realities affirmed by Christian faith easily can become uncritical, and in two different ways. First, the historical contingencies that contributed to the formation of democratic capitalism can be mistaken for logical necessities. Such an error leads to the presumption that, because it first emerged in a Western civilization decisively influenced by biblical religion, democratic capitalism must be a uniquely valid expression of authentic Christian faith. Second, the moral ambiguity of life as actually experienced in our society, personal as well as communal, can be obscured easily by a theological correlation with the "ideal" of democratic capitalism. Now rendered sacrosanct by its association with central theological doctrines, the articulated ideal can become a cover-up hiding the discrepancies between the actual performance of the system and our transcendent aspirations toward the common good.

There is ample evidence that Novak's theology of economics was meant to minimize the risk of these distortions, on both counts. Regarding the first tendency, he clearly dissociates his project from any uncritical religious legitimation of democratic capitalism:

> It is essential not to confuse the transcendence of Christianity and Judaism with the survival of democratic capitalism. . . . I do not claim that democratic capitalism is the practice of which Christianity and Judaism are the religions. That is not my view. . . . Judaism and Christianity do not *require* democratic capitalism. It is only that without it they would be poorer and less free. Among political economies, there may be something better than self-correcting democratic capitalism. If so, it is not yet in sight. (1982, p. 336)

The second tendency, in principle, is met by the affirmation of Original Sin which is comprehended within a metaphysics of Emergent Probability in Novak's theology. While remembrance of our complicity in sin is generally useful for deflating "human pretensions of unambiguous virtue" (1982, p. 349), Novak's point also is to lower expectations regarding the realization of God's purposes in any form of political economy, including democratic capitalism. His thoughts on the Incarnation, "a doctrine of hope, but not of utopia" (*ibid.*, p. 341), are meant as well to liberate the defenders of this system from claiming too much for it.

Despite his good intentions, Novak's outline does not succeed as a persuasive theological defense of either democratic capitalism or the choice of business careers within it. Nevertheless, the precise nature of his failure is instructive, if the theology of the corporation is to be given a second chance. Novak's discussion of democratic capitalism fails to be adequately historical in its perspective on both the development of this system of political economy and the forms of business enterprise within it. Let us look at the systemic problem first. Democratic capitalism, according to Novak, is inherently pluralistic insofar as it institutionalizes three independent sectors, a political system, an economic system, and a moral-cultural system, that continually adjust themselves to one another (1982, pp. 171–186). The political system is more or less identified with the government; the economic, with corporations; and the moral-cultural, with churches, universities and the communications media. Each of these systems, in principle, provides checks and balances on the others.

My objection is not that this model of institutional differentiation fails to illuminate contemporary experience, but that Novak's rendering of it tends to mask the nature of the conflicts inherent in the development of the system. The possibility that intractable "contradictions" may undermine the ideal equilibrium discerned among the three is raised, only to be dismissed by Novak as another indication of anticapitalist bias. Not that Novak is blind to disequilibrium as such, but that the symptoms he emphasizes, namely, the alleged encroachment of the government in the economic sphere, or the "unprecedented power" and unchecked ambitions of the "new class" that allegedly dominates the moral-cultural sphere, are depicted as threats to a preexisting harmony. It is not that these threats seem arbitrarily chosen, but that the ideal of harmonious interaction makes it impossible to appreciate the way in which certain historic struggles, notably those of organized labor, were actually constitutive of the system as such.

Novak, for example, mentions his own study, *The Guns of Lattimer* (1978), of the United Mine Workers' strike of 1897 in northeastern Pennsylvania, and the labor massacre that accompanied it. His comment is telling: "Nonetheless, the pluralism of the three systems enabled the miners at Lattimer, at the cost of their own blood, to make their case and ultimately to bring about important transformations in all three systems" (1982, p. 176). His own description of the event, however, suggests a different interpretation. The strike and others like it were significant events in creating and stabilizing the threefold systemic differentiation in the first place. All too often most Americans seem to have experienced only one system, bent on suppressing the human rights and dignity of now one, and then another group of working men and women. The point here, of course, is not simply to set the historical record straight, but to reassert the constructive role of dissent in the development of the system. Without the formation of the coalitions that succeeded in curbing the seemingly limitless power of modern industrial corporations in the period of their infancy, democratic capitalism would not exist today. Novak's version of our history, apparently, cannot admit the profound irony involved in the emergence of a form of capitalism whose very success is due to the organized resistance of forces animated by an anticapitalist bias. This lack of discernment may be one of the casualties of the polemical situation in which Novak positions his theology of democratic capitalism. Once the sense of irony is lost, the full range of morally responsible attitudes one might adopt toward capitalism and business corporations seems considerably narrowed.

Equally perplexing is his failure to appreciate the diverse patterns of organizational development represented within corporations. His only concern seems to be an external one, shaped by the need to refute analyses such as Charles E. Lindblom's *Politics and Markets* (1977), which express legitimate fears of the inordinate political influence of large corporations. Novak seems to think the issue is simply one of size, rather than public accountability. Lindblom, on the other hand, sees a threat to political democracy in the conventionally hierarchical structures of corporate governance. Rather than point out how obsolete Lindblom's generalizations about business management actually are, Novak seems to accept the conventional model and dismiss experimenting in business with managerial styles attuned to participatory democracy as incompatible with the requirements of efficiency in industrial production (1982, pp. 178–180). Once again, the problem is one of focus: Novak's seems concerned about the internal dynamics of corporate management only insofar as it impinges upon the field of public policy, where systemic questions are raised. His focus may present no problems for a theology of democratic capitalism, but it does undercut efforts to envision an adequate theology of the corporation.

Despite these limitations, Novak's theology must be regarded as a genuine contribution to the development of Catholic social teaching. As his less polemical and more discursive later work, *Freedom with Justice: Catholic Social Thought and Liberal Institutions* (1984), makes clear, part of Novak's purpose is to confront "the anti-liberal tradition" within the church by showing the convergences between crucial aspects of papal social teaching and the modified economic liberalism he advocates. Because he is concerned with overcoming the alleged incompetence exhibited by the church's current leadership in debates over matters of economic policy, he hopes to use Catholic social teaching as a vehicle for developing a constructive theology of political economy, parallel to the mature philosophy of John Stuart Mill. He insists rightly that such a theology can proceed only by understanding the social institutions, rather than merely the ideologies, supportive of economic liberalism. The routine performances characteristic of these institutions actually come closer to fulfilling the aspirations of Catholic social teaching than those of any other system of political economy. While *Freedom with Justice* thus adds nothing new to the position staked out more provocatively in *The Spirit of*

Democratic Capitalism, it does establish Novak's claim to represent a valid perspective within the tradition of Catholic social teaching, if there were any lingering doubts about the intellectual origins of his perspective.

The Corporation Theologically Envisioned

If we are to advance the discussion of a theology of the corporation beyond Novak's ground-breaking attempt, we must try first to formulate the question from which the theological significance of this all-too-human institution can be discerned. To answer the question, What, theologically speaking, is a corporation? we must have some prior notion of what it means to speak about anything theologically. As the etymology of the word suggests, all theology must be about God. To speak theologically is to construe the purposes of things in their proper ordering before God. Because the one speaking, presumably, intends to be Christian, the God whose purposes are to be discerned is none other than the Trinity most fully recognized in the confession of Jesus of Nazareth as the Christ, the Incarnate Word. With reference to the unfolding revelation of the Triune God, then, What is a corporation?

In another of the seminal essays that graced the first symposium of the Notre Dame Center for Ethics and Religious Values in Business, *The Judeo-Christian Vision and the Modern Corporation* (1982), James M. Gustafson, in dialogue with Elmer W. Johnson, rather offhandedly provided an illuminating answer to this question when he characterized institutions, including business corporations, as "aspects of the divine governance of the world" (1982, p. 320). Although Gustafson and Johnson meant to focus on the moral character of executive leadership, they identified rightly the unstated premise for any serious theological discussion of business management as a Christian vocation. What does it mean, therefore, for a human institution to be seen as an aspect of the divine governance in the world? Is there anything in the world that is not a part of the divine governance? It all depends on what divine governance turns out to be.

Given the self-consciously Protestant character of Gustafson and Johnson's thinking, their perspective on divine governance is likely to be biblical in its reference. I discern in it an echo of the Letter to the Romans, the perennially contested passage in Chapter 13 on the nature of civil authority:

> You must all obey the governing authorities. Since all government comes from God, the civil authorities were appointed by God, and

so anyone who resists authority is rebelling against God's decision, and such an act is bound to be punished. Good behavior is not afraid of the magistrates; only criminals have anything to fear. If you want to live without being afraid of authority, you must live honestly and authority may even honor you. The state is there to serve God for your benefit. (Romans 13:1–4, The Jerusalem Bible)

To affirm modern business corporations as of divine governance is to extend to them the range of Christian aspirations that conventionally have been attributed to the state. As Johnson points out, "one of the more profound insights of the Judeo-Christian vision is the importance it attaches to institutional arrangements as *enabling conditions for responsible leadership*" (1982, p. 325).

The nature of these enabling conditions is suggested in the passage from the Letter to the Romans. While the metaphor of official appointment and the legal claim to obedience may be open to a variety of interpretations, the role of human institutions in securing God's purposes in the social order is affirmed clearly. Equally clear is the assertion that such institutions exist to serve our benefit, which as such is also service to God. By providing an appropriate system of constraints—as well as opportunities—institutions enable us to act responsibly in concert with one another. These constraints, as Johnson suggests, may be understood within the Pauline perspective on the Law, which functions not just coercively but also educatively in the role of "schoolmaster" (1982, p. 322). The creation and preservation of a social order, however modest, thus is not to be taken for granted. Given the Pauline vision of the redemptive struggle of sin and grace that informs this passage, the actual history in which our institutions currently operate must be regarded as an unnatural one, that is, a situation warped by the disorders that are a consequence of sin. The creation and preservation of institutions that enable us to act responsibly, however imperfect their performance continues to be, must be regarded as part of the ongoing miracle of God's redeeming grace in history.

The forms of governance exercised by human institutions are properly understood as providential to the extent they develop in response to God's activity in this history of redemption. Such institutions are misleadingly regarded as "ordinances of Creation," as if their historical form were permanent and not open to further transformation. Nor are they to be seen merely as manifestations of the so-called "Natural Law" unless, of course, that law itself is explicitly affirmed as itself participating in the history of redemption. A theology of divine governance consistent with the vision affirmed in the Letter to the Romans, thus eliminates any deistic construal of the development of the social order. The providential character of human institutions must be a reflection of the Divine Life shared and communicated to us through the Trinity. Anything short of a Trinitarian interpretation of our history risks misconstruing both the nature of God and the social order that God is achieving through us.

Such theological assertions, or others very like them, would seem conventional in any Christian theology of the political order. That these same affirmations, and the theological corollaries developed in the traditions responsive to them, should be transferred now to the economic order and used analogously to advance our understanding of modern business corporations may need explanation. What are the implications to be drawn from regarding the economic order in this way? First of all, unless economic institutions are aspects of divine governance, it is difficult to make any sense of the Christian vocation affirmed of those who work in them. A genuinely Christian sense of vocation must be an appropriately subjective response to an objective truth about the social location in which such a vocation is discerned. The call to service experienced in a Christian vocation cannot be simply a generalized abstraction regarding the laity's need to achieve holiness in the world. The call must be experienced with reference to specific forms of stewardship, which are themselves in the process of becoming institutionalized; those responding to such a call may thus experience the institutions in which they are serving as forms of covenanted community. In short, unless corporations are affirmed as aspects of divine governance, it is difficult to see how the traditional Christian vocabularies of stewardship, covenant and vocation have any reference to the economic order. And yet, somehow clearly they do.

Second, if corporations are aspects of the divine governance, we must ask ourselves how they relate to the other aspects of God's redeeming presence in the social order. The chief of these, of course, is the church itself and, as the passage from Romans reminds us, the state. The church, of course, is the more significant of the two: Its purpose is to render visible the basic pattern of God's activity in history by becoming the point of spiritual incorporation for all persons and groups within the Body of Christ. The church's form of incorporation is sacramental: By extending the life of the Mystical Body through space and time, it empowers God's would-be collaborators for service in the world. The state, by contrast, oversees all forms of incorporation by establishing the juridical basis, or constitutional order, in which all institutions exercise their various functions. Citizenship is thus not so much a form of incorporation as the acknowledgement of one's membership in civil society as such. The state, therefore, is the ultimate guardian of the human rights and duties operative throughout society; its role in the divine governance is focused appropriately on justice.

The modern business corporation is not, nor could it ever be, a substitute for either the church or the state; its purpose in the unfolding of the

history of the redemption is different from both. The corporation's purpose is to create wealth, that is, to produce the economic resources necessary for authentic social development. It creates wealth by organizing
material and spiritual resources for production. The profits earned and
distributed to its shareholders are but one conventional, though indispensable, token of its effectiveness in fulfilling this purpose. But the effectiveness distinctive of business itself, management theorists like Peter
Drucker assure us, is a result of the unique ways corporations learn to
serve the needs of their customers. The form of service thus institutionalized incorporates a distinctive mix of external competitiveness with
respect to the markets in which such needs are identified, and internal
cooperation by which the productive energies of various groups of people are focused to meet these needs. Given the continually shifting patterns of needs expressed by those whom the corporation is meant to
serve, this form of divine governance is likely to be far more tentative and
improvisational than either the church or the state. This basic instability
itself may be regarded as one impressive sign, however ambiguous, of the
ongoing struggle of the redemption.

The notion that a business corporation operates to bring order out of
the chaos of conflicting economic needs and competing resource alloca-
tion strategies suggests why, thirdly, that such corporations, theologically
speaking, must be distinguished from markets with respect to the divine
governance. Inasmuch as exchange relationships are a natural expression
of human sociality, markets are as close to a natural phenomenon as any
human social practice is likely to be. The specifically economic forms of
exchange, furthermore, seem to be rooted in the exigencies of scarcity,
which itself must be affirmed—as I have argued in a previous presentation at one of these symposia—as part of the inherent limits built into the
basic order of Creation (1989). The logic of economic scarcity, in other
words, ought not to be considered one of the "sinful structures" condemned by Catholic social teaching, and neither should the markets that
arise in response to it.

Nevertheless, left to their own devices, markets generate as much
economic chaos as order. One might as well rely on a tornado to usher in
the warm, gentle breezes of springtime as trust markets of themselves to
create a tolerably just distribution of the economic resources they help
generate. This is true as a matter of logic as well as historical experience.
The economist Joseph Schumpeter reminded us that markets are to be
numbered among the agents of "creative destruction." They are as naturally so as severe weather surely is. The successful gardener does not
waste time trying either to suppress the weather forcibly or to temper it
with moral exhortations. Instead, she learns to discern the signs of its

changing conditions and adapts her cultivation accordingly. The modicum of order thus achieved is similar to the outcome for which business managers doggedly hope. The successful enterprise exercises a degree of control over markets by learning to adapt its production strategies to changing conditions. Economic resources are thus allocated in ways that are meant to capitalize on the market's capacity to maximize wealth, while attempting to minimize the destruction that can be caused by the market's propensity toward extreme fluctuations. It is, in short, the business corporation that has a role to play in the exercise of divine governance; markets, to borrow a phrase from Reinhold Niebuhr, make such governance both possible and necessary.

Fourth, and finally, the distinctive ways in which business corporations and markets typically interact provide additional clues as to the nature of the divine governance. Corporations stand at the intersection of several types of markets, not just those defined by their customers. Unlike a privately held company, a publicly held corporation is accountable to its stockholders whose purposes in investing in a particular firm rarely coincide anymore with the firm's own interests. While the managers of such a corporation clearly owe a fiduciary responsibility to its stockholders, this moral and legal obligation toward the owners of the resources organized in a firm hardly exhausts the responsibilities of management. It has become useful to think of a broader category of stakeholders, including especially the firm's employees to whom and for whom managers are accountable. The manager's vocation with respect to the divine governance will not be understood, apart from an appreciation of the constraints imposed by the diverse and often conflicting interests of the corporation's stockholders and other stakeholders.

The Business Corporation and Catholic Social Teaching

The theological perspective that I have proposed may strike some as a personal idiosyncrasy, a manifestly Calvinistic vision whose peculiar emphases find hardly an echo among the major themes of Catholic social teaching. Indeed, it is true that one searches the tradition in vain for any reflection on modern business corporations remotely resembling its attention to the nature and functions of the state. Furthermore, Catholic social teaching has been extremely reluctant to affirm the providential character of any human institution apart from the church itself, although it does testify to God's historical activity in general terms. Vatican II's *Gaudium et Spes*, of course, issued what amounted to a *Magna Charta* for substantively theological reflection on the social order when it affirmed the church's "duty of scrutinizing the signs of the times and of interpreting them in light of the gospel" (1966, pp. 200–201). Nevertheless, even the pastoral constitution conceptualized this new agenda as a series of highly abstract reflections on "the situation of men in the modern world" (*ibid.*). *Gaudium et Spes* does include a promisingly constructive statement on the "socioeconomic" dimension of this situation, but it does so without benefit of any explicit theory of modern economic institutions.

Despite the tradition's failure to articulate a theology of the modern business corporation, Catholic social teaching may provide exceptional resources for developing one, along the lines previously indicated. The single, most important of these is the principle of subsidiarity, first rendered visible in Pius XI's *Quadragesimo Anno* (1931). Within the framework provided by the vision of the social order implicit in that principle, the themes characteristic of the U.S. bishops' pastoral letter, *Economic Justice for All* (1986), notably, its reflections on the meaning of "solidarity" and "participation," can and ought to be developed with respect to the corporation. The pastoral letter's own exhortations directed at "Owners and Managers" toward the end of Chapter Two (1986, pp. 55–59), as well as the direction of its hope for "completing the unfinished business of the American experiment" in democracy, outlined in Chapter Four (*ibid.*, pp. 145–162), will serve as benchmarks for assessing progress in the development of a theology of the corporation. These resources suggest that considering business corporations as "aspects of the Divine governance of the world" simply cannot be dismissed as a Calvinist conundrum, but may represent the path of constructive development helping to define the future of Catholic social teaching.

Quadragesimo Anno introduced the principle of subsidiarity by way of refining further the vision of the social order implicit in *Rerum Novarum* (1891). Pope Pius XI's concern, of course, was to draw a line on the pattern of corporatist institutional development that had been advocated under the banner of Italian fascism. Subsidiarity, therefore, was meant to define the limits appropriate to state intervention in the social order:

> Nevertheless, it is a fundamental principle of social philosophy, fixed and unchangeable, that one should not withdraw from individuals and commit to the community what they can accomplish by their own enterprise and industry. So, too, it is an injustice and at the same time a grave evil and a disturbance of right order, to transfer to the larger and higher collectivity functions which can be performed and provided for by lesser and subordinate bodies. Inasmuch as every social activity should, by its very nature, prove a help to members of the social body, it should never destroy or absorb them. (1963, p. 147)

The most illuminating commentary on the operative meaning of the principle of subsidiarity remains the bishops' recent pastoral letter, *Economic Justice for All*. Despite the fact that some of the pastoral letters' critics, including Michael Novak, have invoked the principle to resist or narrow the bishops' interpretation of Pope John XXIII's doctrine of economic rights, a more discerning view of the principle's use is evident in the way it serves to frame the challenge of implementing the set of "moral priorities for the nation" centered on the so-called "preferential option for the poor." The principle is quoted in full, an unusual degree of emphasis, as the bishops invite the collaboration of persons situated in different institutional settings with respect to the economy.

As the pastoral letter reminds us, "This principle guarantees institutional pluralism. It provides space for freedom, initiative, and creativity on the part of many social agents. At the same time, it insists that *all* these agents should work in ways that help build up the social body" (1986, p. 51). Consistent with this conventional view, when the bishops turn specifically to the role of "citizens and government," once again the principle is used to circumscribe the limits of public policy intervention with respect to the moral priorities they have outlined: "Government should undertake only those initiatives which exceed the capacities of individuals or private groups acting independently" (1986, p. 62). Lest Americans miss the nuances implicit here, they go òn:

> This does not mean, however, that the government that governs least governs best. Rather it defines good government intervention as that which truly "helps" other social groups contribute to the common good by directing, urging, restraining, and regulating economic activity as "the occasion requires and necessity demands." (*Ibid.*)

Here the bishops are commenting directly on the passage from *Quadragesimo Anno*.

A less conventional, though highly promising constructive application of the principle of subsidiarity emerges in the pastoral letter's groundbreaking chapter on "A New American Experiment: Partnership for the Public Good." The principle is invoked twice, once each regarding the nature of the "partnerships" that can be developed at both the national and the international level (1986, pp. 155,160). The focus here shifts from limiting government intervention to identifying and nurturing the range of private, professional, and quasi-governmental associations capable of entering into non-adversarial patterns of collaboration with government. The role envisioned for these "mediating structures" (*ibid.*, p. 153), with reference to both economic development and the institutionalization of moral responsibility, is truly breathtaking.

Indeed, the "New American Experiment" is illustrated first with reference to the new forms of partnership that are transforming the corporate governance of individual business firms and certain industries. The experiments at issue range from innovative styles of corporate management, to employee stock-ownership plans, all of which are intended to foster a greater sense of accountability through increased participation throughout the enterprise. Indeed, the bishops endorse these experiments not just for their moral promise, which is considerable, but also for their potential to "enhance productivity, increase the profitability of firms, provide greater job security and work satisfaction for employees, and reduce adversarial relations" (1986, pp. 148–149). They recognize also, however, that such efforts may be at risk because of the inordinate pressures of investors too obsessed with immediate returns to allow the innovations adequate time for a fair trial. While they acknowledge the principle of fiduciary responsibility, they call also for a reexamination of the problem of corporate governance "within the bounds of justice to employees, customers, suppliers and the local community" (*ibid.*, p. 152). These issues, of course, lie at the heart of an adequate theology of the corporation.

The extension of the principle of subsidiarity, outlined in these admittedly fragmentary descriptions of the "New American Experiment," might seem like a straw in the wind, were it not for a simultaneous, though unrelated, development at the Extraordinary Synod of Bishops held in Rome in October 1985. The Synod's final document, "The church, in the Word of God, Celebrates the Mysteries of Christ for the Salvation of the World," observed that the principle might help clarify certain points of ecclesiology, especially in regard to Vatican II's notion of "collegiality." Again, the Synod did not articulate the theological presuppositions animating the principle of subsidiarity, but it did confirm that the principle's range of application was not to be limited to a narrow focus on the role of the state in society. Here, too, the point is that the principle may be a remarkably concise way of symbolizing Catholic tradition's tacit ideal of the social order, any social order, to be discerned in any institutional setting and used to evaluate their ultimate organizational effectiveness.

Can this tacit understanding be made explicit? Elsewhere, I have argued that the principle of subsidiarity may be regarded as a practical corollary of the church's faith in the Holy Trinity (1987, pp. 129–138). The Trinity, of course, symbolizes the nature of the community of Divine Persons revealed in Jesus Christ's unique status as the Son of God, the Word Incarnate, and the mission of the Holy Spirit accomplished through his faithful interaction with the will of his Father. Traditional Trinitarian theology, as represented, for example, in the Athanasian Creed, confesses not only the perfect equality and/or reciprocity characteristic of the relations internal to this community, but also the radical subordination of all things external to it. The Divine Life unfolding within the Trinitarian community, formally considered, thus exhibits both egalitarian and hierarchical tendencies, which are distinguishable and justifiable as functional necessities. In short, the Divine Life is one of identity, except for the distinguishable roles that each Person plays in the Mystery of Salvation. The overcoming of sin through grace, accomplished in diverse ways through our interaction with each of these Persons, empowers us for participation in this Mystery. We become sharers in the Divine Life, through participation in the sacraments that communicate the Mystery to us, but not as equal partners. Faith remains the acknowledgement of our absolute dependence or radical subordination to the Divine Life.

Though my evidence for such an assertion can only remain speculative, I contend that the pattern of Divine Life communicated in our graceful relationship to the Trinity is not simply encoded in our souls, as many of the ancient Fathers recognized, notably, St. Augustine of Hippo. The analogies by which we approach an understanding of the Divine Life are inscribed not only in the exercise of human intelligence but also in the organization of human institutions. Institutions, despite their diversity, not only aspire to community, but also achieve whatever degree of social order they afford through the interweaving of egalitarian and hierarchical imperatives. If it is theologically legitimate to discern one vestige of the Trinity in the functioning of the human mind, it seems no less legitimate to discern another in the functioning of human institutions. Besides, such an analogy must hold if institutions are to be regarded theologically as "aspects of Divine governance in the world." If the governance affirmed is already God's own work before it is consciously accepted as our own, the Divine Life must somehow already be encoded in the institutions where we test and fulfill our vocations.

Such a theological affirmation of the meaning of human institutions by no means canonizes them, as if thereby they become sinless and unassailable. Just as the vestiges of the Trinity are as likely as not to be obscured by the routinely ambiguous outcomes of human knowing and willing, so not all forms of organizational development necessarily manifest the pattern of Divine Life. The point of the principle of subsidiarity, however, is to provide us with critical leverage against such obscurities. Properly functioning institutions, to the extent that they adhere to the principle, will render the organizational vestiges of the Trinity less obscure than otherwise they might have been. Like all things, like all of us, they remain radically subordinate to the Trinity, no matter how successful they become in reflecting the pattern of organizational development implicit in the community of Divine Life.

It is worth recalling in this context that both the Trinitarian community of Persons and the principle of subsidiarity exhibit something like a preferential option for egalitarian democracy. Perfect reciprocity is the objective norm, the ideal to which we aspire; and forms of subordination, that is, the routine interventions of a heirarchy of "higher" organizations, are justified only to the extent that they actually empower the "lower" forms, individual persons as well as communities, to achieve their own distinctive purposes. The full unfolding of the Divine Life in history, after all, was occasioned by the Original Sin of our first parents. And as the liturgy of the Easter Vigil reminds us, without that "happy fault" (*O felix culpa. . .*), it is hard to see how we would have apprehended the Divine Life in its fullness. The Trinitarian community of Persons had to intervene to save us from ourselves, just as "higher" institutions are called into being by the dysfunctions encountered by individuals and "lower" forms of community in the vicissitudes of our disordered history. What is at stake here can be only suggested at this point: (1) As the previous remarks indicate, Catholic social teaching already contains a template for developing a theology of the modern business corporation, namely, the principle of subsidiarity; (2) the critical potential latent in this principle will be realized only when its unstated theological premise is articulated; (3) that premise is rooted in the Mystery of the Trinity which is ultimately the only object of genuinely theological reflection.

Even in Catholic social teaching a theology of the corporation must, first of all, be about God or it is about nothing at all. If the principle of subsidiarity provides us with an authentic template for the social order, it does so because its truth is first about God before it is about the proper scale and scope of human institutions. Granted, in invoking the principle, neither *Quadragesimo Anno* nor the bishops' pastoral letter makes this point; nevertheless, it can be inferred from a consideration of at least the pastoral letter's discussion of "solidarity" and "participation." The bishops' discussion of solidarity is explicitly Trinitarian:

> Only active love of God and neighbor makes the fullness of community happen. Christians look forward in hope to a true communion among all persons with each other and with God. The Spirit of Christ labors in history to build up the bonds of solidarity among all persons until that day on which their union is brought to perfection in the Kingdom of God. Indeed Christian theological reflection on the very reality of God as a trinitarian unity of persons—Father, Son, and Holy Spirit—shows that being a person means being united to other persons in love. (1986, pp. 33–34)

Solidarity, in short, is an achievement not to be taken for granted. It is the fullness of community to be realized ultimately in the Kingdom of God. The principle of subsidiarity is a signpost along the path toward that fullness. It helps us to distinguish which organizational development strategies are likely to advance the cause of solidarity.

Equally suggestive, though less theologically articulate, are the pastoral letters' remarks on social "participation." If solidarity is the end-state or envisioned outcome of human socialization, participation signifies the process involved in getting there. It is the object of social justice which, in the bishops' view, specifies the end of justice as a whole, encompassing within the economic sphere both "commutative" and "distributive" justice: "*Social justice implies that persons have an obligation to be active and productive participants in the life of society and that society has a duty to enable them to participate in this way*" (1986, p. 36). Clearly, achieving social justice requires an assessment of institutions with respect to their success in empowering persons for participation. Once again, the principle of subsidiarity, and the Trinitarian template of the social order latent in it, seem reflected specifically in the bishops' concern for social justice and participation.

The polar opposite of social participation, "marginalization," cited in the pastoral letter, helps clarify the meaning that "structures of sin" might have in Catholic social teaching. Marginalization is the general category defining all those conditions, especially those caused by various forms of "discrimination in job opportunities or income levels on the basis of race, sex, or other arbitrary standards" (1986, p. 37) that exclude people and communities from full participation in society. Past institutional arrangements that have contributed to the marginalization of people and communities are truly "structures of sin," not just in the sense that they perpetuate evil, but also insofar as they impede or make a mockery of that solidarity which will, in the perfection of the Kingdom of God, help manifest the Mystery of the Divine Life. The principle of subsidiarity may be useful both for identifying various forms of marginalization, to the extent that these are a result of disorders in the routine exercise of institutional power, and for transforming these same institutions in the direction of the ideal of solidarity.

When we turn from this particular cluster of ideas, the principle of subsidiarity and the twin themes of solidarity and participation, to the bishops' specific exhortation to the "Owners and Managers" of businesses (1986, pp. 55–62), we discover an attempt to initiate a new collaboration between the bishops and the men and women engaged in business. The hopeful and constructive approach, given the suspicions against business that Catholic social teaching often harbored in the past, seems difficult to explain apart from a recognition of the theological significance of the modern business corporation. For the bishops' appeal is not simply born of expediency. It is not just that they recognize, along with John Paul II, the corporation's indispensable role in "organizing human labor and the means of production so as to give rise to the goods and services necessary for the prosperity and progress of the community" (*ibid.*, p. 56). The bishops go beyond this to affirm not only that business people have a "vital Christian vocation" (*ibid.*, p. 59) but also that the corporation and other business institutions have "the duty to be faithful trustees of the resources at their disposal" (*ibid.*, p. 56).

These terms, vocation and trusteeship or stewardship, derive their meaning ultimately from Catholic social teaching's affirmation of the biblical vision of the meaning and use of worldly goods. This vision provides the context in which the pastoral letter discusses the traditional right of private property, and proposes—somewhat offhandedly—a new economic right that seems distinctive of corporations:

> Businesses have a right to an institutional framework that does not penalize enterprises that act responsibly. Governments must provide regulations and a system of taxation which encourages firms to preserve the environment, employ disadvantaged workers, and create jobs in depressed areas. Managers and stockholders should not be torn between their responsibilities to their organizations and their responsibilities toward society as a whole. (1986, p. 59)

If this means what it says, the passage is truly extraordinary for several reasons. First, it may cast light on what is and is not meant by an economic right. Second, it suggests that the bishops already have come to appreciate the spirit of democratic capitalism, and can invoke the principle of subsidiarity for the corporation's own benefit, as well as in the interests of its diverse stakeholders. Finally, it implies a theology of the corporation that would, among other things, clarify its status as the subject of such a right. In puzzling out the basis for such a theology within the tradition of Catholic social teaching, I am highlighting here the only premise that will make such a theology genuinely theological. Ascribing such a right to business corporations makes sense only if corporations are, in fact, "aspects of Divine governance in the world."

A Second Chance for Catholic Social Teaching

Space and time do not permit me here to address the range of issues raised by Reich's *The Work of Nations: Preparing Ourselves for 21st*

Century Capitalism. His work suggests, however, that a concern to advance a theology of the corporation beyond the preliminary sketches outlined by Novak is motivated by more than just a desire to round off things. If Reich's analysis is at all on target, there is a terrible urgency to this proposal, for his is an argument about a transformation of the political economy that cannot be addressed at the abstract, systemic level at which both Novak and the bulk of the tradition of Catholic social teaching usually have operated. The need for critical reflection at the intermediate or institutional level is required here, precisely because it is an understanding of the new patterns of organization currently transforming business corporations that are creating a new order—or new level of disorder, if you will—in our political economy.

There is good news and bad news for Catholic social teaching in Reich's analysis. The bad news is that the range of experiments, represented by innovative styles of corporate management, are contributing to a situation in which the limited solidarity taken for granted in the conventional view of a national economy is eroding quickly. Even to continue analyzing the current U.S. situation in terms of a "national economy" is to fall victim to conceptual obsolescence. This suggests the conventional assumption that the cause of social justice can be advanced by mobilizing U.S. Catholics for more effective participation in the formation of national economic policy may also be obsolete. Federal intervention may not be the way to overcome the evils generated by the U.S. economy, primarily because the fundamentals of the economy in this country are increasingly beyond the scope of government regulation.

The good news, however, is that the internationalist vision that has always informed Catholic social teaching as a tradition and that has always circumscribed the limits to excessively nationalistic conceptions of the public agenda of U.S. Catholics may now come into its own as uniquely relevant for creating a system of international accountability for the capitalism of the twenty-first century. Reich's analysis describes a world in which the tradition's vestigially premodern ideal of international order now appears supremely relevant, if not uniquely indispensable, to a postmodern global economy in which corporations at the cutting edge of the system are beyond the control of any existing regulatory frameworks. The postmodern corporation is an emerging international institution. The forms of partnership accountability envisioned in the U.S. bishops' pastoral letter will have to be revised accordingly.

The second chance for Catholic social teaching is not just a chance to get beyond the ideological polarizations of the Roaring Eighties. If Reich's analysis is on target, we will need a theological understanding of the corporation that is as appreciative of its internal dynamisms as it has been critical of its external outcomes. For what is at stake in the transformation of traditional corporations into the global enterprise networks described by Reich is undeniably the result of a breakthrough in the organization of human intelligence and creativity, although one that also has generated more than its share of the dislocations that raise the cry for social justice. An adequate theology of the corporation, it is hoped, will help Catholic social teaching make the most of this second chance. It may do so by showing how it is possible to pursue the twenty-first century's agenda for social justice in the global economy firmly and fearlessly, without falling into the trap of pointlessly adversarial politics.

Twenty

Trade Unions, Catholic Teaching and the New World Order

George G. Higgins

What follows is a sampling of my personal recollections about the reception and implementation in the United States of *Rerum Novarum* and the follow-up encyclicals of Pope Leo XIII's successors. I will address this subject as a skim-the-surface, social-action bureaucrat who has spent most of his life far removed from the academy but who has benefited from and is grateful for the in-depth research in which so many of you have long been engaged as full-time professionals in social ethics and the social sciences.

Looking back fifty years, half-way back to *Rerum Novarum*, I am struck first of all by the fact that we tend now to approach the social encyclicals and other relevant church documents with a greater sense of historical consciousness and we are less inclined to understand them talmudically than was formerly the case. My former colleague, Father John F. Cronin, who in years gone by was the preeminent popularizer of Catholic social teaching in the United States, touched upon this point twenty years ago in his own published recollections about the reception of the encyclical *Quadragesimo Anno* and related documents:

> It never occurred to us that these documents were both historically and culturally conditioned. We realized that [*Quadragesimo Anno*] was clearly addressed to the major industrial areas of the world. But it did not occur to us how much of the "mind set" was Italian and Germanic. Most of us never heard of form criticism. Probably we would not have dared to use it on documents of the magisterium even if we had known what it meant.

A casual survey of scholarly commentaries on *Rerum Novarum* in several different languages clearly validates Cronin's argument. My own reading or rereading in recent months of a representative sampling of these commentaries and historical studies clearly demonstrates that it is impossible to understand Leo's encyclical or any of the more recent encyclicals without examining the historical context within which, and often in response to which, the documents were written. Failure to examine these papal documents in their historical setting has led some to exaggerate their strengths and others to exaggerate their weaknesses. It has also led even scholars of some repute to find a greater degree of unbroken continuity between the successive encyclicals than the facts would seem to warrant.

Curiously, one of the better commentaries on the historical development of Catholic social teaching from Leo XIII until recent times was written two decades ago by a non-Catholic historian, Richard L. Camp.[1] Professor Camp, a sympathetic critic of the encyclicals, starting with *Rerum Novarum*, finds a distinct evolution in papal social teaching which, in his view, cannot be explained simply as an effort of Leo XIII's successors to bring him up-to-date. In short, Camp thinks it is naive to exaggerate the strengths of *Rerum Novarum* and equally naive to find too much continuity in Catholic social teaching. On the other hand, his refined sense of historical consciousness prompts him, even when he is pointing to weaknesses in *Rerum Novarum*, to give due credit to Leo XIII for its strengths. Specifically, for example, he argues at one point (as many of today's neo-conservative critics of Catholic social teaching also are wont to do) that Leo XIII and some of his successors placed too much emphasis on the distribution of wealth and not enough on the need for greater productivity. But even here his criticism of *Rerum Novarum* is tempered by his understanding of the historical context in which Leo was writing. No one can deny, he says, that the distribution of wealth was in fact a serious problem in Leo's time and no knowledgeable person would argue today that the workers' place in society in 1891 or their share of the national wealth was satisfactory even in England or in the United States and other advanced industrial nations. He concludes:

> *Rerum Novarum* met these issues directly and proposed a balanced, pragmatic blueprint for the regeneration of the proletariat within existing economic institutions which could enable the laborer to take his place as a respected and dignified member of society. . . . He saw the need for the church to speak for the workingman, and he inspired Catholics to make the laborer's cause their own. Had he done nothing else his place in history as a great pope would still have been secure.

By and large, other critics of *Rerum Novarum* and more recent papal encyclicals are loath to say loud and clear that even today, as in 1891, the distribution of wealth remains a serious problem.

Examining *Rerum Novarum* in its historical context also serves to remind us that the encyclical was received differently in different nations because of their varied histories and traditions. To cite but one example, Catholics in Europe in 1891 were divided over the issue of "Catholic" or "Christian" versus "neutral" trade unionism. This debate, which carried over on the continent well into the twentieth century, never caught fire in the United States, thanks to the leadership of Cardinal James Gibbons of Baltimore and several of his fellow bishops in warding off a threatened papal condemnation of the Knights of Labor, the leading labor federation in the United States during the latter part of the nineteenth century. From the time of Gibbons to the present day, Catholic workers in the United States have been free to belong to "neutral" unions, and no attempt has been made to establish sectarian "Catholic" or "Christian" unions.

As Father John Pawlikowski, professor of social ethics at the Catholic Theological Union in Chicago, has pointed out in his own commentary on *Rerum Novarum*, the most direct and lasting effect of the encyclical was the impetus it gave to unionization. He points out:

> Although a few American bishops like Cardinal Gibbons and Archbishop Ireland had already given their blessing to unionization and Catholics were already active in union leadership, the encyclical opened the doors to a much more massive and intensive collaboration between American Catholicism and the labor movement.

This one example can serve to substantiate Jesuit Father John Coleman's argument, in a brilliant essay on the development of Catholic social teaching, that despite all the theoretical arguments pro and con about the historical strengths and limitations of *Rerum Novarum* and more recent encyclicals, it is important to note that the encyclicals

> tended to be read, absorbed and commented on mainly by socially involved Catholics who generally gave them a more progressive interpretation than their location in historical context might have warranted. The encyclicals, then, represent in some sense a genuine unified tradition of sane and humane social thought which we both celebrate today and try to bring forward into the future.

Coleman himself is critical of the encyclicals on several scores but, in the end, he concludes that:

> Ultimately the future of this tradition will depend less on our ability to parrot its significant terms . . . and more on our ability to read the

signs of the times in fidelity to the Gospel of human dignity as Leo
and his successors tried to do in their times. History will surely unveil
all too well our shortcomings. May it also—as it does for this legacy
of the popes—show our prophetic vision and courageous action.

It would be difficult to think of a better way of stating the lesson to be
learned by today's Catholics as we go about celebrating the one hundredth anniversary of *Rerum Novarum*.

My second observation has to do with the changing relationship,
since and mainly because of Vatican II, between the Holy See and the
local churches in the area of Catholic social teaching and Catholic social
action. Let me illustrate this point, in an oversimplified manner, by recalling that between 1944 when I first joined the staff of the Social Action
Department of the old National Catholic Welfare Conference and the end
of Vatican II in 1965, there was literally no contact of any kind between
our department at the conference and the Holy See. I do not recall that we
exchanged at any time even so much as a letter, a cablegram, or a telephone call. That is no longer the case, of course. At the present time the
local church in the United States is routinely in contact with the Holy See
and its several congregations. The participation of Cardinal Casaroli at this
Notre Dame conference and the participation of Cardinal Etchegaray,
president of the Pontifical Council on Justice and Peace, at the recent
National Conference of Catholic Bishops/U.S. Catholic Conference
(NCCB/USCC) observance of the Centenary of *Rerum Novarum* can serve
to symbolize this new and potentially very promising relationship
between the local church and the Holy See—this new expression of collegiality in the extended sense of that word.

This changing relationship, which reflects in its own way a new and
better post-Vatican II understanding of ecclesiology, involves more than
simply a new style and new forms of communication at the bureaucratic
level between the local churches and the Holy See. It runs deeper than
that. It involves the local churches, to some extent at least, in the very
process of developing Catholic social teaching. You will recall that Pope
Paul VI, in his Apostolic Letter of 1971, *Octogesima Adveniens*, broke radically new ground in this regard. *Octogesima Adveniens* is written in the
form of a familiar dialogue not only with Catholics and Christians in general, but with all those of goodwill, and carefully avoids the more pontifical style of teaching which so often characterized similar documents in the
not too distant past.

On some matters, of course, Paul VI states his own convictions very
firmly, but never in such a way as to force his opinions on the reader
or to short circuit or foreclose the dialogue. On matters that are purely

contingent, those open to varying viewpoints which lend themselves to a variety of solutions, he carefully refrains from trying to say—or even leaving the impression that he is trying to say—the last and final word. Indeed, he goes out of his way to emphasize that it is neither his ambition nor his mission "to utter a unified message and to put forward a solution which has universal validity." His purpose is the more modest one of "confiding" his own thoughts and preoccupations about some, but by no means all of today's more pressing social problems and of encouraging individual Catholics and groups of Catholics, in dialogue with other Christians and all people of goodwill, "to analyze with objectivity the situation which is proper to their own country" and "to discern the options and commitments which are called for in order to bring about the social, political and economic changes seen in many cases to be needed."

One is reminded here of John XXIII's distinctively pastoral style of teaching by Pope Paul's repeated emphasis, in several different contexts, on the legitimate variety or plurality of possible options which are open to people of goodwill and by his related emphasis on the obligation of individual Catholics to form their own opinions on these matters in light of the Gospel message without waiting for directives from their ecclesiastical leaders.

It goes without saying, of course, that the full implications of *Octogesima Adveniens* have yet to be worked out in practice. By way of example, does it follow logically from *Octogesima Adveniens* that there ought to be a more systematic input from the local churches in the drafting of social encyclicals and other universal church documents on Catholic social teaching? This is a question to which, even with the best of goodwill and under optimum conditions, there is no easy answer, given the diversity and complexity of problems confronting a church that today is truly universal in its geographical sweep and spread. In any event, it is an intriguing question and one which, I suspect, will continue to crop up from time to time. It is an old question, of course. Even before Vatican II it was raised by, among others, the late Father Georges Jarlot, S.J., who taught Catholic social teaching at the Gregorian University in Rome for many years. Father Jarlot, a native of France, hardly can be accused of prejudice when he said that the church's social teaching, prior to the Council, was inevitably European and even, like John XXIII's two encyclicals, Italian. His specific reference to John XXIII's two encyclicals, *Mater et Magistra* and *Pacem in Terris*, is somewhat surprising because, of all the social encyclicals since *Rerum Novarum*, these two seem the least European and the most universal in style as well as in content. Be that as it may, Father Jarlot's overall characterization of the church's social teaching "prior to the Council" is valid.

A German scholar, Phillippe Herder-Dorneigh, went one better than Father Jarlet, again before Vatican II, when he said that in addition to being too European in content and too "curial" in style, the social encyclicals have been too theoretical or abstract in their approach to social problems without reflecting the full range of viewpoints within the universal church sufficiently. He went on to say that the classical period of Catholic doctrine abruptly ended with the death of Pius XII; the braintrust upon which he had depended and in which German Jesuits had played an important role was relegated to the background. New specialists took their place and helped formulate *Mater et Magistra*. This, he noted, marked a step forward, and at the hands of these "new specialists" Catholic social doctrine ceased to be all-encompassing and began to break down into individual pronouncements on concrete situations. He was wrong about that, of course, but the question he was addressing is still with us.

My third observation—again at the bureaucratic level—has to do with the increasing willingness of the Holy See to encourage the local churches to play a more active international role in support of social justice and human rights. Again, let me cite my own experience at the old National Catholic Welfare Conference (NCWC) to illustrate the point. It is my clear recollection that during my first twenty years on the staff of the old NCWC—i.e., between 1944 and 1965—Rome expected the conference to work exclusively within the continental borders of the United States. I am exaggerating, of course, but while a certain amount of significant international work was done by the conference in those days—mainly through the initiative of the late Father Raymond McGowan, one of the unsung heroes of the Catholic social action movement in the United States—this work was, in a sense, bootleg activity and was the tolerated exception to the general rule that the local churches were expected to leave it to Rome to take the initiative in the field of international relations. That is no longer true. Our own NCCB/USCC is involved deeply now in international affairs, with the encouragement and blessing of the Holy See.

I am speaking here, of course, mainly about changes at the bureaucratic level. At the substantive level needless to add, the universal church and the local churches are also more extensively and intensively involved in the field of international social justice than previously. The content of Catholic social teaching before John XXIII was concerned mostly with the socioeconomic problems of individual nation states. Not so today. I will say no more about this, except to add that, sociologically speaking and quite apart from any theological considerations, the role of the Petrine office has taken on, in some respects, more importance than ever before in modern history. At times this may go down hard with Americans, for, even in our better moments (witness the unashamedly super-patriotic rhetoric of a typical State of the Union Message) we are probably more provincial and less cosmopolitan than normally we are willing to admit. For example, in recent years, in the specific field of Catholic social teaching it has become fashionable in some American circles to complain (a bit too peevishly for my taste) that the Holy See has been slow to recognize and to learn from the American political and economic experience. There is a certain merit to this complaint, but to overdo it would be to run the risk of being perceived by intelligent observers in other countries, rich and poor alike, as innocents abroad in a very complex world society. I think we would be well advised to take to heart the cautionary words which the very cosmopolitan and extremely intelligent Cardinal Etchegaray addressed, ever so courteously, to the several hundred delegates attending the recent NCCB/USCC observance of the Centenary of *Rerum Novarum.* "The entire world," the Cardinal said, "cannot be reduced to the United States."

Let me wrap up these random recollections with some remarks about a few of what I consider to be unresolved problems in our implementations of Catholic social teaching.

In my opinion, we have yet to understand in all of its pertinent implications the principle of subsidiarity and the corelative principle of socialization, both of which, taken in tandem, are of central importance in the corpus of modern Catholic social teaching.

First a word about the principle of subsidiarity with its emphasis on the central importance of non-governmental mediating structures in our economy. In my judgment, while rightly giving due prominence to the role of such mediating structures and organizations, we have tended to do so negatively by stressing very one-sidedly their obvious importance as bulwarks against statism and have yet to agree upon a positive and structured role for these organizations in the operation and planning of the economy. I think we have to come to terms, for example, with John Paul II's treatment of this subject in his encyclical *Laborem Exercens.* This document speaks of "a wide range of intermediate bodies," with economic purposes, enjoying "real autonomy" with regard to the public powers and pursuing their aims "in honest collaboration with each other and in subordination to the demands of the common good." It is my impression that many of those in the United States who rightly stress the importance of these intermediate bodies tend to see them as being parallel to the corporate structures in the domestic and world economies and do not really envisage them as being institutionally involved, as autonomous bodies with economic purposes, in the economic decision-making process of either individual nations or of the world community of nations.

358 Shaping a Just Community

I am inclined to think that this limited anti-statist understanding of the role of intermediate structures and organizations accounts, to some extent, for the massive and menacing lack of concern in conservative circles about the growing weakness of American unions, to cite but one of the more important of all of the so-called intermediate structures in our society. I regret to say it, but the silence of the conservative community in the United States on this issue has been thunderous in recent years.

Robert A. Nisbet is one of the few conservative social and political philosophers who strongly laments the decline of organized labor in the United States, but even he tends to think of unions one-sidedly as powerful forces in support of capitalism and as bulwarks against political invasion of economic freedom. In his book, *The Quest for Community*, published in 1958 and recently made available again in a new edition, Nisbet writes:

> The labor union and cooperative are foremost among new forms of association that have served to keep alive the symbols of economic freedom as such. It should be remarked, they have been the first objects of economic destruction in totalitarian countries. . . . The individual entrepreneur, it may be observed, is less dangerous to the totalitarian than the labor union or cooperative. For in such an association, the individual can find a sense of relatedness to the entire culture and thus become its eager partisan.

Nisbet goes on to say:

> The mythology of individualism continues to reign in discussions of economic freedom. By too many partisans of management the labor union is regarded as a major obstacle to economic autonomy and as partial paralysis of capitalism. But to weaken, whether from political or individualistic motives, the social structures of family, local community, labor union, or industrial community, is to convert a culture into an atomized mass. Such a mass will have neither the will nor the incentive, nor the ability to combat tendencies toward political collectivism.

These are welcome words, coming at a time when some of the most influential employer organizations in the United States are calling insistently for a union-free environment and gleefully—as in the case of the United States Chamber of Commerce—predicting the demise of the American labor movement. Now that the Iron Curtain has come down, it is time for scholars of Nisbet's stature in the conservative community to stress not only the negative role of unions as indispensable bulwarks against statism but also their positive role in the proper ordering of economic life in the United States.

I suspect that we have tended to shy away from this problem for fear of being accused of hankering unrealistically and ahistorically for some outmoded form of European corporativism—a subject which, because it was widely confused with Italian, Spanish and Portuguese forms of fascism or semi-fascism, led many critics to repudiate *Quadragesimo Anno's* formula for the reconstruction of the social order. Admittedly, that is an understandable and salutary fear but it should not intimidate us from thinking through in very practical and pragmatic American terms the implications of John Paul II's emphasis on the economic role of free and autonomous unions in the proper ordering of economic life.

It might be useful in this regard to revisit John XXIII's encyclical, *Mater et Magistra.* Pope John carefully avoided giving his approval to any particular method of organizing or reorganizing economic life. Moreover, even his terminology was somewhat different from that of Pius XI in his encyclical *Quadragesimo Anno* and, in his later encyclical on communism, *Divini Redemptoris,* Pius XI used the terminology of "corporativism" which, in English, has been freely translated into the Industry Council Plan. John XXIII, on the other hand, was preoccupied mostly with the practical aspects of the problem and avoided using this kind of terminology. He was a pastor and not a jurist. He knew all about the discussions raised by the formulas of Pius XI and Pius XII and the misunderstandings these discussions had caused. So he kept from any formulizing and even went so far as to avoid using their words "corporation" and "corporative organization."

It would appear to be partially correct, then, to say that John XXIII was less interested than was Pius XI in the so-called Industry Council Plan. Pope John's approach to the problem of social reconstruction and his terminology was less theoretical and more flexible than that of Pius XI. But it would be a mistake to conclude that Pope John was any less interested than was Pius XI in the basic principles of social reconstruction underlying the Industry Council Plan. These principles can be summarized as follows:

> Economic order will not come naturally, only by free competition, free enterprise and free initiative, although a maximum degree of freedom must always be safeguarded. Intermediate bodies are natural and necessary if we want to avoid State totalitarianism, but not for that reason alone. Institutional cooperation at all levels must be organized between the agents of the economy. Intermediate bodies

must cooperate among themselves and with the government in order to help it play its positive role in the economy for the common good, national and international.

Pope John did not tell us in detail how the principles were to be put into practice. His approach, I repeat, was very flexible. He opened the doors to all kinds of institutional cooperation among those involved at the different levels of production, strongly insisting that any organization of the economy must take into account the national and international common good. The state has a positive role to play and this role must be carried out with respect for legitimate autonomies and with the participation of all involved groups. In substance, this is what proponents of the Industry Council Plan have been saying all along. At times, perhaps, their approach and their terminology have been rather inflexible. If so, *Mater et Magistra* can serve as a timely corrective. One way of moving in the direction of the Industry Council Plan would be to develop a pragmatic system of an American style of co-management or co-determination and new forms of profit sharing and co-ownership.

In my judgment, however, it would be fatuous to talk theoretically about developing new experiments of this kind unless and until there is a reasonably broad consensus in the United States that free and autonomous unions are, in the language of *Laborem Exercens*, "indispensable," especially in highly industrialized economies such as our own. As I have already indicated, however, no such consensus exists at the present time. Quite the contrary. Because I feel very strongly on this subject, on the basis of my own experience during the past fifty years, I will say no more about it for fear of appearing to ride my hobby horse into the ditch. Suffice it to say that, in my judgment, the current decline in union membership in the United States, and the apparent and very paradoxical lack of concern about this phenomenon on the part of so many who theoretically attach so much importance to intermediate structures in our economy, are cause for deep concern. I take my lead in this regard from the writings of the late Monsignor John A. Ryan, widely regarded as the greatest single figure in the Catholic social movement in the United States. At the beginning of the Great Depression, Ryan wrote:

> Effective labor unions are still by far the most powerful force in society for the protection of the laborer's rights and the improvement of his or her condition. No amount of employer benevolence, no diffusion of a sympathetic attitude on the part of the public, no increase of beneficial legislation, can adequately supply for the lack of reorganization among the workers themselves.

These words are as true today as when they were first written more than a half century ago.

Having addressed briefly the principle of subsidiarity, let me say a word in passing about the co-relative principle of socialization—not socialism, but socialization as the term is used in *Mater et Magistra*, a term which acknowledges and even recommends a positive role for the government in promoting social justice. To neglect the implications of this principle in the corpus of Catholic social teaching accounts in part for our having gotten bogged down too often in an ideological debate in the United States about capitalism versus socialism. A prominent American banker, who happens to be a serious and forward-looking student of Catholic social teaching, has trenchantly addressed this subject, at least by indirection, in a paper delivered in June 1991 at a major conference on the Centenary of *Rerum Novarum* at the University of San Francisco.

He says that recent breath-taking developments in Eastern Europe have provided us with an opportunity to take a fresh look at capitalism. This time, he says, we can do so unencumbered by the baggage of the past. By that he means that the examination need no longer involve the issue of capitalism versus communism. Instead, the examination can sharpen its focus on ways to make market-based economies work even better in terms of meeting broad human needs, both material and spiritual. In a sense, he adds, communism had been a rather convenient thing to have around. Its existence served to simplify debate, narrow the options, and discourage rigorous examination; subtleties were frequently not allowed. Attempts at meaningful discourse were often enfeebled by a hardening of the categories. He concludes:

> In short, with one debate seemingly resolved, we can now focus our energy and our attention on eliminating the significant faults and inadequacies of capitalism that we know to exist, while at the same time preserving those special properties that embue the markets with their special genius.

I hope he is right about that, for we have been bogged down long enough in an either/or, black and white debate about capitalism versus communism. During the long Cold War between the communist East and the capitalist West, we had a plausible excuse for diverting so much of our energy to this debate, even though the debate was often oversimplified at times and reflected national and geopolitical rivalries rather than pure principle. Unfortunately, however, the debate, at least in the United States, turned into an argument, not only about the Soviet style of communism versus the Western style of capitalism, but also about democratic capitalism versus democratic socialism. It is regrettable that the debate so often took such an ideological turn. I say this because both democratic capitalism and democratic socialism carry so much partisan baggage *and* are fraught with so much ambiguity that they have become, all too often, little more than shibboleths. And while shibboleths are fun to argue about, they are less meaningful even to intellectuals, and much less useful to economic practitioners in the unsettled nineties than those who are ideologically stuck with them seem to think they are. What is needed at this stage in our history is a non-ideological objective study of the U.S. economy.

It is cause for rejoicing that this kind of non-ideological, pragmatic reexamination of the U.S. economic system is belatedly under way in the health care field, to cite but one example.

Until a few years ago, debate about health care in the United States was a fruitless exercise in simplistic ideological rhetoric. Any program, no matter how modest, aimed at giving the government a significant role in the restructuring of the health care system was labelled "socialized medicine." Year after year, it was the same old irrelevant debate about free-market capitalism versus socialism, and all the while the health care system kept going from bad to worse. At the present time, the system is so bad that it can only be described as a national crisis.

Fortunately the debate recently has taken a turn for the better. The *New York Times* reported on April 8, 1991, that a survey on health care taken among chief executives of the nation's largest corporations has found that 91 percent of them say a fundamental change or complete rebuilding of the health care system is needed. The survey also found that 73 percent of the executives said that the problem could not be solved by corporations working on their own. A majority said that some degree of government intervention would be necessary.

The *New York Times'* summary of this survey was carried in the Business Section of the paper. In my opinion, it merited front-page coverage, for its implications for the future are almost revolutionary. Common sense is beginning to displace sterile capitalism versus socialism rhetoric in the debate about the crisis in health care. Drastic increases in the cost of the health care system have convinced the majority of corporate executives that something must be done without delay. After trying and failing to get a grip on medical costs themselves, they have accepted the idea— which they once thought to be heretical—that change must be national not piecemeal or local. At a minimum, they see an important role for the government in restructuring the system, although, understandably, they do not want the government to run the entire system. Moreover, an increasing number of corporate executives are prepared now to cooperate with organized labor and other interested parties in hammering out the details of a viable national solution to a problem which is now completely out of hand. That is revolutionary and, to repeat, is cause for rejoicing.

We will not be alone in addressing this challenge because, contrary to the conventional wisdom of recent decades, we are witnessing unexpectedly a revival of interest in Catholic social teaching as, for example, in the phenomenally widespread observance here in the United States of the anniversary of *Rerum Novarum*.

I began my remarks by quoting from an article by my former colleague, Father John F. Cronin. Let me quote again from that article:

> About 1966, there developed a sudden and dramatic turning away from the traditional methods of Catholic social teaching and social action. Encyclical courses were dropped from colleges and seminaries. Even updated books based on the social magisterium ceased to sell.

Cronin goes on to say that "prediction is hazardous, but it seems that the golden era of Catholic social teaching beginning in 1891, has ended by 1971.

I feel certain that Father Cronin, who unfortunately has been an invalid for many years but is still of very sound mind, would be more than happy to concede that history has invalidated this prediction—happy, that is to say, to observe in his declining years that interest in Catholic social teaching, far from having ended in 1971, seems to be on the upswing.

Notes

1. E. G. Brills, *The Paper Ideology of Social Reform*, 1969.

Contributors

Jean-Yves Calvez, S.J., is chief editor of *Etudes* and, since 1953, professor of philosophy at the Institute of Political Studies in Paris. He is a member of the Pontifical Council of Justice and Peace (1990); was director of the Center for Research and Social Action (CERAS) 1984–85; appointed regional assistant for France and Italy (1978–83); and was elected president of the Institute of Social Studies in the Catholic Institute of Paris (1960–67). He is the author of several books, including *Développement, emploi, paix; Une éthique pour nos sociétés; La Politique et Dieu; Introduction à la vie politique; Eglise et société économique*; and *La Pensée de Karl Marx*.

John B. Caron is the retired chairman and president, for thirty-three years, of Caron International, a textile manufacturing firm. The company's domestic operations were sold in 1989, but Mr. Caron continues as a consultant. He was graduated in chemical engineering from the University of Notre Dame (1945) and is a member of its Board of Trustees. He was chairman and continues to be a board member of the *National Catholic Reporter* and Technoserve, a Third World development organization. He also served in the United States Navy. Mr. Caron's principal interests are Third World development, education, peace/security issues, and the role of religion in society.

Agostino Cardinal Casaroli was appointed Secretary of State by Pope John Paul II in 1979, as well as Prefect of the Council for Public Affairs of the Church and president of the Pontifical Commission for Vatican City State (until 1984). Also in 1979 he was created Cardinal. He entered the Pontifical Ecclesiastical Academy in Rome (1937) and gained his doctorate at the Lateran Athenaeum (1939). He was ordained a priest in 1937 and in 1940 entered the service of the Secretariat of State. He served as moral consultant of the Roman Group of the Union of Businessmen and Managers (1957–79). Until his retirement as Secretary of State in 1990, Cardinal Casaroli was very active in the international arena on the subject of human rights and was the architect of the church's strategy in Eastern Europe.

Joan Chittister, O.S.B., is the executive director of Benetvision: A Center for Research and Resources in Contemporary Spirituality, Erie, Pennsylvania, and is a fellow of the Institute of Spirituality at Saint Mary's College,

Notre Dame. She was prioress of the Benedictine Sisters of Erie (1978–90), president of the Conference of American Benedictine Prioresses (1974–90), and president of the Leadership Conference of Women Religious (LCWR) in 1976. Sister Chittister is on the executive board of the Ecumenical and Cultural Institute at St. John's University, Collegeville, Minnesota, and is a member of the board of directors of the *National Catholic Reporter.* She received her Ph.D. in communication theory from Pennsylvania State University. Her publications include *Womanstrength: Modern Church, Modern Women; Job's Daughters: Women and Power; Wisdom Distilled from the Daily: Living the Rule of St. Benedict Today;* and *Wings of Change: Women Challenge the Church.*

M. Shawn Copeland, O.P., is assistant professor of theology and black studies at Yale University Divinity School. She received her Ph.D. in systematic theology from Boston College in 1991. Honors and fellowships include: Dissertation Fellow, The Fund for Theological Education, New York (1987–88); Danforth Graduate Fellow, The Danforth Foundation, St. Louis, Missouri (1980–86); and University Fellow, Department of Theology, Boston College (1979–83). Professor Copeland was executive director of the National Black Sisters' Conference, Pittsburgh, Pennsylvania (1973–76), and has lectured at Harvard University Divinity School, Boston College, the Episcopal Divinity School in Cambridge and St. Norbert College in DePere, Wisconsin.

Richard T. De George is University Distinguished Professor of philosophy, professor of business administration, and director of the International Center for Ethics in Business at the University of Kansas. He received his Ph.B. from the University of Louvain, Belgium (1955), and his M.A. (1958) and Ph.D. in philosophy (1959) from Yale University. He was a research fellow at Yale, Columbia, and Stanford Universities and the Hoover Institution, the Charles J. Dirksen professor of business ethics at Santa Clara University (1986), and is a specialist in Russian and East European thought. Professor De George was president of several academic organizations, including the American Philosophical Association and the Society of Business Ethics. He has written widely in the field of applied ethics, is on the editorial boards of the *Business and Professional Ethics Journal* and the *Journal of Business Ethics,* and has published sixteen books, including *Competing with Integrity in International Business; Business Ethics; The New Marxism;* and *Ethics, Free Enterprise, and Public Policy.*

Amitai Etzioni is the first University Professor of George Washington University. He served as the Thomas Henry Carroll Ford Foundation professor at Harvard Business School (1987–89); as senior adviser in the White House (1979–80); was guest scholar at the Brookings Institution (1978–79); and professor of sociology at Columbia University (1958–78). He founded the international Society for the Advancement of Socio-Economics and was its first president (1989–90). In 1968 he founded the Center for Policy Research at George Washington University and has been its director since its inception. He received his M.A. from the Hebrew University (1956) and his Ph.D. from the University of California-Berkeley (1958). Professor Etzioni has consulted widely for government agencies, the National Science Foundation, the President's Commission on the Causes and Prevention of Violence, and the White House during several administrations. He is the editor of *The Responsive Community*, a communitarian quarterly, and has published fourteen books, including *The Spirit of Community: Rights, Responsibilities and the Communitarian Agenda; An Immodest Agenda; The Active Society;* and *A Comparative Analysis of Complex Organizations.*

J. Bryan Hehir is professor of the Practice in Religion and Society, Harvard Divinity School, and faculty member at the Harvard Center of International Affairs. He was the Joseph P. Kennedy professor of Christian ethics at the Kennedy Institute of Ethics, and professor of ethics and international politics at the School of Foreign Service, both at Georgetown University (1984–92). He served in various consulting capacities at the U.S. Catholic Conference for twenty years. In addition to receiving nineteen honorary degrees, he received his Th.D. from Harvard University (1977) and an M.A. from St. John's Seminary in Boston (1962). Father Hehir was a MacArthur Fellow, John D. and Catherine T. MacArthur Foundation (1984–89), received the Albert Koob Award, National Catholic Education Association (1986), and the Letelier-Moffitt Memorial Human Rights Award, Institute for Policy Studies (1983).

Peter J. Henriot, S.J., is director of the Jesuit Centre for Theological Reflection in Lusaka, Zambia. He is engaged in research and educational programs relating to social issues in Zambia and elsewhere in Africa and is involved in local pastoral work. Since 1989 he has worked in village grass-roots development programs in southern Zambia. From 1971 to 1988 he was on the staff of the Center of Concern in Washington, D.C., serving for eleven years as executive director. He received his Ph.D. in political science from the University of Chicago and did post-doctoral work at Harvard University. He received a Th.D. from the Graduate Theological Union in Berkeley. He is the author of *Opting for the Poor: Challenge for North Americans* and co-author of *Catholic Social Teaching: Our Best Kept Secret* and *Social Analysis: Linking Faith and Justice.*

Theodore M. Hesburgh, C.S.C., became president emeritus of the University of Notre Dame in 1987, after heading the institution for thirty-five years. His major retirement role is developing several Notre Dame institutes and centers he was instrumental in founding, principally the Institute for International Peace Studies and the Kellogg Institute for International Studies. He is also a founding member of the first private foundation allowed to organize in Russia, the Foundation for the Survival and Development of Humanity. Father Hesburgh began his studies in 1934 at Notre Dame and continued at the Gregorian University in Rome, Holy Cross College in Washington, D.C., and Catholic University of America, where he received his doctorate in 1945. He has held fourteen presidential appointments, the most recent being a director of the U.S. Institute of Peace, and was a charter member of the U.S. Commission on Civil Rights, created in 1957, which he chaired from 1969 to 1972. President Lyndon Johnson bestowed on him the Medal of Freedom in 1964. Father Hesburgh is the author of several monographs and four books: *The Humane Imperative: A Challenge for the Year 2000; The Hesburgh Papers: Higher Values in Higher Education;* his autobiography, *God, Country and Notre Dame;* and *Travels with Ted and Ned.*

Msgr. George G. Higgins served for more than three decades as "Mr. Social Action" at the National Catholic Welfare Conference and its successor organization, the United States Catholic Conference. He received his Ph.D. in 1944 from the Catholic University of America. Msgr. Higgins has been active in the AFL-CIO, the Leadership Conference on Civil Rights, the Bishops' Advisory Comittee for Catholic-Jewish Relations, and as advisor to the chairman of the U.S. Delegation to the Belgrade Conference on Human Rights. He is co-author of *Organized Labor: Reflections of a Labor Priest,* and writes a weekly syndicated column, "The Yardstick," and book reviews and articles in *Commonweal* and *America.*

John W. Houck is professor of management and co-director of the Notre Dame Center for Ethics and Religious Values in Business. A former Ford and Danforth Fellow, he has earned both an A.B. and a J.D. degree from the University of Notre Dame, an M.B.A. from the University of North Carolina–Chapel Hill (1959), and a LL.M. from Harvard University (1963). He has lectured and conducted workshops on the role of religious and humane values in business. In addition to articles and reviews, he has published *A Matter of Dignity: Inquiries into the Humanization of Work* and *Academic Freedom and the Catholic University.* With Oliver F. Williams, C.S.C., publications include *A Virtuous Life in Business: Stories of Courage and Integrity in the Corporate World; The Common Good and*

U.S. Capitalism; Catholic Social Teaching and the U.S. Economy: Working Papers for a Bishops' Pastoral; The Judeo-Christian Vision and the Modern Corporation; and *Full Value: Cases in Christian Business Ethics.*

Denis E. Hurley, O.M.I., serves in the honorary role as chancellor of Natal University in South Africa. He was Archbishop of Durban, South Africa, from 1951 to 1992; previously, he served as Vicar Apostolic of Natal with the rank of bishop, and as curate to several parishes in South Africa. He was president of the Southern African Catholic Bishops' Conference (1952–60, 1981–87), and founded the ecumenical agency for social concern, known as Diakonia, in Durban (1976). He has been a member of the International Commission on English in the Liturgy since its inception in 1964 and its chairman since 1975, and served as president of the South African Institute of Race Relations (1965–66). In addition to being the recipient of several honorary degrees, Archbishop Hurley received the Civic Honours of the City of Durban (1972) and was named Chevalier of the Legion of Honour (France) in 1975. He obtained his Licentiate in philosophy at the Angelicum, and Licentiate of theology at Gregorian University in Rome. Among the several books he has authored are *Catholics and Ecumenism: Prospects and Problems; South Africa, 1961;* and *Human Dignity and Race Relations.*

Richard P. McBrien is the Crowley-O'Brien-Walter professor of theology at the University of Notre Dame and former chair of the department. A priest of the Archdiocese of Hartford, he obtained his doctorate in theology from the Gregorian University in Rome. He was president of the Catholic Theological Society of America and the 1976 recipient of its John Courtney Murray Award for distinguished achievement in theology. Father McBrien has authored twelve books, including *Catholicism* (winner of the Christopher Award), *Caesar's Coin: Religion and Politics in America,* and *Report on the Church: Catholicism after Vatican II.* He has published articles and reviews in several journals, and writes a syndicated weekly theology column for the Catholic press, which several times has won awards from the Catholic Press Association.

Dennis P. McCann is professor and chair of the Department of Religious Studies and co-director of the Center for the Study of Values at DePaul University in Chicago, where he has taught since 1981 in the fields of Roman Catholic studies, religious social ethics and business ethics. He also became the first annual holder of the Wicklander chair in professional ethics at DePaul University (1991–92). He received his S.T.L. in theology from the Gregorian University in Rome and his Ph.D. in theology from the University of Chicago Divinity School. His publications include *Christian Realism and Liberation Theology* and *New Experiment in Democracy: The Challenge for American Catholicism.*

Marcos McGrath, C.S.C., has been Archbishop of Panama since 1969. In 1982 he was president of the National Commission for the Family (CONAFA) in Panama and president of the Panamanian Episcopal Conference (1964–72). He was a member of the First (1967) and Second (1969) Post-Conciliar Synods of Bishops, the Council of Permanent Secretariat of the Synod (1970), the Synods in 1971 and 1974, and the Vatican Council for the Unity of Christians (1984). He worked in various capacities with the Council of Latin American Bishops (CELAM) from 1963–79. In Chile, 1953–61, he held several positions at San Jorge Secondary School, and was professor and subsequently dean of theology at the Catholic University of Chile. Archbishop McGrath received his doctorate at the Angelicum in Rome, after studying at the Paris Theological Institute and Holy Cross College in Washington, D.C.

Michael Novak holds the George Frederick Jewett chair in religion and public policy at the American Enterprise Institute for Public Policy in Washington, D.C., where he serves also as director of social and political studies. As former ambassador, he headed the U.S. Delegation to the Conference on Security and Cooperation in Europe (1986) and to the United Nations Human Rights Commission in Geneva (1981, 1982). Mr. Novak received his B.T. at the Gregorian University in Rome (1958), continued his theological studies at Catholic University, and earned his M.A. in the history and philosophy of religion at Harvard University (1966). He is the author of many articles, essays, reviews, weekly or monthly columns, and over twenty books, including *The Catholic Ethic and the Spirit of Democratic Capitalism, Free Persons and the Common Good, Taking Glasnost Seriously,* and *The Spirit of Democratic Capitalism.*

Peter J. Paris has been the Elmer G. Homrighausen Professor of Christian Social Ethics at Princeton Theological Seminary since 1985, and Senior Fellow, Mathey College, Princeton University, since 1988; previously, he taught at Vanderbilt University Divinity School (1972–85). He has served as president of the Society of Christian Ethics and of the American Academy of Religion. He received his M.A. (1969) and Ph.D. in ethics and society (1975) from the University of Chicago. He was ordained a Baptist minister in Canada in 1959. Professor Paris was a research fellow at Harvard University Dubois Institute, received a Ford fellowship, Center for Urban Studies, University of Chicago (1968–70), and a University of

Chicago fellowship (1965–68). His publications include *Black Religious Leaders: Conflict in Unity* and *The Social Teaching of the Black Churches,* and numerous journal essays.

William Pfaff is an author and political journalist. He was one of the earliest members of the policy research group, the Hudson Institute, and from 1971 to 1978 was deputy director of its European affiliate in Paris, Hudson Research Europe, Ltd. Previously, he had been an executive of the Free Europe Committee in New York (parent organization of Radio Free Europe) and editor of *Commonweal.* He was graduated in English from the University of Notre Dame in 1949. Mr. Pfaff has lectured widely and held a Rockefeller Foundation grant in international studies. His several books include *Condemned to Freedom;* and *Barbarian Sentiments: How the American Century Ends,* which was nominated for a National Book award. Its French translation was awarded the City of Geneva's Prix Jean-Jacques Rousseau as best political book of 1990. His political essays have appeared in the *New Yorker* since 1971, and he writes an editorial-page column for the *International Herald Tribune* in Paris which is syndicated internationally by the *Los Angeles Times.*

Paul E. Sigmund is professor of politics at Princeton University, specializing in political theory and Latin American politics. He received his M.A. (1954) and Ph.D. (1959) from Harvard University. He was a fellow at the Woodrow Wilson International Center for Scholars (1985–86), at the National Endowment for the Humanities (1980–81), and at the Center for International Studies, Princeton University (1972, 1974). He has published sixteen books and 150 articles, including *Nicholas of Cusa and Medieval Political Thought, Natural Law in Political Thought, St. Thomas Aquinas on Ethics and Politics, Liberation Theology at the Crossroads: Democracy or Revolution?* and a translation from Latin of *Nicholas of Cusa: The Catholic Concordance.*

Oliver F. Williams, C.S.C., is associate provost, co-director of the Notre Dame Center for Ethics and Religious Values in Business, and a member of the faculty of the department of management at the University of Notre Dame, where he researches and teaches in the field of business, society, and ethics. He holds a Ph.D. in theology from Vanderbilt University and had the experience of a research year at Stanford University Graduate School of Business. Former chair of the Social Issues Division of the Academy of Management, he is the author of *The Apartheid Crisis,* co-author of *Full Value: Cases in Christian Business Ethics,* and co-editor of *A Virtuous Life in Business: Stories of Courage and Integrity in the*

Corporate World, The Making of an Economic Vision, The Common Good and U.S. Capitalism, Co-Creation and Capitalism: John Paul II's Laborem Exercens, and *The Judeo-Christian Vision and the Modern Corporation.* Father Williams has published articles in numerous journals, including *California Management Review, Journal of Business Ethics, Harvard Business Review,* and *Business Horizons.*

Index